# *Goethe's World*

# *Goethe's World*

AS SEEN

IN LETTERS AND MEMOIRS



EDITED BY BERTHOLD BIERMANN

A NEW DIRECTIONS BOOK

*Typographic Design by Maurice Serle Kaplan*

MANUFACTURED IN THE UNITED STATES BY THE BELGRAVE PRESS AND CHAS. H. BOHN & COMPANY, BOOKBINDERS, NEW YORK CITY

*New Directions Books are published by James Laughlin*

NEW YORK OFFICE — 500 FIFTH AVENUE

## CONTENTS

*The pieces marked with an asterisk are translated by Walter Sorell.*

CONTENTS

## ILLUSTRATIONS

ILLUSTRATIONS

# INTRODUCTION

THE STORY of Goethe's life is supported by a wealth of documentary evidence rarely found in other life stories. Besides Goethe's own contributions, autobiographical writings, letters and diaries, a myriad of notes and reports by his contemporaries preserve the image of his personality. The diligent scrutiny of scholars has made the world of which Goethe was center and high point accessible to all who want to enjoy the spectacle of a singularly rich and productive life.

Of Goethe's autobiographical writings only the story of his youth was completed. Under the slightly ambiguous title of "Truth and Poetry", it immediately intrigued his contemporaries. The poet himself stated that his intention was to give a genuine biographical record and that, by the two-faced title, he simply wanted to put the reader on guard against the fallacies of the author's memory. The fact that Goethe told us the true story of his youth, however, does not mean that he told us all of it. He had little likeness to Jean Jacques Rousseau who indulged in the delights of confession. Goethe preferred to gloss over events which, recalled in detail, would have pained him. With loving care he described the idyl at the parson's house at Sesenheim where he met Friederike Brion, but he scarcely mentioned the parting in the autobiography. "Those were painful days, the memory of which has not remained with me," was the cryptic allusion to the end of a love affair which almost meant death for Friederike. That the sufferings were not all hers, we can only imply from a study of his poetic productions.

The precaution which Goethe took to veil his deeper feelings was the cause of much misunderstanding. Margaret Fuller, who professed the greatest admiration for his poetic genius, thought it necessary to defend Goethe thus: "Pardon him, world, that he was too worldly. Do not wonder, heart, that he was so heartless." In our days psychological penetration has revealed more of Goethe's complex personality. We are inclined to see him as an artist burdened with an extreme sensibility, who, after near defeat in his early experiences, had good reason to watch over his emotional balance.

Goethe's first courtship, the romance of the fifteen-year-old boy with Gretchen, ended in a nervous breakdown. The tempestuous love affair of the student with Käthchen Schönkopf was followed by an almost fatal illness. When Goethe was faced with a conflict of passion and friendship in his love for Charlotte Buff, he was as close to self-annihilation as Werther, the hero of the novel which made the twenty-four-year-old author famous. Though he saved himself through his creative genius and later talked rather mockingly about Werther and his gloomy followers, nevertheless, there remained something of the Werther-mood in him throughout life. He was thirty-seven and the respected minister of the Duke of Saxe-Weimar when he wrote to Frau von Stein: "I am revising the novel of Werther, and I always think that the author was wrong not to shoot himself after having finished his manuscript." Again passion without hope of fulfillment almost destroyed him. We know from the episode with Ulrike von Levetzow that even the aged Goethe despite all his composure and bearing was never secure, and the disposition for great passion and tragedy was always present. When the seventy-four-year-old poet had to realize the impossibility of a marriage with the girl of nineteen, he was lost in despair as in the days when he wrote his Werther. He became dangerously sick, and his physicians were at a loss what to do; they could not find a physical cause for the illness.

It is necessary to read the letters of the young Goethe fully to realize the intensity of his passions. In these effusions all is still in the natural state, not yet fashioned by a long process of intellectual and moral self-discipline to the composed dignity which distinguishes the mature man. We sense the immense élan with which the youth starts out for life; we remark how experience saddens him; we see him in danger of being paralyzed by depressive moods and a morbid preoccupation with sickness. All emotions tend to the extreme—his love and devotion, his jealousy and his despair. The style of Goethe's early writings reflects this exalted state of mind; some passages of the letters, though written in prose, belong rather to poetry.

In later years Goethe dictated most of his correspondence to a secretary, a method which accounts for a certain ceremoniousness in his style. Compared with masters of the epistolary art of the eighteenth century his letters seem deficient in elegance of expression. Though Goethe does not entertain his correspondents so gracefully, he compensates by imparting knowledge. He used the stimulus of correspondence to clear his own impressions and ideas, and if he had little or no personal matter to relate, he put down observations and general reflections which might otherwise have found a place in his writings. Later, it was easy for him to publish parts of his correspondence, such as the letters from Switzerland and Italy, by simply cutting out all personal allusions. When he edited his correspondence with Schiller, the result was mainly a spirited conversation between two eminent writers about the problems which occurred in their literary workshops. In a letter to his friend Zelter, Goethe reported how an early experience set him on guard against the habit of writing letters devoid of substance. He used to work as a young man with a high church dignitary who, through his influential position and a personal interest in literary affairs, was obliged to carry on an immense correspondence. As he was a man of kindly disposition, he tried in his letters to satisfy all demands made on him, and adopted a certain style which veiled the emptiness of his answers. He appeared to say something important to everyone, whereas in reality, it was mere politeness. Goethe then says: "I took a solemn oath, never under similar circumstances—my celebrity at the time already threatened me with these—to give in to such practice, since if I did so, all pure and sincere relations with my fellow men would in the end be dissolved and scattered to the winds."

Goethe's diaries fill thirteen volumes in the complete edition of his writings. Impressive as the mass of notes is, the material does not yield very much on the poet's inner life. The diary is really an intimate journal only in the first years at Weimar—full of introspective observations, reflecting the relentless effort to satisfy the urge for moral improvement. He feels heavily the burden of his official duties and tries to adjust himself to the exigencies of his position, not out of ambition, but because he earnestly desires to prove useful to the little country. For some time the study of administrative problems even alienates him from literature. The strictly private aspect of the diary is underlined by the fact that Goethe uses a code for the names of the high personages of the Weimar court. He employs astronomical symbols, and thus Frau von Stein is significantly represented by the sign of the Sun.

But as time goes on, the diary tends more and more to become a mere enumeration of facts. The names of visitors are recorded, the topics of conversation mentioned, the letters received and sent off are listed; a word of comment or a general reflection rarely interrupts the report of daily transactions. The entries in the handwriting of a secretary, carefully classifying the different items in little paragraphs, make these pages look like columns in a ledger. And indeed, the diary was for Goethe something like a register where he preserved the account of the most precious of his possessions—his time. There was a grain of superstition in this exactitude, as if the continuity of life could be endangered through lack of evidence. Upon regaining consciousness after a dangerous illness, one of his first requests was to know if the secretary had continued his diary. Goethe complained bitterly when he heard that he had not done so.

For decades Goethe's fame attracted visitors to Weimar who wanted to see the great man face to face. Naturally, their reports have a certain uniformity, since they deal mainly with the poet's demeanor. No one who met Goethe for the first time failed to be impressed by his majestic eye, and even the sarcastic Heinrich Heine was no exception. In other respects the opinions differed. What seemed to one the natural dignity in the poet's bearing was felt by another as stiffness and coldness. As Goethe did not feel at ease with strangers, the conversations at such meetings rarely yielded much. He could no longer escape celebrity through an assumed name as he had done in his youth while travelling, but could only protect himself against obtrusive curiosity through an air of polite indifference. He warmed up when the visitor could offer some knowledge which was of special interest to him. Foreign guests, in particular, were likely to arouse his interest, as they could provide information about their home countries.

Though some visitors were certainly disappointed, little adverse criticism of Goethe was voiced openly. But, in the privacy of literary circles where his domineering position was resented by younger and less favored writers, anecdotes circulated about the poet's selfishness and vanity. A young American, Joseph Green Cogswell, was extremely prejudiced against Goethe whom he knew only from this gossip. The young man went with great apprehension to see "this strange beast," as he termed him in a letter written before his visit. It was a great surprise for Cogswell to find in Goethe a man without a trace of affectation who explained in detail the objects in the mineralogical cabinet of Jena and showed the most sincere interest in him and the circumstances of his home country. When Cogswell made a farewell visit to Goethe two years later, he wrote home: "I know not when I was more touched at parting from a person to whom I was bound by no particular tie, than from him."

The intimate Goethe as he appeared in his family circle or in a tête-à-tête with a trusted companion was described in the memoirs of his disciples who had the opportunity of observing him in daily intercourse. Conscious of the importance of their rôle, they recorded the poet's remarks and opinions as an authentic commentary on his life and work. They not only received instruction but also rendered the master an important service. They gave him a chance to discuss freely ideas not intended for his writings which were destined for a large public. Goethe never again developed his conception of death and immortality in such detail as in the conversation with Johannes Falk on the day of Wieland's funeral. The concurrence of an event which touched him profoundly and the presence of a sympathetic listener was necessary to induce him to disclose ideas which probably occupied his mind for some time. Riemer, long associated with Goethe as his secretary, unfortunately presumed that he knew everything about the master. He discredited Falk's reporting, because he himself had never had a similar conversation. How unjust! Goethe, though he valued Riemer's scholarly qualities, obviously did not respect his poetic imagination enough to share such daring speculations with him. On the other hand, he confided to Riemer epigrams of worldly wisdom which might have shocked the pious Falk. Long experience had taught him that man grasps only knowledge which he can assimilate to his own personality.

While Goethe resembles a priest of Nature's mysteries in Falk's presentation and has the traits of a Greek sage in Riemer's description, he has the gentle authority of a father conferred on him by Eckermann in his famous volume of conversations. No doubt, Goethe was all this on occasion and still more. In later years Goethe no longer took part in the life at the court of Weimar, and Friedrich von Müller became a sort of mediator between him and society. In this advantageous position, he was able to observe the poet in an attitude less visible to others—that of sarcastic critic of men and society. On his visits Müller informed him of the political and literary developments and entertained him with gossip and anecdotes from the court. Sometimes Goethe was provoked into making comments on the folly of men in general and the Germans in particular. Müller, a man who wanted to believe in the progress of mankind, then felt torn between his admiration for the poet and his indignation about Goethe's skeptical attitude. On such a day, when he had no encouraging words from the poet to record for posterity, he remarked in his diary: "Today he displayed that sarcastic humour and that spirit of sophistic contradiction which cause such displeasure." After all, the poet who created the character of Mephistopheles might well be tempted to assume occasionally this rôle.

Among the weighty men who surrounded Goethe, Bettina Brentano appeared as a guest from another world. Passionate and capricious, with the freakishness of an elf, she relied mainly on her imagination in her love for Goethe. She aspired to be the poet's most faithful disciple but interpreted his works in a very personal manner and absorbed nothing from his teachings. Bettina's book, "Goethe's Correspondence with a Child," once very popular with the readers, intrigued scholars for a long time. Since the originals of the correspondence have been published, we know that she mingled facts and fiction in her record; when the discrepancy between her own ardent letters and Goethe's carefully styled messages became too obvious, she added suitable passages. In spite of all that, Bettina had remarkable talents and an instinct to discern true genius. She considered it her special mission to bring Goethe and Beethoven together, and the meeting actually took place at Teplitz in Bohemia in 1812.

The reports about this event are fragmentary. After the first meeting, Goethe gave a sympathetic characterization of the composer in a letter to his wife. "I have never seen an artist more intense, more powerful, more sincere," he wrote. "I understand well how strange he must feel in this world." Though in later years Beethoven remembered with great pleasure his conversations with Goethe, he was somehow irritated by the poet's refined way which did not suit his conception of genius. He wanted to demonstrate his independence, and the occasion came when they were walking together and met the Empress of Austria and her entourage. Beethoven later told Bettina proudly what had happened: "We saw them from afar approaching, and Goethe slipped away from me and stood to one side. Say what I would, I could not induce him to advance another step, so I pushed my hat on my head, buttoned my overcoat, and went, arms folded, into the thickest of the crowd. Princes and sycophants drew up in a line; Duke Rudolph took off my hat, after the Empress had first greeted me. Persons of rank know me. To my great amusement I saw the procession defile past Goethe.

Hat in hand, he stood at the side, deeply bowing." Goethe kept silent about this scene and only alluded to it, in a letter to Zelter in which he pitied Beethoven for his growing deafness, considering it a cause of his unsocial behavior.

It is doubtful if a closer bond would have formed between Goethe and Beethoven even under more favorable circumstances. After Schiller's death Goethe relied more and more on men who, though experts in their fields, did not bear the stamp of genius. He spoke enthusiastically of Byron, yet the English poet was someone far away, whose originality and extravagance could not bother him personally. For his friendships, Goethe preferred a man like Heinrich Meyer, a mediocre painter but a great connoisseur of the history of art, who helped him to arrange his rich art collections. Another man after his own heart was Zelter, realistic and reliable in all affairs, with a solid knowledge of the structure of music. Anyone who could contribute to his scientific information was welcome. Goethe frankly admitted what he had gained from others, directly through their advice and more indirectly as objects of his study of human nature. "My work," he said to Soret, "is that of an aggregation of beings taken from the whole of nature—it bears the name of Goethe."

The rich documentary record provided by Goethe's contemporaries was supplemented by a variegated pictorial record. But just as no single observer was able to retain all of the poet's many-sided personality, no artist could hope to display it in one portrait. The differences in the portraits of Goethe even when they belong to the same period are often puzzling. The temperament of the painter and his artistic principles determined this or that attitude of the poet; as a result, different characteristics were stressed. The public favored idealized representations, and some artists complied too willingly to this trend.

Goethe himself preferred realistic pictures of his friends and employed the designer Schmeller to make accurate drawings of interesting visitors. In regard to his own portrayal, he was indifferent after having seen so many unsatisfying attempts. Even well-recommended artists had difficulty in getting him to consent to a few sittings. The reason that he granted the request of Ludwig Sebbers to paint his portrait on a large porcelain cup was probably that the technique of porcelain-painting interested him. He allowed Sebbers fourteen sittings for this curious picture and was so pleased with the artist's work that he sat again for a drawing. Heinrich Meyer gave Goethe his expert view of Sebbers' performance in the following words: "I do not know any portrait of you which represents your features, your attitude, and your visible being more truly." The kind face painted by Sebbers on fragile material and the powerful profile-drawing (known only from reproductions, as the original disappeared) complement each other very well. They transmit to us something of the impression of majesty and benevolence which Goethe's visitors experienced, and which Grillparzer expressed thus: "He looked like a king, and again like a father."

* * *

I am too well aware that the selections I present in the following pages give only glimpses of Goethe's world. Vast as the material is, much of it had to be put aside as it would need lengthy explanation to a reader not familiar with the history of German literature. For a similar reason I could only touch upon an important field of Goethe's activity—his scientific studies. On the other hand, I favored English sources and tried to keep the record of American visitors as complete as possible. The information necessary for the understanding of the documents is contained in separate introductions and occasionally additional comments. Details are explained briefly in the text. For more information the reader may consult the biographical index.

A large part of the German sources is not yet translated. Mr. Walter Sorell contributed new translations from German texts and revised the bulk of the older translations. For advice and encouragement in the preparation of this book, I owe thanks to Mr. Charles Neider. I profited from Mr. Peter Behrendt's critical suggestions during my work. Mrs. Gerda Meyerhof assisted me graciously in the selection of the illustrative material. I want to thank the library of Harvard University for permission to reproduce a photograph and Yale University Press for permission to include reproductions of documents of which the originals are part of the William A. Speck collection in the Yale University Library. The right to reprint a selection from William Emerson's Journal has been courteously granted by Columbia University Press. My task was facilitated through the privilege of using the fine Goethe collection of the Columbia University Library.

BERTHOLD BIERMANN

*New York, September, 1948*

PART ONE

# *Passion and Genius*

1749-1775

# RECOLLECTIONS OF GOETHE'S MOTHER

*On August 28, 1749, Johann Kaspar Goethe and his wife, Elizabeth, born Textor, were blessed with a son who was baptized Johann Wolfgang. The father, a wealthy citizen of Frankfort on the Main, practiced law and held the title of "Imperial Councillor." The poet's mother belonged to a distinguished Frankfort family; her father was the chief magistrate of the Free City of Frankfort for many years. The stories which Goethe's mother loved to tell about Wolfgang's childhood were recorded by a young friend of hers, Bettina Brentano. When the poet began to prepare his autobiography, he asked Bettina for this information and received from her, interspersed in her letters, the following stories of his mother.*

THE BED in which you were born had blue checked curtains. At that time your mother was 18 years of age and had been married for a year. For three long days before you came into the world you made her very unhappy. Furious that necessity forced you out of your original abode and also that the midwife handled you improperly, you were quite blue and without a sign of life when you saw light for the first time. You were sprinkled with wine and your belly was warmed since they despaired of your life. Your grandmother stood behind the bed and when you opened your eyes, she shouted: "Elizabeth, he is alive!"

"At that moment my motherly heart awoke and has lived since in constant enthusiasm to this very hour," your mother told me in her 75th year of age.

When he was 9 weeks old, he had frightening dreams, made a great many strange grimaces and when he awoke, he went into a fit of distressed crying. He often yelled so violently that he lost his breath and his parents were afraid for his life. They bought him a little bell and when they noticed that he became restive in his sleep, they rang the bell and made a rattling noise so that he should forget his dream immediately when he awoke.

He did not like to play with little children, unless they were very beautiful. Once he was taken to a party and he suddenly began to cry. Asked for the reason, he shouted: "I can't stand that ugly child, send it away." He did not even stop crying when he was home again where his mother talked to him about his bad behavior. He could not forget the ugliness of the child, nor calm down. At that time he was 3 years of age.

He grew tenderly attached to his little sister when she was still in the cradle. He furtively put some bread into his pockets and stuffed it into the child's mouth whenever she cried. He became terribly angry when anyone lifted the child, he would then jump up on the people and tear their hair. It was far easier to enrage him than to make him cry.

His mother was strangely surprised that he did not shed a tear when his younger brother Jacob, who was his playmate, died. On the contrary, he seemed to show some kind of anger at the mourning of his family. When, a week later, his mother asked the stubborn child whether he had not loved his brother, he ran into his room and took from under his bed a great many sheets of paper on which he had scribbled lessons and stories. He told her that he had done all this to teach his brother.

Once at harvest time when there were fireworks in all the gardens in Frankfort in the evening and rockets were sent up from all sides, in the farthest fields (to which point the activities did not extend) many will-o'-the-wisps were noticed jumping back and forth, at one time falling apart, at another flocking together and then even beginning to dance figures. As soon as the people stepped closer, one of the will-o'-the-wisps after the other would vanish, some of them would take a few leaps before disappearing, others would remain suspended in midair and then suddenly go out, others remained sitting on hedges and trees. The people did not find anything and went back again; but immediately the dance would start anew, one light after another would reappear and dance around half the town. What was it?—Goethe and many of his comrades who had put lights onto their hats had been dancing outside the town.

"He was extremely peculiar about his clothes," his mother said. "I had to keep three different outfits ready. On the one chair I put his overcoat, long trousers, an ordinary vest and a matching pair of boots; on the second, an evening dress, silk stockings which he had already worn, shoes, and so forth; on the third, I had to keep everything of the best including sword and bagwig. The first mentioned outfit he wore at home, the second when he went to see his acquaintances, the third was his gala dress.

"When I came into his room the next day, I had to put everything in order. His boots would stand on the elegant cuffs and ruffles, his shoes would be lying all over the place. I shook the dust from his clothes, replaced the underwear and put everything right again.

"When one day I took his vest and shook it in the air at the open window rather determinedly, suddenly a great many little stones hit me in the face. I began to curse about it. He happened to come in at that moment and I scolded him. The stones could have put out my eyes, I said. 'Well, none of your eyes has been put out by them,' he said. 'Where are the stones? I must have them back, help me find them again.'

"Now, he must have received these stones from his sweetheart, since he was concerned only about them and nothing else. They were ordinary pebbles and he was greatly irritated because he could not find all of them. Those which were still there he carefully wrapped in paper and took away."

## JUVENILE LOVE

*Goethe experienced the awakening of love as a youth of fourteen. When he was in his sixties, the poet narrated this episode in "Truth and Poetry", his autobiography.*

I WAS quite unexpectedly involved in an affair which brought me near to a great danger, and, for a time at least, into perplexity and distress. The friendly intercourse which I had with the boy Pylades [fictitious name for a playmate] continued beyond my childhood. We indeed saw each other less often, because our parents were not on the best of terms; but when we did meet, the old warmth of friendship revived immediately. Once we met in the pleasant walk made by the avenues between the outer and inner gate of St. Gallus. We had scarcely exchanged greetings, when he said to me, "I have had the same experience as ever about your verses. I read aloud those you recently showed to me to some good friends of mine, and not one of them will believe that you wrote them." "Do not let that trouble us," I answered; "we will write them and enjoy them, and the others may think and say of them what they please."

"Here comes the unbeliever himself," added my friend. "We will not speak of it," I replied; "what is the use? We cannot convert him." "By no means," said my friend; "I cannot let him off so easily."

After a short conversation on indifferent topics my young

comrade, who was but too well disposed towards me, could not suffer the matter to drop without saying to the other, with some resentment, "Here is my friend who made those pretty verses for which you will not give him credit!" "He will certainly not be offended at that," answered the other, "for we do him an honor when we suppose that more learning is required to make such verses than one of his years can possess." I made some casual answer; but my friend continued, "It will not be very difficult to convince you. Give him any theme, and he will improvise you a poem on the spot." I fell in with the proposal, and the other asked me whether I would venture to compose a pretty love-letter in rhyme, which a modest young woman might be supposed to write to a young man, to declare her inclination. "Nothing could be easier," I answered, "if I only had writing materials." He pulled out his pocket almanac, in which there were a great many blank leaves, and I sat down upon a bench to write. They walked about in the meanwhile, but always kept me in sight.

I immediately brought my imagination to bear on the situation, and thought how pleasant it would be if some pretty girl were really attached to me, and wished to reveal her sentiments to me, either in prose or verse. I therefore began my declaration without delay, and in a very short time produced some verses, in form between doggerel and madrigal, and as simple as possible in style, which, when read aloud, filled the sceptic with astonishment, and my friend with delight. The former expressed his desire to keep the poem, and I could hardly refuse, seeing that it was written in his almanac; besides, I was glad to leave such documentary evidence of my capabilities in his hands. He left us with many assurances of admiration and respect, saying he wished for nothing more than that we should often meet; so we settled soon to go together to the country.

Our party actually took place, and was joined by several more young people of the same sort. They belonged to the middle, or, if you will to the lower classes, and were not wanting in brains, and moreover, thanks to their school education, were fairly well informed and had a certain degree of culture. In a large, rich city there are many modes of gaining a livelihood, and they supported themselves by copying for lawyers, and by giving the children of the lower orders more advanced instruction than that of the elementary schools. They helped to prepare other children, who were to be confirmed; then, again, they did errands for business men and merchants, and were thus enabled to enjoy themselves frugally in the evenings, and particularly on Sundays and festivals.

On the way out, while they highly extolled my love-letter, they confessed to me that they had made use of it in a merry jest,—they had copied it in a feigned hand, and, with a few pertinent allusions, had sent it to a conceited young man, who was now firmly persuaded that a lady to whom he had paid distant court was excessively enamoured of him, and sought an opportunity for closer acquaintance. At the same time, they told me in confidence that he now desired nothing more than to be able to answer her in verse; but that neither he nor they had any ability in that direction, so that they earnestly begged me to compose the much-desired reply.

Mystifications are and will continue to be an amusement for idle, more or less intelligent people. A pardonable love of mischief, a malicious spirit of provocation delight those who have neither resources in themselves nor a wholesome external activity. No age is quite above such trivial pleasures. We had often tricked each other when we were children; many games turned upon such mystifications and tricks. The present jest did not seem to me of any greater consequence; I gave my consent. They informed me of many details which the letter ought to contain, and we brought it home already finished.

A little while afterwards I was urgently invited, through my friend, to be present at one of the evening gatherings of their society. The lover, he said, was willing to bear the expense on this occasion, and desired expressly to thank the friend who had shown himself so excellent a poetical secretary. We assembled late enough, the meal was most frugal, the wine drinkable: while as for the conversation, it consisted almost entirely of jokes at the expense of our very foolish young host, who, after repeated readings of the letter, almost believed that he had written it himself.

My natural good-nature would not allow me to take much pleasure in such a malicious deception, and the continual harping on this one theme soon disgusted me. I should certainly have passed a tedious evening, if an unexpected arrival had not revived me. On our entrance the table was already neatly and tidily set, and sufficient wine had been served; so we sat down, and were left to ourselves, without requiring any attendance. However, as the wine ran short at last, one of them called for the maid; but instead of the maid there came in a girl of uncommon, and, when contrasted with her surroundings, of astonishing beauty. "What is it you want?" she asked, after a friendly greeting; "the maid is ill in bed. Can I serve you?" "The wine has run short," said one; "if you would fetch us a few bottles, it would be very kind of you." "Do, Gretchen," said another, "it is only a step or two." "Why not?" she answered, and, taking a few empty bottles hurried out. Her appearance, as she turned her back on us, was even more attractive. The little cap sat so neatly upon her little head, poised gracefully in its turn upon a slender neck. Her whole person breathed a peculiar charm which could be more fully appreciated when one's attention was no longer exclusively attracted and fettered by the clear, calm eyes and lovely mouth. I reproved my comrades for sending the girl out alone at night, but they only laughed at me, and I was soon consoled by her return, as the publican lived only just across the way. "Sit down with us as a reward," said one. She did so; but, alas, she did not come near me. She drank a glass to our health, and left us, advising us not to carry on our revels too late into the night, and not to be so noisy, as her mother was just going to bed. It was not, however, her own mother, but the mother of our hosts.

The girl's image never left me from that moment; it was the first durable impression made upon me by any woman; and as I could find no pretext to see her at home, and would not seek one, I went to church for love of her, and soon discovered where she sat. Thus, during the long Protestant service, I gazed my fill at her. When the congregation left the church I did not venture to accost her, much less to accompany her, and was perfectly delighted if she seemed to observe me and to return my greeting with a nod. Yet I was not long denied the happiness of approaching her. They had persuaded the suitor, whose poetical secretary I had been, that the letter written in his name had been actually sent to the lady, so that he lived in daily expectation of an answer. It was intended that I should write this too; and the roguish conspirators entreated me earnestly, through Pylades, to exert all my wit and employ all my art, to make this composition a masterpiece of elegance.

In the hope of again seeing my fair one, I set to work immediately, and thought of everything that would please me most if Gretchen were writing it to me. I seemed to have expressed myself so completely after her form, her nature, her manner, and her mind, that I could not refrain from wishing that it were so in reality, and lost myself in rapture at the mere thought that something similar could be sent from her to me. Thus I deluded myself, while intending to impose upon another; and so laid myself open to much joy and to much sorrow. By the time I was once more summoned, my work was ready; I promised to come, and did not fail at the appointed hour.

Only one of the young men was at home; Gretchen sat at the window spinning; the mother was busy about the house. The young man asked me to read it aloud to him; I complied not without emotion, glancing at intervals from the paper at the beautiful girl before me; and, as I read, the slight uneasiness and faint flush I seemed to notice only helped me to render with more zest and fire those words which I would fain have heard from her own lips. The cousin, who had often interrupted me with commendations, at last entreated me to make some improvements. These concerned some passages which indeed were rather adapted to Gretchen's

*Above*: Goethe's father and mother

*Below*: Goethe and his sister Cornelia

Goethe's home at Frankfort on the Main

condition than to that of the lady in question, who was of a good family, wealthy, and known and respected in the city. The young man then pointed out the desired changes, brought me writing materials, and took his leave for a short time to attend to some business matters. I remained sitting on the bench against the wall, behind the large table, and made an attempt at the alterations that were to be made, using for the purpose the large slate, which almost covered the whole table, and a pencil that always lay in the window, both of which were used to jot down reckonings or memoranda of various kinds, or even as a means of communication between incoming and outgoing guests.

I had for a while written different things and rubbed them out again, when I exclaimed impatiently, "It will not do!" "So much the better," the girl said gravely; "I am glad it will not do. You should not meddle in such matters." She arose from the distaff, and stepping towards the table, gave me a severe lecture, with a great deal of good sense and kindliness. "The thing seems an innocent jest; it is a jest, but it is not innocent. I have already known several cases, in which our young men, for the sake of mere mischief of that kind, have brought themselves into great difficulties." "But what shall I do?" I asked; "the letter is written, and they rely upon me to alter it." "Trust me," she replied, "and do not alter it; rather take it back, put it in your pocket, go away, and try to put matters straight through your friend. I will also put in a word; for though I am a poor girl, and dependent upon these relations—who indeed do no harm, though they will often risk a good deal for the sake of fun or profit—I held out against them, and would not copy the first letter, as they requested. They wrote it in a feigned hand, and can do the same with this one, unless they devise some other expedient. But you, a young man of good family, rich, independent, why should you allow yourself to be used as a tool in a business which can certainly bring you no good, and may possibly have most unpleasant consequences?" It was a pleasure to me to hear her speak at such length, for as a rule she took small part in the conversation. My feeling for her grew so strong, that, no longer master of myself, I replied, "I am not so independent as you suppose; and of what use is wealth to me, when I may not have the most precious thing I can desire?"

She drew the rough copy of my verses towards her, and read them in soft, low undertones. "That is very pretty," said she, stopping short at a sort of naive conceit; "but it is a pity that it is not destined for any genuine purpose." "That would indeed be desirable," I cried, "and, oh! how happy would that man be who received such a proof of affection from a girl he tenderly loved." "It would not be likely to happen," she answered; "and yet many things are possible." "For example," I continued, "if anyone who knew, prized, honored, and worshipped you, were to lay such a paper before you, and besought you very earnestly, what would you do?" And I once more pushed towards her the paper she had just returned to me. She smiled, considered for a moment, took the pen, and signed her name. I was beside myself with rapture, sprang to my feet, and would have embraced her. "No kissing!" she said, "that is so vulgar; but let us love each other if we can." I had picked up the paper, and thrust it into my pocket. "No one shall ever get it," said I; "the affair is at an end. You have rescued me." "Now complete the rescue," she exclaimed, "and hurry off, before the others come, and you get into trouble." I could not tear myself away from her, but she gently urged me, warmly pressing my right hand in both of hers! Tears stood in my eyes; I thought hers, too, were wet. I pressed my face upon her hands and hastened away. Never in my life had I been in such a tumult of emotion.

The first impulses of love, where youth is still pure and unspoiled, will be free from all taint of sensuality. Nature seems to intend that each sex should find in the other an embodiment of the ideas of virtue and beauty. Thus the sight of this girl, and my love for her, had opened out to me a new world of loveliness and goodness.

## GOETHE TO J. J. RIESE

*The 16-year-old Goethe was sent to Leipzig, as his father had been, to study law at the University, although his propensity for poetry already at that time overshadowed all other interests. This great Saxon commercial city, famous for its annual fairs, also held a leading position in the artistic life of Germany. Goethe's childhood friend, Johann Jacob Riese, to whom this letter is addressed, studied at the University of Marburg at the same time.*

Leipzig, October 20, 1765
6 A.M.

RIESE, Good Morning!

21st, 5 P.M.

RIESE, Good Evening!

I had hardly seated myself yesterday to devote an hour to you, when suddenly a letter reached me from Horn and tore me away from the sheet I had already commenced. Today, too, I shall not remain with you much longer. I am going to the playhouse. There are excellent plays here. But yet—I am undecided! Shall I stay with you? Shall I go to the playhouse? I don't know. Quick! Let the dice decide. But I have no dice! I am going! Goodbye.

Yet wait! I will stay. Tomorrow I can't again, for I must attend a lecture, pay a visit, and then I am invited for the evening. So I will write now. Let me know what sort of life you are leading, whether you often think of me, who your professors are, et cetera, and mind, a long et cetera. I am living here like—like—I don't know what like; yet something

Like a bird that rocks upon a bough
In the loveliest grove, alive with liberty,
Who undisturbed enjoys the gentle breeze
And, with his little wings from tree to tree,
From bush to bush, flits warbling here and there.

In short, picture to yourself a little bird on a green bough, revelling in joy, and you have my life. Today I began my classes. What are they? Is it worth the trouble to ask? . . .

I haven't seen Gottsched [Professor of Literature and influential author] yet. He has married again. A Lieutenant-Colonel's daughter; but you know about it. She is nineteen and he sixty-five years old. She is four feet tall, and he seven feet. She is as thin as a herring, and he as fat as a feather-sack.—I am cutting a great figure here!—But as yet I am no dandy; nor will I become one.—I need the art of being diligent. In society, concerts, the theatres, dinners, suppers and drives, so much is going on just now. Ha! it is capital. But it costs capital too. The deuce, my purse feels it! Stop! Help! Stop! Don't you see them still fly? There went two louis d'or. Help! There goes another. For heaven's sake! Another couple has gone. Dimes are here as pennies are out there in the Reich with you.—And still one may live cheaply here. The fair is over. I shall manage to live economically. Then I hope I'll make both ends meet with 300 thaler—what am I saying?—with 200 thaler a week. Nota bene not including all that which already went to the devil. My board is expensive. Just look at our bill of fare,—fowls, geese, turkeys, ducks, partridge, snipe, grouse, trout, hares, venison, pike, pheasants, oysters, etc. All this daily. Nothing of other vulgar meat, such as beef, veal, mutton, and so forth; I have forgotten how they taste. And this sumptuousness is not expensive, not expensive at all.—I just see that my sheet is almost full and there are no verses on it yet, though I intended writing you some. Another time.

# AN ENGLISH LETTER WRITTEN BY GOETHE

*Together with his father and his sister, Goethe took private lessons in English at Frankfort for a short while. From Leipzig, the 17-year-old youth sent his sister, beside several letters in French, some in English as an exercise and even tried his hand at English verses.*

The II of May, 1766

MY FRENCH SPEECH interrupted by some speedy affair shall remain unfinish'd untill another time, I think to thy great pleasure. I'll say thee the cause thereof: The father, as he writes in an appendix to Lupton's letter, would see if I write as good English as Lupton German. I know it not, but if he should write better than I that is no wonder; if I should have been as long a time in England as he was in Germany I would laugh of ten thousand scoolmasters. Let us speak a little, sister, the father may judge.

Lupton is a good fellow, a merry, infectious fellow as I see it in his letter which is written with a spirit of jest, much laudably moderated by the respect he owes to his master. But one can see that he is not yet acquainted with the fair and delicate manners of our language. Notwithstanding, he writes well. For the present state of the improvement of my English-speaking it goes as good as it can. My Born and his Tutor and I, when we are assembled we speak nothing than English. I learn much by that conversation. But that lovely Friend is gone to Graitze in Voigtland to be inoculated, God may give he returned saved and in good health.

Any words of my self. Sister, I am a foolish boy. Thou knowst it; why should I say it? I am no more a thunderer as I was in Frankfort. I make no more: J'enrage. I am as meek! as meek! Hah, thou believest it not! Many time I become a melancholical one. I know not whence it comes. Then I look on every man with a staring owl-like countenance. Then I go in woods, to streams, I look on the pyed daisies, on the blue violets, I hear the nightingales, the larks, the rooks and daws, the cuckoo. And then a darkness comes down my soul; a darkness as thick as fogs in the October are. Often has Horn the great honors to follow me, I go tête-à-tête with him in the Gardens. A male tête-à-tête! 'Tis pity! But hark ye! In like a situation of my soul, I make English verses (a science more than Lupton), English verses that a stone would weep. In that moment thou shallst have of them. Think on it, sister, thou art a happy maiden to have a brother who makes English verses. I pray thee be not haughty thereof.

## J. A. HORN TO K. L. MOORS

*Johann Adam Horn, a boyhood friend from Frankfort, followed Goethe to the University at Leipzig. As it seems, Karl Ludwig Moors was considered a moral authority by his friends.*

Leipzig, August 12, 1766

To speak of our Goethe! He is still the same proud fantast he was when I came here. If you could only see him, you would either be mad with anger or burst with laughter. I cannot understand at all how a man can so quickly transform himself. At present all his manners and his whole bearing are as different as day and night from his former behavior. Beside being proud he is a dandy too; one may remonstrate with him for his folly as much as one likes,

One may be Amphion and charm stones with a quodlibet,
But no one has brought Goethe to his senses yet.

All his thoughts and efforts are set on pleasing his ladylove and himself. In every circle he makes himself more ridiculous than agreeable. Merely because the lady likes it, he has put on tricks and gestures that one cannot possibly refrain from laughing at. He has adopted a gait which is quite insufferable. If you could only see it! . . . From day to day his company becomes more intolerable to me and he too tries to avoid me whenever he can. I am too plain a man for him to walk across the street with . . .

Do write again to him soon and tell him your opinion; otherwise, he and his ladylove will remain as silly as ever. Heaven only preserve me—as long as I am here—from any sweetheart, for the women here are the very devil. Goethe is not the first who has made a fool of himself to please his Dulcinea. I only wish you could see her just for once: she is the most absurd creature in the world. Her coquettish deportment and her haughty air are all with which she has bewitched Goethe. Dear friend! how glad I would be if Goethe were still what he was in Frankfort! Good friends as we were formerly, we now scarcely endure each other for a quarter of an hour. Yet with time I still hope to convert him, though it is a difficult task to make a coxcomb wise. But I will venture everything for the sake of it . . .

You may write him again what I have told you here. I shall be delighted, if you will do so. I care neither for his anger nor for that of his ladylove. For, after all, he is not easily offended with me; even when we quarel he sends for me next day. So much for him; more another time.

## J. A. HORN TO K. L. MOORS

*The 20-year-old Anna Katherina Schönkopf, called Annette or Käthchen, had Goethe's affection. The girl's father was the proprietor of a wine shop and inn where Goethe and his friends used to have their meals.*

Leipzig, October, 1766

WELL, DEAR MOORS, how glad you will be to learn that we have not lost a friend in our Goethe as we falsely supposed. He has so disguised himself as to deceive not only me but a great many others, and we should never have discovered the real truth of the matter, if your letter had not threatened him with the loss of a friend. I must tell you the whole story as he himself told it to me, for he has commissioned me to do so in order to save him the trouble.

He is in love—it's true—he confessed it to me and he will also confess it to you; but his love, however sad the facts may be, is not culpable, as I first thought. He loves, but not that young lady whom I suspected him of loving. He loves a girl beneath him in rank, but a girl whom—I think I do not say too much—you yourself would love, if you saw her. I am no lover, so I shall write entirely without passion. Imagine a woman, well grown though not very tall, a round, agreeable though not extraordinarily beautiful face, open, gentle, with an engaging air, great candour without coquetry, a very sound mind without having had any great education. He loves her very tenderly with the perfectly honest intentions of a virtuous man although he knows that she can never be his wife. Whether she loves him in return I do not know. You realize, dear Moors, that is a point about which one cannot well ask; but this much I can say to you that they seem born for each other.

Now heed his cunning! That no one may suspect him of such an attachment, he undertakes to persuade the world of precisely the opposite wherein he has been extraordinarily successful. He lives in great style and seems to be paying court to a certain young lady of whom I have told you before. He can see his beloved and converse with her at certain times without giving occasion for the slightest suspicion, and I sometimes accompany him to see her. If Goethe were not my friend I would fall in love with her myself. Meanwhile everyone thinks him in love with Miss—but why should you have to know her name,—and people are fond of teasing him about her. Perhaps she herself believes that he loves her, but the good lady deceives herself.

Since that time he has admitted me to closer confidence, has made me acquainted with his affairs and shown me that his expenditure is not as great as might be supposed. He is more of a philosopher and moralist than ever, and innocent as his love is, he nevertheless disapproves of it. We often dispute about this, but let him take whatever side he will, he is sure to win; for you know what weight he can give to only apparent reasons. I pity him and his good heart which really must be in a very melancholy condition, since he loves the most virtuous and perfect girl without hope. But if we suppose that she requites his love, how miserable must he be on that very account! I need not explain it to you who so well knows the human heart. He has told me that he will write to you one or two things about himself. There is no necessity for me to recommend silence to you on this subject, because you yourself realize how necessary it is.

## GOETHE TO K. L. MOORS

Leipzig, October 1, 1766

My dear Moors,—at last I write you. The confused circumstances in which I find myself will excuse me for having so long been undetermined as to what to do. I have at last made up my mind to disclose everything to you, and Horn has taken upon himself the trouble of writing to you, a matter which by no means would have been agreeable for me. So you know everything. You will have learned from it that your Goethe is not quite so culpable as you thought. Think as a philosopher—and so you must think if you wish to be happy in the world—and what blameworthy aspect has my love then? What is a social position? A mere colour-wash that men have invented to daub over people who do not deserve it. And money is just as miserable an advantage in the eyes of a person who thinks. I am in love with a girl without position and without means, and at this moment I feel for the very first time the happiness that a true affection affords. For the attachment of my maiden I am not indebted to those miserable, trivial flirtations of the lover; only through my character, only through my heart have I won her. I have no need of presents to keep her and I look down with a contemptuous eye upon the expedients by which before now I have purchased the favors of a W. The excellent heart of my Schönkopf is my pledge that she will never fail me until duty and necessity shall bid us part. Were you only to know this excellent girl, dearest Moors, you would forgive me this folly which I am committing in loving her. Yes, she is worthy of the great happiness which I wish her without being able ever to hope that I shall contribute anything to it. Farewell. I will write your brother; it is not pride, it is carelessness which has made me forget him. I must in conclusion impose upon you, in the name of friendship, the most profound silence. Let no person know it; none without exception. You can imagine what harm might hereby come to pass.

## GOETHE TO HIS SISTER

*Cornelia, Goethe's only sister, was his most beloved playmate in the days of his youth. His sister, younger by one year, talented herself in many ways, admired her unusual brother by whom she was willingly guided in her intellectual development.*

Leipzig, October 12, 1767

CERTAINLY, DEAR SISTER, you deserve a very long letter. This morning I reread everything you wrote to me this year and I find I have reason to be very much ashamed of myself. I even shall miss today's lectures to talk with you, although Gellert [esteemed professor and writer] will deliver a speech.

First of all, I must speak of your compositions about which I have kept silent in a somewhat impolite way up to now. I must necessarily laud you and I believe you will be able to think and to write a great many good things when your imagination, your way of approaching a story and the manner in which you tell it will be brought into another but not too different direction. I cannot comment upon it more explicitly without expatiating at great length. Be patient until I shall be with you, then I shall give you instructions in this and various other studies which I have gathered for you and a few other girls.

Only this I can tell you meanwhile; I find that your ideas about most subjects are still very much confused. Though you have fine sentiments as every woman who is like you, they come too easily and are too little thought through. Furthermore, you sometimes say things which, with all my knowledge of the young female, I cannot unravel and understand.

Moreover, I notice that certain books have evidently spoiled your taste in various respects which, like that of most women,

is as variegated in color as a harlequin's dress. This is why I wanted to ask you to read as little as possible and to write much during the year in which we shall still be separated; nothing else but letters and, if this can be done, real letters to me to cultivate the language uninterruptedly; and study the household just as much as the art of cooking and also practice the piano for your own entertainment, for all these things must necessarily be mastered by a girl who wishes to be my pupil (except for languages in which you are especially gifted). Furthermore, I ask you to perfect yourself in dancing, to learn the most common card games and to show great taste in stylish fashion. These latter requirements demanded by so strict a moralist as I am will seem to you very odd, all the more since I lack all three of them; nevertheless, be not be concerned about it and do learn them, their use and advantage will soon become known to you. But this I have to tell you immediately: I do not only ask you not to love them in the least (particularly the two first mentioned) but to flee them; despite it, you must be well versed in them.

Should you have done all this according to my instructions until I come home, I wager my head you will, in a short year, be the most reasonable, well-behaved, pleasant and adorable girl—not only in Frankfort, but in the entire Reich. For, between the two of us, stupidity reigns out there quite strongly. Isn't that a wonderful promise! Yes, dear sister, and a promise which I can and will keep. And tell me, wouldn't I be a great man even if I had not learned anything else here during my stay than to carry out such a great deed? Meanwhile, I tutor the girls here and make various experiments, sometimes I am successful, sometimes not.

# GOETHE TO E. W. BEHRISCH

*Ernest Wolfgang Behrisch, far more advanced in years and life experience than Goethe, was the confidant of his love affairs in Leipzig. The relation to Käthchen Schönkopf was often dimmed through stormy scenes of jealousy, and the arrival of new guests in Schönkopf's inn gave rise only too easily to such scenes. In the November days of 1767 a student, Ryden by name, aroused Goethe's jealousy which led to the dramatic incident which he depicts in this letter to his friend.*

Tuesday, 7 P.M.

HA, BEHRISCH, this is one of those moments! You're gone and the paper is but a cold refuge compared with your arms. Oh God, oh God.—First let me only come to again. Behrisch, cursed be love. Oh, if you could only see, see this unhappy man who is raving and does not know against whom he should rave, you would lament. Friend, friend! Why do I only have one?—

It's now 8 o'clock. The blood in my veins is running more quietly, I shall be able to talk to you more calmly. Whether reasonably? God alone knows that. No, not reasonably. How could a madman talk sensibly? That is I. If there were chains on my hands, I would at least know where to get my teeth through. I gave you a great deal to put up with, now put up with this too. That gabbling, and when you are getting afraid, then pray, I'll say Amen; I myself, I cannot pray. My—Ha! You see! Here it is again! If I could only come to order, or order come to me. My dear, my dear!

Horn was here, I had him come here to read aloud to me, but I have sent him away, he thinks I am in bed. He must not disturb me when I am talking to you. He is a good boy, but when it comes to disturbing someone, he is a master at it.—A thousand things and not the right one.—Oh, Behrisch, Behrisch! My head.

I cut a quill in order to get some relief. Let's see whether we get anywhere. My beloved sweetheart! Ah, she'll be it forever. Look, Behrisch, the moment she makes me rave I feel it thus. God, oh God, why must I love her so! I'll start once more. Annette did—no, she didn't. Patience, patience, I'll tell you everything in order.

On Sunday I went to Doctor Hermann after lunch and returned to Schönkopf's at three. She had gone to Obermann's. For the first time in my life I wished I could be there, but knew no pretext and decided to go to Breitkopf's. I went and could not find peace up there. I was hardly there for a quarter of an hour when I asked the young lady whether she had a message for the Obermann's because of *Minna of Barnhelm* [Lessing's comedy]. She said no. I insisted. She thought I should stay and I thought I wanted to go. Finally, infuriated by my requests, she wrote a note to Miss Obermann, gave it to me and I rushed over with it. How delighted I expected to be. Woe to her! She spoiled my delight. I arrived. Miss Obermann tore the note open, it contained the following words: "What strange creatures those men are! Fickle, without knowing why. Herr Goethe is hardly here when he makes me understand that he prefers your company to mine. He forces me to send you some kind of message, even if it says nothing. However angry I am with him, I nevertheless am grateful to him that he gives me the opportunity to tell you that I am always yours as ever."

After Miss Obermann had read the letter, she assured me that she did not understand it. My beloved read it and, instead of rewarding me for my appearance and thanking me for my affection, she had only coldness and indifference for me until even Miss Obermann and her brother became aware of it. This behavior which she continued the whole evening and the entire Monday caused me so much distress that Monday night I was overcome by fever which tormented me terribly last night, it made me feel cold and hot and forced me to stay home this whole day—well! Oh Behrisch, don't ask that I tell you this calmly and collectedly. God—tonight I sent down for something. My maid brought back the news that she had gone to see a comedy with her mother. I had just had the chills, and at that news the blood in my veins turned into fire! Ha! A comedy! At a time when she knows that her sweetheart is sick. God. That was bad; but I forgave her. I did not know which play it was. What? Could she have gone to the playhouse with those people?—with *those* people! It shook me! I had to know it.—I dressed and ran like a madman to the playhouse. I took a ticket for the gallery. I ran upstairs. Ha, a new blow. My eyes are weak and can't see who is in the loges. I thought I would go completely mad, wanted to rush home to fetch my glasses. A mean fellow standing by my side helped me out of my difficulty, I saw that he had two pair of glasses, I asked him very politely to let me have one, and so he did. I looked down and found her loge—oh, Behrisch—

Yes, I found her loge. She sat in the corner, a little girl beside her, God knows who she was, then Peter, then her mother.—But now! Behind her chair Herr Ryden in a most affectionate position. Ha! Imagine myself! Imagine myself! On the gallery! With a binocular—seeing that! Confound! Oh Behrisch, I thought my head would burst with fury. They played *Miss Sara Sampson* [drama by Lessing]. Frau Schulz rendered the Miss, but I could neither see nor hear anything. My eyes were fastened to the loge, and my heart was dancing. Now he would lean forward so that the little girl sitting beside her could not see anything, now he would step back, now he would lean against her chair and whisper something—I ground my teeth and looked on. I could feel tears well in my eyes, tears from staring at one spot,—I was not able to cry the whole evening.—Then I thought of you, I swear, of you and wanted to go home and write you, but then this sight kept me back and I stayed. God, God! Why had I to pardon her that moment! Yes, that's what I did. I saw how she met his look quite coldly, how she turned away from him, how she hardly answered him, how she seemed to feel annoyed, all that I imagined I saw. Ah, my glasses did not flatter me as much as my soul: I wished to see it. Oh God, and if I had actually seen it, would not her love for me be the last cause to which I should ascribe it?

The clock strikes nine, now it will be over, this confounded comedy. Cursed be it! Now, let me go on with my story. Thus I was sitting for half an hour and did not see anything, not more than I had seen in the first five minutes. Suddenly I was gripped by my fever with its entire intensity, and I thought I would die at that moment; I returned the binoculars to my neighbor and ran home, I did not walk,—and now I have been with you for the last two hours. Do you know a more unhappy person than I am, with such capacities, with such prospects, with such virtues, let me know his name and I shall be silent. The whole evening I tried to cry in vain, my teeth chattered, and when you grit your teeth you cannot weep.

Another pen. Again a few moments of calm. Oh, my friend. The third page already. I could write you a thousand without tiring. Without coming to an end. What miserable person ever got weary of lamenting?

But I love her. I think I would drink poison out of her hand. Pardon me, my friend. I am truly writing in fever, really in a paroxism. But let me go on writing. Better I get rid of my fury thus than that I should beat my head against the wall.

I dozed on my chair for a quarter of an hour. I am certainly very tired. But this page must be covered with words this evening. I have still so much to say.

How will I spend the night? The thought of it makes me shudder. What will I do tomorrow? I'll be calm until I enter the house. And there my heart will start beating and when I'll see her walk or hear her speak, it will beat stronger and after lunch I'll leave. Should I see her, then I'll feel the tears in my eyes and I'll think: God forgive you as I forgive you, and may He give you all those years which you take away from me; that I'll think, look at her and be happy to believe somehow that she loves me, and I'll go again. So it will be tomorrow, the day after tomorrow and so forth.

Look, Behrisch, once I saw "Sara Sampson" with her. How different from today. They were the same scenes, the same actors, and today I couldn't bear them. Ha! all delight rests in us. We are our own devils, we drive ourselves out of Paradise.

I slept again, I am very tired. How will it be tomorrow? My poor head is spinning. Tomorrow I'll go out and see her. Maybe, her unjust indifference will have decreased. If not, then I am sure of another attack of fever, doubly vehement tomorrow night. I don't care! I am no longer master of myself. What did I do the other day when I was carried off by a runaway horse? I could not make it stop, I saw myself dead, at least, I visualized a terrible catastrophe. I dared it and flung myself off. Then I had courage. Perhaps I am not the most courageous man, I am only made to become courageous when in danger. God! My friend! Do you know what I mean? Good night. My brain is in disorder. Oh, if the sun had only returned! Dissatisfaction! I truly no longer know what I am writing.

Wednesday morning.—I have had a ghastly night. I dreamed of Sara. Oh Behrisch, I am somewhat calmer, but not much. I'll see her today. We rehearse our Minna at Obermann's, and I'll be there. Ha, should she continue to show herself indifferent toward me! I could punish her. The most frightful jealousy should torment her. Yet no, no, I can't do it.

Evening, 8 o'clock. Yesterday at about the same time, how different was everything from now. I perused my letter again and certainly I would tear it to shreds if I could be ashamed to appear before you as my real self. This impetuous desire and this just as vehement abhorrence, this rage and this carnal lust will make you see the youth in me, and you will have sympathy with him.

The very thing that turned the world into hell for me yesterday, made it heaven today—and will continue to make it so until it will no longer be able to make it either.

She was at Obermann's and we were alone for a quarter of an hour. It didn't need more time to reconcile ourselves. Shakespeare says in vain: "Frailty, thy name is woman!" it should rather be said about young men. She admitted her injustice, she was stirred by my sickness and she threw her arms around my neck and asked my pardon; I forgave her everything. What did I have to forgive in comparison to what I would not have forgiven her at that moment.

I was strong enough to hide before her my foolishness about the comedy. "Look here," she said, "we were at the playhouse last night, you need not be angry about it. I moved into the very corner of the loge and had Lottchen sit right next to me, so that he shouldn't come to sit beside me. He stood behind my chair all the time, but I avoided as best I could talking to him, I chatted with my neighbor in the next loge and would have liked to sit over there."

—Oh, Behrisch, all this I tried to tell myself yesterday when I saw it, and now she said it herself. She! With her arms around my neck. A moment of pleasure is the substitute for a thousand qualms. Who would want to live otherwise? My distress was gone, an evil that has passed is an asset. The memory of pain that we overcome is a pleasure. And so much for it in exchange! My entire happiness in my arms. The beautiful feeling of shame by which she is so often overcome notwithstanding our familiarity that the power of love again drives her into my arms against all commands of reason; her eyes which close as often as her mouth is pressed onto mine; her sweet smile in the short pauses of our caress which makes her cheeks blush with shame, with love, desire, and fear, this trembling endeavor to free herself from my embrace which shows by its weakness that nothing other than fear would ever make her tear herself away from me. Behrisch, this is bliss for which one likes to bear purgatory. Good night, my head is spinning as it was yesterday, only caused by something else. My fever did not return today, it will hardly return as long as the weather stays as nice as it is. Good night.

## AN IMPROVISED BIBLE LESSON

*Marie Körner, the mother of the poet Theodor Körner, related this scene which took place in Leipzig in her childhood.*

My father worked mainly on little vignettes for the publisher and bookseller Breitkopf; he also made part of his living by giving instruction in his art. Among his pupils was the later so famous Goethe, then sixteen years of age, student of the law; he was one of his most ardent pupils, but one, who, at the same time, was always up to funny tricks or indulging in pieces of folly.

This acquaintance caused our dear mother a great deal of worry and anxiety. When our father would sit, industriously, over his work until the late afternoon hours, his young friend would egg him on to cease working; he would hush my mother's objections by saying that working in the twilight with the thin etching needle has a very bad effect on the eyes, all the more since he must look through the glass. Although my mother replied that looking through a glass would affect the eyes far less than looking into a glass and sometimes even too deeply, the high-spirited student would not give in and would take our father with him to Schönkopf's or to Auerbach's cellar. This acquaintance caused our dear mother many a tear. When however next morning Monsieur Goethe—noble young men were addressed Monsieur—reappeared in our house and mother was giving him a good scolding because he dragged father to such wanton student gatherings where a married man who has a wife and children to care for certainly did not belong, then he knew how to make her friendly again so that she called him the Frankforter Struwel Peter and forced him to have his hair combed which was full of feathers as though sparrows had nested in it. Only when our mother repeatedly asked my sisters and me for our combs, did we bring them, and it took quite a while before his hair was in order again. Goethe had the most beautiful brown hair; he wore it unpowdered, tied at the nape of his neck, yet not like old Fritz did in a stiff pigtail, but so that his thick locks fell loosely down his neck. Goethe never wanted to admit this when I reminded him of it many years later; moreover, he maintained that our mother found particular pleasure in combing his hair and that she ruffled his well-groomed hair in order to be able to straighten it thoroughly.

For the most part, this charming fellow lost the friendship of us children because he preferred fooling around with father's greyhound—it was a graceful little dog called Joli—to playing with us and overlooked many of his unmannerly habits, while he acted the strict educator as far as we were concerned. He always brought some dainty bits with him for Joli; when we, however, annoyance in our eyes, remarked about it, we were given to understand that sweets would spoil our teeth and burnt almonds and chestnuts our voices. Goethe and our father went so far with their wantonness that they put up a small tree, heavy with sundry sweets, for Joli at Christmas; they dressed him up in a red woolen doublet and led him on his two hindlegs to the little table which was richly covered for him, while we had to content ourselves with a package of brown gingerbread which my godfather had sent from Nuremberg. Joli was such an imprudent, yes I dare say, such an unchristian creature that he did not show the least respect for our decorated crib under the Christmas tree, sniffed at everything, snatched the sugary child Jesus out of the crib and crunched it up which made Goethe and my father scream with laughter while we melted into tears. Fortunately, the Holy Virgin, the Holy Joseph and the ox and donkey were made of wood; thus, they were spared such an end.

Our instructions were limited to very few subjects. At eleven o'clock in the morning a shrivelled schoolmaster from Leipzig arrived at our place; he was a proofreader at Breitkopf's printinghouse and wished to give himself the air of a theologist with his black clothes and white ruffles around his neck. He instructed us in reading, writing and arithmetic and was paid a pittance for each hour. What actually topped his attire was his wig falling down in many curls plaited with hair-thin threads. When he entered he would—while still on the threshold—call to us: "Children, your prayer!" Then we said one verse of a song from our hymnbook in unison whereupon we read in the Bible for an hour.

We were all perched together in a single room, and thus it often happened that Goethe came in during our lesson and sat at our father's work table. It once so happened that we had to read aloud a chapter of the Book of Esther, a chapter which seemed to him unfit for young girls. For some time Goethe had listened silently; but suddenly he jumped up from father's work table, snatched the Bible from my hands and shouted at the schoolmaster furiously: "Sir, how can you have these young girls read such w.... stories!"

Our schoolmaster trembled and shook; for Goethe continued his censorious sermon with ever-growing fury until our mother interfered and tried to calm him. The schoolmaster stammered something like "everything is the word of God," whereupon Goethe pointed out: "Examine everything, but retain only what is good and moral!"

Then he opened the New Testament, skimmed through it for a while until he had found what he was looking for. "Here, Doris dear," he said to my sister, "this you may read to us. It is the Sermon on the Mount, everyone of us will like to listen." Since Doris, greatly alarmed, stuttered and could not read, Goethe took the Bible from her, read the whole chapter aloud and added a few quite enlightening remarks such as we had never before heard from our schoolmaster.

Now, this man too got back his courage and humbly remarked: "The gentleman seems to be a *studiosus theologiae;* with God's help he will become a pious worker in the Lord's vineyard and a faithful shepherd of his flock."

"Certainly," our father added jokingly, "he'll bring his barrel into the cellar and feather his nest; he will not be wanting penitent sinners."

Thus the lesson ended quite gaily; everyone was laughing at our father's joke, and, in fact, we did so without knowing why.

## GOETHE TO KÄTHCHEN SCHÖNKOPF

*In September, 1768, Goethe had returned home still suffering from the consequences of a grave haemorrhage which had endangered his life a few weeks previously in Leipzig. New complications arising as soon as he was in Frankfort delayed his recovery for a long time.*

Frankfort, December 30, 1768

MY BEST, my most anxious friend,—Undoubtedly you will have received the news of my recovery from Horn for the New Year, and I hasten to confirm it. Yes, my dear, it has gone by and in future you will have to calm yourself when you hear: He is again laid up! You know, my constitution makes a false step sometimes, and in a week I am generally well again. This time it went badly with me and even looked worse than it was, for it was very painful. But in evil there is also good. I have learned a great many things during my sickness which, otherwise, I would not have learned in my life. Now that all is over I am quite lively again, although I have not left my room for fully three weeks and scarcely anyone visited me but my doctor who, thank God, is an amiable man. What a foolish creature is man! When I was in lively company I was ill-tempered; now that I am forsaken of all the world I am full of vivacity; even during my illness this cheerfulness of mine was a source of relief to my family who were hardly in a position to console themselves, let alone me. In a fit of folly I composed the lines for the New Year which you too will have received and which I had printed for amusement. Besides, I draw a good deal, write fairy tales and am content. God grant me in the New Year everything that may be good for me which he may grant to all of us, and if we ask for nothing else we may certainly hope to receive it. If I could only last till April, I would not mind being made an April-fool of. From then on I hope to improve, more particularly as my health may be expected to improve daily, now that we know what is actually the matter with me. My lungs are as healthy as they can be, but there is something wrong with my stomach. Confidentially I have been given to understand that I may look forward to an agreeable and pleasant mode of living: my mind therefore is cheerful and at ease. As soon as I recover I am to visit foreign countries, and it will only rest with you and somebody else how soon I shall again see Leipzig. Meanwhile I contemplate going to France to see for myself how French life is being lived and to learn the language. Now you can imagine what a polite man I shall undoubtedly have become by the time I see you again. Sometimes the idea strikes me what a preposterous trick it would be, were I to die before Easter despite my fine projects. For that event I ordered a tombstone for the Leipzig churchyard, so that every year on St. John's, my name-saint's day, you may at least visit the St. John's-Manikin and my grave at the same time.

## GOETHE TO FRIEDERIKE OESER

*Friederike was the daughter of the director of the Leipzig Academy of Art, Adam Friedrich Oeser, under whose guidance Goethe received his instructions in drawing. The friendly relationship to the young girl was, above all, based on their common interest in literature.*

Frankfort, February 13, 1769

MADEMOISELLE,—My answer has been long deferred; should I perhaps beg your pardon? Certainly not, if I could do so. If I could say: Mam'selle, excuse me,—I have had many, many things to do at which Hercules might have dislocated his arm; I could not possibly do it. The days were short, my brain owing to the influence of Aries and Aquarius was somewhat cold and damp;—and if I had brought to bear the full string of commonplace excuses, let it not be imputed to myself that I was lazy: If I were in circumstances to say any such thing, I would rather never write at all. Oh, Mam'selle, it was an inopportune composition of my natural humor which tied me for four weeks to my bedpost and four weeks to my chair so that all the time I would just as soon have been bewitched in a cleft tree. And yet they have passed, and I have studied well and thoroughly the chapters of contentment, patience and whatnot of subjects in the book of fate, and have grown somewhat the wiser thereby. You will therefore excuse me if the present letter is more a commentary on yours than a reply to it, because however great the pleasure was which I have had from your letter, I must also take exception to it; and—*Honneur aux dames*—you are wrong, indeed.

We must understand each other better before we proceed further. Assume, then, that I am dissatisfied with you. Like a chronicler I will now begin from the beginning and go on from there to the end, and the letter will grow to be as long as the dissertation of a cathedral canon on a short simple text.

Well, you know of old—at least it is not my fault if you do not know it—that I look upon you as a very good girl who, if so disposed, could easily have it in her power to reconcile an honorable man with the female sex, even though he were as prejudiced as Wieland. If I am wrong, that again is not my fault. For nearly two years I have frequented your house and have seen you almost as seldom as a nightly searching Magus hears a Mandrake whistle.

To speak then of what I have seen—the Church does not pass any judgment on that which is not revealed, said Paris—I do assure you that I have been enchanted by it; but, indeed, philosophers of my stamp generally carry with them Ulysses' bundle of herbs, along with other trinkets, in a sachet, so that the most powerful witchcraft does them no more harm than a drinking bout,—a headache next morning, but the eyes are clear again. Let this be well understood, so that there may be no misconception.

You are fortunate, very fortunate; if my heart were not dead to all sensation just now, I would tell you how fortunate you are, indeed, I would sing it to you . . . You are gentle, sensitive, a connoisseur of charm. This is good for you and your companions, but it is not good for me, and you must be good for me if you want to be a thoroughly good girl. I was once ill and became well again, well enough to reflect with comfort upon my last will. I slunk about in the world like a spirit which, after death, is often drawn to those places which formerly attracted him when he could still enjoy them in the flesh, sorrowfully he creeps to his treasures, and I meekly to my girls, to my friends. I hoped to be commiserated, for our self-love must hope for something, either for love or pity. Mistaken spirit, remain in your tomb! You may weep and wail ever so pitifully and dolefully in your white sheet,—he that is dead is dead; he that is sick is as good as dead; go, ghost, go! if you don't want them to say you are a troublesome ghost.

The stories that led me to these reflections do not belong to this letter. Only one of them will I narrate to you circumstantially, should I still be able to recall it correctly. I came to a girl,—I could have sworn it was you—she received me with a great shout and almost died of laughter that a man could have the ridiculous idea of dying of consumption at the age of twenty. Indeed, she is right, I thought, it is laughable, although as little for me as for the old fellow in the sack who well-nigh died of a beating at which a whole audience almost died of laughing. Since all things in this world have two sides however, and a pretty, agreeable girl can easily make one believe that black is white, and since I am at any rate easily persuaded, the thing pleased me so well that I allowed myself to fancy that it was all imagination and that one would be happy as long as one were pleased, and so forth. And she told me how happy she had been in the country, how she had played blindman's buff and whip-top, had fished and sung, so that I felt as a girl does when reading Grandison: there's a fine specimen of man, she thinks and would like to have such a person for herself. How gladly would I have joined in and made my illness worse. Let a man be what he may, Mam'selle, there is nothing so bad but that fate could not turn it to good account,—your mercilessness towards the poor doomed man during the last few days gave him strength. Believe me, you alone are to blame that I left Leipzig without any special pang. Joy of heart and heroism are as communicable as electricity, and you possess as much of them as an electrical machine has sparks within it. I will see you again tomorrow!—such a farewell to a poor wretch who is about to be chained to the galley is not the most tender. So be it! it gave me strength and yet I was by no means satisfied with it. Between ourselves, let me say, greatness of soul is generally want of feeling. When I consider it well, you acted quite naturally; my departure must have been a subject of indifference to you, but to me, in truth, it was not. I should certainly have wept had I not been afraid of spoiling your white gloves, an unnecessary precaution, for I saw just in the last second that they were of silk and knitted, and then I could have wept again, only it was too late.

But let me conclude. I left Leipzig, and your spirit accompanied me with all the sprightliness of its being. I arrived here and began to make observations for which I had no time before. I looked about for friends and found none, for girls and they were not so compounded as I like. And I was in grief and complained to you in beautiful verses and wondered whether you would commiserate me and comfort the unhappy swain with a letter. Then came a letter! Well, it's true I was cheered, for you cannot imagine the drought which causes one here to pant for agreeable entertainment, but it was no comfort to me. I saw you were of the opinion that poetry and untruth are sisters and that your correspondent might perhaps be a respectable man, but he was also a thorough poet who, from his preference in favor of chiaroscuro, laid on his colors somewhat more strongly and his shades somewhat more darkly than nature does. *Bon.* I will give you credit where you are right . . .

Let it be what it will, the whole affair was an impartial, disinterested reminder for a certain young lady that a really good heart includes compassion too; that the feeding of poor people or of larks is not, by far, the highest degree of feeling; that laughter at real misfortune is just as little a good cure as forgetfulness; that when satisfied ourselves we can, with very little grace, address a discourse on contentment to a hungry man; and, lastly, that the most delightful letter does not possess a hundredth part of the charm of a conversation. Now you might have cast all this and much more in my teeth, and not so gently at all, whereby I should have been confounded and should never have ventured to make any, even the least, of these inopportune observations. If young ladies always knew what they could do if they wished! It is well that it is as it is; I shall be content that they do not know all our weak points. But enough of this subject about which I have written so much, because I hope never again to write about it . . .

How I would enjoy a few delightful evenings with your dear father! I should find so much to say to him. My present existence is devoted to philosophy. Locked in and solitary as I am, my entire apparatus consists of paper and ink, pens and a couple of books. And, by this simple road, I arrive at a knowledge of truth often as far as, or even farther than others with their library knowledge. A great scholar is seldom a great philosopher; and he who, with much labor, has thumbed the pages of many books, despises the easy simple book of nature. And yet it is certainly a poor recommendation for true wisdom that nothing is true but what is simple. Let him who follows the simple path go on his way in silence; humility and prudence best become our footsteps on this path, all of which will eventually meet with due reward. For this I am indebted to your dear father; he was the first to mould my soul in this fashion. Time will reward my diligence so that which has been begun by him can be carried out.

Whenever I start chatting I lose myself as you do; only I cannot find my way back so soon. When I spoke of chatting, this remark applies more to the present letter than it does to yours. It was a little short. Be encouraged by me to write. You do not know how much you do for me in occupying yourself with me for only a little time. And were it only on account of its rarity, you ought to keep up a correspondence with someone in the Reich.

Yet one or two more remarks before I close. My songs, a few of which have had the bad fortune to displease you, will be printed at Easter, set to music. I might have taken the liberty of offering a copy to you with my autograph, were it not that I know how easily you are moved by some trivialities to invectives, as you yourself say at the beginning of your letter which I think, by the way, I have well understood. It is my misfortune that I am so frivolous and that I look at everything from its bright side. Is it my fault that you regarded my songs from the worst aspect? Throw them into the fire and do not look at them when printed; only keep me in favor. Between the two of us, I am one of the resigned poets: if the one poem does not please you, I will write another.

*The Leipziger poems, Goethe's first publication, were brought out as a book of songs in October, 1769, without mentioning the name of the poet. Goethe dedicated the manuscript to Friederike Oeser.*

## GOETHE TO KÄTHCHEN SCHÖNKOPF

*In May 1769, Kätchen became engaged the lawyer Dr. Christian Karl Kanne whom Goethe himself had introduced to the Schönkopf family.*

Frankfort, June 1, 1769

MY FRIEND,— From your letter to Horn I have learnt of your happiness and have seen your joy; you can picture to yourself what my feelings are and what my joy is, if you still can picture to yourself how much I love you. Remember me to your dear doctor and commend me to his friendship. I might well have considered myself guilty of neglect for not writing to you for so long, had you looked forward with impatience to a letter from me. Knowing however that you did not, I therefore did not write; I knew there was a time for you when a letter from me was as little worth your attention as the "Erlangen Journal." Indeed, taking it all in all, I am like a fish out of water and could swear that,—but swear I will not since you might imagine I am not in earnest.

Horn is beginning to improve; when he arrived there was nothing to be done with him. He is so tender, so sensitive about his absent Ariane that it becomes ridiculous. He believes in earnest what you have written to him, namely that Konstanze [Sophie Breitkopf, Horn's beloved] has grown pale from grief. Talking of turning pale, one would suppose that his love could not be very strong; for his cheeks are ruddier than ever. When I assure him that Sophie will learn from her friend's example and gradually realize, etc., he curses me to his heart's content, sends me and my examples to the devil and swears that the characters of tenderness which have been engraven on her heart by the might of his love are indelible. The good fellow does not reflect that maiden's hearts cannot be of marble, nor for that matter should be of marble. The most lovable heart is that which loves the most readily, but that which the most readily loves, forgets the most readily. But he does not think of it and is right in not doing so; it is a horrible sensation to see one's love expire. A lover whose feelings are not requited is not nearly so unfortunate as a forsaken one; the first still cherishes hope and at least does not dread being hated; the other, yes the other—he who has once felt what it is to be cast out of a heart that was his, does not like to think of it, let alone to speak about it . . .

Writing, particularly to you, has grown distasteful to me. If you do not expressly command it, you need not look for a letter from me before October. For, my dear friend, even though you address me as your *dear* friend and sometimes your *best* friend, there is nevertheless always something tiresome about one's best friend. No one asks for preserved beans as long as fresh ones are to be had. Fresh pike are always most esteemed; but when one fears they might spoil one pickles them, particularly when one wishes to lead them astray. It must seem funny to you when you reflect on all the admirers you have salted with friendship, big ones and little ones, crooked or straight ones; I myself laugh when I think of them. Yet you must not altogether break off your correspondence with me, since for a fish in pickle I am still good enough.

Apropos, lest I forget it, I send you herewith a trifle of which you can make what you want, either something for your own head or for another person's hands. The scarf and the fan have not yet advanced a finger's breadth. You see I am candid; whenever I sit down to paint, something sticks in my throat. It is only in spring that the shepherd carves on the trees, only in the flower season does one weave garlands. Pardon me; but the remembrance grows too saddening for me, if I try to do for you what I once did without being more to you than I am now.

August 26, 1769

My dear friend,—I thank you for the interest you take in my health and I must tell you, for your consolation, that the last report on my illness was not altogether well founded. I find myself pretty well, although often undoubtedly less so than I could wish to be. You may readily suppose that nothing but indisposition prevented me from writing long since; perhaps other reasons may shortly hinder you from communicating with me. It is strange that a year ago today I saw you for the last time; it is stupid how different everything looks in one year; I wager that were I to see you again, I should no longer know you. Three years ago I would have sworn it would turn out differently. I maintain, we should swear to nothing. There was a time when I could not cease talking to you; now all my wit will not go far enough to write a page to you, for I can think of nothing that would be agreeable to you. If I could only hear from you that you are happy, that you are happy without exception, I shall be pleased. Do you believe it? Horn sends his greetings to you; he is more unfortunate than I am, but wonderfully as everything is arranged, so his folly aids in curing him of his passion. Farewell, dear friend; greet your dear mother and Peter from me.

I am in a disagreeable mood today. Were I in Leipzig, I would sit at your side and make grimaces. You may remember some such scenes of old. But no; were I beside you, how happy I should feel! Oh, if I could only call back the last two years and a half! Käthchen, I swear, my dearest Käthchen, that I would act more wisely.

December 12, 1769

MY DEAR, my very dear friend,—A dream reminded me last night that I owe you a reply. Not that I had so completely forgotten it; not that I had never thought of you; no, my friend, every day speaks to me about you and about what I owe you. Yet it is strange and a sensation which you too perhaps may know: the memory of absent friends becomes dimmed though not effaced by time. The distractions of our life, acquaintance with new objects, in short every change in our condition works upon our hearts as dust and smoke does on a painting, making the finely-drawn lines quite imperceptible, whilst one does not know how it happens. A thousand circumstances bring you before my mind, a thousand times do I see your image, but as faintly and with as little feeling as if I thought of some stranger. It often occurs to me that I owe you a reply without my experiencing the slightest desire to write to you. When I now read your kind letter, already some months old, and see your friendship and care for one so unworthy, I am shocked at myself; then I feel what a sad change must have come over my heart that I can experience without joy that which formerly would have raised me to the heavens. Pardon me for this! Can one blame a miserable man because he cannot rejoice? My misery has also deadened my feelings toward the good that is still left in me. My body is restored to health but my mind is not yet healed; a quiet, inert calm has overcome me, but that is not to be happy. In this state of rest my power of imagination is so dormant that I can form no image of that which once was so dear to me. It is

Charlotte Kestner, born Buff. After an engraving in the William A. Speck Collection in the Yale University Library

Johann Kaspar Lavater. Original in the William A. Speck Collection in the Yale University Library

only in my dreams that my heart sometimes appears to me as it is; only a dream can recall those sweet images, so recall them that my feelings become alive; as I have already said you are indebted to a dream for the present letter. I saw you; I was beside you as of old; it was so strange that I would rather not tell you about it. In a word, you were married. Could this have been so? I looked at your dear letter and found that the time corresponded. Should it be true, oh, may this be the beginning of your happiness.

Reflecting on it unselfishly, how do I enjoy the thought of knowing that you, my best friend, you above all others who envied you and felt superior to you, are in the arms of an amiable husband and freed from all the unpleasantness to which a single existence, and especially your single existence, was exposed. I am thankful to my dream for having vividly pictured to me your happiness and the happiness of your husband and his reward for having made you so happy. Preserve for me his friendship by remaining my friend, because even your friends you must have in common with him now. If I may believe my dream we shall see each other again, but I hope not too soon; and as far as I am concerned I shall strive to defer its fulfillment, if a man should ever be able to resist fate.

I formerly wrote to you somewhat ambiguously as to what was to become of me. I can tell you more plainly now that I shall change my present residence and move farther from you. Nothing shall remind me of Leipzig any more, not more than an impetuous dream, no friend who might come from there, nor any letter. And yet I can feel that this will be of little help: patience, time and distance will do what nothing else can do, they will blot out all unpleasant reminiscences and return our friendship to life with joy, so that, after a lapse of years, we shall look at each other with quite different eyes but with unchanged heart again. Till then, farewell! Yet not quite till then. Within a quarter of a year you shall have another letter from me, which will tell you of my destination, of the time of my departure and once again, though needlessly, that which

I have already told you a thousand times. I pray you not to reply, but to let me know through my friend if you would like to have anything more from me. This is a sad request, my dearest one, the only one of your sex I may not call friend for this is a word without significance in comparison to what I feel. I desire as little to see your handwriting as to hear your voice; it is sad enough to be so haunted by dreams. Yet you may count on one more letter from me, this I will hold sacred; and a part of my debt shall be discharged, the remainder you must still excuse. Imagine that all our connection would cease, if I would make good this last point . . .

I cannot send you any nuptial ode. I composed several for you, but they gave either too much or too little expression to my feelings. And how could you desire of me a worthy song for a joyous festival? For some time—yes, for a long time past—my verses have been as peevish and as ill-conditioned as my head, as you will observe from most of those already printed and as you will see too from the others if they should be printed . . .

Farewell, dearest friend; receive this letter with love and kindness. My heart could not but speak once more at a time when I was informed only by a dream of an occasion which might have forbidden it. A thousand times farewell, and think occasionally of the tenderest devotion of your—Goethe.

# GOETHE TO J. C. LIMPRECHT

*In Spring, 1770, Goethe went to Strasbourg to continue his juristic studies there. Although under French domination, Strasbourg had a German university. The influence of the pietistic circles with which Goethe had come in contact in Frankfort during his illness is recognizable in his letters to the poor, half-blind student of theology, Johann Christian Limprecht.*

Strasbourg, Good Friday,
April 12, 1770

DEAR LIMPRECHT,—I do not for a moment doubt that you will now be in want of money, for it has occurred to me today, in a very strange way, to send you a louis d'or. It is still better than nothing, methinks, though it is not much; accept it at least as a sign that the days past are not forgotten.

I am a student again and, thank God, I have as much health as I need and cheerfulness in abundance. I still am as I was, except that I stand somewhat better with our Lord God and with his dear Son Jesus Christ. You can deduce from it that I am somewhat wiser and have experienced what it means: The fear of the Lord is the beginning of wisdom. Of course, we do not sing the hosanna before he comes; well and good; even that is joy and happiness: The king must first enter the town before he can ascend the throne.

Furthermore, I wish to hear that your circumstances have improved. You have always had to carry a heavy burden in the world, and finally with your eyes and me. I do not mean my illness; that was a loving-kindness, and a loving-kindness is never burdensome; but when I recall what an unbearable fellow I was during the last summer, it seems to me miraculous that anybody could have endured me. Yet I deserved pity. I had my good burden.

Farewell, and accept this letter in the spirit in which it is is written and sent, without ceremony and with my entire heart.

April 19, 1770

YESTERDAY I received your kind letter of the 28th of March, only a few days after the strange fancy had struck me and made me forward my letter to you on Good Friday night.

I am glad to hear that you are well and preaching, and if you devote yourself to it you must be able to get through the world even without eyes. It is said that Democritos blinded himself so as not to be distracted by this hazardous sense, and in truth if he could do it, he was not wrong: I would often give something to be blind. And yet if it is the case as heretofore that you see twilight where others have day, you do not lose much. For, indeed, everything is twilight in this world, whether a trifle more or less of it, one can find consolation for that.

I am changed, quite changed for which I thank my Saviour; that I am not what I ought to be, I am grateful for that too. Luther says, "I am more afraid of my good deeds than of my sins." And when one is young, one is not perfect in anything.

I have now been here for fifteen days and I find Strasbourg not a bit better or worse than anything else I know upon this earth, that is to say very ordinary,—and yet it has certain aspects which can give one an impulse towards good and evil and which can put a new face on things. Adieu.—Goethe

## GOETHE TO AUGUSTIN TRAPP

*Augustin Trapp whom Goethe knew from school in Frankfort wanted advice in a marriage project.*

Strasbourg, July 28, 1770

I KNOW NOTHING! You have known that for a long time, I should think, and yet you are always questioning me and are surprised when I do not answer. As much as I like to communicate with my friends, and especially with you, my unsettled way of life keeps me from doing so; then whenever I come upon letters that have to be answered and I find questions and inquiries in them to which I am not equal, my laziness gladly uses this excuse to put off the answer into the far distance. I give no thought to the morrow and thank God for it and sometimes His Son too, when I dare, that I am in circumstances which seem to impose a carefree life upon me. How can you wish for advice, for advice in a situation which goes so far beyond my experience, and besides which I do not know anything about the situation nor the person in question.

What else remains to be done? To discuss whether it is well to marry or not. Dear friend, such general reflections make neither the one nor the other wiser than he is and I know far too little about your special case to be able to have a single right idea. Moreover, this is one of those occasions when our prudence, wisdom, speculation or distrust, whatever you like to call it, is of the least help. He who cannot like Eliezer, with complete resignation in the all-pervading wisdom of God, leave the fate of an entire future world to the drinking of the camels is in a bad spot, he cannot be helped. For how could he be advised who will not let himself be advised by God?

Of course, dear friend, what happens to all of us young men

will happen to you too. We do not let our fathers do the courting for us, nor are we easily kept at prayers when our bride is coming. Our affections? What we should do in regard to them? These immature emotions of our hearts, they are fools, and you know what happens when one is fooled by such companions.

On this occasion I could use many nice metaphors, many good moral and even some political thoughts, did I not know the value of words so well. Reflections are very cheap ware; prayers, on the other hand, are a very profitable business; a single elation of our heart in His name whom we call God until we deserve to call him our God, and we are overwhelmed with countless benefits.

One more thing. How is the condition of your health? I beg you to take care of this body with constant vigilance. The soul cannot help looking through these eyes alone, and when they are dim, there is rainy weather all over the world.

I very likely know that as well as anyone else. There was a time when the whole world seemed full of thorns to me as it now does to you. The Physician of Heaven has strengthened the fire of life in my body again, and courage and joy have returned to it.

It will be the same with you when you will be at your best. Farewell. And should you not quite agree with me, it need not worry you; only be convinced of the perfect truth that I am your faithful friend.

# JUNG-STILLING'S MEETING WITH GOETHE

*Heinrich Jung who worked his way out of poverty began to attend the Strasbourg University at the age of thirty to study medicine. In his once very popular autobiography in which he spoke about himself in the third person as "Stilling" and in which he called his friend, an older medical student, "Troost," we find the following description of his first meeting with Goethe.*

THE OTHER DAY at noon Jung-Stilling and Troost went to the dining hall in Strasbourg for the first time. They were the first to arrive and were shown to their seats. Places were laid for twenty at that table, and they saw one after the other enter the room. One in particular came in, spirited, with big bright eyes, a wonderful forehead and a beautiful figure. He attracted Herr Troost's and Herr Stilling's attention. Troost said to Stilling that this must be an eminent man. Stilling affirmed it, but he thought that they both would have a great deal of trouble with him because he considered him an impetuous comrade. He derived his conclusion from the unrestrained behavior this student displayed; but Stilling was very much mistaken.

Meanwhile they learned that this excellent man was called Herr Goethe. Then a theologian, whose name was Lerse, entered. He had a most wonderful personality and was Goethe's favorite, as he rightly deserved, since he was not only a noble genius and a theologian, but he had also the rare gift of quietly making the most pungent satirical remarks in the presence of viciousness. His disposition was uncommonly noble. Someone else took the seat beside Goethe, but I shall say little more of him than that—he was a rare bird with peacock feathers. Another excellent Strasbourger was sitting at the table. His seat was at the head of the table, though it would not have mattered had it been behind the door. His modesty does not permit one to speak in praise of him: it was the actuary, Herr Salzmann. My readers may imagine the most thorough and most sensitive philosopher matched with purest Christianity, then they imagine Herr Salzmann. Goethe and he were bosom friends . . .

Herr Troost was neatly and fashionably dressed. In fact, so was Stilling, too. He wore a dark brown coat and Manchester under-garment, but he still retained a round wig which he wanted to use alternately with his bagwigs. Thus it happened that he wore it that day and had come with it to the table. No one was disturbed by it, only a Herr Waldberg from Vienna. He looked at him and, since he had learned that Stilling's interest lay in religion, he began thus asking him: whether perhaps Adam might have worn a round wig in Paradise?

Everyone laughed heartily except Salzmann, Goethe and Troost; they did not laugh at all. Stilling became infuriated and replied: "Shame on you for this mockery. Such an ordinary joke is not worth being laughed at." Goethe interrupted here and said: "One had better probe a person first, whether he deserves mockery. It is a devilish thing to make fun of a righteous man who did not insult anyone."

From this time on Goethe took an interest in Stilling, visited him, became fond of him, entered into a good fellowship and friendship with him and tried to show his fondness for Stilling on all occasions. It is a pity that so few people know the real heart of this excellent man!

# GOETHE TO FRIEDERIKE BRION

*Goethe made the acquaintance of the Pastor Johann Jacob Brion and his family on the occasion of a visit with his friend Friedrich Leopold Weyland to the little Alsatian village of Sesenheim. At his first meeting with one of the Pastor's daughters, the 19-year-old Friederike, he was deeply impressed by her. The following letter composed immediately after his return to Strasbourg is the only one preserved of Goethe's correspondence with Friederike.*

Strasbourg, October 15, 1770

DEAR NEW FRIEND,—I do not hesitate so to call you. I know very little of the language of the eyes, but at first glance my eye read in yours the hope for this friendship and, I could swear, for our hearts. And you, gentle and good, as I know you, should you not feel the least inclination for me who hold you so dear?

My dear, dear friend, indeed, there is no question whether or not I have anything to say to you; but whether I know just why I am going to write to you at this moment and what I should like to say, that is another matter. A certain inner restlessness tells me that I would like to be with you; and in such a case a little scrap of paper is as true a consolation to me here in the midst of noisy Strasbourg, as ever it can be to you in your peacefulness when you keenly feel the separation from your friends.

You can pretty well imagine the circumstances of our homeward journey, if you were able to see in my looks how sad I felt at parting from you and if you observed Weyland's eagerness to get home, however gladly he would have stayed with you under other circumstances. His thoughts went forward, mine backward, and so, naturally, the conversation could be neither extensive nor interesting . . .

Finally we arrived, and the first thought which occurred to us and which had been our consolation on the road was a plan to see you again soon. There is something so dear in the hope of meeting again. And we with our pampered hearts, when anything makes us the least bit sad, are always ready with the remedy and say: "Dear heart, be quiet; you will not long be separated from those you love; be quiet, dear heart." And then we let it have the picture of our imagination so that, meanwhile, it may have something at least and then it is obedient and quiet like a little child whose mother gives it a doll instead of the apple which it ought not eat.

Enough, here we are, and you can see that you were wrong! You refused to believe that I would dislike the noise of the city after your sweet country joys. Certainly, Mam'selle, Strasbourg never seemed to me so empty as now. I hope, though, it may be better when time will have worn away a little of the memory of our delightful and wanton enjoyment, when I will no longer feel so vividly how sweet, how amiable my friend is. But should I be able or wish to forget it? No, I'll rather keep the little heartache and write to you often.

And now many, many thanks and many sincere remembrances to your dear parents; to your dear sister [the 14-year-old Sophie] many hundreds of–, which I would gladly repay to you.

## SKETCH OF FRIEDERIKE

*Goethe's first visit to Sesenheim was followed by longer stays at the house of the parson where he was considered a future member of the family. In his autobiography Goethe inserts the following description of Friederike.*

THERE ARE WOMEN whom we like best to see in a room, others who look better in the open air. Friederike belonged to the latter. Her whole personality, her figure, never appeared to better advantage than as she walked along a raised footpath; the grace of her carriage seemed to vie with the flowery earth, and the steady brightness of her face with the blue sky. And she carried this refreshing atmosphere which surrounded her, back into the house with her. It was easy to see how clever she was in clearing away difficulties, and with what ease she could smooth away the painful impression left by any small unpleasantness.

The purest joy which we can feel with respect to one we love is to find that she pleases others. Friederike shed a happy influence around her wherever she went. In walks, she flitted about, an animating spirit, and knew how to fill up any occasional gaps which might occur. . . . She was most graceful when she ran. Just as the deer seems to be best fulfilling its destiny as it bounds lightly over the sprouting corn, so the peculiar essence of her nature seemed best to reveal itself as she ran with light steps over mead and furrow, to fetch something forgotten, to look for something lost, to summon a distant couple, or to give any necessary orders. At such times she was never out of breath, and never lost her balance. Hence her parents' great anxiety about her chest must to many have seemed excessive.

## GOETHE TO J. D. SALZMANN

*Johann Daniel Salzmann, an elderly bachelor with literary interests, was Goethe's confidant during his day at Strasbourg. The melancholy tone of the letter points to Goethe's realization that his separation from Friederike was unavoidable.*

Sesenheim, June, 1771

NOW IT IS about time that I came back; I want to and want to, but what can intentions do against the faces around me? The condition of my heart is peculiar and my physical health wavers through the world which is more beautiful than I have seen it for a long time. The most charming neighborhood, people who are fond of me, a round of pleasures. "Are not the dreams of thy childhood fulfilled?" I often ask myself when my eye feeds upon this horizon of delights. "Are not these the fairy gardens for which thou didst yearn?"—They are, they are! I feel it, dear friend, and feel that one is not a whit the happier when one attains what one has wished for. The makeweight the makeweight! which fate throws in the balance for us at every happiness.

Dear friend, it requires great courage not to become downhearted in this world. As a boy I planted a little cherry-tree in sport; it grew and I had the joy of seeing it bloom; a May frost ruined the joy I had with its blossoms, and I had to wait a year, then they grew beautiful and ripe; but the birds had eaten the largest share before I had tasted a single cherry. Another year it was the caterpillars, then a greedy neighbor, then the mildew; and yet when I have a garden of my own I shall again plant cherry-trees. In spite of all misfortunes, there is still enough fruit to satisfy one. I know another pretty story which happened to my late grandfather and which is somewhat more edifying than the cherry-tree tale; but I must not begin it, it is too late for it.

Prepare yourself for an eccentric dish, reflections, sentiments, such as might be properly comprehended under the general title whimsicalities.

Farewell, and if you wish to see me soon again, send me a remittance to set me free, for I have become firmly fixed here. Seriously, be kind enough to give the woman who brings this letter a louis d'or; I was not prepared for so long a time. Write to me, please, and kindly put it into the letter and give the bearer strict injunctions. Adieu, dear fellow, pardon me for everything.

## GOETHE TO HIS GRANDMOTHER

*Johann Wolfgang Textor, the father of Goethe's mother, died in his 78th year. He was chief magistrate of the Free City of Frankfort for many years.*

Strasbourg, 1771

DEAREST GRANDMA,—Our dear father's death, already dreaded from day to day for so long a time, has yet come upon me unprepared. I have felt this loss with all my heart; and what does the world around us mean to us when we lose what we love?

I write to you to console myself, not you, who are now the head of our family, to beg you for your love and to assure you of my tenderest devotion. You have lived longer in the world than I and you must find in your own heart more comfort than I can know of. You have endured more misfortune than I; you must feel far more vividly than I can say it that, through the hand of Providence, the most sorrowful occurrence often takes the most favorable turn for our happiness; that the succession of fortune and misfortune in life is intertwined like sleep and waking, neither without the other, and one for the other's sake; and that all happiness in the world is only borrowed. You have seen children and grandchildren die before you, ceasing their work in the morning of their life; and now your tears accompany a husband to the everlasting Sabbath-rest, a man who has honestly earned his wage. Now he has his rest; and yet the good Lord, whilst he took care of him, has also taken thought for you, for us. He has not taken from us the merry, friendly, happy old man who carried on the affairs of age with the vivacity of youth, who was a leader amongst his fellow citizens and the joy of his family; he has taken from us a man whose life we have seen for some years hanging by a silken thread; his energetic spirit must have felt with painful heaviness the oppressive weight of a sickly body, must have wished itself free as a prisoner yearns to escape from his cell.

Now he is free, and our tears bid him God-speed; and our sorrow gathers us around you, dear mother, to console ourselves, our hearts full of love, with you. You have lost much, but much remains to you. Look at us, love us, and be happy. May you enjoy for a long time yet the temporal reward which you have so richly earned of our invalid father who has gone hence to praise it at the place of requital and who has left us behind as tokens of his love, tokens of time past, for our sorrowful and yet pleasing recollection.

And so may your love for us remain as it was; and where much love is, there is much happiness. I am, with a truly warm heart, your loving grandchild,—J. W. GOETHE

# GOETHE TO J. D. SALZMANN

*After his return from Strasbourg where he had passed his final exams, Goethe was admitted to practice law in Frankfort. But his poetic plans occupied him far more than the juridical practice, above all, his first draft of the historical drama "Götz von Berlichingen."*

Frankfort, November 28, 1771

YOU KNOW ME so well, and still I will bet that you cannot guess why I don't write. It is a passion, an altogether unexpected passion; and you know how things of that sort get a hold on me so that I forget sun, moon and stars over it. You know I cannot live without it, and whatever it may cost I plunge into it. This time no consequences are to be feared. All my genius is concentrated on a certain enterprise whereby Homer, Shakespeare and everything is forgotten. I am dramatizing the history of one of the noblest of Germans [Götz von Berlichingen], rescuing the memory of an honest man; and the great labor it costs me is a really pleasant pastime which one needs here so badly; for it is sad to live in a place where all our activity is concentrated on ourselves.

I have not replaced you, and converse with myself in the fields and on paper. It is true that, when thrown back on itself, my soul soars to flights which collapsed in the distracted life of Strasbourg. Yet even that would be poor company, if I had not turned all the power which I feel within me towards one object and tried to seize and carry it on as far as I can; and what cannot get along by itself, I drag along. When it is ready you shall have it, and I trust you'll have no small pleasure as I shall give new life to a noble ancestor (whom we, unfortunately, know from his tombstone only). Besides, I think you will also love him a little because it is I who present him.

You can see how very simple my occupation is, since I can attend to my practice in extra hours. How often I wish for you so that I could read you a short passage from the work and could hear your judgment and approbation. As for the rest, everything here is dead around me. You may easily guess, however, that I have changed a great deal during these months, for you know how much paper belonged to the diary of my brain every week . . .

I looked for your letter of October 5th and I found a lot more to be answered. My good man, my friends must pardon me, my driving nisus is so strong that I seldom can force myself to take breath and to look backwards, it is also always somewhat painful to me to knot together the torn threads of my imagination.

## GOETHE TO J. G. HERDER

*In Strasbourg Goethe made the acquaintance of Johann Gottfried Herder, his senior by five years. By profession theologist, Herder was at the same time an original and profound thinker whose ideas exerted lasting influence on the young Goethe.*

Frankfort, end of 1771

HERE IN THIS SKETCH which you receive [the first draft of "Götz von Berlichingen"] is the result of my hermit life in this place. It is only a sketch, although it is painted on canvas with my brush and even in some places worked out in detail.

I shall not account for my work to you, my good man, nor will I tell you my present feelings about it, since I have moved away from it, withdrawing to a distance; it would look as if I wished to influence your judgment, because I fear it could stray to a position where I do not wish it. But this I venture to say, that I really worked on it with confidence, devoting to it the best energies of my soul, because I worked with the intention of consulting you. I know that your judgment will not only open my eyes about this piece, but, moreover, will teach me how to regard this work as a milestone from where I have to enter upon a long, long itinerary, and in hours of rest I then may find out how far I will still have to go. Nor shall I undertake any alteration before I hear your voice, for I well know that then a radical regeneration must take place, if it is to see the light.

July, 1772

No DAY goes by without my talking to you, and I often think, "if I could only live with him." It will come, it will come! The youth in his coat of mail wanted to follow too soon, and you ride too fast. Enough, I shall not be idle, I'll follow my path and do whatever I have to do . . .

Pray let us try whether we cannot meet more often. You may feel how you would embrace him who could be to you what you are to me. Let us not, like weaklings, be discouraged, because we must, of necessity, sometimes clash with one another; and when our passions collide, can we not endure such blows? This is far more meant for me than for you. Enough, if you have something on your mind against me, say it outright and in all earnestness, or in anger, with contempt, whatever you feel like . . .

Just one word about "Götz von Berlichingen." Your letter was a letter of consolation; I rated it far lower even than you. Your statement "that Shakespeare has quite spoilt you," I recognized at once in its full force. Certainly, it must be smelted, purified from all dreg, mixed with new and nobler materials and recast; then it shall appear before you again. Everything in it is thought out. That annoys me a great deal. "Emilia Galotti" [Lessing's drama] is thought out too, and neither accident nor caprice ever play the least part in it. With some common sense one can find out the why of every scene, of every word, I might say. Therefore, I am not partial to that piece, in spite of its being the masterpiece it is, nor do I favor my own.

If it were not that at the bottom of my soul there was still so much that foretold, sometimes only vaguely indicating, that I might hope, "if beauty and greatness interweave themselves more in thy feeling, thou wilt do what is good and beautiful, speaking and writing without knowing why thou doest it."

## J. CH. KESTNER ON GOETHE

*Johann Christian Kestner was secretary to the Bremen Legation at the Imperial Chamber at Wetzlar, when, in 1772, Goethe arrived there to study the practice of this Court of Appeal for the whole Empire. Kestner had not only professional qualities as jurist and diplomat, but, moreover, was a man of a rare liberality of mind as the subsequent events in his relation with Goethe should prove. Kestner's characterization of Goethe, the most complete portrayal of the early period, was destined for his friend Friedrich von Hennings, who took great interest in the literary movements of his time.*

IN SPRING, there arrived here a certain Goethe, jurist by occupation, twenty-three years old, only son of a rich father; he came here to gather some practical experience—this was his father's intention—, his own however was to study Homer, Pindar, etc., whatever else his genius, his manner of thinking, and his heart might suggest to him.

At the very first the men of letters here announced him to the public as a brother-in-spirit and collaborator of the "Frankfurter Gelehrte Anzeigen" [literary periodical], parenthetically also as a philosopher, and they did their best to make his acquaintance. As I do not belong to this class of people, or rather am not so often seen in society, I did not meet Goethe until later and then quite by accident. One of the most distinguished of our wits, the Secretary Gotter, persuaded me one day to go with him to the village of Garbenheim—a common walk. There I found him on the grass, under a tree, lying on his back, while he talked to some persons standing around him—an epicurean philosopher (von Goue, a great genius), a stoic philosopher (von Kielmansegge) and a hybrid between the two (Dr. Koenig)—and thoroughly enjoyed himself. He was afterwards glad that I had made his acquaintance under such circumstances. Many things were talked of—some of them very interesting. This time however I formed no other judgment concerning him than that he was no ordinary man. You know that I do not judge hastily. I immediately found that he had genius and a lively imagination; but this was not enough to make me estimate him highly.

Before I proceed further, I must attempt a description of him, as I have since learned to know him better. He has a great deal of talent, is a true genius and a man of character; he possesses an extraordinarily vivid imagination and therefore generally expresses himself in images and similes. He often says about himself that he always speaks figuratively and that he can never express himself literally, but when he is older he hopes to think and to say the thought as it really is. He is ardent in his affections and yet has often great power over himself. His manner of thinking is noble; he is so free from prejudices that he acts as it seems good to him, without troubling himself whether it will please others, whether it is the fashion, whether conventionalism allows it. All compulsion is odious to him.

He is fond of children and can occupy himself with them very much. He is bizarre, and there are several things in his manners, in his outward bearing which could make him disagreeable. But with children, women and a great many people he is nevertheless a favorite. He has great respect for the female sex. He is not yet stable in his principles and is still striving to attain a certain system. To mention something in this connection, he has a high opinion of Rousseau, but is not a blind worshipper of him. He is not what is called orthodox. However, this is not out of pride or caprice, or for the sake of making himself important. On certain significant subjects he opens himself to few and does not willingly disturb the contentment of others in their own ideas. It is true, he hates skepticism, strives after truth and definite ideas on certain fundamental questions; he also thinks that he already has clearly defined ideas on the most important of them, but as far as I have observed it is not yet the case.

He does not go to church or to the sacrament, and prays seldom. For, says he, I am not hypocrite enough for that. Sometimes he seems in repose with regard to certain subjects, sometimes just the contrary. He venerates the Christian religion, but not in the form in which it is presented by our theologians. He believes in a future life, in a better state of existence. He strives after truth, yet values the feeling of it more than the demonstration. He has already done much, is well read, and has many achievements to his credit. But he has meditated and reasoned still more. He has occupied himself chiefly with belles lettres and the fine arts, or rather with all sorts of knowledge, except that which wins bread.

## KESTNER TO F. VON HENNINGS

*Lotte or Lottchen, Kestner's fiancée, was the daughter of Heinrich Adam Buff, who was steward of an institution called the "Deutsches Haus" at Wetzlar. After the death of her mother, the then 19-year-old girl devoted herself to the care of a large family of sisters and brothers, younger than herself. In the following letter to his friend Hennings, Kestner recounts how the delicate relationship between Goethe, Lotte and himself developed.*

It so happened that Goethe was at a ball in the country where my fiancée and I also were. I came late and was forced to ride after them. Therefore, my fiancée drove there with other people. In her carriage was Dr. Goethe who saw Lottchen on this occasion for the first time. He has great knowledge and has made Nature, in her physical and moral aspects, his principal study and has sought the true beauty of both. No woman here pleased him. Lottchen at once attracted his attention. She is young and, although not regularly beautiful, has a very attractive face. Her eyes can be as bright as a spring morning, and especially it was so that day, for she loves dancing. She was gay and in quite a simple dress. He noticed her feeling for the beauty of Nature and her spontaneous wit,—rather humor than wit. He did not know she was betrothed as I came a few hours later; and it is not our custom to show anything but friendship to each other in public. He was excessively gay (this he often is, though at other times melancholy) ; Lottchen quite fascinated him, the more so because she took no trouble about it, but gave herself wholly to the pleasure of the moment. The next day, of course, Goethe came to visit her. He had seen her as a lively girl, fond of dancing and pleasure; he now saw her under another and a better aspect,—in her domestic quality . . .

It could not long remain unknown to him that she could give him nothing but friendship; and her conduct towards him was admirable. The identity of our taste and a closer acquaintance with each other formed between us the strongest bond of friendship. Meanwhile, though he was forced to renounce all hope in relation to Lottchen, and in fact he did renounce it, he could not, with all his philosophy and natural pride, so far master himself as completely to repress his feelings for her. And he has qualities which might make him dangerous to a woman, particularly to one who is sensitive and full of taste. But Lottchen knew how to treat him so as not to encourage vain hope in him, and, moreover, make him admire her manner towards him. His peace of mind suffered. There were many strange scenes in which Lottchen's behavior heightened my regard for her and he, too, became more precious to me as a friend; I was often astonished when I witnessed that love can make such strange creatures even of the strongest and otherwise the most independent men. Most of the time I pitied him and had inner conflicts; for on the one hand, I thought I might not be able to make Lottchen as happy as he could, but, on the other hand, I could not endure the thought of losing her. The latter feeling remained victorious, and in Lottchen I have never once been able to perceive a shadow of the same conflict.

## FROM KESTNER'S DIARY

*Goethe tried in vain to overcome his passion for Lotte. He finally recognized that there was only one way out of a situation which became more and more embarrassing for his friend Kestner: departure.*

September 10, 1772

TODAY Dr. Goethe dined with me in the garden; I did not know that it was for the last time. In the evening Dr. Goethe came to the "Deutsches Haus." He, Lottchen and I had an odd conversation about the life in the other world; about leaving and coming back, etc., a conversation which was not begun by him, but by Lottchen. We agreed that the one who died first should—if he could—give information to the living about the conditions of that other life. Goethe was quite cast down, for he knew that he was to go next morning.

September 11, 1772

THIS MORNING Goethe went away without saying goodbye. He sent me a note with some books. He had long since said that about this time he would make a trip to Coblenz where the military paymaster, Merck [Goethe's friend], expected him, and that he would not say goodbye but depart suddenly. So I had expected it. But I felt that I was nevertheless not prepared for it, I felt it deep in my soul. That morning I came home from my office.

"Herr Dr. Goethe sent this at ten o'clock."—I saw the books and the note and thought it would tell me: "He is gone," and I was quite dejected. Soon after Hans came to ask me if he were really gone. Frau Lange [Goethe's aunt] had taken occasion to send word by a maid: "It was very ill-mannered of

Doctor Goethe to leave without saying goodbye." Lottchen sent back the reply: "Why did you not teach your nephew better?" Lottchen, in order to make sure, sent a box she had of Goethe, to his house. He was no longer there. At noon Frau Lange had again sent word: "I would write Dr. Goethe's mother how badly he conducted himself."—Everyone of the children in the "Deutsches Haus" was saying: "Dr. Goethe is gone!"

At noon I talked with Herr von Born who had accompanied him on horseback as far as Braunfels. Goethe had told him of our conversation last evening. Goethe had left in very low spirits. In the afternoon I brought Lotte the notes Goethe had written her. She was sorry about his departure and while reading tears stood in her eyes. Yet she was glad that he was gone as she could not give him what he desired. We spoke only of him, I could not help thinking of nothing else but him.

## FAREWELL TO LOTTE

*Goethe's notes, the first addressed to Kestner, the others to Lotte, reflect the deep impression made on his mind by the conversation they had on the eve of his departure.*

Wetzlar, September 10, 1772

I'LL BE GONE, Kestner, when you receive this note, I'll be gone. Give Lottchen the enclosed note. I was firmly composed, but your conversation has torn me asunder. At this moment I can say nothing to you but farewell. If I had tarried a moment longer with you I could not have restrained myself. Now I am alone, and tomorrow I shall leave. O my poor head!

I surely hope to return, but God only knows when. Lotte, how it moved my heart to listen to you, knowing it was the last time I saw you! Not the last time, and yet I am going away tomorrow. What spirit led you to this conversation? It gave me occasion to say all that was in my heart. Ah, I was more intent upon this world down here, upon your hand which I kissed for the last time! The room to which I shall never return, and your dear father who saw me to the door for the last time! I am now alone and may weep. I leave you happy and shall always remain in your hearts. And I shall see you again, but not 'tomorrow' is 'never.' Tell the boys: "He is gone." I cannot write any more.

September 11, 1772

MY LUGGAGE is packed, Lotte, and the day is breaking; another quarter of an hour, and I am gone. The pictures which I forgot and which you will divide among the children may serve as an excuse for my writing to you, Lotte, as I have nothing to write. For you know everything, you know how happy I have been these days. Though I am going to the dearest, to the best people,—but why away from you? Well, it is so, and it is my fate that I no longer can add tomorrow and the day after tomorrow to today—which I have so often done in jest. Be cheerful under all circumstances, dear Lotte. You are happier than a hundred others; but do not be indifferent, and I, dear Lotte, am happy that I can read in your eyes that you believe I shall never change. Adieu, a thousand adieus!

# THE VISIT OF THE BEGGAR STUDENT

*Ludwig Friedrich Höpfner was Professor of Law at the University of Giessen and collaborator at the "Frankfurter Gelehrte Anzeigen" for which Goethe wrote literary pieces.*

ONE DAY a young man, carelessly dressed and awkward in his bearing, announced his visit to Höpfner at Giessen with the express remark that he urgently must talk to the professor. Höpfner, though occupied with the preparations for a lecture, received the young man. His whole manner while entering and taking his seat made Höpfner surmise that he faced a student who found himself in financial difficulties. Höpfner's premonition found corroboration in the fact that the young man began the conversation by speaking of his family's background and their pecuniary circumstances in the most explicit detail whereby, from time to time, he made him understand that they were not of the best.

With the hour of his lecture approaching, the professor decided very soon to let the young man have some money without further ado thereby making an end to this painful conversation. However, as soon as he made his intention clear by looking for his purse in his pockets, the alleged beggar student turned the conversation to scientific questions and soon removed the suspicion that he might have come to accept a gift of money. But as soon as the young man noticed that the professor had changed his opinion about his intentions, the conversation was directed into its previous channels and the student's insinuations that he was out for financial help became more and more obvious. Thus several times Höpfner found himself on the point of offering some money to the young man and soon after thinking better of it; the student then left quickly keeping the professor doubtful and guessing about this enigmatic visit.

When, on the evening of the same day but somewhat later than usual, Höpfner entered the place where the instructors of the university used to gather socially, he found everything there in an uproar. Quite a great many people were present and grouped around a single table, some sitting, some standing, in fact, some of the learned gentlemen stood on chairs to look over the heads of their colleagues into the center of those gathered from where the sonorous voice of a man emerged who enchanted his listeners with his fiery talk.

To Höpfner's question as to what was going on they replied: Goethe from Wetzlar has been here for the last hour. The conversation had gradually reached the point where Goethe was doing almost all the talking and everyone was listening to him, surprised and enchanted.

Höpfner, desiring to see the poet, stepped on a chair, looked into the circle and beheld his beggar student transformed into a youth looking like a young god.

## GOETHE TO J. CH. KESTNER

*The secretary to the Brunswick legation in Wetzlar, Karl Wilhelm Jerusalem, shot himself with a pistol which he had borrowed from Kestner on the pretext of needing it for a journey. The unfortunate love for the wife of one of his colleagues had finally driven this gifted young man to this desperate action. Goethe knew Jerusalem, who was the son of an influential theologian, from the days he spent in Leipzig.*

Frankfort, November, 1772

UNHAPPY JERUSALEM! The news was shocking and unexpected

to me; it was dreadful to receive this news as an accompaniment to the pleasantest gift of love. The unfortunate man! But the devils, those infamous men who enjoy nothing but the chaff of vanity and who have pagan lust in their hearts, who preach idolatry and inhibit healthy nature, who overstrain and ruin man's drives are guilty of this misery—of our misery. May the devil, their brother, take them! If that confounded parson, his father, is not to be blamed for it, God forgive me that I wish he may break his neck like Eli. Poor lad! When I returned from a walk where I met him in the moonlight, I said: he is in love. Lotte must still remember that I laughed about it. God knows, loneliness has undermined his heart—For seven years his face has been familiar to me, though I have talked little with him. On my departure I took with me a book of his; I will keep that and the memory of him as long as I live.

*The news of this suicide stimulated Goethe to compose the novel, "The Sorrows of Werther," in which he painted the dangers of his own passion for Lotte by describing Jerusalem's fate.*

## GOETHE TO J. CH. KESTNER

Frankfort, December 25, 1772

CHRISTMAS DAY, EARLY. It is still night, dear Kestner. I have risen in order to write again by the morning light which makes me recall pleasant remembrances of past days. I have had some coffee made to honor the festival, and I will write you until it is day. The watchman has already sounded his tune; it woke me up. Praised be thou, Jesu Christ. I very much like this time of the year and the songs one sings; and the cold which has set in makes me fully happy. Yesterday I had a magnificent day. I was afraid for today, but it has begun well and so I am not anxious about its end. Last night I already promised the two dear silhouettes hovering over my bed like angels of God to write to you. I had pinned up Lotte's silhouette immediately on my arrival; whilst I was in Darmstadt they put my bed in here, and behold Lotte's picture hung at its head which made me very happy; Lenchen [Lotte's younger sister] is now on the other side. Thanks for the nice picture, Kestner, it accords far more with what you write me of her than anything I had imagined; thus it is always with us who guess, imagine and foretell.

The watchman has turned toward me again, the north wind brings his melody to me as if he were blowing before my window.

Yesterday, dear Kestner, I was in the country with a few good fellows; our merriment was very noisy, and shouts and laughter from beginning to end. This is not quite appropriate to the coming hour, but what cannot be brought about by the blessed Gods when it pleases them; they gave me a joyful evening, I hadn't drunk any wine, I could enjoy nature with clear eyes. It was a beautiful evening, when we returned it had become night. Now I must tell you there is always a congenial feeling in my soul when the sun has long gone down, and night spreads from the east towards the north and south, and only a circle of the fading evening still shines out from the west. See, Kestner, where the country is so flat there is the most splendid view; I have looked long at the sun thus in younger and warmer times, setting on my wanderings. On the bridge I stood still. The dark town on the other side, the quietly shining horizon, its reflection in the stream made a wonderful impression on my soul, an impression I fully absorbed. I ran to the Gerocks [childhood friends of Goethe], made them give me pencil and paper, and I drew, to my great joy, the whole picture glowing as it was in my mind. They were all pleased with it, they felt everything I had done, and then only was I certain of what I did. I begged them to cast lots for it; they refused and wanted me to send it to Merck. Now it hangs on my wall and makes me glad today as it did yesterday.

We had a wonderful evening together, like people on whom fortune has bestowed a great gift, and I fell asleep thanking the Saints in Heaven that they are willing to give us childlike joy as a Christmas present. As I crossed the market place and saw the many lights and toys, I thought of you and the boys, how you would come to them, at that moment, a heavenly messenger with the gospel, and how the book, opened up, will edify them. Could I have been with you, I would have liked to light up such festive wax-candles, so that it might have shone on their little heads as a reflection of the splendor of Heaven.

The gate-keepers are coming from the burgomaster and rattle the keys. The first gray of day comes to me over the neighbor's house, and the bells call together a Christian congregation. I feel very much elated up here in my room which for a long time I have not liked as much as I do now. It is decorated with the most well-chosen pictures which wish me a friendly good morning. Seven heads after Raphael, inspired by the living spirit; I copied one of them and am satisfied with it, though not overpleased. But my dear girls, Lotte is there and Lenchen too. Tell Lenchen I wished so ardently to come and kiss her hands like the Monsieur who writes such affectionate letters. He is, indeed, a poor gentleman! I would line and stuff a coverlet for my daughter with such love letters, and she ought to sleep under it as peacefully as a babe. My sister laughed heartily, she too has had such *billets doux* since her youth. But those things must be as repugnant as a rotten egg to any sensitive girl.—The comb is exchanged, not so beautiful in color and shape as the first, but I hope more useful. Lotte has a little head, but it is some head.

The day is coming on in strength; if happiness were as quick in advancing we should soon celebrate a wedding.

## GOETHE TO J. CH. KESTNER

Frankfort, January 28, 1773

THAT WAS a wonderful twenty-four hours. Last night I adorned my fair friends [the two Gerock girls] for the ball although I did not go with them myself. For one I put together, out of the fulness of her wealth, an egret of jewels and feathers and ornamented her splendidly. And once I thought: if you were but with Lotte and were decking her out like this. Then I went with Antoinette and Nanny upon the bridge for an evening walk. The water was very high, it rushed by loudly, the ships were all crowded together. We greeted the dear sad moon kindly, and Antoinette found everything as beautiful as in Paradise and everyone so lucky who can live in the country, on ships and under God's sky. I gladly left her those sweet dreams and would add a few more to them if I could. We went home, and I read and translated Homer to them which is now our favorite reading. The others had gone to the dance.

Last night a terrible storm woke me up at midnight. When it raged and howled I thought of the ships and Antoinette and thought myself well off in my civilized bed. Hardly had I fallen asleep again when the beat of the drum, the alarm and cry of fire awakened me: I jumped out of bed and to the window and saw the glow, bright but distant. I dressed myself, and off I was. A large spacious house, the roof in full flame. And the glowing stanchions, the flying sparks, and the storm in fire and clouds. It was tremendous. It kept burning, downwards and round about. I ran to our grandmother who lives over there. She was just about to remove the silverware. We brought all the valuables into safety, and then awaited the will of fate. It lasted from 1 o'clock until broad daylight. The house with its wings and outbuildings, and also the neighbors' workshops lie in ruins. The fire is stifled, not extinguished. They have it under control, it will not break out again. And now I wish you a good meal. With my mind a bit exhausted, rather as if I had danced, and with other images in my head. How will my dancers have got home? Adieu, dear Lotte, dear Kestner.

## GOETHE TO J. CH. KESTNER

Frankfort, March, 1773

THAT YOU DID NOT receive the rings [for the wedding ceremony] a week ago is not my fault. Here they are, and they ought to please you. I, at least, am satisfied with them. They are the second pair. A week ago the fellow sent me a pair so botched and bungled—away! he had to make new ones and they are nice, I think. Let them be the first links to a chain of happiness which shall bind you to earth as if it were Paradise. I am yours, but from henceforth not at all curious to see you or Lotte. And on Easter day which will, it is to be hoped, be your wedding day, her silhouette shall be removed from my room, or perhaps even the day after tomorrow, and it shall not hang there again until I hear she is a mother; then a new epoch begins, and I shall no longer love her but her children, though a little for her sake, but that does not matter; and should you ask me to be godfather, my spirit shall rest doubly on the boy, and he shall make a fool of himself over girls who are like his mother.

Be happy, then, and go. I am glad you are not coming to Frankfort; if you came, I would leave. To Hanover then, and goodbye. I have sealed up Lotte's ring, as you told me. Adieu.

Goethe. Oil painting by G. M. Kraus, 1775

Elizabeth (Lili) Schönemann

*Enclosed note to Lotte*

MAY THE REMEMBRANCE of me be ever with you, like this ring, in your happiness. Dear Lotte, after a long time we shall see each other again, you with the ring on your finger, and I ever yours.

April, 1773

GOD BLESS YOU, you surprised me [the marriage took place a week earlier]. On Good Friday I was going to make a holy sepulchre and bury Lotte's silhouette. So she hangs there still and shall keep hanging until I die. Farewell. Greet your angel and Lenchen; she must become the second Lotte, and everything will go well with her. I wander in deserts where there is no water, my hair is my shade and my blood my well. And yet your ship, just in port, with gay flags and shouts, makes me glad. And below and above God's heaven I am your friend and Lotte's.

## GOETHE TO J. CH. KESTNER

Frankfort, August, 1773

MUCH GOOD LUCK for everything you undertake, and to your good wife all the joys of life.

I cannot blame you for living in the world and making acquaintance with people of rank and position. To associate with great people is always advantageous to him who knows how to make use of them in moderation, who knows how to respect them as I respect the gunpowder whose force brings down a bird from the air, as though there was nothing more to it. But they also know how to evaluate nobility and usefulness, and a young man like you must hope, must aspire to the best place. Good heavens! even if you do it only for your wife's sake.

As far as domestic joys are concerned, it seems to me, that chancellor as well as secretary participate in them, but I would like to be prince and not let them be taken from me. Therefore, live in God's name according to your own heart against the censurer as well as against the flatterer. I like to listen to them, to listen until they weary me . . .

And now for my dear Götz! I rely upon his good disposition, he will go on and last. He is a child of man with many faults, and yet withal one of the best. Many will be shocked at its outer appearance and a few rough corners, but I have already so much approbation that I am astonished. I do not think that I shall so soon do anything that will please the public again. Meanwhile I go on working, whether or not the whirlpool of affairs may please to use me for something better.

*The reworked drama "Götz von Berlichingen" appeared in print as Goethe's first independent work in June 1773. The treatment of the subject, free from all dramatic rules, and the popular language of this piece made a strong impression on the literary youth.*

## GOETHE TO CHARLOTTE KESTNER

Early on Christmas Day, 1773

IT IS A YEAR AGO that I wrote you at this very hour, my dear ones; how much has changed since. That I have not written you for so long has its reasons in my life being all confused.

I thank you, dear Lotte, that, in exchange for my cobweb [Goethe had sent her material for a dressing gown], you have presented me with a letter. If I had hoped for that, my present would have been selfish. I have certainly kissed the letter a hundred times. There are moments in which one especially realizes how dearly one loves one's friends . . .

The passage in your letter in which you hinted at the possibility of my being closer to you [Goethe was supposed to join the Kestners at Hanover], grieves me intensely. Ah, that has been my dream as long as you have been away. But it will probably remain a dream. My father, indeed, has nothing against my taking up service with other people, and neither love nor the hope of an office keeps me here—and so it seems as if I could dare to see once more what it is like out there.

But, Kestner, the talents and the physical strength I have I need too much for myself. I have always been accustomed to act only according to my instinct, and with that no service could be rendered to any prince. And moreover, until I have learned political subordination—'They are confounded people, those Frankforters,' President Moser used to say, 'one can't do anything with their stubbornness.' And even it were not so, amongst all my talents my jurisprudence is the smallest one. That little bit of theory and common sense won't do—here my law practice goes hand in hand with my knowledge; I learn every day and go ahead at an ordinary pace. But as member of a court—I have hitherto guarded myself from playing a game in which I was the most inexperienced at the table—well—but I would like to know whether your words were anything more than desire and fancy.

## GOETHE TO G. A. BÜRGER

*The poet Gottfried August Bürger was, above all, known for his ballads. Some of them have become very popular with the German speaking people.*

Frankfort, February 12, 1774

I SEND YOU a copy of the second edition of my "Götz von Berlichingen." I have been wishing for a long time to write to you and the few hours which I have been spending with your friend Tesdorpf have decided me to do so.

I rather pride myself on being the one to break down the paper curtain between us. Our voices have often met and our hearts too. Is not life short and barren enough? Should not those walk together whose paths run in the same direction?

Whenever you do some work, send it to me; I will do the same. That will encourage us. You will only show it to the friends of your heart, and I'll do the same. And I promise never to copy anything.

Tesdorpf has been with me on the ice; my heart has gone all out for that kind soul. Farewell. Goethe

## PORTRAIT OF LAVATER

*The Swiss pastor and poet Johann Kaspar Lavater visited Frankfort in June, 1774. He was preparing his great work on physiognomy to which Goethe also later made contributions. In his autobiography, Goethe recounts his impressions of this visit.*

OUR FIRST MEETING was a cordial one; we embraced in the most friendly way, and I found him just what I expected from the many portraits of him I had seen. I saw before me, in full life and activity, an individual of unique distinction, whose like the world has not seen and will not see again. Lavater, on the contrary, betrayed at once by some singular ejaculations, that I was not what he had expected. Thereupon, I assured him, with that realistic spirit which was natural to me and had been increased by cultivation, that since God and nature had been pleased to make me in such fashion we must rest content with it. The most important of the points on which we had been least able to agree in our letters, became at once subjects of conversation, but we had no time to discuss them thoroughly, while something happened to me that I had never before experienced.

For our part whenever we wished to speak of serious matters touching the soul or heart, we were wont to withdraw from the crowd, and even from all society, because among so many modes of thought, and different degrees of culture, it is difficult to be understood even by the few. But it was not so with Lavater, he liked to extend his influence as far as possible, and was never at ease except in a crowd, where he could find scope for his wonderful talent for instruction and entertainment, based on his great knowledge of physiognomy. He had the power of discriminating persons and minds, which enabled him to understand at once the mental state of all around him. And whenever his penetration was met by sincere confession, or true-hearted inquiry, he was able, from the abundance of his internal and external experience, to satisfy everyone with an appropriate answer.

The deep tenderness of his look, the marked sweetness of his mouth, and even the honest Swiss accent which made itself heard through his High German, besides many other of his distinguishing features, immediately placed all whom he addressed entirely at their ease. Even the slight stoop in his carriage, and slightly hollow chest, contributed not a little to counterbalance in the eyes of the remainder of the company the weight of his commanding presence. Towards presumption and arrogance he could behave with tactful self-possession, for while seeming to yield he would suddenly bring forward some great and noble view, which could never have crossed the mind of his narrow-minded opponent, holding it before him like some great diamond shield, yet at the same time so skillfully moderating the light which flowed from it, that such men felt themselves instructed and convinced,—so long at least as they were in his presence. Perhaps with many the impression continued to operate long afterwards, for even conceited men may be good at heart; all that is necessary is to soften by gentle influences the hard shell which holds the fruitful kernel.

What caused him the greatest pain was the presence of persons whose outward ugliness must irrevocably stamp them as decided enemies of his theory of the significance of form. These usually displayed a considerable amount of common sense, and even superior gifts and talents, in vehement hostility and paltry attacks upon a doctrine which appeared offensive to their self-love; for it was not easy to find any one so magnanimous as Socrates, who interpreted his faun-like exterior as a tribute to his acquired morality. To Lavater the hardness, the obduracy of such antagonists was horrible, and his opposition to them often passionate; just as the smelting fire must attack the resisting ore as troublesome and hostile.

## GOETHE TO CONSUL SCHOENBORN

*The Danish diplomat Friedrich Ernst Schoenborn, greatly interested in literature, made Goethe's acquaintance in Frankfort before he departed for his post as consul in Algiers.*

Frankfort, June 1, 1774

On May 25th I received your letter; it gave us all long-awaited joy. I immediately cut this new pen to crowd an equivalent sheet full for you, but it is only today, June 1st, that I find time to write to you.

In the night from the 28th to the 29th a fire broke out in our Judengasse which spread quickly and terribly; I contributed my drop of water, and the most wonderful, deepest and most manifold feelings rewarded me on the spot for my trouble. On this occasion I again learned to know the common people more intimately and again became convinced that they are the best people.

I thank you heartily for going into so great detail of your journey in your report; in return you shall hear everything from our Reich. I have written to Klopstock [famous poet] and sent him something at the same time. Do we need mediators to communicate with each other?

I have composed a variety of new things: a story with the title, "The Sorrows of Werther," wherein I create the figure of a young man who, endowed with deep pure feelings and real penetration, loses himself in fantastic dreams, undermines himself by meditation, until at last, shattered by additional unfortunate passions, especially a hopeless love, he sends a bullet through his head. Then I have worked on a tragedy, "Clavigo," a modern anecdote, dramatized with all possible simplicity and truth; my hero, an undecided man, partly great and partly little, the counterpart to Weislingen in "Götz," or rather Weislingen himself presented in the entity of a main character; scenes are to be found here which I could only indicate in "Götz" in order not to weaken the chief interest. I have had a disgraceful thing printed on Wieland under the title, "Gods, Heroes, and Wieland," a farce. In it I attack him in a mean way because of his faintheartedness in the presentation of those giants of a vigorous world of fable. Little by little, I shall try to send these things to you in Marseille whenever there will be an opportunity; the post cannot take much across the sea.

I have mapped out a few more plans for great dramas, that is to say I have found interesting details for them in reality and in my heart. My "Caesar," which will not please you, seems also to take shape. I devote myself to criticism not at all. I send little things to Claudius and Boie [editors of a literary periodical], I will add a few of them to this letter. I have not been away from Frankfort, but I have led such a dissipated life that I lacked new sensations and new ideas.

*The works mentioned in Goethe's letter were published soon thereafter, with the exception of "Julius Caesar," a work the poet soon abandoned. Christof Martin Wieland, who was as amiable a person as a writer, did not take Goethe's parody amiss and, later on, the heartiest friendship developed between these two men.*

# J. CH. KESTNER TO GOETHE

*The publication of "The Sorrows of Werther" in the fall 1774 turned out to be a literary sensation. The heroes of this short novel in letters, Werther, full of Weltschmerz, and the lovable Lotte became more popular than any other characters of fiction before. What was of main interest to the average reader, namely the genuine lifelike presentation of the characters, was for the Kestners, however, who had served as models for it, a source of great apprehension.*

Hanover, October, 1774

YOUR "WERTHER" might have given me great pleasure, since it could have reminded me of many interesting scenes and incidents. But as it is, it has, in certain respects, given me little edification. You know I like to speak my mind.

It is true, you have woven something new into each person, or you have fused several persons into one. So far good. But if, in this interweaving and fusing, you had taken counsel of your heart, you would not have so prostituted the real persons whose features you borrowed. You wished to draw from nature, so that your picture might be truthful; and yet you have combined so much that is contradictory, that you have missed the very mark at which you aimed. The distinguished author will revolt against this judgment, but I appeal to reality and truth itself when I pronounce that the artist has failed.

The real Lotte would, in many instances, be grieved if she were like the Lotte you have painted. I know well that it is supposed to be a composition of two characters; but the Mrs.

H. [the beloved of the unfortunate Jerusalem] whom you have partly woven in would have also been incapable of what you attribute to your heroine. But this expenditure of fiction was not at all necessary to your end, to nature and truth, for it was without any such behavior on the part of a woman—a behavior which must ever be dishonorable even to a more than ordinary woman—that Jerusalem shot himself.

The real Lotte, whose friend you want to be, in your picture which contains too much of her not to give her away completely, is, I think—but no, I will not say it: it pains me already too much only to think it. And Lotte's husband? You called him your friend and God knows that he was it, is with her—

And that miserable creature of an Albert! In spite of its being an alleged picture of imagination and not a portrait, it has nevertheless such traits of an original (only external traits, it is true, thank God, they are only external) that it is easy to guess the real person. And if you wanted him to act the way he does, was it necessary to have made him such a blockhead? So that you might step forward and say, look here what a fine fellow I am!

*Kestner's reproach refers, above all, to one passage at the end of Goethe's novel in which Lotte, covered with kisses by the desperate Werther, almost confesses that she loves him. Albert, Lotte's husband, is presented as a dull person whose lack of understanding was partly to be blamed for Werther's suicide.*

# GOETHE TO J. CH. KESTNER

*After the immediate excitement had gone, Kestner was, as it would seem, ready to pardon his friend for his indiscretion. It is Kestner's second, unknown letter to which Goethe replies.*

Frankfort, November 21, 1774

YOUR LETTER, KESTNER, is here in front of me! on a strange desk, in a painter's studio, because yesterday I began to paint in oils. I have your letter here and must reply thanks to you! Many thanks, dear friend, you are always good!—Oh, that I could embrace you, that I could kneel before Lotte one minute only and all, all should be explained and blotted out which I could never make clear through volumes of paper! Could you feel the thousandth part of what "Werther" is to a thousand hearts, you would not figure out the cost you had to pay. Now read this clipping and return it exactly as you find it in the letter. You sent me Henning's letter [Kestner's friend], he does not accuse, he excuses me. Dear brother Kestner! If you would only wait, you will be helped. I would not for my own life's sake recall "Werther," and believe me, believe in me, your anxieties, your gravamina will vanish like spectres of the night if you have patience, and then—within a year, I promise you in the most loving, truest and the most fervent manner to sweep away—as a pure north wind does fog and vapor—everything that may still remain of suspicion, misinterpretation, etc. among the gossiping public, although they are a herd of swine.—"Werther" must, must be! You don't feel him, you perceive only me and yourself, and what is pasted on, as you call it,—and, in spite of you and others, is interwoven. If I am still alive, it's you to whom I must say thanks—therefore you are not Albert—well, now—

Press Lotte's hand heartily from me and tell her: to know that her name is uttered with awe by a thousand sacred lips is surely an equivalent for anxieties which would hardly, apart from everything else, vex one long in every-day life where one is exposed to every gossiping woman.

If you are good and do not bicker, then I'll send you letters, cries, sighs for "Werther," and if you have faith, believe me that all will be well and that gossip is nothing; then take to heart your philosopher's [Henning's] letter which I have kissed.

Oh, you! that you did not feel how people embrace you and comfort you and find consolation in your, in Lotte's, virtue in contrast to the misery which terrifies you even in fiction? Lotte, farewell. You, Kestner—love me—and stop wrangling.

Please, don't show this note to anyone! It is between you two! Let no one else see it! Adieu, you dear ones. Kestner, kiss your wife and my godson for me.

And remember my promise. I alone can devise means to put you completely out of reach of all gossip, beyond the breath of suspicion. I have it in my power, but it is too soon yet. Greet your Hennings very heartily from me.

Yesterday a girl said to me she did not think that Lotte was such a pretty name! It has such a peculiar sound in Werther. Another wrote the other day: "I beg you, for God's sake, not to call me Lotte any more! Lottchen or Lolo—whatever you like—only not Lotte, until I am worthier of that name than I am now." O magic power of love and friendship!

# K. VON KNEBEL TO F. BERTUCH

*Karl Ludwig von Knebel had made Goethe's acquaintance in Frankfort as traveling-companion of the young Duke of Saxe-Weimar, Carl August, in December, 1774. This connection finally led to Goethe's appointment in Weimar.*

YOU MAY HAVE LEARNED from Wieland that I made Goethe's acquaintance and that I think very highly of him. I can't help it, but I swear that all of you people who have the right mind and heart will think as I do when you know him. This will always remain one of the extraordinary phenomena in my life. Perhaps the newness of the experience was too much of a surprise to me; but what can I do about it when natural causes bring forth natural reactions in me.

What does our Wieland say to Goethe's letter to him? If only he would never become angry with him. Not two other people in the world would find a quicker understanding than Wieland and Goethe should they get together. I am certain, and can see in everything, that Klopstock and Goethe have not understood each other nearly so well. Goethe's mind is very much occupied with Wieland's writings. This is from where their friction stems.

Goethe is constantly living in an inner struggle and uproar, since everything makes an intense impression on him. This causes his spiritual attacks, the wantonness which certainly does not emanate from a wicked heart, but from the magnitude of his genius. It is the need of his mind to create antagonists with whom he can fight; and he surely won't select the worst for this purpose. He spoke to me with quite particular respect of all those persons whom he attacked. But that fellow is bellicose, he has the spirit of an athlete.

As he is the greatest, most singular personality I have ever come across, he once made the statement—on an evening in Mainz—quite sadly: "Now that I am on good terms again with all these people, with the Jacobis and Wieland—I don't like it at all. It is the condition of my soul that, as soon as I find something which I consider the ideal of perfection for a time, I must also have something as an ideal for my wrath. I know they are all eminent people, but just because of it; what harm can I do to them? What isn't straw will go on living in spite of everything, and the wave of approval, even if it be turned away for a while, again falls back on them."

I had to laugh heartily about naivete of this kind, for the spirit of adjustment is out of place in him. How ever it may be, I could think myself into the possibility of his situation and laughed at him. He loves the eldest of the Jacobis above everyone. He even honored me by finding conspicuous similarities between him and myself. Meanwhile he finished a script, as he assured me, which is to be the most wicked he ever has done of this kind. He even dragged in a woman from Frankfort with whom Jacobi has a liaison. She adjured him for heaven's sake to let her read the script and swore she would not take anything amiss. But he asserted bluntly that it was impossible for any woman in the world not to resent those passages. Now he is waiting for Jacobi to come to Frankfort; he must read it to him, and then he will tear it to pieces.

That much about Goethe! But all this is of little importance. The serious part of his mind is very venerable. I saw a pile of fragments he has written, among other things part of an opus on Doctor Faustus in which are quite extraordinarily beautiful scenes. He drags his manuscripts out of all corners of his room. He had worked on the "Sorrows of Werther" for two months and he assured me that he had not erased one line in the original manuscript. Six weeks for his "Götz von

Berlichingen." He is doing another one again, and dozens of others yet—but about all this some other time.

*Indeed, Goethe must have destroyed the lampoon on the brothers Georg and Fritz Jacobi, for it has never become known. The scenes of Faust about which Knebel spoke belonged to a fragment which is now called "Urfaust." This fragment was lost for a long time until a copy of it was discovered in 1887.*

## GOETHE'S BETROTHAL AND RENUNCIATION

*In the last part of his autobiography, written when he was in his eighties, Goethe gives the story of his betrothal to Elizabeth Schönemann. Lili, as the girl was called by her friends, was the daughter of a rich Frankfort banker and seventeen years of age when Goethe first met her in 1775. Goethe's narration, which in the original is interrupted by numerous digressions, is re-arranged here to give a chronological record of this relationship.*

A FRIEND one evening entreated me to go with him to a little concert to be given in the house of an eminent merchant of the reformed persuasion. It was already late; but yielding to my love of acting on the spur of the moment, I went with him, respectably dressed, as usual. We were shown into a room on the ground floor,—their spacious ordinary family sitting room. There was a large company assembled, a piano stood in the middle of the room at which the only daughter of the house sat down immediately, and played with considerable facility and grace. I stood at the far end of the piano, that I might be near enough to watch her bearing and appearance; there was something childlike in her manner, and the movements she made in playing were unconstrained and easy.

When she had finished her sonata, she stepped towards my end of the piano; we merely bowed without entering into conversation, for a quartet had already been started. At the close of it, I drew somewhat nearer and made some polite compliment; telling her what pleasure it gave me that my first acquaintance with her should at the same time make me acquainted with her talent. She made some graceful reply and we both kept our places. I saw that she observed me closely, and that I was really standing inspection; but I took it all in good part, since I had something charming to look at in my turn. Meanwhile, we were observing each other, and I will not deny that I was aware of a sweet and gentle attraction. Social demands and the varied entertainment prevented any further approach this evening. But I must confess that I was anything but displeased, when, on taking leave, the mother gave me to understand that they hoped soon to see me again, while the daughter seemed not indisposed to join in the request. I did not fail to repeat my visits at suitable intervals, since I was sure of finding cheerful and intellectual conversation, which seemed free from all tendency to more passionate feelings. . . .

On the strength of my writings, people gave me credit for knowledge of the human heart, as it was then called, and from this point of view our conversations invariably possessed ethical interest. But how could we discuss our inner feelings without coming to mutual disclosures? So it was not long before, in a quiet hour, Lili told me the history of her youth. She had grown up in the enjoyment of all social advantages and worldly pleasures. She described to me her brothers, her relations, and all the circumstances of her life; only her mother remained in respectful obscurity. Little weaknesses, too, were remembered; and among them she could not deny, that she had been made conscious of a certain power of attracting others, and, at the same time, of a certain tendency to drop them again. So in the course of our discussion, we came at last to the important point, that she had exercised this power upon me, but had been punished for it, since she had been attracted by me also. These confessions flowed from so pure and childlike a nature, that by them she made me entirely her own.

We were now necessary to each other, we had grown into the habit of seeing each other; but how many a day, how many an evening till far into the night, should I have had to deny myself her company, if I had not reconciled myself to seeing her in her own circle! This was a source of manifold pain to me. My relation to her was that of one person to another—I looked upon her in her character of a beautiful, amiable, highly accomplished daughter; it was like my earlier attachments, but was of a still higher kind. Of outward circumstances, however, of the inevitable constant mixing with society I had never thought. An irresistible longing possessed me; I could not be without her, nor she without me; but owing to her surroundings, and the interference of individual members of her circle, how many days were spoiled, how many hours wasted! . . . .

She, whom I was accustomed to see only in a simple dress which was seldom changed for another, now stood before me in all the splendour of fashionable elegance; and yet it was still herself. Her grace and kindliness of manner remained as usual, only I should say her power of attraction was more conspicuous;—perhaps, because brought into contact with a number of persons, she seemed called upon to express herself with more animation, and display different sides of her character according as this or that person approached her. At any rate, I could not deny, on the one hand, that these strangers were in my way, while on the other I would not for a great deal have missed the pleasure of witnessing her social gifts, and of seeing that she was capable of taking her place in a wider and more public sphere.

Though decked with ornaments, it was still the same breast that had opened to me its inmost secrets, and into which I could look as clearly as into my own; they were still the same lips that had so lately described to me the state of things in which she had grown up and spent her early years. Every look that we interchanged, every accompanying smile, bespoke a noble feeling of mutual comprehension, and I was myself astonished, here in the crowd, at the innocent secret understanding which had grown up between us in the most human and most natural way.

But with the returning spring, the pleasant freedom of the country was to knit these relations still closer. Offenbach on the Main showed even then the beginnings of a considerable city, which promised to develop in the future. Beautiful and, for those times, splendid buildings were already erected. The largest of these was inhabited by Uncle Bernard—to call him by the name adopted by his family—extensive factories adjoined; d'Orville [relative of Lili] an energetic young man of amiable qualities, lived opposite. Contiguous gardens and terraces, reaching down to the Main, and affording free egress in every direction into the lovely surrounding scenery, filled both visitors and residents with supreme content. The lover could not find a more desirable spot for indulging his feelings. . . .

If, because of my multifarious avocations, I could not pass whole days in the country with her, yet the clear evenings gave us opportunity for prolonged meetings in the open air. Lovers will take pleasure in the following incident.

Ours was a condition of which it stands written: "I sleep, but my heart wakes." Light and darkness were alike to us; the light of the day could not outshine the light of love, and the night was turned into brightest day by the radiance of passion.

One clear starlight evening we had been walking about in the open country till it was quite late; and after I had seen her and her friends home to their several doors, and finally had taken leave of her, I felt so little inclined to sleep that I immediately set off on another ramble. I took the high-road to Frankfort, giving myself up to my thoughts and hopes; I seated myself on a bench, in the purest stillness of night, under the gleaming starry heavens, that I might belong only to myself and her. My attention was attracted by a sound quite near me, which I could not explain; it was not a rustling, nor a rushing noise, and on closer observation I discovered that it was under the ground, and caused by the working of some little animal. It might be a hedgehog, or a weasel, or whatever creature is in the habit of burrowing by night. Having set off again towards the city and gone as far as the Roederberg, I recognized, by their chalk-white gleam, the steps which led up to the vineyards. I ascended them, sat down, and fell asleep.

When I awoke, the dawn had broken, and I found myself opposite the high wall, which in earlier times had been erected to defend the heights on this side. Sachsenhausen lay before me, light mists marked the course of the river; it felt cool and pleasant to me. There I waited till the sun, rising gradually behind me, lighted up the landscape lying before me. There lay the spot where I was again to see my beloved, and I returned slowly to the paradise where she still slept.

On account of my increasing circle of business, which, from love of her, I was anxious to establish and extend, my visits to Offenbach became more rare, and hence arose a somewhat painful predicament: it seemed as if I were neglecting and wasting the present for the sake of the future. As my prospects were now gradually improving, I took them to be more promising than they really were, and I thought the more of coming to a speedy decision, since so public an intimacy could not go on much longer without causing embarrassment. And, as is usual in such cases, we did not expressly say so to one another; but the feeling of perfect mutual satisfaction, the full conviction that a separation was impossible, the confidence reposed by each in the other,—all this produced such a seriousness, that I, who had firmly resolved never again to become involved in a protracted connection of the kind, and who found myself, nevertheless, again in the trammels, without the certainty of a happy issue, was in truth beset with deep depression of spirit, and in the endeavor to shake it off I plunged more and more into uninteresting worldly affairs, from which I could only hope to derive profit and satisfaction at the side of my beloved.

In this strange situation, such as many others, no doubt, have painfully experienced, there came to our aid a certain lady who was a friend of the family, and possessed an intimate knowledge of all the persons and circumstances involved. She was called Mademoiselle Delph; she and her older sister managed a little business in Heidelberg, and on several occasions had owed much to the kindness of the chief banking-house in Frankfort. She had known and loved Lili from her youth; she was a person of character, grave and masculine in appearance, with an even, firm, rapid step. She had had peculiar reason to adapt herself to the world, and hence she understood it, in a certain sense at least. She could not be called intriguing; she was accustomed to watch developments for a long time, and to keep her conclusions to herself: but then she had the gift of seeing an opportunity, and if she found people wavering betwixt doubt and resolution, when everything depended upon decision, she would bring such force of character to bear on the situation, that she seldom failed to accomplish her purpose. Properly speaking she had no selfish ends; to have accomplished something, to have carried something through, especially to have brought about a marriage, was reward enough for her. She had long since comprehended our position, and, in repeated visits, had carefully observed the state of affairs, so that she had finally convinced herself that the attachment must be encouraged; that our plans, good in intention, but not prosecuted with sufficient energy and resolution, must be promoted, and this little romance brought to a close as speedily as possible.

For many years she had enjoyed the confidence of Lili's mother. Introduced by me to my parents, she had made herself agreeable to them; for in an Imperial City, brusqueness of manner like hers is seldom offensive, and backed by cleverness and tact, is even welcome. She was fully acquainted with our wishes and our hopes; her love of doing something made her see in them a call upon her good offices; in short she entered into negotiations with our parents. How she began it, how she removed the difficulties which must have stood in her way, I do not know; but she came to us one evening and brought their consent. "Take each other by the hand!" cried she, in her pathetic commanding manner. I stood opposite to Lili and offered her my hand; she, not indeed hesitatingly, but still slowly, placed hers in it. After a long breath we fell into each other's arms with deep emotion.

It was a strange decree of overruling Providence, that in the course of my singular history, I should also have experienced the feelings of one who is betrothed. I may venture to assert, that for a moral man it is the pleasantest of all recollections. It is delightful to recall those feelings, which are difficult to express and almost inexplicable. The previous state of things is entirely changed; things before absolutely antagonistic are now reconciled, the most inveterate differences adjusted; the promptings of nature, the warnings of reason, tyrannizing impulses, and the sober law, which before kept up a perpetual strife within us, all enter into friendly unity, and at the festival, so universally celebrated with solemn rites, that which was forbidden is commanded, and that which was penal is raised to an inviolable duty.

The reader will learn with approval that from this time forward a change took place in me. If my beloved had hitherto been regarded by me as beautiful, graceful, and attractive, now her worth and excellence claimed my respect and consideration. She was as it were a double person: her grace and loveliness belonged to me,—that I felt as before; but the dignity of her character, her self-reliance, her absolute reliability, remained her own. I beheld it, I comprehended it, I delighted in it as a store of wealth, the interest of which I was to share as long as I lived.

There is depth and significance in the old remark: no one

remains long on the summit. The consent of the parents on both sides, obtained in such a characteristic manner by Demoiselle Delph, was considered final, without comment and without further formality. For as soon as something ideal—and in truth a betrothal such as ours merits the name—is brought face to face with reality, then when all seems to be settled, a critical time ensues. The outward world is utterly unmerciful, and rightly, for it must assert its authority once for all; the self-confidence of youthful passions is very great, but we see it only too often shattered upon the rocks of opposing realities. A young couple who enter upon married life, unprovided with sufficient means, cannot look forward to a life of honeymoon bliss, especially in these times; the world immediately presses upon them with uncompromising demands, which, if not satisfied, make the young couple appear ridiculous.

Of the insufficiency of the methods which I had seriously adopted for the attainment of my end, I could not have been aware beforehand, because they would have been adequate up to a certain point; but now that the realization of my hopes was drawing nearer, I saw that matters were not quite what they ought to be. The illusion which passion finds so convenient, was now exposed in all its inconsistency. My house, my domestic circumstances, had to be considered in all their details, in the light of sober common sense. . . . When I tried to fancy myself bringing her to my home, somehow she did not seem to suit it exactly; just as when I went to her parties I had been obliged to change and re-change the style of my clothes for fear of appearing ridiculous by the side of those gay and fashionable worldlings. But no such change was possible in the domestic economy of a substantial burgher-house, rebuilt in accordance with an old-fashioned splendour which gave as it were a conservative character to the establishment. Moreover, even after our parents' consent had been gained, it had not been possible to establish friendly relations or any intercourse between our respective families. Different religious opinions produced different habits; and if the amiable girl wished to continue her former mode of life, she would have found neither opportunity nor space in our moderate-sized house. . . .

On my return [from a journey to Switzerland] I did not, I could not, avoid seeing Lili; our attitude towards one another was tender and considerate. I was informed that she had been fully convinced in my absence that she must break off her intimacy with me, and that this was the more necessary and indeed more practicable, since I had made my meaning sufficiently clear by my journey and voluntary absence. Nevertheless, the same spots in town and country, the same friends, acquainted with all our past, could scarcely leave us untouched—we who were still lovers, although drawn apart in a mysterious way. It was an accursed state, in some way resembling Hades, the meeting-place of the sadly happy dead. There were moments when departed days seemed to revive, but instantly disappeared, like vanishing ghosts.

Some kind people had told me in confidence, that Lili, when all the obstacles to our union were laid before her, had declared that for love of me she was ready to renounce her present life with all its ties, and to go with me to America. America was then, perhaps, even more than now, the Eldorado of all who felt unhappy in their present position. But the very thing which should have raised my hopes, only depressed them the more. My handsome paternal house, only a few hundred steps from hers, offered certainly more tolerable prospects than the uncertain and distant surroundings beyond the ocean; still I do not deny that in her presence all hopes, all wishes sprang to life again, and irresolution was stirring within me.

# GOETHE TO AUGUSTE ZU STOLBERG

*The young Countess Auguste zu Stolberg wrote to Goethe, under the impression of his "Werther," without revealing her identity in her first letter. Goethe felt so attracted by this unknown correspondent that he confided in her his most intimate feelings in his desire for communication. Although the correspondence with her was continued for many years, Goethe and Auguste never met.*

Frankfort, February 13, 1775

PICTURE TO YOURSELF, my dear, a Goethe clad in a laced coat and covered from head to foot in tolerably consistent finery, illuminated by the meaningless splendour of sconces and chandeliers, amidst all kinds of people. He is arrested at the card-table by a pair of beautiful eyes and, in varying dissipation, driven from company to concert and thence to a ball, he frivolously pays court to a pretty blonde [Lili Schönemann]. There you have a picture of the present Carnival-Goethe who recently stammered forth to you a few lines of gloomy deep feelings, but who delays writing to you because in your presence he feels his deficiency.

But then there is another Goethe, in a gray beaver coat, with brown silk necktie and boots, who thinks he can already feel the spring in the whisking February air and to whom his dear wide world will soon reopen. Living, striving and working in himself, he sometimes seeks to express in words, according to his power, the innocent feelings of youth in little poems or the strong spices of life in various dramas; or he draws the forms of his friends and his neighborhood and his beloved household goods with chalk upon grey paper.

He does not ask—neither to his right nor to his left—what people think of what he did. He knows while working he ascends a step higher, because he will leap at no ideal, but, fighting and playing, will have his feelings develop to creative ability. This is the Goethe from whose mind you are never absent, who, suddenly, early in the morning, feels a summons to write to you and whose greatest happiness is to live with the best persons of his time.

So here, my best friend, is very varied news of my condition. Now do the same and entertain me with yours, so we shall come closer to each other and believe we can see each other—because, this I can tell you right away, I shall often entertain you with many trifles just as they cross my mind.

One more thing. What makes me happy are the many noble people who, amongst the many that are insignificant and unbearable indeed, come from all parts of my country to where I live, sometimes passing, sometimes staying. We only know what we are when we find ourselves reflected in others.

Moreover, should it ever be disclosed to me who and where you are, it would make no difference; when I think of you I feel nothing but equality, love, and closeness! And so remain to me as I surely remain to you, through all the ups and downs of life, always yours.

Offenbach, March 6, 1775

WHY SHOULDN'T I write to you, why lay down the pen again for which I have so often reached? How I have thought of you all the time! And now!—I'm in the country among very dear people, in expectation. Dear Augusta, God knows I am a poor fellow. The 28th of February we danced out the close of Carnival. I was there among the first in the room, walked up and down, and thought of you—and then—much joy and love surrounded me. The next morning, as I came home, I was going to write to you, but I left it and talked a great deal with you. What shall I tell you, since I cannot quite explain to you my present position, as you do not know me.

Dearest, remain kind to me. I wish I could rest on your hand, repose in your eyes. Great God! what is the heart of man? Good night. I thought I should get better whilst writing. In vain, my head is overstrained, adieu.

It is night; I wanted to go into the garden, but had to remain standing under the doorway, it is raining hard. I have thought a great deal of you, thought that I had not yet thanked you for your silhouette. But how often have I already thanked you for it, how is mine and my brother Lavater's physiognomical faith again confirmed. This pure intellectual forehead, this sweet firmness of the nose, these dear lips, this well-defined chin, the nobility of the whole! Thank you, dearest, thank you.

Today has been a wonderful day, I have drawn,—written a scene. Oh, if I did not write dramas now, I would perish! Soon I'll send you one written. If I could only sit opposite you and weave it into your heart!—Only take care, my dear, that it does not leave your hands. I don't want this to be printed, for I wish in the future, if God will, to bury or to finally settle my women and children [his poetic productions] in a little corner; without flaunting it in the face of the public. I am so sick of the unearthing and dissecting of my poor Werther. Whenever I enter a room I find the Berlin pack; one blames it, the next praises it, a third says it is tolerable, and the one irritates me as much as the other—come now, you must not think ill of me for that. It does not interest me deeply, it does not move or affect me in regard to my works which are always only the stored up joys and sorrows of my life—though I find it is much more reasonable to shed chicken's blood than one's own.

*Goethe's remark refers to a parody of "Werther" which was published in Berlin. In it the hero loads his pistol with chicken blood before attempting to commit suicide, remains alive and becomes a happy husband.*

# GOETHE TO G. A. BÜRGER

Frankfort, October 18, 1775

WHERE IN THE WORLD I am sitting must be all the same to you. You feel that it is a moment of unrestrained necessity which places the pen in my hand to write you, dear Bürger. Here on the right hand I am warmed by a pleasant fireside, and I am writing to you on a low seat, at a child's little table. I have so much to tell you, but will tell you nothing, and you will understand me and everything. The first moments of composure which by a mad chance, by a *lettre de cachet* of fate, are thrown over my heart, the first after the most desultory, the most confused, the most complete, the fullest, the emptiest, the strongest and silliest three quarters of a year which I ever had in my life. Whatever human nature can collect of contradictions the Fairy Kind or Unkind—what should I call her?—bestowed on me as the New Year's present of '75; in fact, the excellent arrangement was already made with the christening gift; and so let everything take its course. How it will be with me henceforth, God knows! It will be still more restless, still more entangled; and then I shall recall with pleasure the present moment in which I write.

## ON HIS WAY TO WEIMAR

*Goethe had accepted an invitation from the Duke of Weimar, but the chamberlain who was supposed to accompany him did not show up without giving any explanation. Thus Goethe finally departed alone and in all secrecy, since he had taken leave of his friends some time ago. His intention was to go to Italy, but, when he received news from his travelling companion, his destination remained Weimar after all. On the road he made the following entry in his diary:*

October 30, 1775

PRAY THAT YOUR FLIGHT may not happen in winter nor on a Sabbath: this my father had let me know from where he was lying in bed as a farewell warning for my future!—This time, I exclaimed, it is now Monday morning at six without my praying, and, in regard to the rest, do not ask the dear invisible thing that guides and teaches me when and whether I may go. I had packed for the North, and go to the South; I said I would come and do not come; I said I would not come and come! Well, the gate-keepers are tinkling on their way from the burgomaster, let's go ere it dawns and my neighbor, the cobbler, opens his workshop and shutters; let's go. Mother, adieu!

On the Kormarkt [Lili's house] the tinker's boy got himself installed with rattling noises, he greeted the neighbor's maid in the early morning rain. This greeting was full of anxious presentiments of the coming day. Ah, thought I, whoever could—No, said I, there was also a time once—he who has memories should not envy anyone. Lili, adieu, Lili, for the second time! The first time I bade you farwell still full of hope to unite our fates. It has been decided—we must act out our roles separately. However confused it looked from here, I am neither afraid for you nor for myself!—Adieu.

And you! how shall I call you, how? You whom I carry on my heart like a spring flower! How can I take leave of you? With good cheer! It is time now! highest time though—a few days more—and then—oh, fare well! Am I only in the world to writhe in eternally innocent guilt?—

Merck [his friend in Darmstadt], if you should know that I am here close to the old tower and that I pass you who so often was the goal of my itineraries. Riedesel's garden, our beloved sandhill, and the forest of firtrees, and the drilling place—No, brother, you shall not participate in my confusions which, through participation, become only more confused.

Here, then, may lie the foundation stone of my "Diary!" And everything else depends upon the dear thing that has made the plan for my journey.

PART TWO

# *In the Stream of the World*

1775-1788

View of Weimar. By G. M. Kraus

Carl August, Duke of Saxe-Wei

Christoph Martin Wieland

## WIELAND TO J. K. LAVATER

*Weimar, the capital of the Duchy of Saxe-Weimar in Thuringia, was a sleepy country town of 6,000 inhabitants on Goethe's arrival in 1775, a place which had nothing to offer to any visitor but its court life. At that time, the 18-year-old Duke Carl August, married to Princess Luise shortly before, took over the Government which up to then was in the hands of his energetic mother, the widowed Duchess Anna Amalie who acted as regent for her son. The gifted young duke whose eagerness for noble deeds and exploits found no satisfaction in governing his little country looked for distraction in adventurous rides and wanton drinking bouts with a group of his friends to whom Goethe soon belonged. Wieland who, in the following letters, reported to Pastor Lavater of Zurich on the impression Goethe had made on him, had been the mentor of the prince for some years.*

Weimar, November, 1775

I MUST TELL YOU that Goethe is with us since last Tuesday and that I grew so very fond of this wonderful person in three days, that I can see through him entirely, can feel and understand him, and that I am so full of him—which you can much better imagine than I can describe to you . . . I realize that one has to see a person, face to face, in order to really know him. It simply is a necessity with people of Goethe's caliber. I have had Goethe very little to myself as yet. I have to share him with so many people!

January, 1776

Now I have been living with Goethe for nine weeks and live entirely in him, our souls are united; this has come about gradually without any effort and quite unnoticeably. He is—however and from wherever you look at him—the greatest, best, the most magnificent human being God has ever created. To-day there was an hour in which I saw him in his entire grandeur—in his entire, wonderful, sensitive, pure humaneness. Beside myself, I knelt at his side, pressed my soul to his and prayed to God.

February

PRESUMABLY Goethe will stay here for quite some time. He got completely entangled and now he attempts the adventure from which I kept away when I saw that it was saved for someone else. He does his best and, moreover, what a hundred other people could not do in order not to forsake his Lavater. But ah! how much more could and would this magnificent mind of his do, had he not sunk into this our chaos out of which he won't create any possible world, not with all his will power, all his strength. But wasn't I already 38 years old when I became entangled in this impossible adventure, impossible when looked at in broad daylight, when I was induced by a magic imagination and the still stronger magic of the misleading thought of being able to do many good and great things for centuries to come, to do them at this court,—a dangerous adventure and one surrounded by precipices? Goethe is only 26 years of age. How should he, with the impulse of such strength, be able to resist even greater temptations? Because his commanding influence on our princely children, old and young, is incredible. And yet—yet, let us wait and see! If it only doesn't turn out too bad as it otherwise would have, if only something good comes out of it which otherwise would not have happened,—then it would have been worth the trouble!

In my house he is like someone who belongs to us. Here with us he breathes the air of calm and devotion which then helps him bear the hustle and bustle of the great whirl all the better.

## GOETHE TO JOHANNA FAHLMER

Weimar, February 14, 1776

I TRY to adjust myself to the life here and to adjust this life to my needs. I wish I could write to you from the bottom of my heart, but it cannot be done, there are so many threads running through each other, so many twigs from the stem crossing each other that, without a diary, which I have not yet written, there is nothing intelligible to be said. Herder has accepted the appointment of Superintendent General.

Nevertheless, I shall stay here and play my role as well as I can and as long as it pleases me and my fate. If it were only for a few years, in any case it may still be better than the inactive life at home where, with my utmost desire, I cannot do anything. Here, at least, I have some duchies to deal with. At present I only try to make myself acquainted with the country which already gives me a great deal of joy. Also the Duke becomes hereby inspired to work, and, since I know him profoundly, I am in regard to many things thoroughly and completely at ease. I am leading a nice domestic life with Wieland, have lunch and dinner with him when I am not at the court. The girls here are very pretty and well-behaved, I am on good terms with all of them. A noble soul is Frau von Stein, to whom—as you might say—I am attached and firmly drawn. Luise [the Duke's wife] and I only exchange glances and syllables; she is and ever will be an angel. I have very good times with the Duke's mother, and we carry on all sorts of jokes and pranks. You cannot imagine how many good fellows and clever minds are here. We hold together, get on splendidly, dramatize one another, and keep the court at a distance.

## FRAU VON STEIN TO J. VON ZIMMERMANN

*Charlotte von Stein, wife of a dignitary at the Weimar court and mother of several children, belonged to the intellectual circle of the Duchess Anna Amalie. Goethe felt immediately drawn to the gentle Frau von Stein who was his senior by seven years, while—in the beginning—the impression of their being contradictory personalities was predominant in her, as her letters to a friend of hers, the Swiss physician Johann Georg von Zimmermann, prove.*

Weimar, March, 1776

Now I am about to wish you a good night. In the evening, I attended a concert; Goethe was not there. A few hours ago he had been with me and gave me the enclosed note for you. He was cross about your letter which he also read aloud to me. I defended you and confessed that I myself wish he would get rid somewhat of his wild manners for which the people here judge him unjustly, though it really consists of nothing other than hunting and riding horseback in hot haste, cracking his big whip, and all this in the Duke's presence. Certainly, these are not his propensities, but I think he is only doing so for a while to win over the Duke and then to do good. He did not tell me his reasons, defended himself with wonderful explanations, I felt as though he were wrong. He was very nice to me, called me, in confidence, his heart's dearest. This I forbade him in the gentlest tone in the world, warned him not to get accustomed to it, because none other than I could understand it and he, furthermore, often loses sight of certain circumstances. At that he vehemently jumped up from the sofa, saying: "I must go," ran back and forth a few times while looking for his cane, did not find it and rushed out of the door without a goodbye, without saying goodnight. You see, dear Zimmermann, that's how it was with our friend today. Several times already I have had bitter troubles because of him; he doesn't know it and never shall. Once more, good night.—

Well, here is my good morning too. I might even say another 'goodnight' to you before the mail leaves, but I won't be home in the evening and thus must take leave of you in the morning hours.

Yesterday I was supposed to go to see Wieland with the Duke's mother, but I didn't because I was afraid of finding Goethe there. I have surprisingly much on my mind which I must tell this incredible person. It is impossible: He won't get along in the world with his behavior. If our kind moral teacher was crucified, this bitter one will be torn to pieces. Why his constant lampooning? They are all true children of God who tolerates them. And his bad manners, his cursing, his plebeian, vulgar expressions! As soon as it comes to action, it probably will have no influence on his moral attitude, but he corrupts other people with it.

The Duke has changed in a strange way; he was with me yesterday and maintained that all people with respectability and good manners could no longer bear the name of honest men. I admitted that an honest man may often hide under a rough exterior, but certainly just as often under a well-mannered one. That is the reason why the Duke can no longer bear anyone who has not something coarse about him. And all this must be said about Goethe, of a man who thinks and feels for thousands of people, who sees everything so clearly, without prejudice, as soon as he only desires to, who can master whatever he wants. I can feel it, Goethe and I will never become friends; I also don't like his way of treating our sex. In fact, he is what one would call a "coquet"; there is not sufficient respect in his deportment.

Tear this letter to shreds, I feel as though I had perpetrated an ungrateful act toward Goethe, but not to be false to him I'll tell him everything as soon as I find occasion to do so.

## THE DUKE TO MINISTER VON FRITSCH

*To keep his friend in Weimar for a long time, the Duke decided to appoint Goethe to his closest advisory staff, to the "privy council." The first reaction to this step was a ministerial crisis, because President von Fritsch felt the appointment of an outsider without title as an offense and offered his resignation. Only the combined efforts of the Duke and his mother, the dowager duchess, made him remain in office and work together with Goethe.*

Weimar, May 10, 1776

YOUR LETTER of the 24th of April was duly received. In it you tell me your opinion with all the uprightness which I should expect of so candid a man as you. You demand your dismissal from the service, because, as you say, you can no longer sit in a collegium of which Doctor Goethe is a member. As a matter of fact this should not be a sufficient reason to make you come to such a decision. If Doctor Goethe were a man of doubtful character, everyone would approve your decision; but Goethe is upright, his heart is extraordinarily good and tender. I am not the only person pleased with him; men of great insight congratulate me on the possession of such a man. His mental capacity and genius are known. You yourself will understand that such a man would not endure the tedious and mechanical labor of working his way up from the bottom in a Council of State. Not to employ a man of genius in the place where he can make use of his extraordinary talents is to abuse him; I hope you are as convinced of the truthfulness of this statement as I am.

Touching the point that by this means many meritorious people who had some title to this position were set aside, I know of no one in my service who aspired to it; secondly I shall never bestow a position being in such immediate relation to me personally as well as to the weal and woe of my subjects, on the basis of seniority; I shall be guided only by my confidence in the man. As for the judgment of the world which would disapprove of my putting Doctor Goethe in the most important collegium without his having been either a magistrate, professor, councillor on the Board of Domains or councillor on the Government Board,—it does not affect my decision in the least. The world judges according to its prejudices, but I, as well as every other man who wishes to do his duty, do not work for fame, but for the one purpose only to justify myself before God and my own conscience, and I seek to act without any thought of the applause of the world.

In consideration of all this I confess myself greatly surprised that you decide to leave me now, at the very moment when you yourself must, and certainly do, feel how much I need you. Consider how strange it must seem to me that, instead of taking pleasure in giving a capable young man, like the often mentioned Goethe, the benefit of the experience you have gained in twenty-two years of faithful service, you prefer to leave my service in a way which is insulting alike to Doctor Goethe and—I cannot deny it—to me. For it is as if it were a disgrace for you to sit in a collegium with one whom I, as you know, consider my friend, and who has never given occasion to be despised, has rather merited the love of all upright men.

You are your own lord and master, and you may do what you like. I should consider it an injustice to curtail the liberties of anybody, whoever it may be, in such important events of his life, but how I do wish you might come to a different decision!

## GOETHE OR THE DEVIL

*The following anecdote is related by the poet Johann Wilhelm Gleim who benefited contemporary literature by furthering young talents.*

SHORTLY AFTER GOETHE had written his "Werther" I came to Weimar wishing to make his acquaintance. I had brought with me the last Goettingen Musen-Almanac as a literary novelty, and read here and there a piece to the company in which I was passing the evening. While I was reading, a young man, booted and spurred, in a short green shooting-jacket which he held thrown open, had come in and mingled with my audience. I hardly noticed his entrance. He sat down opposite me and listened very attentively. I scarcely realized what there was about him that struck me particularly, except a pair of brilliant Italian eyes. But it was decreed that I should know more about him.

During a short pause in which some gentlemen and ladies were discussing the merits of the pieces I had read, lauding some and censuring others, the gallant young sportsman—for such I took him to be—arose from his chair and, bowing with a most courteous and ingratiating air to me, offered to relieve me from time to time in reading aloud, lest I should be tired. I could not help accepting so polite an offer, and immediately handed him the book. But oh! Apollo and all ye Muses—not forgetting the Graces—what was I then to hear!

At first, indeed, things went on smoothly enough . . . All at once, however, it was as if some wild and wanton devil had taken possession of the young reader, and I thought I saw the incarnate Wild Huntsman before me. He read poems which were not printed in the Almanac at all; he broke out into all imaginable strains and styles. Hexameters, iambics, doggerel verses, one after another, or blended in strange confusion, came tumbling out in torrents.

What wild and humorous fantasies did he not combine that evening! Amidst them, came such noble magnificent thoughts, thrown in, detached and flitting, that the authors to whom he ascribed them would have thanked him on their knees, if such thoughts had come to their minds while sitting at their desks. As soon as the joke was discovered, a general gaiety spread through the room. In one way or another, he dealt everyone present a blow. Even my Maecenasship, which I had always regarded as a sort of duty to excercise towards young savants, poets and artists, had its turn. Though he praised it highly on the one side, he did not forget to insinuate, on the other, that in supporting them I had sometimes backed the wrong horse. In a little fable composed extempore in doggerel verses, he likened me, wittily enough, to a worthy and most enduring turkey-hen sitting on a great heap of eggs of her own and other people's and hatching them with infinite patience; but to whom it sometimes happens that she has a chalk egg put under her instead of a real one, a trick at which she takes no offense.

"This is either Goethe or the devil," I said to Wieland who sat opposite me at the table.

"Both," he replied, "he has the devil in him again today; and then he is like a wanton colt that kicks out his fore legs and his hind legs, and you would do well not to go too near him."

## GOETHE TO FRAU VON STEIN

*For more than a decade Goethe's life stood under the sign of his love for Frau von Stein, a love of unfulfilled passion, but one which purified his being and made him learn to restrain himself. There are more than a thousand letters known which Goethe had written to Frau von Stein, most of them brief messages jotted down on scraps of paper for his beloved, whom he saw in Weimar almost daily. When on journeys, under the impression of a new environment, he wrote more detailed descriptions. The following letter was sent while staying at historical Wartburg where Martin Luther had once commenced work on his Bible translation.*

Wartburg, September 13, 1777

I AM LIVING HERE NOW, my dearest, and I am singing psalms to the Lord who has brought me to such heights and splendor out of pain and darkness. The Duke induced me to move up here. I have nothing in common with those people down there who may be nice people, and they have nothing in common with me: Some of them even imagined they love me, but there isn't too much to it.

My dear, this evening I picture to myself how you will sit down near the moat at the watch-fire in the moonlight, for it will be cool. In Wilhelmsthal [castle with a huge park] it is too low for me and too confined, I could not yet go into the woods as it is still cool and wet. But up here! If I could only send this view to you for which I have but to get up from my chair! How the sad, soft light of the moon lies on the deep green fields, meadows, bushes, woods and groves, here the rocky paths in front of them and there the mountain walls behind them; and how the shadow of the mountain and castle keeps everything buried in the dark and embraces over there the other mountain walls, how the naked pinnacle reddens in the moon, and how the lovely pastures and valleys farther down and the vast country of Thuringia behind it fade in the darkened horizon! My dear, I really enjoy it though I must say that today I still lack an enlivening delight in it. As someone who has been in chains for a long time I first stretch my limbs, but doze with a genuine feeling of gratitude as a thirsty man would seize a glass of water and hardly behold the sacredness of the well and the loveliness of the world.

If I were able to draw it, I would choose a small corner of it only; for nature is too majestic here for any farther look. But what small corners are here!— One should neither draw it nor write about it! However, I wanted to let you know that I live and that I love you very much again as I begin to feel well again. And as consolation in this solitude I fancy that you enjoy receiving a letter or any scribble of mine.

## A CURE FOR A MISANTHROPE

*Goethe gives this description of his first encounter with Friedrich Plessing in one of his later autobiographical writings, "Campaign in France." It was on the occasion of his return journey from France in 1792 that Goethe met Plessing again who in the meantime had gained some reputation as an author and lived as professor of philosophy at Duisburg.*

AMONG A HOST of importunities, addressed to me, both by letter and in person, I received, in the middle of the year 1777, a paper, or rather a pamphlet, dated Wernigerode, and subscribed Plessing, the most wonderful production of the self-torturing kind that I ever beheld. It was plainly from a young man filled with all the knowledge of school and University; but whose learning, nevertheless, did not contribute in the least to his own inward moral tranquility. His handwriting was good and pleasant to read; his style clever and flowing; and, although a tendency to pulpit oratory could at once be perceived, still everything seemed so fresh, and written so from the heart, that one could not help sympathizing with him. But when one's sympathy was allowed to become active and an endeavor was made to get a clearer understanding of the condition of the sufferer, it seemed as if there was in him more of wilfulness than of patience, more of obstinacy than submission, and more of pure selfishness than of ardent longing. In accordance with the propensity of the time, I felt a great desire to see the young man face to face, but considered it inadvisable to ask him to come to me. I had already burdened myself with a number of young men, who, instead of accompanying me on my road towards a purer and higher culture, had lingered on their own path, derived no benefit themselves, and obstructed me in my progress. Hence I allowed the matter to rest till some opportunity should occur for effecting my object. Whereupon I received a second letter, short, but more passionate than the first, in which the writer pressed for an answer and explanation, and implored me most earnestly not to refuse them to him.

But even this renewal of the storm did not trouble me; the second paper affected me just as little as the first; but the habit I had acquired of assisting young men of my own age in affairs of mind or heart, did not allow me to forget him altogether.

The party assembled in Weimar around the excellent young Prince did not readily separate from one another; their occupations and enterprises, amusements, joys and sorrows were all shared in common. But about the end of November, a hunting-party was got up to hunt wild boar in the Eisenach district in order to satisfy the urgent and repeated complaints of the country people; and as I happened to be on a visit there, I was to be of the party, but obtained permission to join them after making a slight detour.

I had a curious, secret journey in view. I frequently heard a strong desire expressed that the Ilmenau mines should be worked again, not only by men of business, but also by persons in Weimar interested in the matter in a general way. Now, although possessing only the most general ideas about mining, I was required, not indeed to give my advice or opinion, but to take an interest in it; and this could not be excited in me in the case of any subject, except by a direct examination of it. I considered it indispensable above all things to get some general understanding, if only superficially, of the nature of mining; in fact, to see things with my own eyes and to grasp them with my mind; then only could I hope to enter further into the details. I had, therefore, for some time contemplated a journey to the Harz, and as this time of the year was usually passed in the open air, in the pleasures of the chase, I felt myself attracted towards it. The winter season had besides, at that time, a great charm for me; and as far as the mines were concerned, neither winter nor summer would be perceptible there. But I must confess that my wish to see my singular correspondent face to face and to test him, contributed in no small degree, too, of my forming this resolution.

Therefore, whilst the hunting party went in another direction, I rode off alone towards the Ettersberg and began the ode, which, under the title of "A Winter's Journey in the Harz," so long remained a riddle among my smaller poems. In the sombre snowclouds, rolling up from the north, and high up in the air, a hawk soared above me. I remained overnight in Sondershausen and reached Nordhausen so early next day that I determined to proceed on my journey immediately after dinner; but it was late at night before I reached Ilfeld, and this was only accomplished with the assistance of guides and lanterns, and not without some risks.

I found a respectable looking inn brilliantly lit up and

some special festivity was apparently being celebrated. At first the landlord did not want to take me in. The commissioners of the supreme courts, I was told, had been busy here for some time past in making arrangements of importance and reconciling various interests; and as this had now been brought to a successful termination, the matter was being concluded with a general feast. But on being urgently remonstrated with, and on some hints being given by my guide that it would be advisable to treat me well, the man offered to give me the room partitioned off from the dining-room, his own special abode, and likewise his large double bed with white hangings. He led me through the spacious brilliantly lighted dining-room, and I had an opportunity of glancing at the merry party.

I had a better opportunity, however, of examining them closely through a hole in the boards of the partition which, undoubtedly, had often furnished the landlord a means for watching his guests. I was greatly amused and looked right up the long well-lighted table, surveying it as one might have the marriage feast at Cana represented in a picture; I had a comfortable view of them from one end to the other: presidents, councillors, and others connected with them, and then secretaries, clerks and assistants. The successful termination of a troublesome affair appeared to produce an equality amongst all those who had taken an active part in it; they were chatting very freely and drinking healths; jokes were bandied about, and some of the guests seemed to be the butts for sallies of wit and jest; in short, it was a high and joyous feast which I could quietly observe in all its peculiarities by the brilliant light of the wax candles, just as if the devil himself had been standing at my side, and treating me with a direct view and insight into some strange state of things. How charming this was to me after the gloomiest of rides among the Harz mountains will be readily understood by lovers of such adventures. It struck me at times as something ghostlike, as if I were looking at a party of merry spectres amusing themselves in some mountain cavern.

After a good sleep, I hastened early next morning, again accompanied by a guide, to the miners' cavern, crept into it, and closely examined the incessant working of the natural phenomenon. Masses of black marble broken down and restored to white crystalline pillars and flat slabs showed me the never-resting activity of Nature. Whilst quietly contemplating the scene, all the miraculous images which a gloomy imagination is so fond of conjuring up out of formless appearances vanished, it is true, but in their place the particular truth stood out all the more purely, and I felt myself greatly enriched by it.

On arriving at the inn in Wernigerode, I entered into conversation with the waiter and found him a sensible person, who seemed to be pretty well acquainted with his fellow-townsmen. I then told him that it was my custom, on arriving at a place where I had no particular introductions, to seek out such young persons as might in any way be distinguished for learning and science; and thereupon asked him to do me the favor to name somebody of this description with whom I might hope to pass the evening pleasantly. Without hesitation the waiter replied that no doubt I should find what I desired in Herr Plessing, the son of the superintendent; that as a boy even he had been distinguished at school and still maintained his reputation for diligence and ability; that people now found fault with his gloomy disposition and did not like him on account of unsocial behavior which led him to shut himself out from society. But that towards strangers he was always polite, as examples could prove, and if I wanted an introduction, it could be got immediately.

The waiter soon brought me word that I might pay Plessing a visit and conducted me to his residence. The evening had already set in, when I entered a large room on the ground-floor, the usual style in ecclesiastical houses, and although it was twilight I could distinguish the young man rather well. I observed some signs of the parents having hastily left the room, to make place for the unexpected visitor.

When the lights were brought in, I had a distinct view of the young man, and he was exactly what his letter had led me to expect; and, like it, he excited one's interest without being exactly attractive.

In order to lead to a more intimate conversation, I described myself as an artist from Gotha and said that, on account of some family matters, I was about to visit a sister and brother-in-law in Brunswick at this unfavorable season.

With great animation he thereupon exclaimed, scarcely allowing me to finish my sentence. "As you live so near Weimar, you have no doubt frequently visited that place which has become so celebrated?" I answered, with perfect simplicity, in the affirmative, and began to speak of Counsellor Kraus, and the Drawing Academy; of Bertuch, Counsellor of the Legation, and his unwearying assiduity; I did not omit either Musaeus or Jagemann; spoke of Wolf, the band-master; and some ladies; described the circle in which these worthy people moved and said they were always glad to see strangers amongst them, who were sure to be well received.

At last he exclaimed somewhat impatiently: "But why do you not mention Goethe?" I replied that I had seen him in the aforesaid circle as a welcome guest, and had even been myself personally well received and kindly treated by him as an artist, but that I could not say much further about him, partly because he lived alone and partly because he belonged to other circles.

The young man, who had listened with restless attention, now demanded me, with some impetuosity, to describe this strange individual who had created such a sensation in the world. Whereupon, with great ingenuity, I gave him a description which was not difficult to do, as the strange person happened to be before me in the strangest of situations; and if Nature had only favored him with a little more sagacity of heart, he could hardly have failed to perceive that his visitor was describing himself.

He had walked up and down the room two or three times, when the maid-servant entered and placed a bottle of wine and some cold supper on the table; he filled both our glasses, touched my glass with his and drank it off excitedly. Scarcely had I, with somewhat less eagerness, emptied mine, when he seized me by the arm with great vehemence and exclaimed: "Oh, excuse my singular behavior! But you have inspired me with such confidence that I cannot help telling you all. This man, from your description of him, ought certainly to have answered me; I sent him a detailed affectionate letter, describing my condition, my sufferings and begged him to interest himself in me, to advise me, to help me; and now months have passed and I have no reply. The very least he could do, was to have sent me a refusal, in return for such unbounded confidence."

In reply to this, I said that such conduct I could neither explain nor excuse; but this much I knew from my own experience that owing to a heavy pressure of things both ideal and real, this, otherwise well-meaning, good-natured and helpful young man, was often unable to do as he pleased, much less to act for others.

"As we have accidentally got that far," he now added with somewhat more composure, "I must read the letter to you; and you can then judge whether it did not deserve some answer, some reply."

I walked up and down the room waiting for him to read it, knowing of course what effect it would produce, and therefore had no fear of making a false step in so delicate an affair. He sat down opposite me and began to read the papers which I knew as well as he did; and nothing, perhaps, ever convinced me more of the truth of the assertion made by physiognomists: that a living being in all its actions and conduct, is in complete accordance with itself, and that every monad, when once it had entered the world of reality, manifests itself in complete unity with its characteristics. The reader was an exact counterpart of what he read; and as the letter had not attracted me first, it did not attract me now in his presence. One could not, indeed, deny the young man one's respect, one's sympathy; in fact, it was this which had induced me to make this curious journey; for an earnest will was visible in him, a noble tendency and aim; but although the tenderest feelings were in question, his manner of reading was without grace, and a peculiar, narrow kind of selfishness was strongly apparent throughout. When he had finished, he asked hastily what I now thought, and whether such a paper did not deserve, nay, demand an answer?

Meanwhile I had obtained a clearer insight into the young man's deplorable state of mind; he had never taken cognizance of the outward world, but had, on the contrary, cultivated his mind by multifarious reading, and directed all his powers and interests inwards; and, not finding any productive talent in the depths of his being, he had gone far to ruin himself altogether. And even the occupation and consolation so gloriously offered us by a study of the ancient languages, seemed to be completely wanting to him.

As I had already proved, both in myself and others, that the best remedy in such cases is to throw ourselves with energy and faith upon Nature and her infinite variety, I made an attempt to apply it in this case also. After a little reflection I answered him in the following way:—

"I think I can understand why the young man, in whom you have placed so much confidence, has remained silent towards you. His present way of thinking is doubtless too different from yours to allow any hope that you could come to any agreement with each other. I have been present during some conversations in the circle spoken of and have heard it maintained that the only way in which a person can escape and save himself from a painful, self-torturing, gloomy state of mind is by a contemplation of Nature and a heartfelt sympathy with the outward world. Even a most general acquaintance with Nature, no matter in what way, in fact any active communication with it, either in gardening or farming, hunting or mining, draws us out of ourselves; the employment of our mental energies upon real, actual phenomena affords by degrees the greatest satisfaction, clearness of mind and instruction; in the same way as the artist who keeps true to Nature, while cultivating his mind, is certain to succeed the best."

My young friend appeared to get very restless and impatient

at this, just as one does when listening to some foreign or confused language, the meaning of which one cannot understand. However, although there seemed but little hope of a successful result, I proceeded more for the sake of saying something, and added that; "To me, as a landscape painter, this appeared very evident, as my particular department of art was in direct communication with Nature. But since that time, I have observed things with more assiduity and eagerness than I had previously done, and not merely noted uncommon and remarkable natural objects and phenomena, but felt myself more full of love for all things and all men." In order not to lose myself in the abstract, I thereupon told him that even this very necessary winter excursion, instead of being irksome, had furnished me with lasting enjoyment. I described to him the course of my journey artistically and poetically, and yet as truly and naturally as I could; I spoke of the snow-clouds which I had that morning seen rolling over the mountains, and the various other appearances that had struck me during the day; I then revealed to his imagination the curious turreted and walled fortifications of Nordhausen, as seen in the twilight; and further, at night, the torrents rushing down the mountain ravines, their waters lighted up now and then, and glistening in the flickering light of the guide's lantern; and, last of all, the miners' caverns.

Here he interrupted me with warmth and assured me that he heartily regretted the trouble he had taken in going to see the latter, short as the distance was; it had not at all come up to the picture he had formed of it in his imagination. After what had passed between us, such morbid symptoms did not annoy me; often had I seen how men throw away the valuable possession of a clear reality for a dismal phantom of their gloomy imaginations! Just as little did it astonish me when, in answer to my question, "How had he pictured the caverns to himself?" he described them in such a way as the boldest scene-painter would scarcely have ventured to do in depicting the fore-courts of Pluto's kingdom.

Upon this I tried other propaedeutic suggestions as expedients for effecting a cure. But these were rejected so emphatically with the assurance that nothing in this world ever could or should content him, that my heart closed itself against him; and I felt my conscience completely freed from the necessity of taking any further trouble about him, considering the fatiguing journey I had undertaken on his account, and the best intentions I had had towards him.

It was already pretty late when he spoke of reading to me his second still more passionate letter, which was, of course, likewise not unknown to me; he accepted my apology for not wishing to hear it then, because of my being too tired, but invited me, in the name of his family, to dine with them the following day; I told him I would let him know early next morning if I could come. We parted peaceably and becomingly. His person left a peculiar impression upon me; he was of middle height, his features had nothing attractive, but neither had they anything repulsive in them; his gloomy presence had nothing uncourteous about it; and he might, in fact, have passed for a well-educated young man, preparing himself quietly in schools and academies, for the pulpit or a professorial chair.

On going out, I found the sky clear and bright with stars, the streets and squares covered with snow; I stopped on a narrow bridge and stood quietly looking at the surrounding objects in the wintry night. At the same time I thought over the adventure and felt quite resolved not to see the young man again; hence I ordered my horse at daybreak, gave the waiter an anonymous note containing my apologies and, at the same time, said many things in praise of the young person to whom he had introduced me, which were true enough, and of which, no doubt, the dexterous fellow made good use for his own purposes.

I cannot say how long it was since I heard anything of my young friend when, quite unexpectedly, one morning a note was delivered to me in my Summer-house at Weimar in which he introduced himself to me. I wrote him a few words to say that I would be glad to see him. I expected a singular scene of recognition; but on coming in he said quietly: "I am not surprised to find you here, the handwriting of your note brought so vividly to my recollection the lines which you left me on leaving for Wernigerode, that I never for a moment doubted that I should here find the mysterious traveler again."

This was a good beginning, and we began talking very cordially together; he endeavored to describe his condition to me, and I, in no way, concealed my opinion from him. I am unable to say now whether I found his mind in a more healthy state, or not; but it cannot have appeared very bad, for we parted after a good deal of conversation, on good terms; but I could not reciprocate the vehement desire he manifested for passionate friendship and the closest intimacy between us.

## GOETHE TO FRAU VON STEIN

Goslar, December 4, 1777

TODAY I have gone through some nasty weather. It is indescribable what the storms in these mountains can brew for us. Storm, snow, hail, rain, and all this on a front of two miles along the north wall of mountainous woods. Almost everything is steaming wet, and I have hardly recovered from it even after eating and drinking, after three hours of rest, etc.—I stood the test of my adventure [his visit with Plessing], in fact, I stood it beautifully and totally, as I foretold and as you will enjoy hearing; because you alone may hear it, the Duke too, but otherwise it must remain a secret. It is base, but wonderful; it is nothing and much—the Gods alone know what they want and what they want to do with us. Their will be done!

Here I am now deeply absorbed in antiquity again. With

an innkeeper who has a great deal of the patriarch about him; there is such a wonderful atmosphere in the house, as with a real student's landlord, that one feels extremely comfortable. —How very much I have again learned to love that class of people one calls the lowly, but which, God knows, is certainly the highest! All virtues are gathered in them, simple-mindedness, modesty, straightforwardness, faithfulness, joy over the little things in life, harmlessness, patience—patience—endurance—I do not want to lose myself in exclamations.

My clothes are hanging around the stove where I now dry them! How little a man needs and how dear that little can become to him when he feels how very much he needs it. When you wish to give me a present in the future, then let it be something that one needs on such a journey.—Take only that little piece of paper in which the Zwieback was wrapped, in how many ways it has served!—You cannot help not laughing here and say: "Finally it will go the way of all paper!"—Enough, it is so.—Really, your watch is a nice legacy!

I do not yet know how this roaming around will end. I am so accustomed to being guided by fate that I no longer feel any haste. Sometimes only, faint dreams of anxiety emerge again; but they too will disappear.

Altenau, December 9, 1777

I DO NOT WANT to examine, nor do I want to have examined the cause of the anxiety which is in me. When I am so alone, I recognize myself again as I was in my early youth running around in the world so completely alone. People still seem to be the same to me, only today I made the following observation. As long as I lived under tension, as long as no one had any compassion with the feelings which came and left me, on the contrary—as it so often happens—, when first the people disregarded me and then looked at me with suspicion because of a few contradictory peculiarities, I got some strangely wrong pretensions despite the sincerity of my heart.—It can't be said like this, I would have to go into detail. Then I felt miserable, exhausted, dejected, mutilated, whatever you want. Now it is strange how much happiness, how much loveliness is in life, particularly in these days of voluntary renunciation.

People rub themselves on me like on a touchstone; I have my fun with their obligingness, indifference, stiffness and coarseness, one or the other. *Summa summarum,* it is the pretension of all pretensions to have none.

My dear! I do not find rest at any place; I have penetrated deeper into the mountains and from here I wish to ramble in the unfrequented places of this country, should I find a guide through the snow. Nightfall already starts here at half past three which is, on the clocks down in the lowlands, certainly not more than three.

Every day I think of the Duke and wish he could enjoy this life with me, but he couldn't take real delight in it; he is still too much pleased with his role of turning the natural into something adventurous, not knowing that one only begins to feel well when the adventurous becomes natural.

Just about this time, in a few days from now, it will be nine years ago that I was fatally sick. In her great distress, my mother opened the Bible and found the following passage as she told me afterwards: "They shall plant vines upon the mountains of Samaria again; the planters shall plant, and shall eat them as common things." At the moment she found consolation in this passage and later a great deal of joy in it.

You can see that things cross my mind helter-skelter.

Maybe, you will already have guessed by now that I am not only living in mines, but am also surrounded by them. Yesterday, my dear, fate payed me a great compliment. The juryman of the mine court was hit by a fragment that came off the rock face and he was thrown to the ground, just one step in front of me. As he was a very robust person, he put his feet firmly against the ground the second it hit him; the piece broke apart and flew down past him; but it nevertheless threw him down with it, and I thought it must have injured his legs at least; but nothing happened to him. A moment later, and I would have stood at the same spot; it was just at a place he intended to show me, and my weak body would have been immediately thrown down and crushed under the heavy load. It was a piece of about half a ton. If only your love be with me and the love of the Gods!

December 10

HOW SHALL I PRAISE the Lord with my quill, what song shall I sing of Him—at this moment when all prose turns into poetry and all poetry into prose? It is hardly possible for me to say with my lips what happened to me: how shall I be able to bring it forth with this pointed quill! My dear, God is treating me like his old saints, and I do not know how it all happens to me. Asking for a sign "that the fleece may be dry and the ground may be wet," then it is so and is the other way too when I wish it, and it is more than anything else the motherly guide to my wishes. The goal of my desire is reached; it hangs suspended on many threads and many threads are hanging down from it. You know how symbolic my life is,—how the gods have their fun with glorifying humility, and you know the devotion with which I can give myself up to a thing from minute to minute, to the most complete fulfillment of my hopes.

I will reveal to you—but do not tell anyone—that I went up the Harz, that I wished to climb the Brocken [the peak of the Harz Mountains]. And now, my dearest, today I was up there, as if it had been quite a natural thing to do though I was assured by all people for the last eight days that it would be quite impossible. But how I did it and the why of it shall be preserved until I see you again. How much I would prefer not to write now!

I said to myself: "I wish to have the full moon out now!" Well, dearest, I step out of the door and there the Brocken with its firs lies in bright moonlight before me. I was up there today, I thought, and have offered my deepest gratitude to my God on the devil's altar.

## GOETHE TO J. F. KRAFFT

*Little is known about the petitioner's fate whose cry for help made such a deep impression on Goethe. Presumably the name "Krafft" is an alias. Goethe supported this unfortunate man, whose privations were aggravated by his hypochondriacal temperament, out of his own pocket until Krafft died in the year 1785.*

Weimar, November 2, 1778

THE MOST CRUEL BLOW to a man struggling against the waves is to see that the willing hand on land lacks sufficient strength to rescue all whom the storm may drive towards his shores; when he—to whom a human life would be the richest yield of justice—must content himself with a little and behold the others perish.

I do not think I am mistaken in the picture of your personality which I derive from your letters, and what grieves me all the more is my inability of affording either help or hope to a man whose demands are so moderate.

Near this pool, which an angel but seldom stirs, hundreds linger for years; a few only can be healed, and I am not the man who, in the meantime, can exclaim: "Arise, and walk."

Accept the little I can give you as a plank thrown out to you, for the moment, to gain time.

Remain for the present season where you are, and in the future I am willing to arrange for some little assistance. Let me know when you receive the money, and how far you think it will go. Should you want a coat, an overcoat, boots or warm stockings, let me know, for I have some to spare.

Accept these drops of balm from the travelling medicine-chest of the willing Samaritan in the spirit in which they are given.

November 23

TODAY I have received your letters of the 17th and 18th of November and have already so far anticipated their contents that I have made most detailed inquiries in respect to any one who might be recommended to me, as wishing to live modestly and quietly in Jena under the protection of the University. Until the answer comes, remain quietly in Gera; the day after tomorrow I shall send you a parcel and give you more information.

You are no burden to me. On the contrary, you teach me how to economize, since I waste a good deal of my income which I might as well save for the benefit of the needy. And do you really think that your tears and blessings are nothing? He who has, must not bless, he must give; yet if the great and the rich of this world distribute wealth and honors, fate has, as a counterbalance, reserved for the poor the privilege of blessing which the happy know not how to covet.

Perhaps soon an opportunity may arise when you may prove useful to me; because not he who makes plans and promises, but rather he who offers faithful service in small matters is most welcome to one who desires to achieve what is good and lasting. Do not hate those poor philanthropists with their stipulations and precautions; with so many adverse experiences one must pray diligently in order to receive, once more, youthful good will, courage, and light-heartedness,—the ingredients of happiness. And, since one can so rarely do anything, it is rather a blessing sent by God when we can help a really unfortunate man.

December 11

I RECEIVED YOUR LETTER of December 7th early this morning. I must tell you, above all, that you shall not be coerced in any way. You shall receive the hundred Taler wherever you may happen to be. But now listen to me.

I know that our own ideas take on the form of realities and, although the picture you have of Jena is a false one, I also know that nothing can be less easily reasoned away than such a hypochondriacal anxiety. For many reasons I thought Jena to be the best place for you. The University and the town have long lost their former character of extravagance and wildness, the students are not worse than anywhere else, and many of them are very reputable people. They are accustomed to seeing so many people come and go that a single individual is not conspicuous. A great many people live there in destitution, so that poverty is neither stigma nor cause for contempt. Nevertheless, it is a town where the necessities of life can be procured.

How terrible it would be to be ill during the winter in the country without assistance! Moreover, the people to whom I mentioned you are respectable householders who, for my sake too, would receive you well. Whatever might happen to you, I would always be able to assist you through one person or another. At any rate, your lodging would be safe. I could be of assistance to you in settling down there; I should only have to answer for board and lodging at present and not pay till afterwards. I should have given you a trifle at the beginning of the year and done the rest on credit. You would have been nearer to me. Every market-day I could send you something, occasionally wine, victuals, utensils which would be of little expense to me and might make your life more endurable. Then, you would have been more closely connected with my domestic arrangements. How annoying is the communication with Gera! Nothing reaches anyone there in time and, moreover, it costs money which is of no good to anyone. Probably you might have stayed in Jena for six months before anyone would have noticed you. For these reasons I preferred Jena, as you would do yourself, if you could only consider the matter with an unprejudiced eye. How about trying it out? Yet I know that a fly can disconcert a man of weak nerves and that no argument avails against it.

Think it over. You would facilitate the matter both to me and to yourself. I promise that you shall be well settled in

Jena. Yet if you cannot bring yourself to take the step, then remain in Gera. At the New Year you will receive twenty Taler and the same amount every quarter at Easter, Midsummer and Michaelmas in advance. I cannot make any other arrangement. Even that amount which I have sent you up to now—having come at the end of the year and quite unexpectedly—has made a hole which I must make good again. Write and tell me how much it was; I have failed to note down one item and now I find an error in my accounts.

If you were in Jena, I might also more easily procure a commission or perhaps some employment for you, make your personal acquaintance, and so forth.

However, act entirely according to your own feelings, and if my arguments fail to touch your feelings and do not convincingly promise rest and revived courage in Jena, then remain in your present state of rest. Begin soon to tell the story of your life and send it to me in instalments. Remain convinced that I approve of everything that can quiet and content you, and that I only chose Jena, because there I hoped—most easily and conveniently to myself—to be able to procure for you the most endurable existence.

## FROM GOETHE'S DIARY

*In January, 1779, the Duke appointed Goethe Director of the War Commission and the Commission of Highways and Canals. On his birthday he was made "Geheimer Rat" (Privy Councillor) whereby he held the same rank as Minister von Fritsch. Although Goethe's official activities expanded a great deal later, his most important task always remained to guide the young Duke as his friend.*

January 13, 1779

I TOOK OVER the War Commission. First session. My mind determined and calm, but caustic. Plunged into these activities these days, full of good hope, certain to go through with it. The pressure of activity does wonders to our soul; if it is discharged, it plays more freely and enjoys life. There is nothing more miserable than a complacent person without work, the most beautiful of all gifts would nauseate him. Difficult to set our bodily machines in motion, and also to keep them going. He who acts finds any manual, and history as well equally ridiculous. But also no prouder prayer exists than that for wisdom, for this has been denied mankind by the gods once and for all time. They only distribute cleverness, give it to the bull according to its horns and to the cat according to its claws, thus they arm all creatures.

That I drink only half as much wine as I did, does me a great deal of good; and since I no longer drink coffee, I am on the most salubrious diet.

February 1

COUNCIL MEETING. Foul air inside. Fritsch's fatal humor. The Duke spoke too much. The thaw got into my limbs and the room was warm. Having eaten with the Duke, gave a few explanations after dinner on: talking too much, dropping affairs, giving oneself away, moderating one's expressions, broaching a subject at the heat of discussion which had better not be mentioned. Also on playing around with military affairs. The Duke still sticks to conventionalities. Wrong application in his case as to what may be found good and worthy in others. Infatuation with outside appearances. I have just made these mistakes in regard to the highways. I'll understand well the war commission, since I have no imagination whatsoever for it and do not intend to bring forth any new ideas; I only wish to know properly and thoroughly what is in existence. The same holds good with the highways.

This point is particularly difficult: If a third person gives some counsel or discovers a flaw and points out the means with which to remove it, it is because this person's egotistic interest so often plays a major part in it. He then wants to have a new budget to get a bonus for himself and his family on this occasion, or new establishments to make life more comfortable for himself, or provide other people with a lifelong income, and so forth. Because of these repeated experiences one becomes so suspicious that one at last almost shuns having anyone wipe off a speck of dust. Therefore it is difficult not to indulge in negligence and inactivity.

August 7

MADE ORDER at home, ran through my papers and burnt all old covers. Times change our concerns. Silent retrospection on life, on confusion, agility, and mental curiosity of youth, how it roams about everywhere to find something that would satisfy it. How I in particular have found delight in secrets and dark imaginative conditions. How I have taken up everything scientific only half-heartedly and have soon given up again, how a kind of humiliating self-complacency runs like a thread through everything I wrote at that time. How short-sighted

I was in human and divine affairs. Of how little use my doings, even the purposeful thinking and writing was, how I have wasted so many days with idle sensations and shadow passions. Now that half my life has gone, I realize I have not covered a good deal of ground, I rather stand here like someone who has saved his life from drowning and whom the sun kindly commences to desiccate.

I do not yet dare overlook the time since October, 1775, during which I have been in the midst of the bustle of the world. May God continue to help me and give the light so that we should not be so much in our own light. He may make us do the proper things from morning until night and may give us a clear notion of their consequences. That we may not be like those people who complain about headaches the whole day and use remedies against them, but drink too much wine every evening. May the idea of the pure—extending to the very bite I take into my mouth—become more and more lucid within me.

## GOETHE TO HIS MOTHER

Weimar, August 9, 1779

My desire to see you once more has up to this time been held in check by the circumstances which made my presence here more or less necessary. But now an opportunity may present itself, in regard to which, however, I must above all ask for the strictest secrecy. The Duke has in mind to enjoy the beautiful autumn on the Rhine. He wishes that I and Chamberlain von Wedel go with him and that we stop at your house; but to avoid the noise and the crowd at the fair we could remain a few days only and then continue on by water. Afterward he proposes to return and to take up our abode with you, and from there to visit the neighborhood.

Whether you take this prosaically or poetically, it is really the dot on the i of your whole past life, because for the first time I would return home well and happy and with all possible honor. Since the wine has turned out so well on the mountains of Samaria I would like to hear the piping too and will hope for nothing less than that you and my father should have open and tender hearts to receive us and to thank God who, in such a manner, lets you see your son again in his thirtieth year. As I have withstood all temptations to slip away from here and to surprise you, I wish to enjoy this journey to my heart's content. I don't expect the impossible. God has not willed that my father should enjoy the fruits so ardently longed for which are now ripe; he has taken his appetite from him, and so it must be. [Goethe's father became feeble-minded] I will gladly ask nothing from his side but whatever the humor of the moment may suggest to him. But I would like to see you really gay and I wish to offer you such a good day as you have never known as yet. I have everything a man can desire—a life in which I daily educate myself and daily grow—and this time I will come to you healthy, without passion, without bewilderment, without restless drives, but like one beloved by God who has passed half of his days and who hopes to derive much good for his future from past sorrows and who has also conditioned his heart for future grief. If I find you happy I shall return with joy to the labor and toil of the day which await me.

Answer me immediately in full. We come, at all events, in the middle of September; I will let you know the details, down to the smallest particular, as soon as I have a reply to this. But inviolable secrecy, for the present, toward my father, Merck, etc. Our arrival must be a surprise to all; I depend upon this. No one here suspects anything of it as yet.

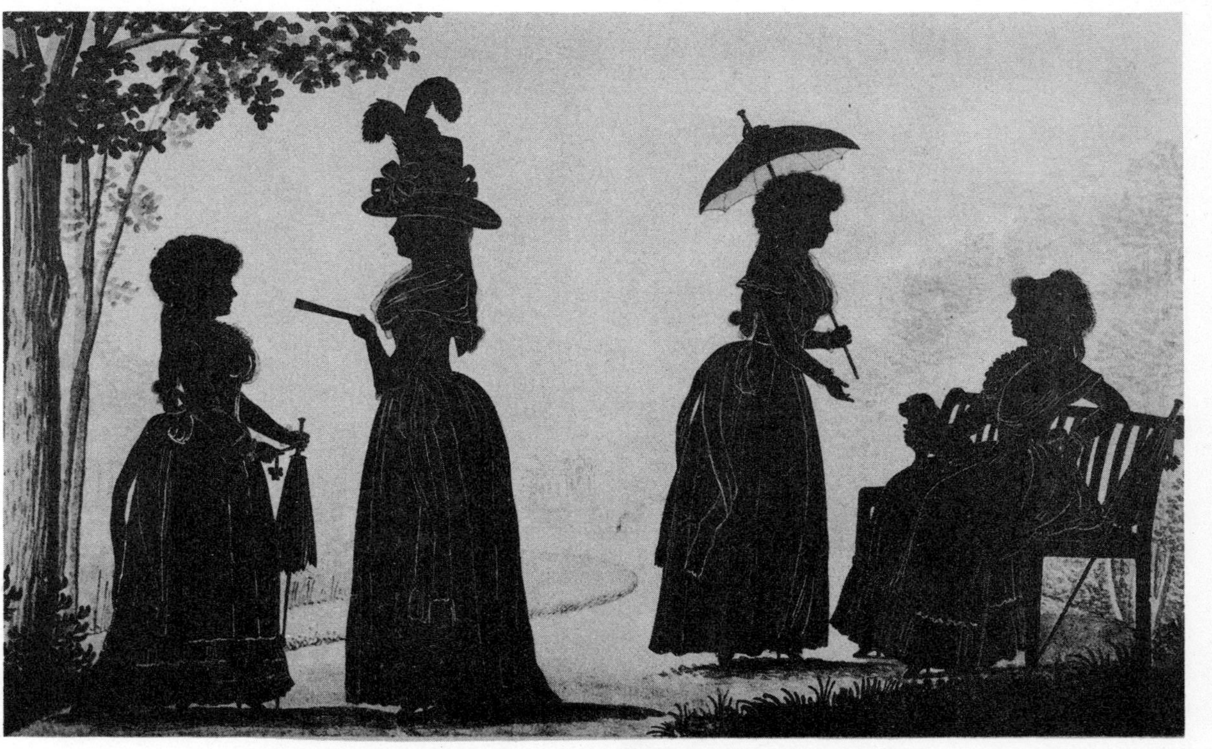

Duchess Anna Amalia (seated) with ladies of the Court

Charlotte von Stein

Goethe

# GOETHE TO FRAU VON STEIN

*After a visit with his parents in Frankfort, Goethe accompanied the Duke on a trip to Switzerland. On his way down there he took the occasion to see two women again who had once been close to his heart: Friederike Brion, the Pastor's daughter from Sesenheim, and Lili Schönemann who had married the Strasbourg banker von Türckheim in 1778.*

Emmendingen, September 28, 1779

ON THE 25TH I took a bypath leading to Sesenheim, while the others continued on their journey. And there I found the family, which I had left eight years ago, all together and I was warmly and well received. As I am now as pure and calm as the air, I welcome the breath of good and quiet people. The daughter of the house had once loved me—more than I deserved and more than others to whom I have given much passion and faithfulness. I had left at a moment when it had almost cost her life. She only touched lightly on it to let me know what was still left from her illness of that time. She behaved most charmingly, with so much sincere friendship, from the very first minute in which she unexpectedly faced me standing on her threshold where we almost collided; it made me feel quite happy. I must also say of her that she did not make the least effort to arouse the old feeling in my soul. She led me to each bower in the garden, and there I had to sit—and it was good so. We had the nicest full moon. I inquired about everything. A neighbor who had often helped us in our artistic endeavors was called to testify that, as recently as eight days ago, he had asked how I was getting along; also the barber came to join us. I found old songs which I had contributed, a carriage which I had painted. We recalled a great many of the funny tricks we had played at that wonderful time, and I found their memory of me as much alive as if I had left them but six months ago. The old people were warm-hearted; they found that I looked younger. I stayed over night and, the next morning at sunrise, I took leave of their friendly faces so that, from now on, I can remember this little corner of the world again with contentment and live in peace with the spirits of these people.

Sunday, the 26th, I again met my party, and we came to Strasbourg toward noon. I went to see Lili and found this beautiful foolish creature playing with a baby of seven weeks, and her mother by her. Here too I was received with surprise and joy. I let her tell me everything and had a good look everywhere, for I soon found to my greatest delight that this good creature was very happy in her marriage. Her husband—from all I could hear—seems to be good, reasonable and very busy; his wealth permits them a nice house, he comes from a respected family, notable citizens; he gives her everything she needs, etc. He was absent. I remained for lunch. In the afternoon I went to the Cathedral with the Duke. In the evening we say a play: *L'Infante di Zamora,* with some quite good music by Paesiello. Then I ate again with Lili and left her in bright moonshine. I can hardly describe the wonderful sensation which accompanied me. As prosaic as my relationship to these people may now be, there is so much of pure and everlasting well-wishing in my feeling. Indeed, there was a real ethereal delight when, on my way to them, I recalled, like counting the beads of a rosary, the truest, the most genuine and lasting of my friendships. Undisturbed by mere passion, the enduring feelings which I have for these people are now coming to the fore in my soul. My remote friends and their fates are now before me like a country whose landscape one sees from a high mountain or like a bird's-eye view.

## GOETHE TO HIS FRIENDS

On the summit of Mt. St. Gothard
November 13, 1779

AT LAST we have fortunately reached the outmost limits of our journey. Here we determined to rest awhile and then to turn our steps toward our dear fatherland. Very strange are my feelings here on this summit where, four years ago, I passed a few days with very different anxieties, sentiments, plans and hopes, and at a very different season of the year, when, without any foreboding of my future fortunes but moved by I know not what, I turned my back upon Italy and ignorantly went to meet my present destiny. I did not even recognize the house again. Some time ago it was greatly damaged by an avalanche; and the good fathers [the Capuchins] took advantage of this opportunity and made a collection throughout the canton for enlarging and improving their residence. Both of the two fathers, who reside here at present, are absent; but, as I hear, they are still the same I met four years ago. Father Seraphim, who has now passed fourteen years in this post, is at present at Milan; and the other is expected today from Airolo. In this clear atmosphere the cold is awful. As soon as dinner is over, I will continue my letter, for I can clearly see we won't go far outside the door.

After dinner

IT IS GETTING colder and colder. One does not like to move from the stove. Indeed, it is most delightful to sit upon it which can be easily done in this country where the stoves are made of stone tiles. But first of all let me tell you of our departure from Realp and then of our journey hither.

Last night, before we retired to our bed the good father showed us his bedroom where everything was in nice order in a very small space. His bed which consisted of a bag of straw with a woolen coverlet did not appear to us as being very meritorious, as we ourselves had often put up with no better. With great pleasure and inner satisfaction he showed us everything—his bookcase and all other things. We praised all we saw; and, parting on the best terms with each other, we retired for the night. In furnishing our room, so that two beds would stand against one wall, both had been made unusually small. This inconvenience kept me long awake until I thought of remedying it by placing four chairs together. It was already broad daylight before we awoke this morning. Coming down, we found everyone with a happy and friendly face. Our guides, on the point of entering upon their return over yesterday's beautiful route, seemed to look upon it as an epoch and as a history with which hereafter they would be able to entertain other strangers; and, as they were well paid, the idea of an adventure became complete in their minds. After this, we partook of a capital breakfast and departed.

Now our road lay through the valley of the Uri which is remarkable for having, at so great an elevation, such beautiful meadows and pastures for cattle. They make here a cheese which I prefer to all others. However, no trees grow here. Sally-bushes line all the brooks, and on the mountains little shrubs grow thickly together. Of all the countries that I know, this is to me the loveliest and most interesting—whether it is that old recollections make it precious to me or that the reception of such a long chain of Nature's miracles excites within me a mysterious and inexpressible feeling of enjoyment. I take for granted that you bear in mind that the whole country through which I am leading you is covered with snow, and that rock and meadow alike are snowed over. The sky has been quite clear, without a single cloud; the hue far deeper than one is accustomed to seeing in low and flat countries; and the white mountain ridges, which stood out in strong contrast to it, were either glittering in the sunshine, or else took a grayish tint in the shade.

In an hour and a half we reached Hôpital—a little village within the canton of Uri, lying on the road to St. Gothard.

Here, at last, I regained the track of my former tour. We entered an inn, and, though it was yet morning, ordered a dinner, and soon afterward began to ascend the summit. A long train of mules, with their bells, enlivened the whole region. It is a sound which awakens all your recollections of mountain scenery. The greater part of the train was ahead of us, and, with their sharp iron shoes, had pretty well cut up the smooth icy road. We also saw a few laborers occupied with covering the slippery ice with fresh earth in order to render it passable. The wish to which I formerly gave utterance, namely that I might one day be permitted to see this part of the world under snow, is now at last gratified. The road goes up the Reuss, as it dashes down over rocks all the way and forms the most beautiful waterfalls everywhere. We stood a long while attracted by the singular beauty of one of them, which, in considerable volume, was dashing over a succession of black rocks. Here and there in the cracks and on the flat edges, pieces of ice had formed; and the water seemed to be running over a variegated black and white marble. The masses of ice glistened in the sun like veins of crystal, and the water flowed pure and fresh between them.

On the mountains there are no more tiresome fellow travelers than a train of mules, their pace being so unequal. With a strange instinct, they always stop awhile at the bottom of a steep ascent, and then dash off at a quick pace to rest again upon the top. Very often, too, they will stop at the level spots, which do occur now and then, until they are forced on by the drivers, or by other beasts coming up. And so those who are walking soon gain upon them by keeping a steady pace and have to push by them in the narrow roads. If you stand still a little while to observe any object, they, in their turn, will pass by you, and you are pestered with the deafening sound of their bells, and brushed hard by their loads which project a good distance on each side of them. In this way we at last reached the summit of the mountain of which you can form some idea by imagining a bald skull surrounded with a crown. Here one finds oneself on a perfect flat surrounded with peaks. Far and near the eye meets with nothing but bare and mostly snow-covered peaks and crags.

It is hardly possible to keep oneself warm, especially as they have no fuel but brushwood here which they are even obliged to handle very sparingly, as they have to fetch it up the mountains from a distance of at least three leagues, because at the summit, we were told, scarcely any kind of wood grows. When the reverend father returned from Airolo he had suffered so much from the freezing cold that, on his arrival, he could hardly utter a word. Although here the Capuchins are allowed to clothe themselves a little more comfortably than the rest of their order, still their style of dress is by no means suited to such a climate as this. All the way up from Airolo, the road was frozen perfectly smooth, and he had the wind in his face. His beard was quite frozen, and it took a long time before he recovered.

We had some conversation together on the hardships of their residence: he told us how they managed to get through the year, what their various occupations were and their domestic circumstances. He spoke Italian only, and so we had an opportunity of putting to use the exercises which we had taken in this language during last spring. In the late afternoon, we went outside the door for a moment so that the good father might point out to us the peak which is considered to be the highest summit of Mount Gothard. But we could hardly bear to stay out a very few minutes, so penetrating and pinching was the cold. This time, therefore, we will remain indoors, tightly shut up, and thus will have time enough before starting tomorrow to again travel in our minds over all the most remarkable parts of this region.

## GOETHE TO J. K. LAVATER

Ostheim, September 21, 1780

THE DAILY TASK which has been meted out to me and which, each day, becomes easier as well as more difficult, requires my presence, waking and dreaming. This duty becomes daily more dear to me and in performing it I wish to equal the greatest men and in no greater duty. This desire to raise the apex of the pyramid of my existence, the basis of which has been given and laid down for me, as high as possible into the air, surpasses everything else and hardly permits me to forget it for even a moment. I must lose no time, I am already advanced in years, and perhaps fate may break me in the middle of my work and the Babylonian tower would remain obtuse and unfinished. At least, it shall be said of it that it was boldly planned, and if I live, my strength will hold out, with God's help, until I reach the top.

Much, too, is due to the charm of a beautiful love with which Frau von Stein seasons my life. One after the other, she has succeeded my mother, my sister and all the women I have loved, and a bond has formed between us as strong as are the bonds of nature. . . .

The Duke is very good and pleasant. If only I could get some more space for him from the gods. The chains by which the spirits lead us, press some of his limbs too tightly, while in others he has the fullest freedom.

## GOETHE TO FRAU VON STEIN

Neunheiligen, March 12, 1781

The messenger you sent me has given me great joy. I was afraid I would not hear from you today and tomorrow, and all the more the good news came unexpectedly. I do not like the idea at all that my letter was misplaced and that you could only be reached so late; I would have wished that you should receive my souvenirs as soon as possible. Your messenger made very good time; he was here before six o'clock this evening.

Our unhappy but beautiful hostess [Countess Jeanette Luise von Werthern-Neunheiligen] is sick and bears it as women are accustomed to bearing illness. This morning we had a long political discussion; she sees even these things intelligently, naturally, and as you would expect from her stand. She loves the Duke more than he loves her, and having seen myself in this mirror, I have realized that you too love me more than we men usually are able to. But I will not give up, I feel challenged to fight for it, and I entreat the Graces that they may give inner kindness to my passion and preserve the mildness from where beauty alone arises.

Keep in mind all the nice things you have to tell me! The spirits of the world have also whispered into my ears a great deal of useful things, indeed, they disclosed beautiful things about me and others.

I hope to find you alone Thursday night, hope to be with you the first few hours. Friday we must dine together and be gay.

I have drawn very little today and nothing at all yesterday; I'll hardly be able to finish a landscape which I intend to leave here. New light dawns on me when I look at the pictures of Everdingen. [landscape painter of the 17th century] Why must we grope in the dark for so long and prowl about in twilight!

Our souls have grown together. I don't want to use many

words, you know that I am inseparable from you and that neither the sublime nor the base can ever keep me away from you. I wish an oath or a sacrament would exist that would make me visibly and legally yours. How much I would hold it in esteem! And my time of probation was long enough to make up our minds. Adieu. Now I can no longer be formal with you, as I have not been able to address you for quite some time in an informal manner.

The messenger promises to be in Weimar in time. I follow him two days later. If possible, you may still receive a letter before I come.

One more thing about the prayers on my trip. The Jews have leather straps which they tie around their arms while praying. Thus I secure your sweet bond around my arm when I address my prayers to you and wish to partake of your kindness, wisdom, moderateness and patience. I entreat you on my knees to complete your work, make a good man out of me! You can do it, not only if you love me; your power becomes boundless if you believe in my loving you. Goodbye!

I hope you feel well. Goodbye! One thing after the other comes to my mind. Goodbye! I could not tear myself away, did not the end of this page separate me from you as the door does at home.

## GOETHE TO HIS MOTHER

Weimar, August 11; 1781

TIME AND QUIET has failed me as yet to reply to your previous dear letter. It gave me great pleasure to see your old and well-known views again expressed in it, and to read them from your own hand. I beg you not to be concerned on my account, and not to allow yourself to be disconcerted by anything. My health is far better than I could ever have hoped for and expected; and as it is adequate to enable me to do, for the most part at least, what is incumbent on me, I have certainly cause to be content with it.

In regard to my position I can say that, notwithstanding great difficulties, it also holds out to me very much that is desirable for me; the best proof of it is that I cannot think of any other possible position for which, at the present moment, I would want to change it. For, with hypochondriacal discontent, to wish oneself out of one's skin into another, is not, it seems to me, very befitting. Merck and others judge my situation very incorrectly. They only see what I sacrifice and not what I gain. They cannot comprehend that I grow richer daily while daily giving away so much.

You will remember the last months I spent with you before I came here; I would have perished in such a continued state of affairs. The disproportion of this narrow and slow-moving bourgeois circle to the broad-mindedness and great agility of my nature would have driven me mad. With my lively imagination and the premonition of all human affairs, I would have always remained unknown in this world and in a perpetual childhood which, mostly through conceit and all its kindred shortcomings, becomes intolerable to itself and to others. How much more fortunate was it to see myself placed in a position with which I could in no way cope and which gave me ample opportunity through many an error of misconception and haste to become acquainted with myself and others; where, left to myself and fate, I passed through so many trials which, to many hundreds of people, may not be necessary, but of which I had the utmost need for my development. And even now, how could I, living my own self, wish for a position more fortunate than the one which holds for me something infinite. Because even if new capacities would daily develop in me, my ideas constantly become clearer, my powers grow, my knowledge widen, my discrimination become more perfect and my spirit more active, I would daily find opportunity to make use of it both in great things and in small.

You see how far I am from the hypochondriacal restlessness which sets so many men at variance with their circumstances, and that only the weightiest considerations or very strange and unexpected events could induce me to leave my post; and it would be also irresponsible toward myself, if I—at a time when the trees which have been planted begin to grow and when one can hope that, during the harvest, the chaff will be separated from the wheat—if I, on account of some discomfort or other, should go away and deprive myself of shade, fruit and harvest.

Meantime believe me that a great part of the good cheer with which I endure and work springs from the thought that all these sacrifices are voluntary and that I need only order the post-horses in order to come and find with you again the necessary and agreeable things of life. For without this prospect and, when in hours of vexation, I am driven to regard myself as a bondman and day-laborer for the mere necessities of life, many things would be much harder for me.

May I always hear from you that your cheerfulness never forsakes you despite my father's present condition. Continue to procure for yourself as much variety as the social life about you offers. It is not very likely that I shall be able to leave here this autumn; at all events, not before the end of September. Yet I shall try to be with you at vintage time. Write me therefore, if it should by any chance fall earlier, due to the favorable summer. Farewell. Greet my old, dear friends.

## GOETHE TO HIS FRIENDS

*On September 3, 1786, Goethe left Carlsbad where he had stayed for the cure, to start on his long desired journey to Italy. His secret departure under an assumed name appeared almost like a flight from the petty circumstances of Weimar. Frau von Stein was deeply hurt by this sudden parting. The eighteen months' stay in Italy marked a decisive epoch in the poet's life. Besides studying the master works of art Goethe devoted himself with special effort to the drawing of landscapes. At that time his activity as a writer was mostly given to the reworking of his older writings for the complete edition to be published by Göschen. The diaries and letters from this journey were later published by Goethe in his "Travels in Italy."*

Rome, November 1, 1786

AT LAST I can speak freely and greet my friends with good humor. May they pardon my secrecy and what has been an almost underground journey to Italy. For scarcely to myself did I dare say where I was hurrying—even on the road I often had my fears, and it was only as I passed under the Porta del Popolo that I felt certain of reaching Rome.

And now let me also say that a thousand times, in fact, that I always think of you while being so close to these objects which I never believed I should visit alone. It was only when I saw that everyone had his body and soul tied to the north and that all longing for those countries was utterly extinct among them, that I resolved to undertake the long solitary journey and to seek that centre towards which I was attracted by an irresistible impulse. Indeed, for the last few years it had become with me a kind of disease which could only be cured by the sight and presence of the absent object. Now I may confess the truth: It reached at last such intensity that I did not dare look at a Latin book, or even an engraving of Italian scenery. The craving to see this country was over-ripe. Now that it is satisfied, my friends and country have once more become very dear to me and my return to them is a wished-for object, in fact, it is the more ardently desired, the more firmly I feel convinced that I bring with me so many treasures for personal enjoyment or private use that they may serve others as well as myself for edification and guidance for my lifetime . . .

Over the mountains of the Tyrol I have as good as flown. Verona, Vicenza, Padua, and Venice I have carefully looked at; hastily glanced at Ferrara, Cento, Bologna, and scarcely seen Florence at all. My anxiety to reach Rome was so great—and it so grew with me every moment—, that to think of stopping anywhere was quite out of the question; even in Florence I only stayed three hours. Now I am here at my ease and, as it would seem, shall be tranquilized for my whole life; for we may almost say that a new life begins when a man finally sees with his own eyes all those things which he has partially absorbed by reading or hearing of it. Now all the dreams of my youth have become real, the subjects of the first engravings I ever remember seeing (several views of Rome were hung up in an anteroom of my father's house) stand bodily before my sight, and all that I had long been acquainted with through paintings or drawings, engravings or wood-cuts, through plaster of Paris and cork models are here collectively presented to my eye. Wherever I go I find some old acquaintance in this new world; it is all just as I had thought it, and yet all is new. The very same I can say of my own observations and my own ideas. I have not gained any new thoughts, but the older ones have become so defined, so vivid and so coherent that they may almost pass for new ones.

When Pygmalion's Elisa, which he had shaped entirely in

accordance with his wishes, and had given to it as much of truth and nature as an artist can, moved at last towards him and said, "I am!"—how different was the living form from the chiselled stone.

In a moral sense, too, how salutary is it for me to live among a wholly sensual people for some time, of whom so much has been said and written and whom every stranger judges according to the standard he brings with him. I can excuse everyone who blames and reproaches them; they stand too far apart from us, and it is difficult and expensive for a stranger to associate with them.

November 5

I HAVE NOW BEEN here seven days and gradually have formed in my mind a general idea of the city. We go from one place to another, and while I am thus making myself acquainted with the plan of old and new Rome, viewing the ruins and the buildings, visiting this and that villa, the grandest and most remarkable objects are slowly and leisurely contemplated. I do but keep my eyes open and see, then go and come again, for it is only in Rome that one can really prepare oneself for Rome.

Let us confess that it is a sad and melancholy business to prick and track out ancient Rome in new Rome; however, it must be done, and we may hope at least for an incalculable gratification. We meet with traces both of majesty and of ruin, which alike surpass all conception; what the barbarians spared, the builders of new Rome made havoc of.

When one thus beholds an object two thousand years old and more, but so manifoldly and thoroughly altered by the changes of time, and yet sees, nevertheless, the same soil, the same mountains and often indeed the same walls and columns, one becomes, as it were, a contemporary of the great counsels of Fortune. Thus from the very beginning it becomes difficult for the observer to trace Rome following Rome, and not only new Rome succeeding to the old, but also the several epochs of both old and new in succession. I endeavor, first of all, to grope my way alone through the obscurer parts, for this is the only plan by which one can hope fully and completely to profit by the excellent introductory works which have been written from the fifteenth century to the present day. The first artists and scholars have occupied their whole lives with these objects.

And this vastness has a strangely tranquillizing effect upon you in Rome, while you pass from place to place in order to visit the most remarkable objects. In other places one has to search for what is important; here one is oppressed and borne down with numberless phenomena. Wherever one goes and casts a look around, the eye is at once struck with some landscape, forms of every kind and style; palaces and ruins, gardens and statuary, distant views of villas, cottages and stables, triumphal arches and columns, often crowding so close together that they might all be sketched on a single sheet of paper. One ought to have a hundred hands to write, for what can a single pen do here; and then by the evening one is quite weary and exhausted with the day's seeing and admiring.

Pardon me, my friends, if in the future you find me rather chary of my words. On your travels you usually rake together all that you meet on your way; every day brings something new, and you then hasten to think about it and to pass judgment on it. Here, however, we come into a very great school indeed where every day says so much that we cannot venture to say anything of the day itself. Indeed, people would do well if, staying here for years together, they observed a Pythagorean silence.

November 8

My strange, and perhaps whimsical, incognito proves useful to me in many ways that I never would have thought of. As everyone feels obliged to ignore who I am, and consequently never ventures to speak to me of myself and my works, they have no alternative left but to speak of themselves, or of the matters in which they are most interested, and in this way I become circumstantially informed of everyone's occupation and of everything remarkable that is being produced. Councillor Reiffenstein good-naturedly humors this whim of mine. As, for special reasons, he could not bear the name which I had assumed, he immediately made a Baron of me, and I am now called the "Baron gegen Rondanini ueber" (the Baron who lives opposite the Palazzo Rondanini). This characterization is sufficiently precise, especially as the Italians are accustomed to speaking of people either by their Christian names, or else by some nickname. Well, I have gained my object and escape the dreadful annoyance of having to give to everybody an account of myself and my works.

November 9

I FREQUENTLY STAND STILL for a moment to survey the heights I have already won. With much delight I look back to Venice, that grand creation that sprang out of the bosom of the sea, like Minerva out of the head of Jupiter. In Rome, the Rotunda, both by its exterior and interior, has moved me to offer a willing homage to its magnificence. In St. Peter's I learned to understand how art, no less than nature, annihilates the artificial measures and dimensions of man. And in the same way the Apollo of Belvedere has again taken me away from reality and carried me away. For as even the most correct engravings furnish no adequate idea of these buildings, so the case is the same with respect to the marble original of this statue as compared with its plaster models of which I formerly knew a great many that were very beautiful.

November 10

I AM NOW HERE living with a calmness and tranquility to which I have for a long time been a stranger. My practice of seeing and taking all things as they are, my fidelity in letting the eye be my light, my perfect renunciation of all pretension, have again come to my aid and made me calmly, but most intensely, happy. Every day has its fresh remarkable object, every day its new magnificent paintings, comprising a whole which a man may long think and dream of, but which, with all his power of imagination, he can never reach.

Yesterday I was at the Pyramid of Cestius, and in the evening on the Palatine, on the top of which are the ruins of the palace of the Caesars standing there like walls of rock. Of all this, however, no idea can be conveyed! In truth, there is nothing little here; although, indeed, occasionally something to find fault with,—something more or less absurd in taste, but even this is part of the general grandeur here.

When I then return to myself, as everyone so readily does on all occasions, I discover within a feeling which infinitely delights me—one, indeed, which I may even express. Whoever looks around here with earnestness and has eyes to see, must become solid, he cannot help apprehending an idea of solidity with a vividness which is nowhere else possible.

The mind becomes primed with capacity, with earnestness without severity, and with strength of character with joy. For me, at least, it seems as if I had never before so rightly estimated the things of the world as I do here; I rejoice when I think of the blessed effects of all this on the whole of my future being. And let me jumble together the things as I may, order will somehow come into them. I am not here to enjoy myself after my own fashion, but to busy myself with these great objects, to learn and to improve myself before I reach my fortieth year of age.

## GOETHE'S MOTHER TO HER SON

Frankfort, November 17, 1786

DEAR SON,—An apparition from the nether world could not have surprised me more than your letter from Rome. I could have shouted for joy that the wish which had been in your heart from earliest youth has now found fulfillment. For a man like you, with your knowledge, with your pure and great vision for all that is good, great and, beautiful, for one with such an eagle eye, such a journey must mean happiness and fortune for the rest of his life—and not only for you, but for all who are lucky enough to live within the sphere of your activity. The words of the late Klettenberg will always remain in my memory: "When your Wolfgang goes to Mainz he brings with him more knowledge than others who come back from Paris or London." How I would have loved to see you at your first sight of St. Peter's!!! However, you promised to visit me on your way back, and then you must describe everything to me in full detail . . .

Here follows an exact and faithful description of my inner and outer well-being. My life flows quietly on like a clear brook. Disquiet and commotion were never agreeable to me, and I thank Providence for my days. To thousands such a life would seem monotonous, but not to me; the quieter my body is, the more active are my thoughts. Thus I can pass an entire day, hour after hour, completely alone, then I wonder that evening has set in and I am as happy as a queen—and one does not need more in this world than to be happy and content. The latest news from your old acquaintances is that Papa La Roche is no longer in Speyer, he has bought a house in Offenbach and thinks he wants to end his days there. The others of your friends are still what they were, not one has made such giant strides as you (but we were always the lackeys, as the late Max Moors once remarked).

When you come here, all these people must be invited and handsomely entertained—game, roasts, poultry—it will be really splendid!

Dear son, a humble doubt just occurs to me as to whether this letter may reach you. I do not know where you are living in Rome, you are there half incognito, as you wrote. Let us hope for the best. But before you come, let me hear from you, otherwise I should be thinking that every post-chaise is bringing my only beloved one—and I do not like to be disappointed in my hope. Farewell, dearest, and think often of your faithful mother—Elizabeth Goethe.

## J. H. W. TISCHBEIN TO LAVATER

*The painter Johann Wilhelm Tischbein, who had settled in Italy many years previously, became Goethe's guide to the art treasures of Rome. His Goethe portrait, the beginning of which is here reported, belongs with the most popular Goethe pictures.*

Rome, December 9, 1786

You were right in everything you said about Goethe. He is certainly one of the most splendid human beings one could ever get to know. Imagine the indescribable joy I had a few weeks ago! Goethe came here quite unexpectedly, and now he is living in my apartment, right next to me; thus I enjoy the company of this most singular and clever man from morning till night. What pleasure this is for me you can easily picture to yourself, as you know Goethe's qualities and my respect for great men. Goethe is a real man such as I only dreamt of seeing in my wildest imagination. I commenced work on his portrait and will do it life size as he is sitting on the ruins and thinking about the fate of human actions.

I found him the way I thought he would be. I had not imagined such great placidity and calm in this lively and sensitive personality, nor that he would feel familiar with whatever is mentioned. Moreover, what I like in him is the simplicity of his life. He asked for a small room where he could sleep and work undisturbed and for quite simple food which I can easily provide for him, since he is content with so little.

Now he sits there and works every morning to finish his "Iphigenia" [drama in verse], working until nine o'clock, then he goes out to see the great works of art here. You can easily imagine, knowing the sincerity of his thoughts, with what an eye and what knowledge he looks at everything. He is little disturbed by the great men of the world, he does not accept nor pay any visit beside those of artists. They wanted to honor him as was done with the great poets who had been here before him, but he refused it politely pretending loss of time and thus kept away from all semblance of vanity. It certainly honors him as much as if he had been really crowned on the Capitol.

## GOETHE TO HIS FRIENDS

*Goethe kept up an animated exchange of thoughts with the many-sided and well-educated writer Karl Philipp Moritz. Moritz suffered from a very painful fracture of his arm, the result of a riding accident.*

Rome, January 6, 1787

I HAVE JUST COME from Moritz, whose arm is healed and out of its bandages. It is well set, and firm, and he can move it quite freely. What during these last forty days I have experienced and learned as nurse, father confessor, and private secretary may prove of benefit to us hereafter. The most painful sufferings and the noblest enjoyments went side by side throughout this whole period.

Yesterday, to relieve the eye, I had set up in our sitting room a cast of a colossal head of Juno, the original of which is in the Villa Ludovisi. This was my first love in Rome; and now I have gained the object of my wishes. No words can give the remotest idea of it. It is like one of Homer's songs.

I have, however, deserved the proximity of such good company for the future, for I can now tell you that "Iphigenia" is at last finished—i.e. that it lies before me on the table in two tolerably concordant copies of which one will very soon begin its pilgrimage to you. Receive it with all indulgence, for, to speak the truth, what stands on the paper is not exactly what I intended; but still it will convey an idea of what was in my mind.

You complain occasionally of some obscure passages in my letters which allude to the oppression which I suffer in the midst of the most glorious objects in the world. With all this my fellow traveler, this Grecian princess, has had a great deal to do, for she has kept me hard at work when I wished to be sight seeing.

I am reminded of that worthy friend of ours, who had long determined upon a grand tour which one might well term a voyage of discovery. After he had studied and economized several years, with a view to this object, he decided, at the last minute, upon eloping with the daughter of a noble house at the same time thinking that both go well together.

With no less caprice, I determined to take Iphigenia with me to Carlsbad. I will now briefly enumerate the places where I held special converse with her.

When I had left the Brenner behind me, I took her out of my large portmanteau, and placed her by my side. At the Lago di Garda, while the strong south wind drove the waves on the beach and where I was at least as much alone as my heroine on the coast of Tauris, I drew the first outlines of the new draft which afterwards I filled up at Verona, Vicenza and Padua, but most diligently at Venice. After this, however, the work came to a standstill, for I hit upon a new design, namely of writing an Iphigenia at Delphi which I would have immediately carried into execution, had not the fear of distraction and a feeling of duty toward the older piece prevented me from doing it.

In Rome, however, I went on with it and proceeded with tolerable steadiness. Every evening before I went to sleep I prepared myself for my morning's task, which was resumed immediately I awoke. My way of proceeding was quite simple. I calmly wrote down the piece and tried the melody line by line and period by period. You will soon be able to judge what has been thus produced. In fact, doing this work I have learnt more than I have accomplished.

*The first draft of "Iphigenia in Tauris" in prose dates from the year 1779. Shortly afterwards the play was performed in which the beautiful actress Corona Schröter played Iphigenia. Goethe himself acted the part of Orestes. After Goethe had reworked the play several times it received its final form of iambic metres in Rome.*

## K. PH. MORITZ TO J. H. CAMPE

Rome, January 20, 1787

WHAT THE GOOD and humane Goethe has done for me during these forty days which kept me lying motionless on one spot in constant pain cannot be expressed in words of gratitude, I, at least, shall never forget it. In this dreadful situation in which everything got together to augment the indescribable pain I suffered and to make my condition dangerous and at the same time hopeless, it was he who has been to me everything one man can be to another. Daily he visited me more than once and sat up with me several nights. He worried about every trifling matter which could be of help and relief to me, and he looked for everything that would somehow cheer me up. And how often, when I was about to despair and to yield to my pain, his presence instilled in me new courage, and since I wished to appear strong before him, I often became really strong.

At the same time, he was the guiding spirit of good will among my countrymen now living here in great number whose friendly behavior toward me shall never slip my memory. Almost everyone of them was with me the other day; they all offered to sit up with me during the night. Goethe made them draw lots for it to determine each one's turn, and in no time all nights were taken so that everyone had a few turns only. Then he had another twelve persons draw lots for the hours of daytime so that one person should be with me for one hour during the day to afford me steadily changing company. Everyone was immediately ready for it; the hours during the day were thus taken and everyone kept them properly.

Even the people with whom I live were moved by the love and friendship of so many people toward one of their compatriots that they followed their example and did for me, during these forty days, the most cumbersome services any person needs who is forced to lie still, and they did it without grumbling and with the greatest eagerness. All this together instilled in me some kind of confidence in my fate again. I thought: though it brought me down, nevertheless, it will not let me sink!

## GOETHE TO HIS FRIENDS

Rome, February 21, 1787

I TAKE ADVANTAGE of a few moments in between packing to mention a few things I have hitherto omitted. Tomorrow we set off for Naples. I am anxiously looking forward to seeing the new scenery which is supposed to be inexpressibly beautiful and hope, in this paradise of nature, to gain new freedom and pleasure for the study of ancient art on my return to sober Rome.

Packing up is much easier for me now that I can do it with a merrier heart than I had some six months ago, when I had to tear myself from all that was most dear and precious to me. Yes, it is now a full half year since; and of the four months I have spent in Rome, not a moment has been lost. This means a great deal, but still does not say too much.

That "Iphigenia" has arrived, I know,—may I learn at the foot of Vesuvius that it has met with a hearty welcome.

That Tischbein, who possesses as glorious an eye for nature as for art, is to accompany me on this journey is of the greatest importance to me. Still, as genuine Germans, we cannot throw aside all purposes and thoughts of work. We have bought the best of drawing-paper, and we intend to sketch away; although, in all probability, the multitude, the beauty and the splendor of the objects will limit our good intentions.

One victory I have gained over myself. Of all my unfinished

poetical works I shall take with me none but the "Tasso," for which I have the best hopes. If I could only know what you are now saying of "Iphigenia," your remarks might be some guide to me in my present labors; for the plan of "Tasso" is very similar, though the subject is even more confined and will be more elaborately finished in its details. Still I cannot tell as yet how it will eventually turn out. What already exists of it must be destroyed; it has been kept in a drawer for too long, and neither the characters nor the plot, nor the tone of it are at all in harmony with my present views.

*For a long time Goethe's mind was occupied with the tragic fate of the Italian poet Torquato Tasso whose life at the court of Ferrara had some similarity with his own at Weimar. During his stay in Italy he wrote essential parts of the drama in iambic feet and completed the play soon after his return.*

## GOETHE TO HIS FRIENDS

Caserta, March 16, 1787

NAPLES is a paradise: in it everyone lives in a sort of intoxicated self-forgetfulness. It is even so with me; I scarcely know myself—I seem quite an altered man. Yesterday I said to myself: Either you have always been mad, or you are so now . . .

In this country one first begins to understand what vegetation is and why man tills the fields. The flax here is already near to blossoming and the wheat a span and a half high. Around Caserta the land is perfectly level, the fields worked as clean and as fine as the beds of a garden. All of them are planted with poplars, and from tree to tree the vine spreads; and yet, notwithstanding its shade, the soil below produces the finest and most abundant crops possible. What will they be when spring comes! Up to now we have had very cold winds, and there has been snow on the mountains.

Within fourteen days I must decide whether to go to Sicily or not. Never before have I been so tossed backwards and forwards in coming to a resolution: Every day something occurs to recommend the trip; the next morning some circumstance is against it. Two spirits are contending for me.

I say this in confidence and for my female friends only, not a word of it to my male friends. I am well aware that my "Iphigenia" has fared strangely. The public was so accustomed to the old form, certain phrases adopted from frequent hearing and reading were familiar to it; now it sounds quite different, and I clearly see that no one, in fact, thanks me for my endless endeavors. Actually, such a work is never finished. It must, however, pass for such as soon as the author has done his utmost, considering time and circumstances.

But all this will not be able to deter me from trying a similar operation with "Tasso." Perhaps it would be better to throw it into the fire. However, I shall adhere to my resolution, and since it must be what it is, I shall make a singular work of it. On this account, I am pleased to find that the printing of my works makes such slow progress; and then, again, it is well to see oneself threatened by the compositor at a distance. Strangely enough, even in one's most independent actions, one expects, nay, requires a stimulus.

If in Rome one can readily set oneself to study, here one can do nothing but live. You forget yourself and the world; and to me it is a strange feeling to go about with people who think of nothing but enjoying themselves. After his long love of art and long study of nature, Sir William Hamilton, who still resides here as ambassador from England, finally has discovered the most perfect work of nature and art in a beautiful young woman. She lives with him: an English woman of about twenty years of age. She is very pretty and has a beautiful figure. He has had made for her a Greek costume which is extremely becoming. Dressed in this costume, with her hair loose and a couple of scarfs, she exhibits every possible variety of posture, expression and look, so that one finally really thinks all this a dream. One beholds here in perfection—in movement, in ravishing variety—all that so many thousands of artists would have liked to be able to produce. Standing, kneeling, sitting, lying down, grave, sad, playful, exulting, repentant, wanton, menacing, anxious—one follows the other, one creates the next mood. With wonderful taste she suits the folding of her veil to each expression and, with the same scarf, makes every kind of headdress. The old knight holds the light for her, and enters into the exhibition with his whole soul. He thinks he can discern in her a resemblance to all the most famous antiques, all the beautiful profiles on the Sicilian coins—aye, of the Apollo Belvedere itself. This much, at any rate, is certain—the entertainment is unique. We spent two evenings on it with thorough enjoyment.

Naples, March 20

THE NEWS that an eruption of lava had just commenced, which, taking the direction of Ottajano, was invisible at Naples, tempted me to visit Vesuvius for the third time. Scarcely had I jumped out of my cabriolet, at the foot of the mountain, when the two guides, who had accompanied us on our previous ascent, immediately appeared on the scene. I had no wish to do without either, and took one out of gratitude and custom, the other for reliance on his judgment,—and the two for the greater convenience.

Having ascended the summit, the older guide remained with our cloaks and refreshment, while the younger followed me, and we boldly went straight towards a dense volume of smoke which broke forth from the bottom of the funnel; then we quickly went downwards by the side of it, till at last, under the clear sky, we distinctly saw the lava emerging from the rolling clouds of smoke.

We may hear an object spoken of a thousand times, but its peculiar features will never be caught till we see it with our own eyes. The stream of lava was small, not broader perhaps than ten feet, but the way it flowed down a gentle and rather smooth plain was remarkable. As it flowed along, it cooled both on the sides and on the surface, so that it formed a sort of canal, the bed of which was continually raised as a result of the molten mass congealing beneath the fiery stream, which, with uniform action, precipitated right and left the scoria which were floating on its surface. In this way a regular dam was finally thrown up in which the glowing stream flowed on as quietly as any mill-stream. We passed along the rather high dam, while the scoria rolled regularly off the sides at our feet. Some cracks in the canal afforded opportunity of looking at the living stream from below, and, as it rushed onwards, we observed it from above.

A very bright sun made the glowing lava look dull; but a moderate steam rose from it into the pure air. I felt a great desire to go nearer to the point where it broke out from the mountain; there, my guide declared, it immediately formed vaults and roofs above itself on which he had often stood. To see and experience this phenomenon we again ascended the hill in order to approach this point from the rear. Fortunately, at this moment the place was cleared by a pretty strong wind but not entirely, because all around it the smoke eddied from a thousand crannies; and now at last we stood on the top of the solid roof which looked like a hardened mass of twisted dough and projected so far outwards that it was impossible to see the welling lava.

We ventured about twenty steps further, but the ground on which we stepped became hotter and hotter, while around us rolled an oppressive steam which obscured and hid the sun. The guide, who was a few steps ahead of me, soon turned back, seized me and hurried out of this Stygian exhalation.

After we had refreshed our eyes with the clear view and

washed our mouths and throats with wine, we went round again to look for any other peculiarities which might characterize this peak of hell towering in the midst of a Paradise. I again observed attentively some chasms, which looked like so many Vulcanic forges, emitted no smoke, but continually shot out a steam of hot glowing air. They were all tapestried, as it were, with a kind of stalactite that covered the funnel to the top, with its knobs and chintz-like variations of colors. In consequence of the irregularity of the forges, I found many specimens of this sublimation hanging within reach, so that, with our staves and a little contrivance, we were able to hack off a few and to secure them. I saw in the shops of the dealers in lava similar specimens, labeled simply "Lava." I was delighted in having discovered that it was volcanic soot precipitated from the hot vapor, distinctly exhibiting the sublimated mineral particles which it contained.

The most glorious of sunsets, a heavenly evening, refreshed me on my return; but I felt how all great contrasts bewilder the mind and senses. From the terrible to the beautiful—from the beautiful to the terrible, each destroys the other and produces a feeling of indifference. Certainly, the Neapolitan would be quite a different creature, did he not feel himself thus hemmed in between God and the devil.

## DIARY OF A SEA VOYAGE

At Sea, Thursday, March 29, 1787

A FRESH AND FAVORABLE BREEZE from the north-east is not blowing this time, as it did at the last sailing of the packet. But, unfortunately, a direct head-wind comes from the opposite quarter, the south-west—and so we are experiencing how much the traveler by sea depends upon the caprice of wind and weather. Impatient as we were we whiled away the morning either on the shore or in the coffee-house; at last, at noon we went on board, and, as the weather was extremely fine, we enjoyed the most glorious views. Not far from the Mole, the corvette lay at anchor. With an unclouded sun the atmosphere was hazy, giving a tint of the most beautiful blue to the rocky walls of Sorrento which were in the shade. Naples which is so alive and full of sunshine glittered brilliantly with countless colors. It was not until sunset that the vessel began slowly to move from her moorings; then the wind which was contrary drove us over to Posilippo and its promontory. All night long the ship went quietly on its way. She is a swift sailer, built in America, and is well fitted with cabins and berths. The passengers cheerful, without being boisterous: Opera singers and dancers, on route to Palermo.

Friday

By daybreak we found ourselves between Ischia and Capri—perhaps not more than a mile from the latter. The sun rose magnificently from behind the mountains of Capri and Cape Minerva. Kniep [Goethe's traveling companion] diligently sketched the outlines of the coasts and the islands in several of their beautiful views. The slowness of the passage was favorable to his labors. We were making our way but slowly under a light side-wind. We lost sight of Vesuvius about four, just as we came in view of Cape Minera and Ischia. These, too, disappeared in the first evening hours. The sun set in the sea, attended by clouds and a long streak of light, reaching for miles, all of a brilliant purple. This phenomenon was also sketched by Kniep. At last we lost sight altogether of the land, and the watery horizon surrounded us, the night being clear, with lovely moonlight.

However, I could only enjoy these beautiful sights for a few moments, because I was soon overcome by sea-sickness. I went to my cabin, chose a horizontal position and, abstaining from all food and drink except white bread and red wine, soon found myself pretty comfortable again. Shut out from the external world, I let the internal have full sway; and, as a tedious voyage was to be anticipated, I immediately set myself a heavy task in order to while away the time profitably. Of all my papers I had only brought with me the first two acts of "Tasso," written in poetic prose. These two acts were quite similar to the present ones in regard to their plan and evolution, but, written fully ten years ago, had something soft and hazy about them which soon disappeared while, in accordance with my later notions, I made form more predominant and introduced more of rhythm.

Saturday

THE SUN ROSE BRIGHT this morning from the water. About seven we overtook a French vessel which had left Naples two days before us, so much faster was our vessel, but still there was no prospect of the end of our passage. We were somewhat cheered by the sight of Ustica, but, unfortunately, on our left, when we ought to have had it, like Capri, on our right. Towards noon the wind became directly contrary, and we did not make the least way. The sea began to get rough, and every one on board was sick.

I kept in my usual position, and the whole play was thought over and over, and through and through again. The hours passed away, and I should not have noticed how they went by, had it not been for the roguish Kniep on whose appetite the waves had no influence. When, from time to time, he brought me some wine and some bread, he took a mischievous delight in expatiating on the excellent dinner in the cabin, the cheerfulness and good nature of our young but clever captain, and on his regrets that I was unable to enjoy my share of it. So, likewise, the transition from joke and merriment to queasiness and sickness, and the various ways in which the latter manifested themselves in the different passengers, afforded him rich material for humorous descriptions.

At four in the afternoon the captain altered the course of our vessel. The mainsails were again set, and we steered direct for Ustica behind which, to our great joy, we discerned the mountains of Sicily. The wind improved, we bore rapidly towards Sicily, and a few little islands appeared in view. The sunset was murky, the light of heaven being veiled beneath a mist. The wind was pretty fair for the whole of the evening; towards midnight the sea became very rough.

Sunday

About three in the morning a violent storm. Half asleep and dreaming, I went on with the plan of my drama; in the meantime there was great commotion on deck; the sails were all taken in, and the vessel pitched on the top of the waves. As day broke the storm abated and the sky cleared up. Now Ustica lay just on our left. They pointed out to us a large turtle swimming a great distance off; I could easily discern it as a living point through my telescope. Towards noon we were clearly able to distinguish the coast of Sicily with its headlands and bays, but we had got very far to the leeward, and tacked on and off. Towards the middle of the afternoon we came nearer to the shore. With the weather being clear and the sun shining bright, we saw quite distinctly the western coast from the promontory of Lilybaeum to Cape Gallo.

A shoal of dolphins accompanied our ship on both bows and continually shot ahead. It was amusing to watch them as they swam along, covered by the clear transparent waves at one time, and at another springing above the water, showing their fins and spine-ridged back and their green and gold glittering sides.

As the land was directly on our lee, the captain steered for a bay behind Cape Gallo. Kniep did not fail to seize the opportunity to sketch the many beautiful scenes rather in detail. Towards sunset the captain made again for the open sea, steering northeast, in order to make the heights of Palermo. I ventured several times on deck, but never interrupted for a moment my poetical labors; and thus I became pretty well master of the whole play. With a cloudy sky, a bright but

Goethe in the Roman Campagna. Oil painting by J. H. W. Tischbein, 1786

The pyramid of Cestius, near Rome. Drawing by Goethe

broken moonlight, the reflection on the sea was infinitely beautiful. The painters—in order to heighten the effect of their pictures—generally lead us to believe that the reflection from the heavenly luminaries on the water has its greatest breadth nearest to the spectator where it also possesses its greatest brilliancy. On this occasion, however, the reflection was broadest at the horizon and, like a sharp pyramid, ended with sparkling waves close to the ship. During the night our captain again frequently changed the tack.

Monday

THIS MORNING, about eight o'clock, we found ourselves facing Palermo. The morning seemed to me highly delightful. During the days that I had been shut up in my cabin, I had got on pretty well with the plan of my drama. I felt quite well now and was able to stay on deck to observe the Sicilian coast attentively. Kniep kept on sketching and by his accurate, but rapid, pencil many a sheet of paper was converted into highly valuable mementoes of our delayed landing.

## ENGLISH LESSONS AND LOVE

*Goethe spent the time from June, 1787, to April, 1788, in Rome again. In depicting his second Roman sojourn—published 40 years later,—Goethe revived the recollection of his tender relationship with the beautiful Maddalena Riggi of Milan.*

AT THE BEGINNING of October under mild, joyous, splendid weather, we enjoyed a regular *villeggiatura* in Castel Gandolfo, getting quite initiated and naturalized into the center of this incomparable region. Mr. Jenkins, the opulent English art-dealer, occupied a very stately mansion there, the former residence of the Jesuit General, where numerous friends found no lack of rooms for comfortable accommodation, of salons for gay parties, of arcades for delicious pleasure walks.

One will obtain the best idea of such an autumn residence, if one thinks of it as of a watering-place. Persons formerly altogether strangers are here, by accident, brought into the most immediate contact. You meet each other at breakfast, at dinners, in walks, in pleasure excursions; you join in conversation both earnest and jocular; in a trice, before you are in the least aware of it, you are friends and confidants. Small wonder, that here where there is not even the diversion which illness and convalescence themselves give to the mind, but where the most perfect leisure reigns all around—small wonder, that the most decided elective affinities operate here with even unusual force. Councillor Reiffenstein had—and rightly too—deemed it advisable for us to repair there at an early date so that we might find time and scope for our walks and artistic wanderings among the mountains, before the crowds should flock in and solicit our participation in common entertainments. We were therefore the first visitors to the place and, in this well-planned expedition, following the lead of our experienced guide, we reaped the greatest enjoyment and instruction.

After a time, however, I noticed the arrival of a truly pretty young Roman young lady and her mother, close neighbors of ours in the Corso. Since my "milording," they had returned my greeting with more than usual friendliness, yet I had never addressed them, though I had frequently passed close by them as they sat in the evening in front of their door. On the contrary, I held faithfully by my vow not to divert my mind from my main business by getting involved in any such relationships. Now, however, in this new sphere we found ourselves all at once brought together like quite old acquaintances. That concert offered material for an opening conversation, and really nothing pleasanter can be conceived than the cheerful natural speech of a Roman lady relating in a lively, graceful manner some action of real life, discoursing rapidly, yet distinctly in the sweet sounding Roman tongue and all in a noble accent, even elevating the middle-class above their station, imparting a certain nobility even to the most natural and common things. I was indeed aware of such qualities and properties, but had never before come on such an enjoyable display of them.

At the same time they introduced me to a young lady of Milan, the sister of a clerk of Mr. Jenkins, a young man who by reason of his efficiency and uprightness was held in great favor by his principal. The two young ladies appeared to be intimate friends.

These two beauties—for beauties they really deserve to be called—stood not in harsh but yet decided contrast to each other. The Roman lady of dark brown hair, brown complexion, brown eyes, and of a somewhat earnest and reserved manner; the Milan lady of light brown hair, of clear soft skin, eyes almost blue, of an open, gracefully inquiring, rather than forward, manner. I sat engaged in a kind of lottery game between the two ladies and had taken the Roman lady into partnership with me in the play. In the course of the game it happened that I tried my luck with the Milan beauty as well, by bets or otherwise. In short, with her, too, there sprang up a kind of partnership, and in my simplicity I did not notice that this divided interest on my part was not favorably regarded till at last, when the play was over, the mother finding me apart, assured the respected stranger—politely indeed, though with maternal earnestness—that having once taken up with her daughter, it was not good manners to show such attentions to another. In a *villeggiatura* it was deemed etiquette for persons who had once so far struck up a partnership with each other to keep together to the end in the exchange of innocent graceful attentions. I made my best excuses and explained to her that it was not possible for a stranger to divine such rules, since it was the custom in our country to show to each and everyone of the ladies of one party the same deference and politeness, all the more in the case of two ladies who were intimate friends.

Unfortunately, however, while I was thus trying to excuse myself, I found, in the strangest manner, that my affections had taken a decided bias in favor of the Milan beauty. I found that impetuously, swiftly as lightning, I had been attracted to her, a fate not so unusual in the case of a vacant heart which in its complacent and tranquil confidence fears nothing, desires nothing, till all at once it comes into the immediate presence of an object it cannot but esteem superlatively precious. In such a moment there is no presentiment of the danger lurking in the flattering features which bewitch us.

Next morning we found ourselves—all three—alone, and my predilection towards the Milan lady increased. She had the great advantage over her friend that a tone of aspiration was observable in all her utterances. She complained not of neglected but of all too circumscribed education. We are not taught writing, she said, for fear we would write love letters. We would not be taught reading, had we not to busy ourselves with the prayer books; and as to foreign languages, nobody will think of instructing us in them; I would give everything to learn English. I often hear Mr. Jenkins with my brother, Madame Angelica, Signor Zucchi, and Signori Volpato and Camuccini talking in English to each other, and I listen to them with a feeling of envy, and the yard long newspapers lie there before me on the table, containing news of all the world, as I see, and I know not what they say!

"It's really a pity," said I, "as English is so easy to learn. You could understand it in a short time. Let us at once make an experiment," I continued, taking up one of the endless English papers lying about in a heap.

I glanced swiftly into it and found an article recording how a lady had fallen into the water but fortunately had been rescued and restored to her friends. There were circumstances complicating the case and rendering it interesting: It was doubtful whether she had voluntarily plunged into the water to drown herself and which of her admirers, the favored or slighted one, had ventured in to her rescue. I pointed out the passage to her, requesting her to peruse it carefully. I then translated all the substantives to her and examined her to see whether she kept their meaning in mind. Very soon she looked over the positions of these principal and root words, and made herself familiar with the place they took in the periods. I next went over the qualifying, acting, determining words, drawing her attention to the manner in which they animated the whole, and catechised her for a long time, until at last, without any challenge on my part, she read out the whole piece to me as though it were Italian, her pretty figure all in graceful agitation during this exercise. Hardly ever have I seen such joy of heart and mind as she expressed while thanking me in the most charming manner for the insight I had given her into this new world. She could hardly keep her composure, as she perceived the possibility of atttaining the fulfillment of her most ardent desire—already experimentally attained so soon.

The company had increased, and Angelica [the painter Angelica Kauffmann], too, had arrived; at a large covered table I was assigned a place at her right, and while the others were mutually offering places, my pupil, who stood at the opposite side of the table from me, hesitated not a single moment to make her way round and sit down beside me. My serious neighbor appeared to notice this with some surprise, nor did it need the glance of a shrewd woman to suspect there must have been some previous passage, and that in fact a friend, who had until then avoided the ladies even to the extent of dull courtesy, had at last fallen an easy conquest into the hands of one of them.

Outwardly, no doubt, I still put up a good show, but was betrayed by a certain embarrassment I showed in dividing my attentions between my two neighbors. I endeavored to entertain my elder, tender and now silent friend by enlivening talk, while by a friendly, quiet, but rather deprecating interest

I tried to compose my new acquaintance who would still expatiate on the foreign language and, as if blinded by a light she had long been waiting for, could not at once readjust herself to the situation.

This state of excitement into which I had fallen was, however, destined to undergo a remarkable revolution. Towards evening I was looking for the young ladies and found the elder ones in a pavilion offering the most splendid of views. My eyes swept round the horizon, but something else than the picturesque landscape hovered before them; the whole scene was pervaded by a tint not to be ascribed solely to the setting of the sun, or the murmurs of the evening zephyrs. The glowing illumination of the elevated points, the cool, blue dusk deepening in the hollows, all this pictured itself to me as more glorious than it ever seemed before in oil or water colors. I could not contemplate it all enough, yet I felt a longing to leave the place and pay homage to the last glimpse of the sun in a small and sympathetic company.

Unfortunately, however, I could not refuse the invitation of the mother and her neighbors to join them, especially as they had made room for me at the window commanding the finest view. Listening to their speeches I could not help observing how they constantly and endlessly turned on the subject of "dowry." All kinds of requirements were discussed, the number and quality of the different gifts, the bestowals of the family, the varied contributions of male and female friends, still in part a secret, and endless other details; all this I had patiently to hear, since the ladies had gotten hold of me for a late walk.

The conversation at last came to the subject of the bridegroom's merits. He was favorably enough described, on the other hand they would not conceal his defects hoping, however, that the grace, the understanding and the amiability of his bride would suffice to mitigate and subdue them in the future wedded state.

At last when the sun was just sinking in the distant sea and, through the long shadows and broken rays of light, afforded an invaluable view, I asked, impatient of all this discourse, yet in the most modest manner, who, then, was this bride? With surprise they inquired whether I was ignorant of what was universally known. It then, for the first time, occurred to them that I was no neighbor but a stranger.

It is now, of course, unnecessary to say what horror seized me when I learned that it was the very pupil who had but lately become so dear to me. The sun set, and under some pretext or other I withdrew from the company that all unwittingly had stung me so cruelly.

The transformation of tender affections one has for a time heedlessly indulged, into the most painful of experiences when one awakens and finds them all a dream, is a matter of everyday occurrence. Perhaps, however, some peculiar interest will be felt in the present case in which a lively mutual good will is nipped in the bud, and the presentiment of all the future bliss which such a relation promises is at once blasted. I came home at a late hour, and early next morning, excusing myself from attendance at dinner, I set off with my portfolio under my arm, on a long excursion.

Years of sufficient experience made it possible for me to collect myself at once, though the effort was painful. "It would be strange, indeed," I exclaimed, "should a fate like Werther's seek thee out in Rome to destroy for thee conditions of so much consequence, and up to now so well maintained."

I again turned instantly to nature as a subject for landscapes, a field I had been meanwhile neglecting, and endeavored to copy her in this respect with all possible fidelity. I was, however, more successful in mastering her with my eyes. All the little skill in technicalities I possessed, hardly sufficed for the most unassuming sketch. All the sensuous fulness, on the other hand, which that region offers us in rocks and trees, in hills and declivities, in peaceful lakes and lively streams, all this was grasped by my eye more appreciatively, if possible, than ever before, and I could hardly resent the wound which had to such degree sharpened my inward and outward sense.

From this point onwards I must dispose of my experience in few words. Crowds of visitors thronged the house, and the houses of the neighborhood. It was now possible for people to avoid each other without appearance of singularity, and a cordial politeness, to which I was disposed by my thwarted affection, caused me to meet with a good reception everywhere in society. My behavior was generally pleasing and I encountered no unpleasantness, no misunderstanding except once at the hands of our host, Mr. Jenkins. I had once brought home with me, from a wide tour among the mountains and woods, the most delicious mushrooms, and handed them over to the cook, who, highly pleased at securing an article of food, rare and greatly prized in those districts, prepared them in the most tasty manner, and placed them on the table. Everyone praised them as exceedingly savory. When, however, in my honor it was betrayed that I had gathered them in the fields, our English host took umbrage, though only in secret, at a stranger having contributed to the banquet a dish of which the head of the house knew nothing, which he himself had not ordered and arranged; it was not good manners for anyone to surprise him at his own table and supply dainties of which he, the host, could give no account. All this Councillor Reiffenstein had to set forth diplomatically to me after dinner to which, suffering as I was from an inward pain that had little connection with the matter of mushrooms, I modestly rejoined that I had supposed the cook would report the matter to his master, but that in future, should any like delicacies fall into my hands during my rambles, I should not fail to lay them personally before our excellent host for his own examination and satisfaction. To be candid, it must be confessed that this generally ambiguous article of food had been put on the table without due examination. The cook had of course assured me of the fact—which he also called to his master's memory—that such a vegetable, as a particular rarity, was seldom indeed, but in every case with great satisfaction, prepared for the table at this season of the year.

This culinary adventure suggested to me, in my quiet humor, the thought of how, infected by a quite peculiar poison, I had myself, by a similar imprudence, fallen into the danger of poisoning a whole party.

It was easy for me to carry out the resolution I had adopted. I contrived at once to evade the English lessons by absenting myself in the morning, and never again approached the pupil I secretly loved, except in the company of several persons.

Very soon this relationship, too, adjusted itself in my busy mind; and that in a very pleasing way. For as I now regarded her as bride, as a future spouse, her character elevated itself in my eyes out of the state of trivial girlhood. And now, turning to her the old affection, but in a higher, unegoistic form, as one who has emancipated himself from the trammels of giddy-minded youth, I very soon attained the friendliest easy feeling in relation to her. My service—if my free attentions towards her may be so named—was altogether innocent of importunity and, on meeting her, partook rather of the character of reverence. She, too, when she came to understand how the relationship in which she stood was known to me, had reason to be perfectly satisfied with my behavior. The rest of the world, moreover, seeing how I mixed freely with everyone, noticed nothing or put no ill construction on anything, and so the days and hours pursued their quiet, comfortable course.

## GOETHE TO HIS FRIENDS

Rome, February 23, 1788

I AM INDUSTRIOUS and happy, and in this state of mind I await the future. Daily it becomes clearer to me that the particular element to which I was destined by birth was poetry and that in the next ten years, for which at most I may work, I ought to cultivate this talent and still produce some good work, since the glow of youth made it possible for me to be successful without any great study. My lengthened residence in Rome will have the advantage of making me renounce the practice of painting and sculpturing.

March 1

It has been a week of rich experience for me, and seems like a month in my memory. First I drew up a plan for "Faust," and I trust it will be a successful one. To write this play now is, of course, a very different thing from what it was fifteen years ago. I think it will lose nothing by its long suspension, especially as I now believe I have recovered the thread. Also in respect to the tone in general I feel content. I have already written out a new scene, and if I fumigate the paper, nobody, I should think, would recognize it from the old. The long rest and seclusion I have enjoyed have wholly restored me to the *niveau* of my own powers, and I find it remarkable how much I resemble my own old self and how little my soul has suffered from the many years and events. The old manuscript, when I see it before me, sometimes gives me many thoughts. It is my earliest utterance on the subject, its main scenes written off-hand without a rough draft. Now, the paper is so yellow with age, so out of order—since the different leaves have never been stitched together—so brittle and fretted away at the edges, that it really looks like the fragment of an old codex. And as I transplanted myself into an earlier world by thinking and divining in that past period, I now transplant myself again, by means of this old production, into a past time I myself have lived through.

*The Faust manuscript enriched with new scenes was for the first time published in Goethe's collected works in 1790.*

## GOETHE TO THE DUKE

Rome, March 17, 1788

I HASTEN to answer your friendly hearty letter with a cheerful "I'm coming!" Thus my desire and wish, my very first intention is being fulfilled. I can feel deeply the scope of your kindness, my first and only appreciation will be an unconditional expression of sincerity. The tact with which you treat me makes me avoid all so-called delicacies which, upon closer scrutiny, often seem to be for the most part nothing but pretensions . . .

Taking all this into consideration, I can only arrive at home by the middle of June, therefore I will have to ask one more favor of you: Will you kindly, after my arrival, grant me the vacation already permitted me while I was absent. Because of my strange and indomitable disposition which has made me suffer a great deal, even in complete freedom and enjoyment of the most desired happiness, it is my wish to find myself on your side and to find my wish reflected in yours to draw the final conclusions on my journeys and to include the greater amount of my reminiscences and thoughts about art in the last three volumes of my writings.

I may as well say that I found myself again in this one year and a half of solitude; but as what?—As an artist! You will be better able to judge and to avail yourself of what else I may be. Due to your constantly active life you have continuously broadened and intensified sovereign knowledge of how to make use of people, as everyone of your letters has clearly shown. I wish to subject myself to your judgment. Let me be your guest, let me complete the full scope of my existence and enjoy life at your side, then my strength will be easily directed hither and thither according to your will like a new spring from great heights, accumulated and purified. Your opinion about me, as shown in your letter, is so wonderful and honorable that I feel ashamed. I can only say: Master, here I am, do with your servant as you will. Any post, any spot you reserve for me I will gladly accept, I will gladly come and go, fill my post and leave it.

Anything I said up to now and asked for, has been based on the assumption that you don't need me immediately, not really. Without the certainty that you would be highly satisfied with my substitute, I would never have gone away or stayed away for so long. By all means, he is the man equipped for such positions which I only held to yield them to a more able man at the right moment. How glad I am that it now has come.

*According to his wishes Goethe was freed from the burden of administrative work after his return. He kept the supervision over the institutes of science and art in the Duchy. In the year 1791 the managership of the newly founded court theatre was added to his duties.*

PART THREE

# *Weimar's Golden Age*

1788-1807

# FRIEDRICH SCHILLER TO C. G. KÖRNER

*While Goethe was still in Italy, Friedrich Schiller came to Weimar to seek a source of income at this art-loving court. The twenty-eight-year-old poet had by then made a great impression on the youth of Germany with his attacks against tyranny as expressed in his first plays. Goethe who in Italy had turned to the ideal of moderation and purity of form, was not too fond of such productions. However, the antagonistic trend of their literary efforts did not prevent him from advocating Schiller's employment as a professor of history at the University of Jena. As for the rest, he did not pay much attention to his young colleague who, pressed by constant financial troubles, ruined his delicate health by working too hard. Christian Gottfried Körner, to whom Schiller reported his first meeting with Goethe, had been for years the confidant of his literary plans.*

Rudolstadt, September 12, 1788

AT LAST I can tell you something about Goethe, and I am sure you are anxiously waiting for such a report. Almost all of last Sunday I spent in his company, on which day he paid us a visit with Frau Herder, Frau von Stein and Frau von Schardt, your Carlsbad acquaintance. His appearance greatly lessened the idea I had conceived from hearsay of his imposing and handsome person. He is of middle height, and carries himself rather stiffly. His countenance is not an open one, but he has a very expressive and lively look, and it is a great pleasure to look into his eyes. In spite of his air of great seriousness, there is a great deal of benevolence and kindness in it. He is brown-haired and seemed to me to look older than he can actually be, according to my calculations. His voice is exceedingly pleasing and his conversation flowing, lively and amusing. It is a pleasure to listen to him; and when he is in a good mood which seemed to have been the case on this occasion, he is fond of talking and takes an interest in what he says. Our acquaintance was soon made and without the slightest formality. Of course, there were too many people and everyone was too eager to catch a word from him, so that I could not be much alone with him or to speak with him on any other than commonplace topics.

He likes to speak of Italy and does so with a kind of passionate memory of this country; his account has given me the most pertinent and the liveliest ideas of the country and the people. He especially portrayed in vivid colors how the Italians—more than any other European people—live in the enjoyment of the present, because the mild climate and fruitful soil lessen their needs and provide for them more easily. All their vices and virtues are the natural consequence of a fiery sensuality. He protested vehemently against the assertion that the Neapolitans are idle people. He claimed that a child of five years of age begins to earn his livelihood there; but of course it is neither necessary nor possible for them to devote whole days to labor as we do. At Rome the unmarried women are virtuous, but all the worse is the immorality of the married women. At Naples it is exactly the reverse. Altogether, he finds a great approximation to the East in the treatment of the other sex in Italy. Rome, he said, will only please a stranger after he has resided there a considerable time. Living in Italy is not more expensive than in Switzerland, if *as* expensive as there. To a stranger, the filth is something unbearable.

He spoke highly of Angelica Kauffmann, both in regard to her genius and heart. She is said to be well off, and he spoke with great enthusiasm of the noble use she makes of her fortune. Neither her love for the arts nor her assiduity have suffered from the fact that she is a wealthy woman. He seemed to have passed many hours in her house and to feel the separation from her with tender sadness.

I intended to tell you many more things gleaned from his conversation, but they will come back to my memory on some other occasion. On the whole, the high idea I conceived of him is not in the slightest degree lessened by his personal acquaintance. But I doubt whether we shall ever become very close to each other. Many things which are still of interest to me, for which I have still to wish and to hope have had their day with him. He is so far ahead of me—not so much in years as in experience of the world and in self-development—that we shall never be able to meet on the road. From the very beginning, his whole life has run in the opposite direction to mine; his world is not my world; our notions and viewpoints seem essentially different. But from so short an interview it is hard to form a judgment. Time will show.

Weimar, February 2, 1789

It would make me unhappy to be a great deal in Goethe's company: he never warms towards even his best friends, nothing touches him. Indeed, I believe he is an egotist of the first water. He possesses the talent to captivate people and to obligate them by small as well as great acts of courtesy, but he always manages to remain free himself. By acts of benevolence he makes men aware of his existence, but only like a God without giving himself—he seems to me the personification of a well-calculated system of boundless selfishness. Men should not tolerate such a being near them. He is hateful to me for this reason, though I cannot help admiring his mind and thinking of him as a great man. In thinking of him I compare him with a coy and prudish girl whom you must make pregnant to humiliate her in the eyes of the world. He has aroused in me a most curious mixture of hatred and love, a feeling not unlike that which Brutus and Cassius must have entertained for Caesar. I could murder his personality and then again love it with my very heart.

Goethe has great influence upon my wish to make my poem as perfect as possible. His judgment means a great deal to me. He spoke most favorably about the "Gods of Greece"; he only found it too long, and he was perhaps right in his judgment. His mind is mature, and his opinion at least in regard to me is rather against me than in my favor. As my great object is to hear the truth about myself, he is the very man among all others who can render me this service. I shall get his opinion through others, for I shall never speak to him about myself.

## GOETHE TO CHRISTIANE

*Goethe made the acquaintance of vivacious Christiane Vulpius soon after his return from Italy. Having grown up in simple circumstances, Christiane could not claim any literary education, but she showed energy and circumspection in taking care of Goethe's household. Since the birth of the boy August on Christmas Day, 1789, Goethe regarded his relationship with Christiane, without doubt, as that of a marriage, although the church wedding did not take place before 1806. In August, 1797, Goethe departed for an army camp in France to join the regiment of the Duke of Weimar. He left his family in the care of his friend Heinrich Meyer in the house on the Frauenplan which shortly before had been given to him as a gift by the Duke.*

Trier, August 25, 1792

YOU CAN NEITHER KNOW nor imagine where Trier [city on the

Moselle River] is situated in the world; the worst is that it is far from Weimar and that it is far from you. I am feeling quite well. I saw my mother and my old friends again, travelled through beautiful but also ugly country, and had to put up with bad roads and severe thunderstorms. I am here, approximately one more day's journey from the army, in an old parson's nest which lies in a pleasant spot. Tomorrow I leave and expect to be in camp by the day after tomorrow. As soon as possible I'll write to you again. You may be quite at ease about me. I hope to be on my way back very soon. My only wish is to see you and the little one again; one certainly does not realize what one possesses as long as one has it. The gift package seems to have arrived and given you pleasure. When I return I shall bring you many things; I do wish it will be rather soon. Goodbye.

Give my regards to Meyer and be my true sweetheart. Adieu, dear angel, I am entirely yours.

Praucourt, August 28

Yesterday I arrived in the Duke's camp, I found him quite well and cheerful, and I am writing to you in his tent in the midst of the noise of the people cutting wood on the one side and burning it on the other. There is an almost unabated rain, people can't get dry either during the day or at night, and I can be very content with having found a place in the Duke's sleeping wagon to pass the night. Victuals are scarce and expensive, everybody is astir and busy making his existence only a bit more bearable. Notwithstanding, people are mostly cheerful and crack jokes about the different happenings here and there. Two captured flags were brought in yesterday, sky blue, rose red and white, and several horses, two cannons and guns, and rain and dirt were immediately forgotten over them.

Don't be troubled about me, I love you very much and will come back as soon as possible. Kiss the little one of whom I think so often,—as well as of everything that surrounds you, kohlrabi and so forth. Goodbye, my dearest.

Verdun, September 2

YOU MUST HAVE, my dear child, a letter from me very soon again. We are already deeper in France, the camp is near Verdun. The town did not want to surrender and had to be fired upon last night. It is a horrifying sight, and one had better not think of having some loved ones there. Today she will surrender and the army will move on toward Paris. Everything moves so fast that it seems I will be with you soon. I did well to go so soon. I am rather well, in spite of missing my comfort and especially my darling. Keep on loving me, take good care of the house and the garden, give my regards to Herr Meyer, kiss the little one and eat your kohlrabi in peace. Don't worry about me. Goodbye, I love you dearly. I'll bring you a gift from Paris, it will be even better than the gift package.

September 8

WE ARE STILL near Verdun, but it seems we'll move forward very soon. I am quite well and have no time to be a hypochondriac. If it would be possible to have you around I would not wish for anything better. I always think about you and the little one and, picturing myself visiting you in the house and garden, I already think how nice everything will be when I come back. [The house was being remodeled.] You only must go on loving me and don't be too generous in making eyes at people.

Before we depart from here I'll dispatch a basket full of liqueur and sweets. Enjoy some of it with Herr Meyer and keep the rest. I am sending you more things for the household. When this letter arrives, you probably will be living in the front wing. Prepare everything well and prepare yourself to become a sweet little cook. After all, there is nothing better than loving each other and being together. Goodbye and remain mine. I love you dearly.

September 10

I HAVE WRITTEN many letters to you and I don't know when

they will reach you. I neglected to number the pages and now begin to do it. Again you will learn that I am well. You know that I love you dearly. If only you could be with me now! Everywhere here are large beds and you would not have to complain as you do sometimes at home. Ah! my darling! There is nothing better than being together. We shall always remind each other of it, when we are together again. Imagine! We are so near Champagne and can't find a good glass of wine. It shall be better on the Frauenplan, if only my sweetheart will take care of the kitchen and cellar.

Be a good hausfrau and prepare a nice home for me. Take care of the little boy and keep loving me.

Only keep loving me! because sometimes in my thoughts I am jealous and imagine that someone else could be more to your liking, since I find many men more handsome and agreeable than myself. But you must not see that, because you must think me the best one, because I love you terribly much and don't like anyone but you. I often dream about you, all kinds of confused things, but always that we love each other. And it shall remain like that.

I ordered two feather beds and pillows stuffed with feathers and different other good things through my mother. Only be sure that our little house will be nice, everything else will be taken care of. I'll find sundry things in Paris, another gift package will come from Frankfort. A basket with liqueur and sweets will be dispatched today. There should be always something added to the household. Keep on loving me and be a faithful child, everything else will take care of itself. As long as I did not possess your heart, what did anything else mean to me; now that I have it, I would like to keep it. In return I am yours too. Kiss the child, give my regards to Meyer, and love me.

September 27

I RECEIVED your letter with the big ink-blot and I am glad that you and the little one are well, that you are quietly enjoying the comfort and good things I left for you. I picture to myself how you cut and work on the materials of the gift package. Don't cut up the beautiful laces, because they are just figured out for a beautiful ruffle. If you are a good sweetheart you will have much joy when I come home loaded with all kinds of good things. I hope to be in Frankfort soon again and that will seem like being with you again.

We experience much hardship, we especially suffer from bad weather. From that I'll recuperate in your arms very soon. By the way, I am quite well and cheerful. Maybe I can tell you more in my next letter. Goodbye. Kiss the little one and love me and put everything right when you move to the front wing.

## GOETHE UNDER FIRE AT VALMY

*The advance of the allied armies on Paris which was begun with great hopes and in which Goethe participated attached to the suite of the Duke of Weimar, came to a standstill at Valmy on September 20, 1792. The often mocked French troops of the Revolution put up surprising resistance under the command of General Kellermann, a resistance which thwarted the strategic plan of the allied armies. Goethe wrote about the events of this historic day in his "Campaign in France."*

THE air of secrecy which, from time to time, necessarily surrounded this march, made us suspect that, before the night was over, we should break up and advance; but the dawn came, and with it a drizzling rain began to fall; it was quite daylight before we were in motion. As the Duke of Weimar's regiment formed the vanguard, some hussars, who were acquainted with the road to our destination, were made to accompany the first squadron as the foremost of the whole column. We now advanced, sometimes at a sharp trot, over fields and hills without a bush or tree; in the distance only, to our left, we saw the Argonne forest; the drizzling rain struck more sharply in our faces; but shortly afterwards we perceived an avenue of very fine poplars, which lay directly across our path. It was the main road from Châlons to St. Menehould, being the way from Paris to Germany; we were led across it, and away into unknown regions.

Some time before this we had seen the enemy, encamped and drawn up in front of the forest, and could also perceive that fresh troops were arriving; it was Kellermann, who was just about to join Dumourier, in order to form his left wing. Our troops were most eager to pounce upon the French, officers as well as men were most ardent in their desire that the General should instantly make the attack; our rapid advance, too, seemed to indicate that such was his intention. But Kellermann had placed himself in too favorable a position and commenced the cannonade about which so much has been said, but the violence of which at the time cannot possibly be described, or even recalled in imagination.

The main road was already a long way behind us, and we kept storming towards the west, when all at once an adjutant came galloping up, ordering us to go back again; we had been led too far, and were now ordered to recross the road and to draw up with our right flank close upon the left side of it. This was done, and we thus made our front against the outwork of La Lune, which was visible on a hill, about a mile ahead of us, close to the road. Our commander came up to us, bringing with him the half of a horse-battery; we received orders to move forward under cover of it and came upon an old driver of the baggage-waggons, lying stretched upon the ground, the first victim of the day. We rode on unconcerned and had a nearer view of the outwork. The battery set up there was firing away fiercely.

Soon, however, we found ourselves in a curious situation; cannon-balls were flying wildly amongst us, without our being able to make out whence they came; for we were advancing behind a friendly battery, and the hostile guns on the opposite hills were much too distant to be able to reach us. I kept to one side of the front and had the most extraordinary view: balls were falling by dozens in front of the squadron, not rebounding, luckily, for they sank into the soft ground, but mud and dirt bespattered men and horses. The black horses admirably held together by their gallant riders snorted and plunged; the whole mass, without separating or falling into confusion, fluctuated to and fro.

A curious sight brought other times to my mind. In the first rank of the squadron the standard was waving to and fro in the hands of a handsome boy; he held it firmly, but against his will was being waved by his frenzied horse; his sweet face, singularly but naturally enough, even at this fearful moment, brought the still sweeter face of his mother up before me; and I could not help thinking of the peaceful moments I had spent in her presence.

Finally, the command came to retreat down the hill: this was done by all the cavalry regiments with great order and steadiness. Only a single horse, Von Lottum's, was killed, although the rest of us, particularly those on the outside of the right wing, should all, properly speaking, have been killed.

After we had withdrawn out of the range of the inexplicable fire and had recovered from our surprise and bewilderment, the riddle was solved: we found the section of the battery, under whose cover we fancied we had been marching, far down in a hollow, of which there are a great many in this district. It had been dislodged from above and had gone down into a ravine on the other side of the road, and thus we had not noticed its retreat. Hostile guns had taken its place; and what was intended for our protection, very nearly became the means of our destruction. The fellows only laughed at us when we reproached them and assured us jestingly that it was much better down here in the valley.

When, however, we afterwards saw with our own eyes how this horse-battery had had wearily to be dragged across difficult marshy terrain, we could not but again reflect upon the critical situation into which we had brought ourselves.

Meanwhile the cannonade continued without interruption. Kellermann occupied a dangerous post at a mill by Valmy towards which point the fire was principally directed; a powder-waggon exploded there, and we rejoiced in the mischief which was thus probably done to the enemy. Hence all those who were exposed to the fire and those who were not, remained merely spectators and listeners. We stayed upon the road from Châlons and halted near a signpost which pointed out the road to Paris.

Therefore, we had this city in our rear now, and the French army stood between us and our native land. Stronger barricades were perhaps never placed in any path and they caused the greatest apprehension to one who had been for four weeks incessantly studying a map of the theatre of war.

However, the necessities of the moment make good their claims even in spite of dangers that might be impending. Our hussars had been lucky enough to capture several waggons of bread which were on their way from Châlons to the army, and they brought them up along the high road. Now, in the same way, as it appeared strange to us to be posted between Paris and St. Menehould, the people at Châlons could never imagine that the enemy would be found on the road leading to their army. For a few pieces of gold the hussars gave up a part of the bread; it was of the finest white kind; a Frenchman is terrified of a morsel of black bread. I distributed more than one loaf among my immediate followers on the condition that they save a share for me for the ensuing days. I found occasion for another piece of foresight. A rifleman belonging to the retinue had likewise purchased a thick woollen blanket from these hussars. I came to an agreement with him that he should let me have it for three consecutive nights, for eight pence a night, and that he should have it during the daytime. He considered the bargain a very advantageous one; the blanket had cost him a florin, and in a short time he would have his money back again with interest. However, I had also reason to be satisfied; my precious woollen coverings from Longwy had remained behind with the baggage; and now, amid the general want of shelter and covering, I had obtained a second protection besides my cloak.

All this took place with the accompaniment of the uninterrupted thundering of cannons on each side; this day ten thousand shots were fired by which, on our side, only twelve hundred men fell, and these, moreover, to no purpose. The sky was cleared by the tremendous concussion; for the cannon were fired exactly like platoon firing, irregularly, stopping and then commencing again. At one o'clock in the afternoon after a pause of some duration, the cannonading was at its height; the earth literally trembled, and still there was not the slightest change in the positions. Nobody knew what would be the result.

I had heard so much about cannon-fever that I wanted to know what kind of thing it was. Ennui and a spirit which danger of any kind excites to daring, in fact, even to rashness, induced me to ride up composedly to the outwork of La Lune. This was again occupied by our people; but it presented the wildest picture. The roofs were shot to pieces, stacks of corn scattered about, men mortally wounded lay stretched upon them here and there, and occasionally a spent cannon-ball fell and rattled among the ruins of the roofs.

Quite alone, and left to myself, I rode away along the heights to the left and could plainly survey the favorable position of the French; they were stationed in the form of a semicircle, with the greatest composure and security; Kellermann, on the left wing, was the easiest to reach.

I fell in with good company on the way. Officers of my acquaintance, belonging to the general staff and the regiment, and greatly surprised to find me here. They wanted to take me back with them. But I told them I had a special objective in view, and they left me, without further discussion, to my well-known but strange caprices.

I had now got right into the region across which the cannon balls came zooming. The sound of them is curious enough and seemed composed of the buzz of humming-tops, the gurgling of water, and the whistling of birds. The balls were less dangerous because of the wetness of the ground; wherever one fell it stuck fast. And thus my foolhardy ride in search of experience was secured at least against the danger of the balls rebounding.

In the midst of these circumstances I soon noticed that something unusual was affecting me; I paid close attention to it, and still the sensation can be described only by comparison. It seemed as if I were in some extremely hot place and quite permeated by the heat, and I felt altogether one with the element in which I was. My eyes lost nothing of their strength or clearness of sight, but it seemed to me as if the world had a kind of brown-red tint, which made the situation as well as the surrounding objects look more terrible. I was unable to perceive any agitation of my blood; but everything seemed rather to be swallowed up in the glow of which I speak. This makes it clear why such a condition can be called a fever. It is remarkable, however, that the feeling of horror and anxiety arising from it is produced in us solely through the ears. For the thunder of the cannons, the howling, whistling, and crashing of the balls through the air is the actual cause of these sensations.

After I had ridden back and was again in perfect security, I remarked with surprise that the glow in me was completely extinguished, and not the slightest feverish agitation remained. Besides, this condition is one of the least desirable; and, indeed, among my dear and noble comrades, there was scarcely one who expressed a sincere wish for it.

Thus the day had passed away; the French stood immovable, Kellermann having acquired a more advantageous position. Our people were withdrawn from under fire, and it was exactly as if nothing had happened. The greatest consternation was diffused amid the army. That very morning they had thought of nothing short of spitting all the French and of devouring them; nay, I myself had been tempted to take part in this dangerous expedition from the unbounded confidence I felt in our army and in the Duke of Brunswick. Now, everyone went about morosely, no one looked at his neighbor, or if he did, it was but to curse or to swear. Just as night was setting in, we had accidentally formed ourselves into a circle, in the middle of which not even the usual fire could be kindled; most of us were silent, only a few conversed, in fact, the power of reflection and judgment seemed to be wanting in everyone. At last I was called upon to say what I thought of the state of affairs, for I had been in the habit of enlivening and amusing the company with brief remarks. This time I said: "From this place and from this day forth commences a new era in the world's history, and you can all say that you were present at its birth."

At such times, when nobody had anything to eat, I claimed a morsel of the bread captured that morning; there also remained about as much as would fill a brandy-bottle of the wine so freely used the day before; and I had therefore completely to abandon the part of conjuror so boldly played while seated by the fire the night before.

The cannonade had scarcely ceased when rain and wind again commenced and made our condition most uncomfortable on the spongy clay soil, exposed as we were to the weather. However, as a natural result of long watching and agitation of mind and body, sleep claimed its right as night drew near. We had lain down behind an elevated part of the ground which protected us from the cutting wind, when it occurred to somebody that for this night we should bury ourselves in the earth and cover ourselves with our cloaks. Preparations were immediately made for this and several holes were dug with implements supplied by the horse artillery. Even the Duke of Weimar did not despise this kind of premature burial.

I now demanded, on payment of eight pence, the blanket mentioned above, wrapped myself in it and spread my cloak over me, without feeling its dampness much. Ulysses, I am sure, did not repose with greater comfort and satisfaction in the cloak which he obtained in a similar way.

All these preparations were made contrary to the wish of the Colonel who called our attention to the fact that the French had a battery upon the opposite hill, behind a copsewood, and they could bury us in real earnest and annihilate us at their pleasure. But we were loath to abandon the sheltered spot and our sagaciously invented snuggery; and this was not the last time I had occasion to observe that people do not avoid danger to put themselves to inconvenience.

## DAVID VEIT TO RAHEL LEVIN

*At the time this letter was written, David Veit was a student of medicine in Jena. Rahel Levin, who later became well known under the name of her husband, Varnhagen von Ense, belonged with the most enthusiastic admirers of Goethe since her earliest youth.*

Gotha, March 30, 1793

I WOULD HAVE LIKED to write to you already from Weimar, but we had to make haste and had to come here quickly via Erfurt, where I am accommodated very comfortably in a beautiful inn.

I have really seen all the great names, Goethe, Wieland, Herder, and I have talked to each one of them rather at length.

We arrived in Weimar at eleven o'clock, changed in a lightning hurry and observed, during the changing, the arrival of the Duke of Rudolstadt's family at the same inn, nimble princes and several princesses, one of whom is passable.

Afraid that Goethe might have to appear at court now, we did not take any time to brush our clothes, but immediately went to him, accompanied by a hired lackey, making our way among the cheers of the expectant crowd. We were told by his servant that, at the moment, a Duke was with him who hardly would leave before one o'clock and we should not come back before two o'clock. I did not let him frighten me away, but told the servant he should announce us as people from Berlin who brought with them a letter from Hofrat Moritz, whereupon we were led two flights up. Downstairs before reaching the first landing we saw the life-sized statues of Apollo and Antinous with all their paraphernalia standing in niches. This landing leads into a hall adorned with various magnificent portraits. From this room we went into a small lovely one which we entered simultaneously with Goethe whom we had seen walking from the other wing of the house through several rooms when we had still been in the hall. He did not have us wait for two minutes. The first thing that caught my attention and you will wish to know, was his figure.

He is far taller than the average man and in proportion to his size heavy set and broad-shouldered. If you remember my uncle Solomon Veit, you have the similarity of figure, but Goethe is still taller and heavier. His forehead is extraordinarily beautiful, more so than I have ever seen before. The eyebrows in the painting [by Johann Heinrich Lips] are well done, but his completely brown eyes are lower set than in the portrait. His eyes are spirited, but do not show the devouring fire of which people speak so much. He has already wrinkles beneath his eyes and rather big bags. All in all, he looks his age of about forty-four to forty-five and the painting is certainly too youthful, unless it is true what everybody claims in Weimar that he aged considerably during his stay in Italy. His nose is actually aquiline, but the dent in the center peters out rather gently. (While he put several questions to my uncle, I looked at him from the side and watched his reflection scrutinizingly in the mirror.) His mouth is very nice, small and very expressive, but deformed, when he smiles, by his strongly crooked teeth. He looks rather serious when he does not talk, but not at all sullen, and there is no idea or trace of conceit in him. Even the silliest person would dislike conceit in a man who in speech and manner is as simple as any businessman. He has a full face, with rather hanging cheeks. As a whole the painting is pretty good, but it gives, after all, not the right impression of him; you certainly would not recognize him.

His face is of a masculine, very dark brown color. The color of the hair somewhat lighter. He wears his front hair completely shaven, combed out at both sides and very smooth, and a long, white powdered pigtail. I don't understand the stock in the portrait at all. The painter Lips must have put on this trimming. His stock is one of the usual as worn by sedate men, buckled in the back, smooth and narrow in front, and not much visible because of the shirt collar covering it. His lingerie is elegant, the jabot only a bit showing. His clothes: a blue coat with woven buttons, double collar (one covering the shoulder, the upright one not very high), a narrow striped vest made of Manchester or a similar fabric and —one supposes trousers. The coat covered them. Ordinary calf leather boots. All in all, he could be a minister, a war counsellor, a privy councillor, maybe an official, but no scholar and certainly no artist. Everyone in Berlin would take him for a native. He received us extremely politely; coming toward us he looked at us in a friendly way, his look as usual serious, but without any arrogance as it seems. When not addressing anyone, his eyes are cast down, his hands behind his back.

The room in which we were standing (he did not ask us to sit down) was decorated with green wall paper, very modern. Paintings and portraits all around. It was about the size of Frau Herz' study, a complete square: two mahogany tables, one mirror, six armchairs, and white silken cushions with green and white stripes. He retained us a quarter of an hour (longer rather than shorter), then he smiled meaningly and —we understood. He accompanied us from the hall and was very polite at our leave taking. The whole reception was very formal, rather cool and general, but much warmer than I expected.

# THE BEGINNING OF A FRIENDSHIP

*The year 1794 became important for Goethe because of the beginning of his friendship with Friedrich Schiller. In the "Annals," a sketchy continuation of his autobiography, Goethe depicted how this meeting was brought about.*

THE RELATIONSHIP to Schiller which all at once developed gave me satisfaction beyond all my wishes and hopes—a relationship which I may rank among the highest that in later years fortune prepared for me. And, indeed, I owed this happy event to my studies in connection with the 'Metamorphosis of Plants,' whereby a situation was brought about which helped clear away all the misunderstandings that had long kept me at a distance from him.

After my return from Italy where I had sought to cultivate myself to greater clarity and purity in all branches of art, in the meantime disregarding everything that was going on in Germany, I found poetical works more or less recent in great repute and exercising extended influence, works which, alas! were extremely repugnant to me. I mention only Heinse's 'Ardinghello' and Schiller's 'Robbers.' The former author was hateful to me because he tried to ennoble and support sensuousness and abstruse modes of thought with the aid of painting and sculpture; the latter, because a forceful but immature talent had poured over the country in full torrent just those ethic and theatrical paradoxes from which I was endeavoring to clear myself.

Not that I blamed either of those talented men for what they had undertaken and achieved. Man cannot deny himself to work in his own way; he makes trials at first unconsciously, crudely, then at each successive stage of culture with ever

Goethe. Engraving by J. H. Lips, 1791

Christiane Vulpius. Drawing by Goethe

increasing consciousness. In this way so much that is excellent and absurd has been dispersed over the world, and confusion has emerged out of confusion.

The noise, however, excited in the country, the applause universally bestowed on those extravagant monstrosities by wild students as well as by the refined ladies of the court frightened me, for I thought to see all my endeavors entirely lost. The subjects in which, and the ways and means by which I had educated myself, appeared to me thrust aside and blocked. And what hurt me most was that all my friends conjoined with me—Heinrich Meyer and Moritz as well as the artists Tischbein and Bury, directing the minds of men in their province in a kindred spirit with my own—they all seemed likewise endangered. I was greatly bewildered. I would have willingly renounced the study of plastic art, the practice of poetry, had it been possible. For what chance was there of excelling those productions of genius and of wild form? Imagine my situation! I aspired to nurture and to convey the most pure perceptions, and here was I hemmed in between *Ardinghello* and *Franz Moor!* [A depraved character in Schiller's first play]

Moritz who likewise returned from Italy and stayed with me for some time, passionately confirmed with me in these views; I avoided Schiller who was staying in my neighborhood in Weimar. Nor was the appearance of 'Don Carlos' destined to bring me nearer to him. I rejected all attempts in this direction on the part of persons who were equally close to him and to me, and in this fashion we lived near to each other for some time.

His essay on 'Grace and Dignity' was just as little fitted to reconcile me with him. He had joyfully absorbed and adopted the Kantian philosophy, highly exalting the subject while seemingly setting limits to it. This philosophy developed the extraordinary characteristics which nature had planted in him, and, in the sublime feeling of freedom and self-determination, he was ungrateful to the great mother, who certainly did not treat him like a stepmother. Instead of regarding her as self-existent, alive, bringing forth her births, from the lowest to the highest, according to fixed laws, nature was to him the product of certain empiric forms innate in man. Some hard passages, setting my confession of faith in a false light, I could even directly trace as referring to myself; and if they were written without allusion to me, the matter appeared in my eyes all the worse, because it only disclosed the more unmistakably the immeasurable abyss between our ways of thinking.

Meeting was not to be thought of. Even the mild entreaties of Dalberg who appreciated Schiller according to his merits had no effect; indeed, the arguments with which I opposed any communion with him were difficult to refute. It could not be denied that two intellectual antipodes were further removed from each other than by one diameter of the earth, and, since they could be considered being opposite poles, could never be brought into one. That, nevertheless, there *was* some point of affinity between them will appear from the following.

Schiller moved to Jena where I did not see him either. At this time, with incredible effort Batsch had started a natural research association, having as a basis of study handsome collections and considerable apparatus. I usually attended their formal sittings, and once I found Schiller there. As we happened to leave at the same time, a conversation developed between us. As it seemed, he had been interested in the lecture, but observed with sharp understanding and insight and to my great pleasure, how such a dismembered way of treating nature was not calculated to engage the layman who would, otherwise, willingly take part in such studies.

To this I replied that perhaps it was not attractive even to the initiated, and that undoubtedly there was another way of going to work, presenting nature not sundered and detached, but operative and alive, striving with sure determination out of a whole into parts. He desired further light on this subject, but did not conceal his doubts; he could not admit that such a view of nature was, as I maintained, the presentation of experience.

By then we reached his house, and the conversation tempted me to enter. I set forth in a lively manner the metamorphosis of plants and, with many characteristic strokes of the pen, caused a symbolic plant to arise before his eyes. He perceived and observed it all with great interest, with a decided power of comprehension. But when I finished he shook his head and said, "That is no observation, that is an idea." I was startled, chagrined in a certain measure; for the line dividing us was by this expression most palpably indicated. An assertion in *Grace and Dignity* recurred to my mind, the old grudge was about to flame up in me again. I controlled myself, however, and answered, "It can be anything but disagreeable to me to have ideas without knowing it, and even to see them with my eyes."

Schiller, who possessed much more tact and practical prudence than I and—maybe also on account of the 'Horen' [a literary periodical] which he was about to bring out—was disposed to attract rather than repel me and thus answered like an accomplished Kantian. And since my obstinate realism gave rise to a lively debate, a lengthy battle was fought and then an armistice declared. Neither of us could boast of being the victor, each deemed himself invincible.

Sentences like the following made me quite unhappy: "How can ever experience commensurate with an idea be given? For just therein consists the peculiarity of the latter that experience can never come up to it." If he deemed what I considered experience an idea, there must after all be something intermediary, something relational between the two. The first step was however taken. Schiller's power of attraction was great, he held fast all who approached him. I took part in his plans and promised to forward to him for his 'Horen' a great deal that was lying in my drawer.

His wife [Charlotte von Lengefeld], whom from her childhood I was wont to love and appreciate, contributed her part towards a lasting relationship. Our common friends were all glad and so, by means of a dispute between object and subject, the most fundamental of all disputes—one, indeed, perhaps never to be wholly settled—we sealed an alliance which has lasted without interruption and has been, both for ourselves and others, the instrument of much good.

For me, in particular, it was a new spring in which everything secreted in my nature burst into joyous life, in happy fellowship, all seeds opening, and tender growths shooting up with increased vitality. Our reciprocal letters give the most immediate, the purest, the completest testimony to this fact.

## SCHILLER TO GOETHE

*The correspondence between Schiller and Goethe gives us insight into the co-operation of two outstanding men of letters who, through their common goals, were constantly brought closer together. The beginning of this correspondence was marked by Schiller's profound analysis of Goethe's "nature," which, by elucidating the difference between these two personalities, showed, at the same time, the possibility of a fruitful complement.*

Jena, August 23, 1794

YESTERDAY I received the pleasant news that you had returned from your journey. Now we can hope again to see you among us soon which I, on my part, most heartily wish. My recent conversations with you have put the whole store of my ideas into a state of motion, for they dealt with a subject which has actively engaged my thoughts for some years past. Many things about which I could not make up my own mind have received new and unexpected light from the contemplation of your mind (for so I must call the general impression of your ideas upon me). I needed the object, the body, to several of my speculative ideas, and you have made me find the right track. Your calm and clear way of looking at things keeps you from getting onto any by-roads into which speculation as well as arbitrary imagination merely following its own bent are so apt to lead one astray. Your correct intuition grasps everything and even far more perfectly than what any analysis laboriously endeavors to unearth, and only because this lies within you as a whole, the wealth of your mind is concealed from yourself. Unfortunately, we are only aware of what we can take apart. Therefore, minds like yours seldom know how far they have penetrated and how little cause they have to borrow from philosophy which, in fact, can only learn from them. Philosophy can merely dissect what is given it, but the *giving* itself is not the work of the analyst but of genius which combines things according to objective laws under the obscure but safe influence of pure reason.

Though from a distance only, I have long watched the course which your mind has pursued and have followed, with ever renewed admiration, the path which you marked out for yourself. You seek the necessary in nature, but you seek it by the most difficult route, by one which all weaker minds would take care to avoid. You look at nature as a whole, when you want light thrown on her separate parts; you look for the explanation of the individual in the totality of all her various manifestations. From the simple organism you ascend, step by step, up to those that are more complex to form finally the most complicated of all—man—out of the materials of nature as a whole. Thus, so to speak, imitating nature in creating him, you try to penetrate into his hidden structure. This is a great and truly heroic thought which sufficiently shows how your mind keeps together the whole wealth of its conceptions in one beautiful entity. You can never have expected that your life would suffice to attain such an end, but to have struck out such a path is worth more than reaching the end of any other; and you, like Achilles in the Iliad, made your choice between Phthia and immortality.

Had you been born a Greek, or an Italian for that matter, and had you from infancy been placed in the midst of the most exquisite nature and an idealised art, your path would have been infinitely shortened, perhaps even rendered entirely superfluous. In that case, you would have taken up the form of the necessary on your first perception of things and the grand style would have been developed in you with your first experience. But being born a German, and your Grecian spirit having been cast in this Northern mold, you had two choices only. Either to become a Northern artist or, with your power of thought, to supply your imagination with all that which reality withheld from it and thus to create Greece within you by a reasoning process. At that period of life when the soul, surrounded by defective forms, constructs its own inward nature out of outward circumstances, you had already assumed a wild Northern nature, and your victorious genius, rising above its materials, then discovered this want from within and became convinced of it from without through its acquaintance with Greek nature. You had then, in accordance with the better model which your developing mind created for itself, to correct your old and less perfect nature, and this could be only done by following certain leading ideas. However, this *logical* direction which a reflecting mind is forced to pursue, is not very compatible with the aesthetic state of mind by which alone a reflecting mind becomes creative. Therefore, you had to achieve one task more: for inasmuch as your mind had passed over from intuition to abstraction, so you had now to go back and retranslate ideas into intuitions and to change thoughts into feelings, because only through them can genius be productive.

It is somewhat in this manner that I imagine the course pursued by your mind, and whether I am right or not, you will know best. However, what you yourself can hardly be aware of (as genius ever remains the greatest mystery to itself) is the beautiful harmony between your philosophical instinct and the purest results of your speculative mind. Indeed, at first sight it seems as if there could not be any greater opposites than the speculative mind which proceeds from an entity and the intuitive mind which proceeds from variety. If, however, the former seeks experience with a pure and truthful spirit and the latter seeks law with self-active and free power of thought, then the two cannot fail to meet one another half way. It is true that the intuitive mind has only to deal with individuals, the speculative mind only with species. But if the intuitive mind is genial and seeks the nature of the Necessary in experience, then individuals will be produced, but they will possess the character of the species; and again, if the speculative mind is genial and does not lose sight of experience when rising above it, then it will indeed produce species only, but with the possibility of individual life and with a well-founded relation to actual objects.

But I find that instead of sending you a letter I am writing an essay—will you pardon me and ascribe it to the lively interest with which the subject has filled me, and should you not recognize your own image in this mirror, I sincerely ask you not to flee from it on that account.

## GOETHE TO SCHILLER

Ettersburg, August 27

On the anniversary of my birthday which will take place this week, I could not have received a more pleasant gift than the letter in which you draw the sum total of my existence in such a friendly manner and in which, by your sympathy, you encourage me to a more assiduous and active use of my powers.

Pure enjoyment and true usefulness can only be reciprocal, and it will be a pleasure to me to unfold to you what the conversation with you has meant to me, how I, too, regard those days as an epoch in my life and how content I feel in having gone on my own way without any particular encouragement. For it seems to me that after so unexpected a meeting we cannot but wander on in life together. I have always highly valued the frank and rare earnestness which is displayed in all that you have written and done, and I may now claim that, more especially during these latter years, it is you who made me acquainted with the course your mind has taken. If we make it clear to one another which point we have so far reached at present, the better our common work will progress without interruption.

All that concerns me, inside and outside, I will gladly tell you. Since I am fully aware that my undertaking exceeds the measure of human capabilities and their earthly duration by far, I should like to deposit many things with you and thereby not only preserve them, but give them life.

Of what great advantage your sympathy will be to me you will soon see for yourself when, after a closer acquaintance, you discover in me a kind of obscurity and hesitation which I cannot entirely master, though I am distinctly conscious of their existence. But such phenomena are often found in our natures, and we quietly submit to them as long as they do not become too tyrannical.

I hope to be able to spend some time with you soon, and we shall then talk over a great many things.

## SCHILLER TO GOETHE

Jena, August 31

ON MY RETURN from Weissenfels where I met my friend Körner from Dresden, I received your last letter but one, the contents of which pleased me for two reasons. First, I perceived from it that the view I took of your mind coincides with your own feelings, and secondly that you were not displeased with the candor with which I allowed my heart to express itself. Our acquaintance, though it comes late, awakens in me many a delightful hope and is to me another proof of how much better it often is to let chance have its way than to forestall it with too much officiousness. However great my desire was to become more closely acquainted with you than is possible between the spirit of a writer and his most attentive reader, now I can clearly see that the very different paths upon which you and I have moved, could not, with any advantage to ourselves, have brought us together sooner than at the present time. But now I hope that we may travel over the rest of our life's way together and, moreover, do this with more than usual advantage to each other, inasmuch as the last travelers who join company on a long journey have always the most to say to one another.

Do not expect to find any great store of ideas in me; that is what I shall find in you. My need and endeavor is to make much out of little, and when you once come to know my poverty in all so-called acquired knowledge, you will perhaps find I have sometimes succeeded in doing this. Since the scope of my ideas is small, I can more rapidly and frequently run through it and for that reason I can use my small resources with more effect and can, by means of form, produce that variety which is wanting in the subject matter. You strive to simplify your great world of ideas, I seek variety for my small means. You have to govern a whole realm, I only a somewhat numerous family of ideas which I would very much like to be able to extend into a little world.

Your mind works intuitively to an extraordinary degree and all your thinking powers seem to have come to an agreement with your imagination to be their common representative. In reality this is the most a man can make of himself, if he only succeeds in generalizing his perceptions and in making his feelings his supreme law. This is what you have endeavored to do and what, in a great measure, you have already achieved! My understanding works more in a symbolizing manner and thus I vacillate, as a hybrid, between ideas and perceptions, between law and feeling, between a technical mind and genius. This is what made me appear rather awkward both in the field of speculation as well as in that of poetry, particularly in my earlier years; because the poetic mind generally got the better of me when I ought to have philosophized, and my philosophical mind when I wanted to write poetry. Even now it often enough happens that imagination intrudes upon my abstractions and cold reason upon my poetical productions. If I could obtain such mastery over these two powers as to assign to each its limits through my freedom, I might yet look forward to a happy fate. But, unfortunately, just when I have begun to know and to use my moral energies rightly, illness seizes me and threatens to undermine my physical powers. I can scarcely hope to have time to complete any great and general mental revolution in myself. But I will do what I can and when, at last, the building falls, I shall perhaps after all have snatched from the ruins what was most worthy of being preserved.

You wanted me to speak about myself, and I have made use of this permission. I make these confessions to you in confidence and venture to hope that you will receive them in a kindly spirit.

Today I shall refrain from entering into details about your essay which will at once lead our conversations on this subject on to the most fertile track. My own researches—entered upon by a different path—have led me to an almost similar result at which you have arrived, and in the enclosed papers you will perhaps find ideas which coincide with your own. I wrote them about a year and a half ago, for which reason as well as on account of the occasion for which they were penned (they were intended for an indulgent friend), there is some excuse for their crudeness of form. These ideas have since then received in me a better foundation and greater precision which may possibly bring them much nearer to yours.

## GOETHE TO SCHILLER

Weimar, September 4

I HAVE READ with much pleasure the manuscripts you sent me as well as the fragment of your essay on the Sublime, and again I have become convinced that we are not only interested in the same subjects, but that we agree in our way of viewing them in most cases. I can see that we have the same ideas on all main points, and as far as the differences of our viewpoints are concerned, of our mode of connecting thoughts and of our manner of expression, they merely arise from the wealth of the object and from the corresponding variety of the subjects. Now I would like to ask you to let me know all you have written or published on this matter, so that we may overtake the past without loss of time.

In this connection I have another proposal to make. Next week the Court goes to Eisenach for two weeks, and I shall be alone and more independent than I will have the chance of being for some time to come. Will you come and pay me a visit during that time, and stay with me? You could take up any kind of work you like without being disturbed. We would converse together at convenient hours, would see those friends in whom we are both most interested, and I think we shall not part without having spent our time together to some purpose. You could live exactly as you like and arrange everything as if you were at home. I would be able to show you the main part of my collections, and many threads of interest would tie us closer together. After the fourteenth you will find me free and ready to receive you.

I shall reserve much that I have to say till you come, and in the meantime wish that all things may go well with you.

## SCHILLER TO GOETHE

Jena, September 7

I ACCEPT with pleasure your kind invitation to come to Weimar. At the same time I earnestly request you not to make any alterations in your household arrangements on my account, for, unfortunately, the spasms from which I suffer oblige me to stay in bed all morning, because they leave me no peace at night and, in fact, I am never well enough even during the day to venture with certainty to count on any fixed hour. You must, therefore, allow me to look upon myself as a perfect stranger in your house, one to whom no attention is paid, so that by being left to myself I may escape the embarrassment of making anyone else dependent on my state of health. Arrangements which would make other people comfortable are my most dangerous enemies, for I need only decide to do a thing at a particular time and I shall certainly find it impossible to accomplish it.

Excuse these preliminaries which I am obliged to settle beforehand to make it at all possible for me to stay with you. I only ask for the pitiful liberty of being allowed to be an invalid in your house.

## SCHILLER TO GOETHE

*For many years Goethe worked on his novel "Wilhelm Meister's Apprenticeship," in which he undertook to delineate the intellectual and moral development of a young son of a bourgeois family. This work which contains a great many autobiographic traits was, after several revisions, finished in 1796. Schiller took a lively interest in this work and his constructive criticism induced Goethe to make a series of improvements.*

Jena, July 2, 1796

I HAVE NOW RUN through all the eight books of your novel, very hurriedly, it is true, but the subject matter alone is so large that I could hardly get through it in two days' reading. Therefore, I ought still not to say anything about it today, for the surprising and unparalleled variety which is concealed in it—in the strictest sense of the word—is overpowering. I confess that what I have as yet grasped correctly is but the *continuity,* not the *unity,* although I do not doubt for a moment that I shall become perfectly clear on this point also, if, as I think, in works of this kind the continuity is more than half the unity.

As, under the circumstances, you cannot exactly expect to receive from me anything thoroughly satisfactory, and yet wish to hear something, you must be content with a few remarks. These, however, are not altogether without value, inasmuch as they will tell of direct impressions. To make up for this, I promise you that our discussions about your novel shall continue throughout the month.

To give an adequate and truly aesthetic estimate of a whole work, as a work of art, is a serious undertaking. I shall devote the whole of the next four months to it, and that with pleasure. Besides this, it is one of the greatest blessings of my existence that I have lived to see this work of yours completed, that it has been written while my faculties are still in a state of growth and that I may draw inspiration from this pure source; further, the wonderful relation that exists between us, makes it seem to me a kind of religious duty to make your cause my own, and so to develop all that is real in my nature that my mind may become the clearest mirror of that which exists beneath this covering, and that I may deserve the name of being your friend in the higher sense of the word. How vividly have I felt at this time that excellence is a power, that it can influence selfish natures only as a power, and that—as contrasted with excellence—there is no freedom but love.

I cannot say how much I have been moved by the truth, the beautiful vitality and the simple fulness of your work. My agitation is certainly greater than it will be when I have completely mastered your subject, and that will be an important crisis in my intellectual life; but, on the other hand, this agitation is the effect of the Beautiful and only of the Beautiful, and is merely the result of my reason for not having yet been able to master my feelings. I now quite understand what you meant by saying that it was the Beautiful, the True that could often move you to tears. Calm and deep, clear and yet incomprehensible like nature, your work makes its influence felt, it stands there, and even the smallest secondary incident shows the beautiful equanimity from which all has emanated.

July 5

NOW THAT I have obtained a fuller insight into your novel as a whole, I cannot say enough of how successful you have been in the choice of the character of your hero, if indeed such things can be said to be chosen. No other character would have been as appropriate to be the *bearer* of the incidents, and, leaving entirely out of consideration the fact that the problem could be given to and solved only by such a character, still no other would have been as well suited for the *presentation* of the whole. Not only did the *subject* itself require this particular character, but the *reader* also was in need of him.

His predisposition to meditation holds the reader back at the most rapid point in the course of the action, and obliges him constantly to be looking forward and backward and to think of everything that is taking place. He gathers—so to speak—the spirit, the significance, the inward nature of everything that goes on around him, converts every obscure feeling into an idea and thought, expresses each individual thing in a general form, places the meaning of everything more clearly before us, and while he thus fulfills his own character, he at the same time most perfectly fulfills the aim of the whole.

The rank and the outward position from which you have selected him makes him specially fitted for this. A new world is opened up to him which makes a vivid impression upon him, and while he is engaged in trying to assimilate it for himself, he leads us into its midst and shows us what there is reality in it for man. His mind possesses a pure and moral image of humanity, with it he tests every outward manifestation of this image. And while on the one hand experience aids him in more accurately fixing his wavering ideas, these very ideas, this inward feeling in turn again corrects experience. In this manner the character helps you wonderfully in discovering and interpreting what is essentially human in all the events and relations that occur. His mind is indeed a faithful but certainly not a mere passive mirror of the world and, although his imagination influences his perception, still the latter is after all only idealistic not fantastic,—poetical, but not wildly extravagant; it is not founded upon any caprice of the wayward imagination, but upon a beautiful moral freedom.

Exceedingly true and admirable is the picture you give of him in his dissatisfaction with himself, when telling Theresa the story of his life. His value lies in his mind, not in what he effects, in his aspirations, not in his actions; therefore, as soon as he is about to give an account of his life to another person, it must appear to him wanting in purpose. On the other hand, a Theresa and similar natures can always calculate the value of such characters in ready money, and can always vouch for them by some outward object. Furthermore, it is a very beautiful and delicate trait which we find in Theresa's character, namely that she has a mind, a sense of justice to appreciate this higher nature; her clear soul feels the necessity of being able to mirror even that which she herself is not. Thus you have at once raised her above all those narrow-minded natures unable to rise out of their miserable selves, even in their imagination. Lastly, that a mind like Theresa's should so believe in a mode of viewing things and of feeling, entirely alien to her own nature, as to be able to love and esteem the heart which is capable of it, is at the same time a beautiful proof of its objective reality which must delight everyone who reads the passage.

Another thing that pleased me very much in this Eighth Book was that Wilhelm is beginning to feel himself of more consequence in face of the imposing authorities, Jarno and the Abbot. This too is a proof that he has pretty well gotten over the years of his apprenticeship, and Jarno on that occasion answers quite according to what I feel: "You are bitter, that is all very well and good, but if only you would get thoroughly angry it would be better still." I confess that without this proof of self-assuredness in your hero, it would be unpleasant to me to think of him as so closely connected with this class of people, as happens subsequently through his union with Natalie. What with his predilection for the aristocracy and his honest distrust of himself and his class—which he, on so many occasions, clearly shows—he does not seem to be altogether capable of maintaining his perfect freedom in this relation, and even here, when you show him to be more courageous and more self-reliant, one cannot refrain from being in a certain degree anxious about him. I ask myself will he ever be able to forget the bourgeois class, and must he not do so, if his destiny is to be fully and well developed? I fear he will never wholly forget it; he has, it seems to me, reflected too much about it; what he at one time saw so distinctly beyond himself, he will never be able to make his own. Lothario's noble presence as well as Natalie's twofold merit of birth and heart will always keep him in a certain state of inferiority. I sometimes become uneasy about him, when I think of him as the brother-in-law of the Count, who does not temper the elevation of his rank by anything aesthetic, but rather renders it the more conspicuous by pedantry.

As for the rest, it is admirable that—with all due respect for certain outward and positive forms—the moment there is any question about what is purely human, you make birth and rank count completely for nothing; and, moreover, as is only fair, without wasting a word on the subject. But what I consider obviously beautiful, you will hardly find approved by the general public. Many people will think it strange that a novel which has so little "Sansculottism," which, in fact, in several passages seems more inclined to speak in favor of the aristocracy, should wind up with three marriages, all three of which are *mésalliances*. Although I do not wish to have anything in the development different from what it is, nevertheless, I would not like to see the true spirit of your work misunderstood because of trifles and casual circumstances; therefore, I would like to have you consider whether it would not be possible to prevent people from forming a false judgment by putting a few words "into Lothario's mouth." I say Lothario's mouth, for he is the aristocratic character. He, consequently, will be most credited by readers of his own class, moreover, in him the *mésalliance* is most conspicuous. This would, at the same time, be an opportunity—and one that does not often occur—of showing Lothario's character in its full development. I do not mean to say that this should be done at the very point where the reader would apply the words: on the contrary, it would be better were the remark to come from Lothario as the natural expression of his mind, and not as a rule for any single case.

As far as Lothario is concerned, it might indeed be said that Theresa's being an illegitimate child and belonging to the middle class of society was a family secret; but—others might say—it is all the worse, because he has to deceive the world in order to give his children the advantages of his rank. You will yourself know best how much or how little regard need be paid to this.

This is all for today. You have now heard all kinds of things from me, and you will, I foresee, have more yet to hear, I wish that some of my suggestions could be of service to you.

## GOETHE TO SCHILLER

Weimar, July 7

I THANK YOU sincerely for your refreshing letter and for communicating to me what you feel and think about my novel, more especially about the Eighth Book. If it accords with your mind, you cannot fail to see your own influence in it, for I should certainly never have been able to finish it—at least not in the way it is done—had it not been for the friendly relation which subsists between us. A hundred times when I was talking to you about theory and practice, my mind was dwelling upon the situations which you have now lying before you, and I was silently judging them according to the principles on which we were agreed. Even now your friendly warnings are guarding me from one or two striking errors. In the case of some of your remarks I saw at once what had to be done, and I shall introduce the alterations in the new transcript.

How seldom, in the business and transactions of ordinary

life, do we find the sympathy we want, and in the case of high aesthetics it is hardly to be expected, for how few persons judge a work of art by itself, how few are able to grasp it as a whole, and even then it is only sympathy that can see all that it contains, and only pure sympathy also that can in addition see what it lacks. And how much more might be added to express the special relation in which I stand to you alone. . . .

I had proceeded thus far directly upon receiving your first letter, when outward and inward obstacles kept me from writing further. I feel, moreover, that even were I quite calm I could not give you any replies to your observations. What you suggested to me must be made practicable, so that the Eighth Book may have the full enjoyment of your sympathy. Kindly continue to make me acquainted with my own work; I have already in thought worked out many of your suggestions. Next Wednesday perhaps I will send you a summary of what I think of doing.

## SCHILLER TO GOETHE

Jena, July 8

As YOU CAN LET me keep the Eighth Book a week longer, I will confine my remarks for the present to this Book in particular. When the whole work is once out of your hands and in the wide world, we can talk more about the form of the whole, and you will, I hope, then give me an opportunity of correcting my judgment.

I would like to draw your attention to two points in particular before the final closing of the Book.

Your novel, as it stands, resembles an epic poem in several instances, among other things in that it possesses machinery which in a certain sense represents the gods or ruling fate. The subject demanded this.

Meister's years of apprenticeship are no mere blind effort of nature: they are a kind of experiment. A secretly working higher force, the powers of the Tower, accompany him with their attention, and, without interrupting nature in her free course, watch and lead him at a distance to an object of which he has and should not have any idea. Gentle and undefined as this influence is from without, it nevertheless really exists, and it was indispensable to the attainment of the poetic purpose. *Years of apprenticeship* convey the idea of relationship; they demand their correlative, *years of mastership;* and indeed the idea of the latter must explain and furnish a basis for the former. But the idea of mastership—which is but the work of ripe and full experience—cannot guide the hero of the novel. It can and dare not stand *before* him as his aim and object, because had he thought of the aim, he himself would have attained it; while guiding him, therefore it must stand *behind* him. In this way the whole receives a beautiful purpose, without the hero himself having any aim. The understanding, then, finds its work accomplished, while imagination fully maintains its freedom.

The fact is that you have even in this particular matter—the only object in the whole novel that is actually expressed—avoided all heaviness and harshness; the same holds good in the case of Wilhelm's being secretly led by Jarno and the Abbot. And furthermore that you have drawn the motives more from a capricious mood, a human trait, than from a moral source, is one of those beauties that belong peculiarly to yourself. The *idea* of machinery is thereby suppressed while its effect continues, and all that concerns form remains within the bounds of nature, only that the result is greater than what nature would have accomplished had she been left to herself.

In spite of all this, I would have liked you to have brought the significance of this machinery—its necessary bearing upon the internal character of the work—a little more clearly before the reader. For the reader should in all cases be allowed a clear insight into the economy of the whole, even though this has to be concealed from the persons represented. Many readers will, I fear, believe that that secret influence is merely for dramatic effect, a device to increase the complication, to create surprises and such things. The Eighth Book does indeed give an *historical* interpretation of all the single incidents brought about by this machinery, but it gives no sufficiently satisfactory *aesthetic* interpretation of the inner spirit of the poetic necessity of these contrivances. I myself was not convinced of this till I had read it a second and a third time.

If, in fact, there were anything else to find fault with in the work it would be this, "that considering the great and deep seriousness that pervades all the single parts and by which it produces so powerful an effect, too much scope is allowed to the play of the imagination." It seems to me that you have in this case carried the free grace of the movement somewhat further than is compatible with the poetic seriousness and that, due to your just horror of everything that is heavy, methodical and stiff, you have approached the other extreme. I think I have noticed that a certain condescension towards the weak side of the public, has induced you to make more use of dramatic purposes and dramatic contrivances than is necessary or appropriate in a novel.

If ever there was a poetic narrative that could dispense with the aid of the marvellous and the surprising, it is this novel of yours; and such a work could very easily be injured by what is useless to it. It might happen that the reader's attention will be directed more to what is accidental and that his interest is taken up with solving riddles when it should have been concentrated on the inward spirit of the work. It might happen, I say,—and do not we both know that this has already happened?

Now the question is whether this fault—if fault it is—might not still be obviated in the Eighth Book. However, it would apply only to the representation of the idea; in regard to the idea itself nothing remains to be desired. Therefore, it would merely be necessary to bring to the fore all that the reader has until now treated too frivolously, and to justify the theatrical incidents which he may have looked upon as the mere play of the imagination, by connecting them more definitely with the most serious import of the work, also in face of reason, as indeed is done *implicite,* but not *explicite.* It seems to me that the Abbot is very well fitted to be charged with this duty, and he would thereby have a further opportunity of recommending himself to the reader. It would, perhaps, not be superfluous if, in the Eighth Book, mention were made of the principal reason why Wilhelm is made a subject of the Abbot's pedagogical plans. These plans would thus receive a more special application, and Wilhelm's personality would also appear of more importance to the company.

You have, in the Eighth Book, thrown out various hints as to what you wish your readers to understand by the terms Apprenticeship and Mastership. When examining a poetical production it is chiefly the purport of ideas that comes into consideration, particularly in the case of a public like ours, and as this is often the only thing that is afterwards remembered, it is of importance that you should herein be thoroughly understood. Your hints are very good, but they do not appear to me to be sufficient. It is true, you would rather have the reader find out more himself than that he should be forthwith instructed by you, but just because you yourself say *something* about it, people will fancy that *all* has been said, and the consequence is that you make the limits of your idea narrower than if you had left it entirely to the reader.

If I had in bare words to define the goal which Wilhelm finally reaches after a long series of aberrations, I should say, "he steps from an empty and undefined ideal into definite, active life, but without losing any of his idealising power." The two opposite paths that lead away from this happy state are represented in your novel, and, moreover, in all possible shades and degrees. From the time of that unfortunate expedition where he wishes to have a play performed, without having thought of its structure, to the moment when he chooses Theresa for his wife, he has, so to speak, onesidedly run through the whole circle of humanity; those two extremes are the two greatest contrasts of which a character such as his is at all capable, and harmony must now necessarily arise out of it. The fact of his passing under the lovely and serene guidance of nature (through Felix) from the ideal to the real, from a lively endeavor to act and to recognize what is real—without however losing that which was real in his first state of endeavor—the fact of his acquiring determinateness without losing his wonderful determinableness, his learning to limit himself, but in this very limit again finding his way to the infinite by means of form, etc.—this I call the crisis of his life, the end of his apprenticeship, and I think all the contrivances in the work seem to unite in the most perfect manner for this purpose. The wonderful and natural relation to his child, and his union with a woman as noble as Natalie, are a guarantee of this state of spiritual well-being, and we see him and leave him on a path which leads to endless perfection.

## GOETHE TO SCHILLER

Weimar, July 9

On a separate sheet I have marked the several passages which I think of altering and filling up in accordance with your suggestions, but besides this I owe you my sincerest thanks for the admonitions contained in your letter of today, and for having directed my attention to the adequate completion of the work. I beg you not to desist from—I might almost say—driving me out beyond my own bounds. The fault you justly notice lies in my inmost nature, in a certain realistic tendency, due to which I take a delight in veiling my existence, my actions, my writings from the eyes of the world. Thus I should always like to travel incognito, to choose the poorer dress in preference to the better one, and, in the intercourse with strangers or acquaintances, prefer a subject of lesser importance, or at least the less important expression, to deport myself with more levity than is natural to me, and thus to place myself as it were between my actual self and what I appear to be. You know very well how this is, and why it is so.

After this general confession I gladly pass over to particulars and must tell you that had it not been for your incitement and instigation, I should—and moreover against my better knowledge and conscience—have abandoned myself to this peculiarity in my novel which would have been unpardonable, considering the great expenditure that has been made upon it, inasmuch as all that is demanded is both easy to perceive and can easily be accomplished.

Thus, were the attention which the Abbot at an early date shows towards Wilhelm clearly expressed, it would throw quite a peculiar light and spiritual luster upon the whole work, and yet I have neglected to do this; hardly have I been able to induce myself, through Werner, to say anything in favor of his outward circumstances.

I broke off the Apprentice's indenture in the Seventh Book, because few maxims on Art and the appreciation of Art are now read. The second half of the letter was to have contained important words on life and the object of life; I thus had the best opportunity through an oral commentary of the Abbot, of explaining and of vindicating the incidents in general, but particularly the events brought about by the Powers of the Tower, and saving this machinery from the suspicion of being a cold necessity demanded by a novel and of giving it aesthetic value, or rather of placing its aesthetic value in proper light. You see that I perfectly agree with your remarks.

There is no doubt that the apparent results expressed by me are much more limited than the contents of the work, and I seem to myself to be like one who, after having set down a number of large figures, one above the other, finally himself wilfully makes an error in calculation in order to lessen the total sum, God knows from what sort of capricious mood.

I also owe you my heartfelt thanks—as well as for many other things—for having in good time spoken in so decisive a way of this perverse manner of mine, and I shall certainly comply with your wishes as far as I possibly can; I need only distribute the contents of your letter in the appropriate places, and the matter is settled. And should it happen to me—for human perversities are difficult to overcome—that the more important words will not come from my heart, I shall beg to add with a few bold pencil strokes that which I, being tied by the strangest necessity of nature, am unable to express.

## GOETHE TO SCHILLER

*For a long time Schiller urged his friend to take up again his "Faust," a work which by its philosophic spirit was particularly close to him. The delay of a planned journey because of the illness of Goethe's friend Meyer was the occasion which gave the poet the opportunity to work on this fragment. On June 23, 1797, he sketched the outline for the continuation of his work, the next day he wrote the poem "Dedication," and within a short time the two prologues were composed.*

Weimar, June 22, 1797

As it is extremely necessary that in my present restless state I should set myself something to do, I have decided to take up my "Faust" and, if not to finish it, to bring it a good deal further at least by breaking up what has been printed and arranging it in large pieces with what is already finished or invented; thus, I am sure, I would further prepare the development of the play which is, in reality, as yet only an idea. I have now taken up this idea and its representation again and have pretty well made up my mind about it. I only wish, however, that you would be so good as to think the matter over on one of your sleepless nights and to tell me the demands which you would require of the whole, and in this manner to narrate and to interpret to me my own dreams like a true prophet.

As the different parts of this poem—as far as its mood is concerned—might be treated differently, provided only that they be kept subordinate to the spirit and tone of the whole, and as, moreover, the whole work is subjective, I can work at it at odd moments and I am therefore at present able to achieve something.

Our ballad studies have again led me on to this misty, foggy path, and circumstances—in more than one sense—advise me to wander about upon it for some time to come.

## SCHILLER TO GOETHE

Jena, June 23

YOUR RESOLUTION to set to work at your "Faust" was indeed a surprise to me, especially just now, when you are thinking of a trip to Italy. But I have once and for all given up the idea of measuring you by the usual standard of logic and I am therefore convinced beforehand that your genius will see you well through the task.

The request you make that I should tell you of my requirements and *desideria* is not so easily fulfilled; but as far as I can I will try to discover your thread, and if that cannot be done I will act as if I had accidentally found the fragments of "Faust" and had myself to work them out. That much I can say here that "Faust"—the piece itself I mean—in spite of its individuality cannot quite ward off the demand for a symbolical treatment which probably corresponds with your own idea anyway. The dualism of human nature and the unsuccessful endeavor to unite in man the godlike and the physical, is never lost sight of and, as the story runs and must run into what is fantastic and formless, people will not be content with concentrating on the subject, but will be led from it to ideas. In short, the demands on "Faust" are both philosophical and poetical and you may turn in whichever direction you please, the nature of the subject will force you to treat it philosophically, and your imagination will have to accommodate itself to serve a rational idea.

But I can hardly tell you anything new by saying this, for you have already, in a great measure, begun to satisfy this demand in what you have already accomplished.

If you now really intend to work on "Faust" I no longer doubt that you will succeed in completing it—a thought in which I greatly rejoice.

## GOETHE TO SCHILLER

Weimar, June 24

Thank you for your first words on my reawakening "Faust." We shall probably not differ in our views of this work, and yet quite a different kind of courage comes over me when I see my thoughts and projects characterized by another person; and your sympathy is fruitful in more than one sense.

To have taken up this work just now is really a wise act,

because with regard to Meyer's health I must expect to pass the winter in the north. I do not wish to be a burden to myself or to my friends by being chagrined at disappointed hopes and, therefore, I have decided, willingly and gladly, to retreat into this symbolical, ideal and hazy world.

First of all, I will now try to finish the large pieces that are already invented and half worked out, put them into some connection with what has been printed and go on in this way until the circle is exhausted.

## SCHILLER TO GOETHE

Jena, June 26

I HAVE NOW again read through your "Faust" and I feel actually giddy from the denouement. This, however, is very natural, for the matter is based upon some special conception, and as long as this is not grasped, a subject much less rich than the present one would put reason into a state of dilemma. What I am anxious about in regard to it is that, in accordance with its character, "Faust" appears to require a totality of material if, at the end, the idea is to appear completely worked out. And I know of no poetic framework for holding together a mass that springs up to such a height. However, you will know what to do.

For instance it was, as I think, appropriate that Faust should be led into active life, and whatever sphere you may select from this mass, it nevertheless seems to me that his nature will demand too great an amount of circumstantiality and breadth.

As far as the treatment is concerned, I find the greatest difficulty in proceeding happily between what is jest and what is in earnest. Reason and sense seem to me in this subject to be struggling as if for life and death. One feels this very much in the present fragmentary state of "Faust," but expectation is led to look at the fully developed whole. The devil gains his point in face of understanding by his realism, and Faust his in the face of the heart. At times, however, they seem to exchange their parts, and the devil takes reason under his protection against Faust.

I find difficulty in the fact that the devil annuls his existence, which is idealistic, by his character, which is realistic. Reason alone can believe in him and it is only understanding that can allow and comprehend his existence as he is.

I am, in fact, very anxious to see how the popular part of the tale will link itself to the philosophical portion of the whole.

## GOETHE TO SCHILLER

Weimar, June 27

Your remarks about "Faust" gave me great pleasure; naturally they coincide very well with my own projects and plans. But I am not so strict with this barbarous composition. I think that I can only hint at the higher demands yet not fulfill them. In this manner, reason and sense will probably beat each other about like two pugilists, and afterwards sit down amicably together. I will take care that the parts are pleasing and entertaining and that they offer food for thought; to the poem itself, which will ever remain a fragment, I may apply our new theory of the epic poem.

## MEMOIRS OF AN ACTRESS

*For many years, Karoline Jagemann was Goethe's most dangerous opponent in the Weimar theatre. Her position as the Duke's mistress enabled her to exert great influence to which even Goethe finally had to bow. After a successful debut in the theatre at Mannheim, Karoline Jagemann appeared on the stage in her native town Weimar for the first time in February, 1797.*

My attitude towards Goethe, after the conclusion of my engagement, was the same I had taken towards the director in Mannheim. During the negotiations which my father conducted with the theatre manager Kirms, Goethe behaved as stiffly and correctly as his outward appearance showed. I do not believe that he was particularly pleased about my engagement, because my position, my talent and my inclinations made it possible for me not to display the same slavish humbleness towards him which he wished to see in the ladies from the theatre. Nevertheless, his reception was exceedingly friendly and polite when I paid him my first visit as a newly engaged member of the staff. There was a certain pedantry in his comportment and stiffness in his posture which, in former years, did not fully display his youthfulness in spite of his classically beautiful face. His well-shaped mouth reminiscent of the Apollo of Belvedere could laugh without being friendly, his large, dark, sharply cut eyes always remained grave when his mouth smiled, and thus disturbed the harmony by which one is so pleasantly moved with even less beautiful features, making his whole appearance impressive, though it did not speak to the heart.

I confess with shame that, at that time, my actions were only decided by my emotions and that I did not ponder over my next step too much. I also do not want to conceal that then I did not know anything of Goethe's best works which might have induced me to pay the customary homage to him. The only thing I had read was the "Götz von Berlichingen" which I had taken from the Duchess' library. I did not think of ingratiating myself with Goethe as the other theatre people had by paying court to Christiane Vulpius, although I was fond of her.

In my childhood days she lived next to us and was a very good-looking, friendly, industrious girl. Her face was fresh and round like an apple, and a pair of burning black eyes looked at you. Her somewhat pouting cherry-red mouth showed a row of beautiful white teeth—since she liked to laugh—and dark brown full curls fell around her forehead and shoulders. She supported her pensioned father and an old aunt by her skill at making artificial flowers, and Goethe made her acquaintance when she was still in poor circumstances. Having been transplanted into plenty and a new enjoyment of life, she did not only make up for the things missed so long, but she also indulged in eating and drinking to such a degree that her naive childlike features took on a bacchantic expression and her figure developed to proportions of obesity. She was always surrounded by the more obscure group of actresses among whom Goethe preferred to select his favorites. Actors tried to get close to her in order to lead a comfortable life and to get good parts. Her parties were mostly rather noisy.

The man whom she adored so deeply sanctioned this manner of living, even showed delight in it whenever she yielded to her desire for pleasure without moderation. At the time when she had become his wife he also permitted her to drive to Lauchstaedt and Jena for a dance where the young gentlemen made fun of her when she had looked so deeply into the punch glass that her tongue got heavy and her face looked as if on fire. Goethe did not think of elevating a creature so close to him when her mind was still capable of being educated, but instead left her to her low instincts.

When I returned from Mannheim, this liaison was officially established and Vulpius lived in Goethe's house, an unheard-of event for the small town. He was the first and only one who dared scorn public opinion without fear, and people thought it all the more offensive since they recognized in it a misuse of the prerogatives afforded him in so many respects through his friendship with the Duke.

## SCHILLER TO H. MEYER

Jena, July 21, 1797

I MOST HEARTILY WELCOME you back on German ground, my dear friend. Our anxiety on your account was often great, and now we sincerely rejoice to hear that your health is again improving.

I am ashamed to think that the first words you receive from me since you left will reach you on your way back to us. As much as I would have liked to talk to you, there was nothing I would have cared to send across the mountains. Undoubtedly, you will have heard from our mutual friend [Goethe] what we were doing here and how we all got along. He will also have told you how often you were in our thoughts. I took great interest in learning from him all that concerned you; how admirably you were using your time, and what treasures you were collecting for us all.

As you know, we too have not been idle here, and least of all could this be said of our friend, who, during these last years, has actually surpassed himself. Of course, you will have read his epic poem [*Hermann and Dorothea*], and you will admit that it is the climax of his achievements so far and of the whole of our modern art. I have watched it coming into life and was almost as much surprised at this process

Friedrich Schiller. Oil painting by Ludovica von Simanowitz

Anne Louise Germaine de Staël-Holstein

as with the work itself. While other men—like ourselves—must collect and test their materials laboriously before they slowly succeed in producing anything tolerable, he only gently shakes the tree and its loveliest fruits, ripe and heavy, fall into his hands. It is inconceivable with what ease he is now gathering the fruits of a well-spent life and of a continued self-education for his own benefit. How important and self-assured are all his steps, and, in regard to himself and the subjects he chooses, his clear-sightedness save him from vain endeavors and from groping about in the dark.

But, since he is now with you, you can convince yourself of all this with your own eyes. You will, however, agree with me that, on the height where he now stands, he should direct his thoughts toward the representation of the beautiful form he has achieved rather than toward the beginning of new subjects; in short, he should now devote himself entirely to poetical practice. When anyone—among the many thousands who strive for such heights—has succeeded in forming himself into a beautiful and integrated entity, then, in my opinion, he cannot do better than to seek every possible form of expression for it, because however far he might still advance, he never could reach any higher.

## GOETHE TO SCHILLER

*Accompanied by Christiane and his eight-year-old son August, Goethe visited Frankfort in August, 1797, in order to introduce his family to his mother. He then continued his journey alone, going to Switzerland where he met his friend Meyer.*

Frankfort, August 9, 1797

I ARRIVED in Frankfort happily and in good health, without having met with the slightest inconvenience, and now seated in a quiet and cheerful room I am reflecting on what it means to start out into the world at my age. At an earlier age, we are impressed and confused by objects, because we are unable to judge or to comprehend them, but, on the other hand, we settle matters more easily, inasmuch as we only take up what lies in our path and pay little heed to what lies to the right or to the left. At a later period we come to know things better; we are interested in a greater number of subjects and we should feel very ill at ease did not calmness and method then come to our assistance. I will now try, as well as I can, to put in order all that has occurred to me within the last week, test my schemes on Frankfort itself, as a city that embraces a great deal, and then prepare myself for my further travels.

The peculiar character of the public in a large city struck me as very remarkable. People live in a perpetual whirl of making money and spending it, and that which we call "mood" can neither be produced nor communicated. All amusements, even the theatre, are meant only to be diversions, and the great fondness of the reading public for journals and romances arises from the fact that journals always, and romances generally, bring diversion to diversion.

I think I have even observed a kind of aversion towards

poetical works, or at all events in so far as they are poetical, which, due to the above reasons, appears to me quite natural. Poetry demands, in fact, it enforces a collected state of mind, it isolates man against his will, it is repeatedly forcing itself on the attention of the reader, and in the wide world (not to speak of the great world) poetry is as inconvenient as a faithful mistress.

I am now accustoming myself to write down what strikes me in the things I see and what I think of them without demanding from myself any very accurate observations or any very mature opinion on the subjects, or even to think of putting them to any future use. When one has come quite to the end of one's journey, the material in hand can then be made use of as subject matter with a greater amount of clarity.

I have been to the theatre several times and also made a methodical plan for forming an opinion of it. I have been gradually trying to fill this up, and it has now for the first time forcibly struck me that in reality a good descriptive account of a journey can be given only when the country described is foreign to the writer, where he is no relation to anyone. No one would ever venture to write about the place where he usually resides, unless the question were a mere enumeration of existing circumstances; the same is the case with everything that is only in some way close to our hearts; above all, one feels that it would be an act of impiety publicly to express even one's most just and moderate judgment on things. These observations lead to good results and show me the way I must pursue. Thus, for example, I am comparing the theatre here with the one in Weimar; when I have seen the one in Stuttgart, perhaps something of general importance may be said about the three, at any rate something that might be expressed publicly.

August 17

A THOUGHT has struck me which, as it may be important for the rest of my journey, I will at once communicate to you so that I may have your opinion in how far it may be right and in how far I am right in allowing myself to be led by it. In following the calm and sober path of an observer, indeed, of a mere spectator, I very soon noticed that the account which I had given of certain objects was, to a certain extent, sentimental, and this struck me so strongly that I was instantly induced to reflect upon the cause and found out the following. In general that which I see and experience combines very well with all my other knowledge and is not unpleasant to me, because I class it with my entire knowledge and it helps to increase my capital. On the other hand, I could not name anything met with on my whole journey that has in any way given rise in me to any feeling of elation so that I am today as composed and unmoved as under the most ordinary circumstances and occurrences. Whence, therefore, comes this seeming state of sentimentality which is to me the more remarkable, because for some time past I have felt no trace of it in my nature, unless the poetic mood could be called so? Might one not be poetically disposed toward a subject that is not wholly poetical itself and thus be in a certain intermediate state?

I have carefully observed the objects which produce this effect and have found to my astonishment that, in fact, they are symbolical. In other words (as I hardly need say), they are eminent cases which, in characteristic variety, stand as the representatives of many others, embrace a certain totality in themselves, demand a certain succession, excite similar and foreign subjects in my mind, and thus, from within as well as from without, lay claim to a certain oneness and universality. Hence they are happy objects for the *man* as they are happy subjects for a *poet;* and as one cannot give them any poetic form, because one recapitulates them to oneself, one has at least to give them an *ideal* form, that is a human form in the higher sense, in fact, what in that much-abused expression is called sentimental. I hope you will not laugh but only smile when, to my own surprise, I tell you that, if I should note down anything of my travels for my friends or for the *public,*

I shall be in danger of writing a *sentimental journey*. Yet I would not as you know, fear any word, even the most deprecatory, if the treatment justified me in what I did and, moreover, if I could be so fortunate as to give the depreciated word back its dignity.

I refer to what you yourself have so beautifully unfolded, to what is the customary language between us, and I ask: When is a sentimental phenomenon (which we dare not despise be it ever so troublesome) intolerable? I answer: When the ideal is directly connected with what is common. This can happen only in the case of an empty style, wanting both in substance and form, for this would annihilate both the idea and the object; the former, which can be significant and occupy itself only with what is significant, and the latter, which can be thoroughly good and right without being significant.

As yet I have found but two such objects: the public square in which I am living—which, in regard to its position and all that takes place in it, is symbolical at every moment; and the area occupied by my grandfather's house, courtyard and garden—which has been converted by wise, enterprising people from its contracted patriarchal condition (as occupied by an old magistrate of Frankfort) into a most useful market-place. The house itself, by a strange coincidence, was destroyed at the time of the bombardment and, although for the most part a mere mound of debris, is worth double what was paid for it to my people eleven years ago by the present proprietors. Now, in so far as it may be supposed that the place will again be purchased and rebuilt by some new speculator, you can easily see that in more than one way it must, and especially according to my view, stand as a symbol of many thousands of other cases in this thriving mercantile city.

In this case, of course, there is moreover the loving remembrance I have of it; but when, having been made observant by these cases, I direct my attention to the further course of my journey not merely to what is *remarkable,* but to what is *significant,* I cannot fail to glean a rich harvest for myself and others. I will first try here and see what I can observe of the symbolical, but intend to study more particularly this subject in regard to places with which I am unacquainted and which I am now seeing for the first time. If I succeed in this, then—without wishing to pursue the experiment very extensively and yet going into the depths in every case and always as far as I may be permitted—I cannot fail to carry away sufficient booty from well-known lands and regions.

Tell me your thoughts on this subject in good time, so that I may be instructed, confirmed, invigorated and cheered. The matter is of importance to me, for it annuls the contradiction which lies between my nature and direct experience and which in former years I was never able to solve immediately and happily. For I confess that I would rather have turned straight home again in order to work out of my inmost being phantoms of every kind than to have again—as until now—to buffet with the million-faced Hydra of Empiricism; for he who does not seek pleasure or advantage from it had better draw back in time.

August 23

YESTERDAY Hölderlin came to see me; he looks somewhat depressed and sickly, but he is very amiable and modestly, almost timidly frank. He spoke about various subjects in a manner that betrayed him as one of your school, and many ideas he has so thoroughly made his own that he could readily take up many things. I advised him to write short poems and to choose in every case a subject of human interest. He seemed still to have some predilection for the Middle Ages in which I could not encourage him.

*Friedrich Hölderlin, at that time twenty-seven years old, was a protégé of Schiller's who had published some of his poems. It was only much later that Hölderlin found recognition as one of the greatest German poets.*

## GOETHE TO SCHILLER

Weimar, November 25, 1797

My best thanks for the letter and parcel I have just received. I can only tell you in haste and so to speak extemporaneously that not only do I agree with you, but that I go much further still. Everything poetical ought to be treated rhythmically; that is my conviction, and the belief that a poetical form of prose might gradually come to be introduced, only shows that the difference between prose and poetry has been completely lost sight of. It is no better than if we heard of a man ordering a dry lake to be made in his park and of the gardener, in trying to solve this problem, making a marsh. These intermediate species are for amateurs and dabblers only, just as marshes are for amphibia. Meanwhile the evil has become so great in Germany that it is no longer noticed–like the goitrous people in Switzerland, who look upon the healthy formation of the throat as a visitation from God. All dramatic works (and perhaps comedies and farces above all others) should be rhythmical; we should then the more quickly be able to judge who has accomplished something. At present the dramatist can do nothing but accommodate himself to public taste, and in this sense one could not blame you if you wished to write your *Wallenstein* [the dramatic cycle on which Schiller worked at that time] in prose; but if you regard it as an independent work, it must of necessity be made rhythmical.

In any case the century in which we are living must be forgotten if we are to work according to our convictions, for such tomfoolery in the way of principles as is universally in vogue at present has probably never existed in the world before, and what good the new system of philosophy is to accomplish remains still to be seen.

Poetry is certainly based on the empiric pathological condition of man, and yet which of our excellent connoisseurs and so-called poets would admit this nowadays? Has a man like Garve—who claims to be a man of thought and is considered a sort of philosopher—the faintest notion of such an axiom? Does he not look upon you as a worthy poet merely because you amused yourself with delivering aphorisms on Reason in poetic language, which is no doubt permissible but not praiseworthy. How gladly would I permit such prosaic natures to start back in horror at so-called immoral subjects, if only they had some feeling for the higher poetic moral, as, for instance, in your "Polycrates" and "Ibycus," and could delight in it.

Let us—since Meyer too has brought with him from Italy a spirit of grim asceticism—become more and more strict in principle and more sure and pleasing in execution! The latter can be accomplished only by keeping our eyes fixed within the frame while at work.

December 9

THE NEWS that you could not come to us this winter has greatly disappointed our actors. It seems they had intended to do themselves honor in your presence. I have consoled them with the hope that you may probably pay us a visit in the spring. Our theatre is very much in need of a new impetus of this kind, which I myself am unable to give it. The difference between him who is in command, and him who gives aesthetic guidance to such institutions is much too great. The latter must affect the feelings and must therefore show feeling himself; the former must hide his in order to hold together the political and economic form. I do not know whether it is possible to combine free reciprocal influence with mechanical causality, at all events, I have not yet succeeded in accomplishing the feat.

I can very well imagine the condition in which you are working. When not possessing a lively pathological interest in my subject, I too have never been able to work out any tragic situation and have, therefore rather avoided than sought it. Can it perhaps have been one of the merits of the ancients that the highest pathos was with them merely aesthetic play, whereas with us the truth of nature has to cooperate in producing a work of this kind? I do not know myself sufficiently well to judge whether I could write a genuine tragedy, however, I shudder at the mere thought of such an undertaking and feel almost convinced that such an attempt might upset me altogether. . . .

I shall be busy for another two weeks with the preliminary arrangements for bringing the new theatrical contracts into order, and other such matters; after that, however, I shall certainly hasten to the solitude of the Jena palace during the day time and to our talks in the evening.

Probably I won't bring Meyer with me, for I have again found that I can work only when in a state of absolute quiet, and that not only conversation, but even the presence of dearly loved persons about me totally divert the stream of my poetic inspiration. Now I might be in a kind of despair—as every trace of productive interest has disappeared in me—were it not that I feel certain to find it again during the first week of my stay in Jena.

## GOETHE TO SCHILLER

*The remodeled Weimar Theatre opened on October 12, 1798, with the prologue of Schiller's Wallenstein cycle. Goethe, who contributed many ideas to his friend's work, planned the première of the first part, "The Piccolominis," as a gala performance on the occasion of the Duchess' birthday.*

Weimar, December 25, 1798

I CONGRATULATE you on having been compelled to finish your work! for I will in no way deny that I have lately been beginning to despair of its getting finished.

Considering the way in which you have treated your "Wallenstein" during these last years, it was impossible to think of any inner cause that would have led to its completion, just as little as wax would become hardened as long as it was left in front of a fire. You will yourself not realize how much you have gained till you have left the subject behind you. I look upon the gain as infinite.

Your room in the palace will be put into perfect order, and I hope you will not find anything wanting; whatever else you may need will be ready for you. Do not let anything detain you, but make up your mind straightway to come on the 2nd of January, for we have a great many things to settle if we are to have things ready by the 30th; the worst part of it is that this deadline cannot be extended.

December 27

THE BEARER of this note represents a detachment of hussars which has orders to arrest the Piccolominis, both father and son, in whatever manner it can; and, should it not succeed in getting complete possession of them, at all events to deliver them up piecemeal. Your Excellency is entreated to give all possible assistance to this laudable undertaking and may demand of us any service in return.

By gracious appointment, the Melpomenean Commission of Enquiry into the mischief created by the Wallensteins.

Goethe and Kirms

*This jesting note of Goethe and the theatre manager, Franz Kirms, referred to the two heroes in Schiller's drama, Octavio and Max Piccolomini, officers in Wallenstein's army.*

## MADAME DE STAËL'S VISIT

*The Baroness von Staël-Holstein had incurred Napoleon's hatred because of her writings and was forced to leave France. At the end of 1803 she came to Weimar with her friend, the writer Benjamin Constant, in order to collect in personal conversations material for a book on intellectual life in Germany. In his "Annals" Goethe reported his impressions of this spirited woman.*

Madame de Staël arrived in Weimar in the beginning of December while I was still busy with the program in Jena. What Schiller wrote to me on December 21 served to present to me a clear picture of the mutual relations which her presence created:

"Madame de Staël will appear to you entirely as you have already a priori construed her in your mind. She is all of one piece, and there is not one foreign, false, pathologic trait in her. Therefore, in spite of the immense distance separating you from her nature and way of thinking, you feel perfectly at ease with her, you are inclined to listen to everything she says and to say everything to her. The French culture presents her clearly and in a highly interesting light. In all we understand by philosophy, that is in every ultimate and supreme judgment, you are in controversy with her and you remain so in spite of all arguments. However, her temperament and her feelings are better than her metaphysics, and her beautiful mind elevates itself to the faculty of a genius. There is nothing she will not explain, penetrate into, take the measure of; she makes no obscure or inaccessible statements; what she cannot illumine with the torch of her understanding has no existence for her. She has, therefore, an utter horror of the ideal philosophy which, in her opinion, leads to mysticism and superstition, and this is to her the close air in which she suffocates. She lacks understanding for what we call poetry; of works of this kind she can appropriate only the passionate, oratorical and general. Not that she would be carried away by anything false, she is only unable always to recognize the genuine.

"From these few words you will perceive how the clarity, decision and intellectual vivacity of her nature cannot work otherwise than beneficially. The only annoyance is the quite unusual nimbleness of her tongue; to keep up with it, you must be all ears. Since even I get along quite tolerably with her notwithstanding my lack of proficiency in French, you with your greater practice will find communication with her a very easy affair."

As it was impossible for me to leave Jena before my business was done, many more descriptions and accounts reached me as to how Madame de Staël behaved and what reception she was getting, so that I could pretty well anticipate the part I would have to play. . . .

Madame de Staël sent ever more pressing intimation of her presence; my work was finished, and for many reasons I decided to return to Weimar. Yet this time again I felt the evil effects of staying in the Castle in winter. The dearly bought experience of 1801 had failed to teach me the lesson of prudence. I returned with a severe catarrh which, though not dangerous, confined me for some days to bed and then for weeks to my room. In this way a part of the stay of this singular woman became historical to me, hearing, as I did, from my friends a report of all that happened in society. The intercourse between us had to be carried on first by notes, next in tête-à-tête conversations, afterwards in a very small circle. This was perhaps the most favorable way in which I could become acquainted with her and, as far as possible, she with me.

Her presence, both intellectually and bodily, had something charming about it, nor did she seem to take it amiss when, as far as the latter was concerned, people showed themselves not insensible toward her. How often might she have transfused into one feeling sociability, good will, affection, and passion! Once she said, "I never trusted a man who has not once been in love with me." It is a pertinent remark, for when once a man—as happens in love—has opened his heart and committed himself, he is forever committed, and it is impossible for him to harm, or leave unprotected, a creature formerly loved.

With decided impetus she pursued her purpose of learning the conditions under which we lived, interpreting them according to her own conceptions. She made all inquiries about each of us individually, and as a woman of the world sought to obtain a clear view of our social relations, and with her feminine powers of mind to penetrate into our more general modes of thought and all that is understood by philosophy. I had no reason whatsoever to disguise myself in her presence, on the contrary, I was disposed to meet her with entire frankness in spite of the fact that people even then were not likely to understand me. But there was one circumstance which forced me into reticence. I had just received a newly published French book containing the correspondence of two ladies with Rousseau. They actually had mystified the inaccessible, shy man. Engaging his interest by some trifling affair, they contrived to entice him into a correspondence which, after they carried on the joke long enough, they collected and published.

I expressed to Madame de Stael my disapproval of such conduct. She, however, took the matter lightly, in fact, she seemed to approve it and gave me, in no dubious terms, to understand that she was planning the same game with us. That was quite enough to make me wary, to put me on my guard and, to a certain extent, seal my lips.

The great talents of this high-minded and high-spirited authoress are evident to everyone, and the results of her travels through Germany are a sufficient testimony of the good use she made of her time.

She had different things in mind; she wanted to know Weimar, in its moral, social and literary aspects, and obtain exact information on all those points. Then she wanted to make herself known, having as much at heart to spread her own views as to fathom our mode of thinking. Nor did she stop at that. She aimed at producing an impression on the senses, the feelings, the mind: she wished to incite people to activity, with the lack of which she reproached us.

Since she had no idea of what is meant by duty, no idea of the quiet, composed attitude obligatory to him who sets himself seriously to the performance of duty, she expected people to concern themselves with everything, to accomplish something at any given moment, just as she expected people to speak continually at a party and to get matters going.

The Weimar people are certainly capable of enthusiasm, perhaps of false enthusiasm from time to time, but French wit was not their forte, least of all at a time when French ascendancy threatened the whole world, and men of quiet penetration anticipated the inevitable trouble which in the next year was to bring us to the verge of ruin.

In reading and reciting, Madame de Staël was also bent on gathering laurels. I asked to be excused one night when she was reading "Phaedra" [Racine's play] and she was by no means satisfied with the moderate German applause.

To philosophize at a party means to carry on a lively conversation on insoluble problems. This was her peculiar pleasure and passion. Of course, she pursued this exercise in speeches and colloquies into a domain of thought and feeling where properly God and the individual soul alone ought to hold communion. Moreover, as a woman and a French woman, she would stick positively by her main positions, actually without listening to what anyone else said.

All this provoked an evil spirit in me so that I treated everything that came up in a contradictory, dialectic, problematic way and often drove her to despair by obstinate antitheses. In this predicament she first appeared in a truly amiable light, while her nimbleness in thought and reply displayed itself most brilliantly.

Several times I still had the occasion of speaking to her alone. But she always managed to annoy me in her peculiar way. On the most important events she would not allow you a moment's time for reflection and in discussing momentous affairs, in dealing with the gravest questions, she would passionately demand of you to be as swift in your movements as though you were catching a shuttlecock.

An anecdote may here be in point. Madame de Staël came to me one evening before the court time, and, the minute she had greeted me, exclaimed with vehemence: "I have important news to tell you. Moreau [a distinguished French general] has been arrested, along with some others, and accused of treason against the tyrant!" Like everyone, I had for a long time been interested in this noble man and followed his ways and actions. In silence I recalled the past to try—in my way—the present by it and to make inferences as to the future, or at least conjectures in that direction. The lady changed the conversation, diverting it as usual to various indifferent topics, while I, still brooding over the old subject, was not immediately ready with replies to her remarks. Therefore, she began again the reproaches I had often heard before. I was this evening, as usual, *maussade,* and no cheerful conversation could be held with me. This made me really angry. I assured her she was incapable of any real sympathy; she stormed in on you, stunned you with a severe blow, and then at once called on you to join in a frolic, to skip with her from one subject to another. This outburst of mine pleased her, she wanted to arouse passion, no matter what. To reconcile me she went carefully through the particulars of the unfortunate event she had referred to, displaying great insight into the whole situation as well as into the characters of the people involved.

Another anecdote will likewise show how gay and easy it was to live with her if you would only take things in her way. On the occasion of a supper at the Duchess Amalia's attended by a great many people, I sat at a distance from her and was quiet and thoughtful this time too. My neighbors reproached me for it, and there was a slight ripple at our end, the cause of which at last reached the ears of the high ranking guests. Madame de Staël, hearing the complaint about my silence, expressed herself on the matter as usual, adding, "In general I do not like Goethe when he has not drunk a bottle of champagne." To this I said, half aloud, so as to be heard by those sitting next me: "Then on more than one occasion we must have been drunk together." A moderate laugh broke out. She demanded to know the cause. No one was able and willing to translate my words into French in their proper sense until at last Benjamin Constant, who sat next me, on her continued importunity, volunteered to put an end to the matter and to satisfy her with a euphemistic phrase.

No matter, however, what may be thought and said of such things later on, the great and important influence she exercised on the course of affairs cannot be denied. That work of hers on Germany, which sprang from such social gatherings, must be regarded as a powerful machine cleaving the first considerable gap into that Chinese wall of antiquated prejudices which divided us from France, bringing us into spiritual communication with the country beyond the Rhine and finally beyond the Channel, and so enabling us to exercise vital influence on the more distant West. Let us therefore bless those annoyances and conflicts of national peculiarities which at the time seemed by no means to our profit.

## GOETHE DEPICTED BY MADAME DE STAËL

Goethe possesses superior talents for conversation; and whatever we may say, superior talents ought to enable a man to talk. We may, however, produce some examples of silent men of genius: timidity, misfortune, disdain, or *ennui,* are often the cause of it; but, in general, range of ideas and warmth of soul naturally inspire the necessity of communicating our feelings to others; and those men who will not be judged by what they say, may not deserve that we should interest ourselves in what they think. When Goethe is induced to talk, he is admirable; his eloquence is enriched with thought; his humor is, at the same time, full of grace and philosophy; his imagination is impressed by external objects, as was that of the ancient artists; nevertheless his reason possesses far too much the maturity of our own times. Nothing disturbs the strength of his mind, and even the defects of his character, ill-humor, embarrassments, constraints, pass like clouds round the foot of that mountain on the summit of which his genius is placed.

What is related of the conversation of Diderot may give some idea of that of Goethe; but, if we may judge by the writings of Diderot, the distance between these two men must be infinite. Diderot is the slave of his genius; Goethe never holds the powers of his mind in subjection: Diderot is affected from the constant endeavor to produce effect; but in Goethe we perceive disdain of success, and that to a degree that is singularly pleasing, even when we have most reason to find fault with his negligence. Diderot finds it necessary to supply by philanthropy his want of religious sentiments: Goethe is inclined to be more bitter than sweet; but, above all, he is natural; and, in fact, without this quality, what is there in one man that should have power to interest another?

Goethe possesses no longer that irresistible ardor which inspired him in the composition of "Werther," but the warmth of his imagination is still sufficient to animate everything. It might be said, that he is himself unconnected with life, and that he describes it merely as a painter. He attaches more value, at present, to the pictures he presents to us, than to the emotions he experiences; time has rendered him a spectator. While he still bore a part in active scenes of passion, while he suffered, in his own person, from the perturbations of the heart, his writings produced a more lively impression.

As we do not always best appreciate our own talents, Goethe maintains at present, that an author should be calm when he is writing a passionate work; and that an artist should equally be cool, in order to act more powerfully on the imagination of his readers. Perhaps in early life, he would not have entertained this opinion; perhaps he was then enslaved by his genius, rather than its master; perhaps he then felt that the sublime and heavenly sentiment being of transient duration in the heart of man, the poet is inferior to the inspiration which animates him, and cannot enter into judgment on it, without losing it at once.

At first we are astonished to find coldness, and even something like stiffness, in the author of "Werther"; but when we can prevail on him to be perfectly at his ease, the liveliness of his imagination makes the restraint which we first felt entirely disappear. He is a man of universal mind and impartial because universal; for there is no indifference in his impartiality: he has a double existence, a double degree of strength, a double light, which on all subjects enlightens both sides of the question at once. When it is necessary to think, nothing arrests his course; neither the age in which he lives, nor the habits he has formed, nor his relation with social life: his eagle glance falls decidedly on the object he observes. If his career had been a political one, if his soul had developed itself by action, his character would have been more strongly marked, more firm, more patriotic; but his mind would not have taken so wide a range over different modes of perception; passions or interests would then have traced out a positive path for him.

Goethe delights in his writings, as well as in his conversation, to break the thread which he himself has spun, to destroy the emotions he excites, to throw down the image he has forced us to admire. When, in his fiction, he inspires us with interest for any particular character, he soon shows the inconsistencies which are calculated to detach us from it. He disposes of the poetic world, like a conqueror of the real earth; and thinks himself strong enough to introduce, as nature sometimes does, the genius of destruction into his own works. If he were not an estimable character, we should be afraid of this species of superiority which elevates itself above all things, which degrades and then rises up; which affects us, and then laughs at our emotion; which doubts and confirms by turns, and always with the same success.

I have said that Goethe possessed in himself alone all the principal features of German genius; they are all indeed found in him to an outstanding degree: a great depth of ideas, that grace which springs from imagination—a grace far more original than that which is formed by the spirit of society; in short, a sensibility sometimes bordering on the fantastic, but for that very reason the more calculated to interest readers, who seek in books something that may give variety to their monotonous existence, and in poetry, impressions which may supply the want of real events. If Goethe were a Frenchman, he would be made to talk from morning till night: all the authors, who were contemporary with Diderot, went to derive ideas from his conversation, and afforded him, at the same time, an habitual enjoyment from the admiration he inspired. The Germans do not know how to make use of their talents in conversation, and so few people, even among the most distinguished, have the habit of interrogating and answering, that society is scarcely at all esteemed among them; but the influence of Goethe is no less extraordinary. There are a great many people in Germany who would think genius discoverable even in a letter, if it were written by him. The admirers of Goethe form a sort of fraternity, in which the rallying words serve to discover the initiates to each other. When foreigners also profess to admire him, they are rejected with disdain if certain restrictions leave room to suppose that they have allowed themselves to examine works which nevertheless gain much by examination. No man can kindle such fanaticism without possessing great faculties, whether good or bad; for there is nothing but power, of whatever kind it may be, which men sufficiently dread to be excited by it to such an enthusiastic degree of love.

# AN ENGLISHMAN VIEWS WEIMAR

*Henry Crabb Robinson, a law-clerk who had become financially independent through a legacy, decided at the age of 25 to satisfy an interest in philosophy and literature by studying in Germany. During his five years in Germany he acquired a thorough knowledge of the language and literature and got personally acquainted with almost all the prominent men. An acute observer, gifted with a true understanding of great men and their works, Robinson has given us in his letters and reminiscences an intimate picture of German intellectual life at the beginning of the 19th century.*

We arrived late on November 19, 1801 at the Eagle Hotel, Weimar; and the next two days belong to the most interesting in all my life. They were devoted to visits to the most eminent men of their age and country.

Our first call was at the house of the aged Wieland. The course of my late reading had not led me to form overwhelming ideas of his mental greatness, though as a *litterateur* he is one of the first writers of his country. He is not less universally read and admired in Germany than Voltaire was in France. His works amount to more than fifty volumes, all written for the many. He resembles a French wit in the lightness of his philosophy, in the wantonness of his muse (though it is by no means so gross), and in the exquisite felicity of his style. But he surpasses Voltaire in learning, if not in philosophy; for Wieland is no school-philosopher,—he belongs to the sensual school of Locke. And his favorite opinions are those of the common-sense, sceptical school. He is a sworn foe to the Kantian metaphysics, and indeed to all others. In his writings, as in his person and manners, he is a perfect gentleman. He received us with the courteous dignity of a sage, who accepted without *hauteur* the homage of his admirers. His pale and delicate countenance was plain, and had something of the satyr in it. He wore a black skull-cap. The marble bust by Schadow, which I have the good fortune to possess, is an exact likeness of him. . . .

He spoke with great feeling of his wife, who had died a few weeks before. "I help myself with illusions," he said; "anyone whom I have once loved never dies to me. They are absent only from my outward senses, and that to be sure is painful. My wife was my good angel for thirty-five years. I am no longer young,—my recollection of her will never grow less." He spoke in a faint half-whisper, as from the bottom of his throat. . . .

My companions then took me to Professor Meyer, who introduced us into the presence of Goethe,—the great man, the first sight of whom may well form an epoch in the life of any one who has devoted himself seriously to the pursuit of poetry or philosophy.

I had said to Seume that I wished to *speak* to Wieland, and *look* at Goethe,—and I literally and exactly had my desire. My sense of his greatness was such that, had the opportunity offered, I think I should have been incapable of entering into conversation with him; but as it was, I was allowed to gaze on him in silence. Goethe lived in a large and handsome house,—that is for Weimar. Before the door of his study was marked in mosaic: SALVE. On our entrance he rose, and with rather a cool and distant air beckoned to us to take seats. As he fixed his burning eye on Seume, who took the lead, I had his profile before me, and this was the case during the whole of our twenty minutes' stay. He was then about fifty-two years of age, and was beginning to be corpulent. He was, I think, one of the most overwhelmingly handsome men I ever saw. My feeling of awe was heightened by an accident. The last play which I had seen in England was *Measure for Measure,* in which one of the most remarkable moments was when Kemble (the Duke), disguised as a monk, had his hood pulled off by Lucio. On this, Kemble, with an expression of wonderful dignity, ascended the throne and delivered judgment on the wrongdoers. Goethe sat in precisely the same attitude, and I had precisely the same view of his side-face. The conversation was quite insignificant. My companions talked about themselves,–Seume about his youth of adversity and strange adventures. Goethe smiled, with, as I thought, the benignity of condescension. When we were dismissed, and I was in the open air, I felt as if a weight were removed from my breast, and exclaimed: *"Gott sei Dank!"* Before long I saw him under more favorable auspices; but of that hereafter.

Goethe has been often reproached for his *hauteur,* and Bürger made an epigram which the enviers and revilers of the great man were fond of repeating. I believe, however, that this demeanor was necessary in self-defence. It was his only protection against the intrusion which would otherwise have robbed him and the world of a large portion of his life.

The same evening I was introduced to one who in any place but Weimar would have held the first rank, and who in his person and bearing impressed everyone with the feeling that he belonged to the highest class of men. This was Herder. The interview was, if possible, more insignificant than that with Goethe,–partly perhaps, on account of my being introduced at the same time to a distinguished publicist, to use the German term, the eminent political writer and statesman Friedrich Gentz, the translator of Burke on the French Revolution, author of several Austrian state papers against France, and the great literary advocate of the Austrian cause. I naturally kept in the background, contenting myself with delivering a letter which Madame de la Roche had given me. But Herder sent for me the next day. He had a fine clerical figure, and reminded me of Dr. Geddes. His expression was one of great earnestness. Though he filled the highest ecclesiastical office the little state of Weimar afforded, yet the greatness of Goethe seemed to throw him into the shade; and this, perhaps, prevented him from appreciating Goethe's genius. For the present I shall content myself with saying that we had some controversial talk,—I not assenting to his contemptuous judgment of the English lyric poets, and he declaring the infinite superiority of Klopstock's Odes to all that Gray and Collins had ever written. We talked also about our English philosophers, and he gave me a shake of the hand for my praise of Hartley. Herder was a partisan of Locke.

Before I left Weimar I called on the one other great poet, Schiller, of whom unhappily I have as little to say as of the others. Indeed we were with him but a few minutes. I had just time to mention Coleridge's translation of "Wallenstein" of which he seemed to have a high opinion. The translator was a man of genius, he said, but had made some ridiculous mistakes. Schiller had a wild expression and a sickly look; and his manners were those of one who is not at his ease. There was in him a mixture of the wildness of genius and the awkwardness of the student. His features were large and irregular.

On Saturday night we went to the theatre, where I saw "Wallenstein's Death," performed in the presence of the author. Schlegel somewhere says: "Germany has two national theatres,—Vienna with a public of 50,000 spectators, Weimar with a public of 50." The theatre was at this time unique; its managers were Goethe and Schiller, who exhibited there the works which were to become standards and models of dramatic literature. Schiller had his seat near the ducal box, Goethe an arm-chair in the center of the first row of the pit. In general, theatres, whatever their size and beauty may be, are after all mere places where people, instead of sitting to enjoy themselves at their ease, are crowded together to see something at a distance, and it is considered a sort of infringement on the rights of others to take knee or elbow room. Here, on the contrary, I found myself in an elegant apartment, so lightly and classically adorned, and so free and easy in its aspect, that I almost forgot where I was. In the pit the seats are all numbered, each person has its own, and each seat has arms. The single row of boxes is supported by elegant pillars, under which the pit loungers stroll at pleasure. The boxes have no division except in front. They are adorned, too, by elegant pillars, and are open below: instead of the boards commonly placed in front are elegant iron palisades. There are no fixed seats, only chairs, all of which, in front, are occupied by ladies. The gentlemen go into the pit when they do not, as courteous cavaliers, wait behind the chairs of their fair friends. The box in front is occupied by the Duke and Duchess with their suite, of course without the dull formality attending a Royal presence at Drury Lane. I beheld Schiller a great part of the evening leaning over the ducal box and chatting with the family. In the performance of this evening, I was pleased with Graff as the hero, and with Mademoiselle Jagemann as Thekla. She was a graceful and beautiful creature, the leading actress of the company. . . .

In March 1804, I had a re-introduction, and not a mere formal one, as the first was, to Goethe. It was at the theatre. He was sitting in his arm-chair, in the front row of the pit. I had repeatedly taken a seat near enough to him to have an occasional glimpse of his countenance, but I never presented myself to his notice. On the evening of which I write, I was sitting immediately behind him. Benjamin Constant [French writer and statesman] came in with him, and after shaking hands with me, whispered my name to Goethe, who immediately turned round, and with a smile as ingratiating as his ordinary expression was cold and forbidding, said: "Do you know, Mr. Robinson, that you have affronted me?"—"How is that possible, Herr Geheimrat?"—"Why, you have visited every one at Weimar excepting me." I felt that I blushed, as I said: "You may imagine any cause, Herr Geheimrat, but want of reverence." He smiled and said: "I shall be happy to see you at any time." I left my card, of course, the next morning, and the next day there came an invitation to dinner; and

I dined with him several times before I left the neighborhood of Weimar.

It was, I believe, on the very evening on which he spoke to me in the theatre, that I asked him whether he was acquainted with our *Venice Preserved.* "O, very well,—the comic scenes are particularly good." I actually started at so strange a judgment. "Indeed, in England those scenes are considered so very bad that they are never acted."—"I can understand that; and yet, on reflection, you will perceive that those scenes are quite essential to the piece. It is they alone which account for, and go near to justify, the conspiracy; for we see in them how utterly unfit for government the Senate had become." I recognized at once the truth of the criticism, and felt ashamed of myself for not having thought of it before. In all his conversation he spoke in the most simple and unpretentious manner, but there was in it remarkable significance,—a quiet strength, a power without effort, reminding me of what I read of a painting, in which a man was wrestling with an angel. An ignorant man abused the picture on the ground that in the angel there was no sign of effort,—no muscle was strained. But this was designed to show its angelic nature. It is the same in the Greek sculpture of the gods.

When Madame de Staël returned from Berlin, and brought A. W. Schlegel [translator of Shakespeare] in her train, I dined at Goethe's with Schlegel, Tieck the sculptor, and Riemer. I was struck by the contrast between Schlegel and Goethe. Nothing could exceed the repose of Goethe, whereas on Schlegel's part there was an evident striving after pun and point. Of these I recollect nothing but that Boettger was his butt, whom he compared to Bardolph. From Goethe I remember a word or two of deep significance. He said to Schlegel: "I am glad to hear that your brother means to translate *Sakuntala.* [Indian drama rendered into English by Sir W. Jones.] I shall rejoice to see that poem as it is, instead of as it is represented by the moral Englishman." And there was a sarcastic emphasis on the word "moral." He then went on: "But in truth, I hate everything Oriental." By which, probably, he meant rather that he infinitely preferred the Greek to the Oriental mind. He continued: "I am glad there is something that I hate; for, otherwise, one is in danger of falling into the dull habit of literally finding all things good in their place,—and that is destructive of all true feeling." This casts some light on his sentiments respecting the two religions which had their origin in the East. And yet this might have been a transient feeling, for in less than ten years he withdrew himself from the contemplation of the miseries which then surrounded him, and took refuge in the study of Oriental literature. The result is given in his *West-Eastern Divan*.

Were I a younger man, and did I fancy myself competent to the task, I would collect and translate all that Goethe has written on Judaism and Christianity. It should be published without note or comment,—for it is unlike anything I have ever met with from believer or unbeliever, and it is absolutely unique. In one of his private letters to Lavater, he makes a distinction, for which our ordinary language has no equivalent. He says, "I am by no means *anti-Christian,* not even *un*-Christian, but I am indeed *not*-Christian." The difference between un-Christian and not-Christian may be conceived.

It was at no great distance from this time that I called on Goethe to see whether I could induce him to act as a mediator between the Duke and the students, in the quarrel that threatened a withdrawal of the best young men of the University. Having listened to my representations, he coolly said: "It is one of these police matters, in which both parties are right. The students, seeing the matter from their point of view, are perfectly in the right. But then the Duke is equally in the right; he has his own mode of looking at things from his point as sovereign."

During these occasional visits, I saw Goethe's table companion, the mother of his child. As is well known, she afterwards became his wife. She had an agreeable countenance, and a cordial tone. Her manners were unceremonious and free. Queer stories are told of her undignified ways and the freedom of her intercourse with him when she was young; but she had outgrown all such eccentricities when I saw her.

## HEINRICH VOSS TO FERDINAND SOLGER

*In the year 1805 Goethe's health was seriously endangered. At the beginning of February his condition was alarming. The young philologist Heinrich Voss, a regular visitor in Goethe's house, reports here about the crisis in his disease which finally led to improvement.*

Weimar, February 8, 1805

STARK, Professor of medicine, came from Jena the same night (it was on Friday) and declared that there would be hope for Goethe could he live until Sunday morning. But already that very night the sickness turned, the cramps subsided, the fever relented, and our dear friend slept peacefully through more than half the night. At eleven o'clock he called me to his bedside, because he had not seen me in three days. I was greatly moved when I came to him and could not with all my might suppress my tears. Then he looked in my face very friendly and lovingly, held out his hand and spoke words which touched me to the core: "Dear child, I stay with you. You no longer have to cry." I reached for his hand and kissed it instinctively several times, but I could not utter a word.

From this day on Goethe improved rapidly. I watched at his side during the night from Saturday to Sunday, and there and then I could observe the progress he made. As he woke up for the first time at twelve o'clock, he asked anxiously: "Did I talk again in my sleep?" Good for me, that I could truthfully deny with a clear conscience what I would have denied anyhow. "Good!" he said after a pause, "that again is a step toward improvement."—

Then I coaxed him very much, and he patiently took his medicine, but with reluctance. Furthermore, I was supposed to rub his body with alcohol twice during the night, as the doctor had ordered. It was only with effort that I could convince him to let me do it. But as I did not give up and coaxed him more and more, he finally said very quietly: "Go ahead, for heaven's sake!"

Then once he woke out of a dream in which he had attended a tournament. He related to me this dream with great pleasure and at this moment his expression was that of energy and vitality, completely Goethe again, in spite of his sickness.

I was overwhelmingly touched by his really fatherly and tender thoughtfulness for myself (whether I would not prepare some coffee for myself—drink a glass of wine, and so forth), always calling me his "good Vosschen." When afterwards he fell asleep again and the lamp shed its soft light on his face, he appeared to me as full of suffering as someone who just begins to emerge from a bottomless misery and still bears all the traces of it in his face. Just then I remembered the stories of the wild doings of his youth to which I had listened so often, and I could not restrain myself from comparing both conditions at their worst.

Two days after that night he got up for the first time and ate a boiled egg. He soon again consented to my reading to him. But he was hard to please in this respect: Goethe asked for entertaining stories and as you know they are not being written nowadays. I got him Luther's writings and read them aloud. That he took for one hour. But then he began to curse and to yell about the confounded devilish imagination of our reformer who populated and personified the whole visible world with the devil.

At this occasion we had a pleasant talk about the advantages and disadvantages of reformation and about the advantages of the Catholic and Protestant faith. I fully agreed with him when he accused the Protestant religion of loading too heavy a burden on each individual. Previously a burden of conscience could be taken from you by others, now the burdened conscience must bear it alone and loses by it the strength to reach harmony with itself again. He said, confession should have never been taken away from man. It was a beautiful and true word, he uttered, as it became very clear to me at that moment. I myself had been in this condition before. When last summer everything happened to induce my moving from Weimar to Würzburg, I did not find any consolation as long as I was in my room; but every time when I came to Goethe and opened my heart to him like to a father confessor (even all of my innermost weaknesses), then I returned to my solitude strengthened with new courage. All my life I shall be grateful to him for this kind action. The day after Goethe had listened to Luther, he asked to have this book taken out of his room.—Now Goethe is reading the novels by Cervantes with great pleasure.

## SCHILLER'S DEATH

*Schiller, whose health was very delicate from early youth and who wrote his works while in constant struggle with disease, died a few months after his 45th birthday in May, 1805. Goethe commemorated the parting of the friend in his "Annals."*

DUE TO two dreadful fires which happened in succession within a few nights of each other and by which I was personally endangered, I was thrown back into the bad state of health from which I was endeavoring to recover. Schiller felt himself in an equally bad plight. Our personal meetings were interrupted, we exchanged flying messages. Some of his letters written in February and March still testify to his sufferings, to his activity, to his resignation and his ever more and more vanishing hopes. At the beginning of May when I dared go out, I found him ready to leave for the theatre, I did not wish to keep him from it, a sense of uneasiness held me back from accompanying him, and so we parted in front of the door of his house, never to see each other again. In the state in which I was, physically and mentally, a state which needed all my strength to keep me on the surface, no one dared to bring to me, in my loneliness, the news of his decease. He had departed on the 9th, and now all my troubles assailed me doubly and threefold.

As soon as I recovered my strength, I looked about in quest of some serious work. My first thought was to complete "Demetrius." [Schiller's unfinished play] From the time when he played with the idea of doing it to the very end we had frequently talked over the plan. In the midst of his work Schiller liked to discuss with himself and others, pro and con, as to how any particular work was to be done. He would just as little tire of listening to other people's opinions as of scrutinizing his own from this and that point of view. Thus, I accompanied him, side by side, through all his works from "Wallenstein" onward, for the most part in a peaceful and friendly way, though sometimes when at last the play was ready for performance I would get into lively discussions with him on certain points, till in the end the one or other of us gave way.

In the play of "Demetrius" too, his ardent and aspiring spirit took in too wide a scope. I saw how he was inclined to construct the exposition in a prelude, now like "Wallenstein," and now like the "Maid of Orleans," how he gradually narrowed his field, compressed the salient points and began to work on this and that part. One event attaining predominance in his mind over another, I was ever at his side with counsel and co-operation. The piece became as vital in me as in him. It was therefore my passionate desire to continue our intercourse with each other to the undoing of death, to keep alive his thoughts, views and intentions, down to the smallest particular, and to raise for the last time our wonted co-operation to its highest climax, a co-operation so often tested by the editing and reworking of our own and foreign plays. Thus by continuing his existence, his loss seemed to me cancelled. I hoped to unite our mutual friends. The German theatre for which we had worked together—he creating and molding, I instructing, practising and executing—should not be entirely forsaken on account of his departure until the arrival of another similar spirit. In short, all the enthusiasm which despair stirs up in us on the occasion of a great loss had taken possession of me. My hands were free from all other work; in a few months I would have finished the piece. To see it played simultaneously in all theatres would have been the most magnificent obsequies which he could have prepared for himself and his friends. I had the feeling of being well again, of being consoled.

Unfortunately, however, many hindrances blocked the execution of this design, hindrances which care and prudence might perhaps have overcome, but which my passionate impetuosity and confusion only aggravated. Obstinately and precipitately I gave up the idea, and even now I dare not think of the situation into which I felt myself plunged. It was only then that Schiller was torn from my side and that his companionship was denied me. My artistic imagination was forbidden from busying itself with the catafalque I intended raising for him, a catafalque which should outlast his burial longer than in the case of the one at Messina. Now it was that my imagination turned to follow the corpse to the grave which had desolately closed in on him. Now for the first time I began to feel how he turned to dust. Intolerable pain got hold of me, my bodily sufferings secluded me from all company and I sank into the saddest loneliness. My diary records nothing

Goethe. Oil painting by F. Jagemann, 1806

Bettina Brentano

of that time, its blank leaves indicate my blank state, and what scraps of news may elsewhere be found only testify how I followed current business without further interest, and instead of directing it let myself be directed by it. In later days, how often had I to smile quietly to myself when sympathetic friends missed Schiller's monument in Weimar. The thought was always present with me how I could have raised the most joyous monument in honor of himself and our co-operation.

## AN INVITATION TO VIENNA

*Professor Heinrich Luden from Jena who met Goethe in August, 1806, at à party in von Knebel's house, gave the following account of his meeting with the poet.*

AT THE BEGINNING the conversation was conducted in the usual way. But hardly a quarter of an hour had passed when Goethe undertook to entertain the party. And he entertained them in a wonderful way. He told anecdotes and adventures of his recent visit in Carlsbad characterizing the people vividly and making jokes and puns. The more attention we all gave to his words and the more we appreciated his tales, all the more generously did he seem to pour out his boundless wealth of stories and to enjoy doing so. The party grew very animated and from time to time broke into hearty laughter, comparable only to the laughter of the immortal gods. Goethe joined in the laughter, though moderately, but seemed to watch it with great pleasure carried away by the wish not to let it die. . . .

I remember more than one anecdote Goethe told. But I don't dare tell them. At any rate, there would be too much missing of grace and piquancy, of Goethe's eyes, voice, and gestures. Because he did not only relate stories, he acted them. Repeatedly he returned to talk about two old countesses whom he had met. Allegedly, they were of tremendous girth displaying therefore an admirable immobility the moment they were seated. However, they retained a fluency of tongue without ever having to gabble. They had the voices of virgins, which turned very often—whenever they got animated or felt they had to show a certain dignity—into a crowing or cooing twitter. Goethe said, "I myself found the strange ball-like figures of these ladies very peculiar. I could not understand how anybody could ever achieve such massiveness, nor had I ever thought the elasticity of the human skin so limitless. But as soon as I was honored by having dinner with the noble ladies, everything became clear to me. All of us know after all what drinking and eating means, and I think we usually give striking evidence of it to our wonderful hostess. But their eating—let alone drinking—exceeded all my imagination. Each of the two ladies ate, for instance, six hard-boiled eggs with spinach, they cut every egg into half and swallowed it with as much ease as an ostrich might swallow half a horse-shoe."

Incidentally, Goethe repeated a few of the noble ladies' remarks about the effect of the Carlsbad mineral water upon their bodies, about the course of events, about the social parties, and also gave their evaluations of writers and works of art that were grand, naive, droll, baroque, and hair-raising. Continuing seriously he said that there was a lot of truth in these remarks and judgments and that he had learned a great deal from these ladies.

Another anecdote might be told, because it amused us so much by the way in which it was presented. I will transmit it in Goethe's words. How it was done, however, everyone must picture to himself.

"As it is my habit to walk up and down, I very often passed an old man of about 78 to 80 years of age who, supported by a gold-topped cane came along the same street, also walking up and down. I learned that he was a former Austrian general, a man of high repute descended from an old and noble family. I noticed several times that the old man looked at me scrutinizingly and, as soon as I had passed, may have even stopped and turned around. It did not strike me as unusual, as things of that sort had happened before. But, on one of my walks, I stepped aside somewhat to look at something, I do not recall what it was. Then the old man came toward me in a very friendly manner, baring his head slightly, whereupon I naturally returned the greeting in a polite manner. He addressed me as follows:

"If I'm not mistaken you are Herr Goethe?"—"Correct."—"From Weimar?"—"Correct."—"If I'm not mistaken you write books?"—"Oh, yes."—"And poetry?"—"Yes."—"It's even supposed to be good stuff."—"Hm."—"Haven't you written a lot?"—"Hm! Passable."—"Is rhyming difficult?"—"So, so!"—"It probably depends on the mood, how well one has eaten and drunk, isn't it so?"—"It almost seems so."—"Well, look here! Then you shouldn't sit tight in Weimar, you'd better come to Vienna."—"I've thought about it already."—"Well, look here, it's nice to be in Vienna, there you can eat and drink well."—"Hm!"—"And people appreciate someone who can rhyme."—"Hm!"—"Yes, and your kind of people—that is if you behave well, you see, and know how to live—are even invited to the first and noblest homes."—"Hm!"—"Do come! Call on me, I have a great many friends, relatives, and some influence. Just write: Goethe from Weimar, met at Carlsbad. The latter is necessary for my memory, because I have a lot to think of."—"I won't fail to do so."—"But, by the way, what have you written?"—"About different things, from Adam to Napoleon, from Ararat to the Brocken, from the cedar to the blackberry bush."—"It's even supposed to be famous."—"Hm! Somewhat!"—"It's a pity that I haven't read anything by you and haven't heard about you sooner. Are there already new revised editions of your writings?"—"Oh yes, that too."—"And will there be some more?"—"I hope so."—"It's too bad, then I can't buy your work. I only buy the very latest editions; otherwise, one always gets annoyed with having a bad book, or having to buy the same book a second time. Therefore, to be on the safe side, I always wait for the death of the author before I buy his books. That's a principle with me and I can't change it, not even for you."—"Hm!"

The party lasted until one o'clock. The conversation became colorless and even dull in the last half hour or so. Finally Goethe looked at the clock. We rose. Then Goethe addressed everyone of us with a few polite words.

## GOETHE'S RESCUE AND HIS MARRIAGE

*The battle of Jena in which the Prussian army was decimated also bore bad consequences for the Duchy of Saxe-Weimar. The Duke had to flee and Weimar got to know all the horrors of war. Friedrich Wilhelm Riemer who reports here about these events had lived in Goethe's house since 1803, first as the teacher of his son August, later as the confidential secretary of the poet.*

TUESDAY, the 14th of October 1806, at seven o'clock in the morning one could hear in Weimar very distinctly the cannonade of the battle of Jena. We noticed this thunder-like platoon fire in Goethe's garden, because the morning wind drove the sound directly there. Later in the day this sound diminished and seemed to cease altogether. Therefore, without being alarmed any longer we sat down to our meal at about three o'clock, but as soon as we had begun to eat we could again hear cannon shots, first singly and then at shorter intervals rather nearby. We got up immediately, the table was quickly cleared. Goethe left through the front rooms, I hurried from the other side through the yard into the garden where I found him already walking up and down. Meanwhile cannon balls whistled above the house. They came from the Altenburg and one of the shells had hit the old theatre.

I ran back through the yard into the house to stay in the downstairs rooms. In the meantime, the Prussian retreat was going on in utter confusion in back of the garden close to the Ackerwand.

I did not see anyone, but heard their shouting and observed the swaying of rifle muzzles and different other weapons beyond the garden wall.

With the fear and expectancy of things to come, with the running back and forth of people who were removing effects left behind by their former Prussian lodgers, one hour may have passed when a frightful quiet fell over the streets and the square before Goethe's house.

Scattered French hussars came galloping to the nearby Frauentor on the lookout for enemies in the town. One of them dared to come farther inside. Goethe's son and I hurried towards them with bottles of wine and beer offering them these refreshments. However, they did not accept anything before they were assured that no Prussian was left in the town. Thereupon the first one, with several others behind him, rode on farther into the town, to where the merchant Martini lived, from where one has a clear view of the entire street leading to the market. When he saw that everything was clear he and the others galloped into the centre of the town.

At the same time, or soon afterwards, I observed Goethe walking at the side of an officer of the hussars toward the market, presumably to reach the castle. I learned only a long time afterwards that this officer who was introduced to me as an acquaintance of Goethe, had very secretly inquired about him. He was a certain Baron von Türkheim, son of Frau v. Türkheim, née Schönemann, who had become famous as Goethe's former sweetheart under the name of Lili.

Goethe sent us a message from the castle saying that Marshal

Ney and some other cavalrymen would be billeted in the house, but we should not admit anybody else.

Soon afterwards sixteen men, mostly Alsatians, were camping in the servant's room, but being too exhausted from the sixteen hours' ride, they only asked for a bed of straw and almost refused food, only refreshing themselves quickly with some bottles of wine and beer.

Meanwhile fire had broken out in the town. Several houses were burning near the castle, the fire was probably, or for certain, set by the French themselves. This was the signal of their entry into Weimar, and therefore they also helped to extinguish it.

In the meantime, utter confusion raged in the town, caused by the arrival of the steadily growing stream of new troops, camping in the squares of the town, pillaging stores and cellars, forcing their way into houses, looting and committing assaults.

Meanwhile Goethe had returned, but the Marshal had not yet shown up, notwithstanding the fact that the table was laid for him and his escort. During all that time the Alsatians slept heavily. The doors were bolted. I stayed in the corridor walking up and down to be at hand in case of the Marshal's arrival and to prevent other people from coming in and, in case of emergency, in order to be able to call the sleeping cavalrymen for help.

While I was alone pacing the corridor in the dark receiving whatever light there was from the mounting flames of the burning houses, a lot of people seeking refuge from the fury and assault of the pillagers were crowded in the back of the house. Some of them helped the lady of the house to prepare food and to carry up the supplies from the cellar for the expected Marshal and his escort. Some complained about the unexpected misfortune and misery which had hit them like lightning, thereby adding to the dismay and restlessness of the occupants of the house who had to keep their heads and to remain collected lest they forget the most important and fitting things in their distress.

It was already late at night and the racket in the streets had not yet subsided. Up to now I had maintained my post unmolested, when suddenly terrific blows with the butt-ends of guns thundered against the door. And when I finally cried: "Who is there?" voices answered demanding entrance. I refused by pointing out that this billet was already taken by the Marshal who was momentarily expected, and besides was occupied by sixteen cavalrymen. But my protests were of no avail. I then woke up a soldier, an Alsatian, who, on entering the house, showed so much good temper that I felt confident he would not be too outraged about the disturbance of his sleep. I requested him to tell his comrades-in-arms that they could not ask nor hope for any reception. He got up, without being annoyed, opened the window, scolded them and told them to return to the bivouac where they had come from to find a better camp or resting place.

It even worked for the moment. They went away scolding and grumbling, and I imagined myself and the house safe. But it did not take long before the knocking was repeated, this time more politely, and they asked very gently to be let in. They were the same men. They claimed only to want a roof over their heads and to be able to rest a while, and tried in every way to arouse my pity. I had to refuse, though with regrets, but finally with the pointed remark that the Marshal was here already and that there was absolutely no space left.

Then they became angry threatening to break in the door. When they detected our low windows and, by looking in, noticed that I stood in an almost roomlike corridor, they were about to break in the windows and to occupy the refused refuge by force. Then I did not deem it advisable to continue my resistance; I pushed back the bolt and let them in. They were two short fellows from the so-called "spoon-guard," as they were then derisively called, but in fact skirmishers fully armed. As they stepped in I repeated once more my explanation and, to prove it, I opened the door to the room where the soldiers slept. They were convinced by what they saw and appeared calmer asking for nothing more than to be able to stay here in this shelter and to get something to eat. I fetched a lamp from the kitchen and some drinks and food, and placed it before them on one of the tables. Some low benches were at hand too, and very soon they took possession of all this and did the bottle full honor. They seemed to like the wine, they became gay and talkative asking different questions and they also inquired about the owner of the house. I excused his absence, but it did not impress them as the truth. They became more and more insistent on seeing him; I was afraid they might try to find the way to his room all by themselves and might then take it out on him. I hurried up to Goethe's room, related in short the course of events and told him that I did not know what else to do but to beg him to come downstairs, to show himself to the fellows and to get them out of the house with more authority than I could summon.

He did it without being or appearing embarrassed. Remembering similar incidents with German soldiers in Champagne he obviously thought that it was now the Germans' turn to take it, and as he was able to adjust himself to everything he did, so he was in this case too. Although he was already undressed being in his voluminous dressing gown–jokingly called by him the mantle of the prophet–he came down the stairs towards them asking what they wanted from him and whether they had not received everything they could possibly expect with the house being full of soldiers already and the Marshal with his escort still to arrive.

His dignified, awe-inspiring appearance, and his fine features seemed to evoke even the respect of these men. Suddenly they turned into polite Frenchmen again, poured another glass of wine and asked him to drink a toast with them. He did it in such a manner that no impartial person would have thought it below his dignity or not befitting the circumstances. After exchanging a few words with them he departed again. They seemed to be satisfied, calmed down and took to the bottle again. But soon they seemed to look around sleepily for a resting place and, since they did not like the bare floor, they made for the nearby staircase by which they had seen their host coming down and leaving. I ran after them, they approached the bedroom prepared for the Marshal and his companion and forced their way in. Argument was of no avail, resistance as impossible as preposterous, so I had to let it happen, hoping only that finally one of the announced adjutants would drive them away successfully.

He came, but only at daybreak. When he entered the house my first words were that his room and bed was already occupied by two marauders whom I had been unable to prevent from doing so. He rushed furiously upstairs and entering the room he brandished his sword in their faces and drove the blackguards out of the beds. They could not get out of the room and house fast enough. I can still see them running past me and, at that time, I was worried that they might take some of the silver with them.

It was bright daylight by then. The Marshal who had passed the night somewhere else arrived. Immediately his bodyguards were stationed in front of the house, and peace and order prevailed again. Having had my first talk with the other occupants of the house I learned that the two marauders I had believed in bed had forced their way into Goethe's room and had threatened his life. But his wife called one of the men who had taken refuge in the house for help, he rescued Goethe from the hands of the drunken soldiers, chased them out and bolted the doors of Goethe's room and anteroom.

Goethe himself did not show any traces of all that; but I was very disconcerted about the danger he had been in without my knowing it.

From this day on Goethe retained a faithful gratitude toward his saviour and his wife who, in general, in these days of horror had shown great steadfastness and skill, though she did not speak French at all. In spite of the terrible amount of food consumed by the soldiers as well as by the Marshal and his wasteful cooks, she managed to keep her house, even giving help to others who were in need and to her protégés in town.

This feeling of gratitude, this realization that, at that moment, he had become indebted to her for his life, was the main motive of speeding up an action which he had in mind for a considerable time, only waiting for a propitious moment to act so that it seemed natural and self-evident, less surprising and easy to arrange, without much ado.

In many instances of his life he had known how to grasp the important and fitting moment. Unexpectedly, something that may have looked like a sudden idea would become reality, though it waited in long and quiet preparation for the igniting spark which an important event alone could justify. This remark does not only refer to his moral actions, but also to him as a poet. And it is natural that man and poet would also herein prove harmonious, as they had their roots in common ground.

Weimar's future existence was at stake. Goethe's fate—even if spared his life—would have been considerably worse than that of his absent sovereign, had Napoleon really executed his threats which, at that time, no power in the world could have prevented, threats which grew very serious in view of the war scenes of conflagration and pillage—but which later could have easily been considered a mere threat.

Other princes would have supported Goethe's sovereign and helped him to his rights sooner or later. But Goethe—having lost everything, estate, fortune and literary treasures, the toil of many years of study—where could he have turned to find protection, maintenance and a fitting occupation? . . .

With this sad prospect of leading a wretched life in the future as a beggar in foreign lands—if permitted to exist at all,—it was only natural and needed no other motivation for binding stronger an attachment with a soul that had proven faithful. And in case of a favorable turn of fate, it had not been more than a justified compensation for all the disadvantages and privations which she may have felt up to now and which might have arisen out of public opinion. He owed her public recognition not only because of his love for her but also because of his feelings for their son, particularly in consideration of his growing up and his impending career.

These twofold reasons induced Goethe to sanction the secret vows of his heart with a formal, public wedding ceremony in the very first days of the abating flood of war and the appearing rainbow of peace.

All friends and admirers of Goethe approved and praised this long expected step. On October 19, the first Sunday after the battle of the 14th, Goethe drove with his wife, his son and myself to the Schlosskirche in the morning. The wedding ceremony was performed in the vestry. The ecclesiastical councillor Günther conducted the ceremony in a dignified manner.

## BETTINA TO GOETHE'S MOTHER

*For Bettina Brentano, who visited Weimar together with her sister and brother-in-law in April, 1807, this journey was something like a pilgrimage. Bettina adored Goethe before she ever met him. A native of Frankfort, she had grown up surrounded by Goethe reminiscences. In his youth the poet had frequented the house of Bettina's grandmother, the writer Sophie von La Roche; later a tender friendship developed between Goethe and her mother, the beautiful Maximiliane Brentano. Bettina was a frequent visitor in the house of Goethe's mother, where her passion for the poet was nurtured by the childhood anecdotes of Frau Rat.*

May 11, 1807

WE REACHED WEIMAR at twelve o'clock and sat down to dinner, but I couldn't eat. The other two lay down on the sofa and went to sleep, for we hadn't slept in three nights. "I advise you," said my brother-in-law, "to take a rest too; it won't make much difference to Goethe whether you go to see him or not, and there's nothing remarkable to see in him anyway." Can you imagine how these words discouraged me? Oh, I didn't know what to do, all alone in a strange town. I had changed my dress and stood at the window and looked at the town clock; it was just striking half-past two. It seemed to me, too, that Goethe wouldn't care particularly about seeing me; I remembered that people called him proud. I constrained my heart to quell its yearning. Suddenly the clock struck three, and then it seemed exactly as though he had called me. I ran down for the servant, but there was no carriage to be found. "Will a sedan chair do?" "No," I said, "that's an equipage for the hospital"—and we went on foot. There was a regular chocolate porridge in the streets and I had to have myself carried over the worst bogs. In this way I came to Wieland, not to your son. I had never seen Wieland, but I pretended to be an old acquaintance. He thought and thought, and finally said, "You certainly are a dear familiar angel, but I can't seem to remember when and where I have seen you." I jested with him and said, "Now I know that you dream of me, for you can't possibly have seen me elsewhere!" I had him give me a note to your son which I afterwards took with me and kept as a souvenir. Here's a copy of it: "Bettina Brentano, Sophie's sister, Maximiliane's daughter, Sophie La Roche's grand-daughter wishes to see you, dear brother, and pretends that she's afraid of you and that a note from me would serve as a talisman and give her courage. Although I am pretty certain that she is merely making a sport of me, I nevertheless have to do what she wants and I shall be astonished if you don't have the same experience."

With this note I sallied forth. The house lies opposite the fountain—how deafening the waters sounded in my ears! I ascended the simple staircase; in the wall stand plaster statues which impose silence—at any rate I couldn't utter a sound in this sacred hallway. Everything is cheerful and yet solemn! The greatest simplicity prevails in the rooms, and yet it is all so inviting! "Do not fear," said the modest walls, "he will come, and he will be, and he will not claim to be *more* than you." And then the door opened and there he stood, solemnly serious, with his eyes fixed on me. I stretched out my hands toward him, I believe, and soon I knew no more. Goethe caught me up quickly to his heart. "Poor child, did I frighten you?"—those were the first words through which his voice thrilled my heart. He led me into his room and placed me on the sofa opposite him. There we sat, both mute, until at last he broke the silence. "You have doubtless read in the papers that we suffered a great bereavement a few days ago in the death of the Duchess Amalia.—"Oh," I said, "I do not read the papers."—"Why, I thought everything that goes on in Weimar interests you."—"No, nothing interests me but you alone, and therefore I'm far too impatient to pore over the papers."—"You are a kind child." A long pause—with me glued in much anxiety to the odious sofa; you know how impossible it is for me to sit up in such well-bred fashion. Oh, mother, is it possible for anyone to forget herself thus?

Suddenly I said, "I can't stay here on this sofa any longer," and jumped up.—"Well," said he, "make yourself comfortable;" and with that I flew into his arms. He drew me on his knee and pressed me to his heart. Everything was quiet, oh, so quiet, and then all vanished. I hadn't slept for so long—years had passed in longing for him—and I fell asleep on his breast. When I awoke a new life began for me.

PART FOUR

# *Master of His Life*

1807-1832

## GOETHE TO F. ZELTER

*Goethe's correspondence with Karl Friedrich Zelter, extending over three decades, bears testimony of a friendship which stood every test of life. Zelter, a natural, uninhibited character, was devoted to Goethe with an admiring love. He came from a family of laborers and he himself had first been a mason, before he could devote himself to his real gift, music. Since 1800 Zelter administered the* Singakademie *in Berlin where he was very successful as teacher and conductor. His admiration for the masters of Church music made him little susceptible to the composers of his time. The partiality of his judgment also influenced Goethe who trusted his advice in all musical questions. Zelter's own compositions, among them many Goethe Lieder, are forgotten today.*

Carlsbad, July 27, 1807

IT IS A LONG TIME, my very dear friend, since you heard from me. I will now shortly tell you what I have been doing in the meantime. I came to Carlsbad in a very poor state of health which was at first so aggravated by a careless use of the waters, common here indeed, but not suitable for me at all, that I got into a miserable condition. After a change of cure and the use of other means, prescribed by Dr. Kapp of Leipzig, things suddenly took a turn for the better. As this has lasted for six weeks I gladly let my friends know of it.

It is eight weeks now since I came here, and I have been occupying myself in different ways at different moments: first of all in dictating short fairy-tales and stories which I have long carried about in my head; then for a time, I took to drawing landscapes and illuminating and am now engaged in classifying my geological opinions relating to the district round about and in briefly commenting on a collection of rock specimens which is on view here.

I have become acqainted with interesting people of all kinds; amongst whom, Reinhard, the French resident, who but lately held an appointment in Jassy and whose fortunes you are sure to have heard of, probably ranks first. As a rule, however, I am very much alone, for in the world one meets only with Jeremiads, which, although they are called forth by great evils, appear nevertheless to be mere hollow phrases, as you hear them in society. When anyone laments over what he and those around him are suffering, what he has lost and fears to lose,–I listen with sympathy and am glad to discuss the matter and to comfort him. But when people lament over the whole thing which is supposed to be lost, but which no one in Germany has ever seen in his life, and much less cared about,–I have to conceal my impatience in order not to appear impolite, or an egotist. As already said, it would be inhuman not to sympathize with a man who feels the loss of his living, the destruction of his career; but if such a man thinks that the world has in the smallest degree suffered in consequence, I cannot possibly agree with him.

Tell me, dear friend, how you are getting on. I have thought of you a thousand times and of what you have accomplished as a private person, without the support of the wealthy and powerful and without any special encouragement. Perhaps what we have most to regret about this political change is mainly this, that under its old constitution Germany and especially the Northern part allowed the individual to cultivate himself as far as possible and that it permitted everyone to do what was right in his own eyes, though there was never any special interest shown in him by the community.

To these general and certainly inadequate reflections which I should like some day to discuss further with you personally

I wish to add a special request which I beg you to comply with soon.

Although we have both voices and orchestra in Weimar and in addition to it, I am the master of such ceremonies, still I never could secure musical enjoyment with any certain regularity, because the odious relations of life and the theatre invariably destroy the higher element for which alone they exist or ought to exist. Schleswig has again sent us two new people, a very good tenor and a kind of assistant rehearser. I have not yet made their personal acquaintance, but they seem to be good and intelligent people. Our opera, as at present constituted, I do not care to interfere with, particularly as I do not thoroughly understand these musical matters. I should therefore prefer leaving the Secular to itself and withdrawing into the Sanctuary.

Now I should like once a week to have sacred part-songs performed at my house, in the same way as at your *Singakademie,* even if it is only the most far-off reflection of it. Help me to do this, and send me some part-songs for voices, not too difficult and with the parts already written out. I will gratefully reimburse you for any expense you may incur. Let me know whether I could get such things, with notes printed or engraved. Canons, too, and whatever you may think useful for the purpose.

You shall always be in our midst, in spirit, and heartily welcome whenever you care to appear in person. Let me have a few lines, for I shall remain here another month, and send me a parcel to Weimar that I may begin at once when I get home. Farewell, and rest assured of my lasting friendship.

# NAPOLEON'S INTERVIEW WITH GOETHE

*Napoleon was at the peak of his might when he assembled the congress of sovereign princes in the Thuringian city of Erfurt. On October 2, 1808, the French Emperor received Goethe, whom the Duke of Saxe-Weimar had called to Erfurt. The following account, which Prince Talleyrand wrote immediately after the interview took place, was published later in Talleyrand's memoirs.*

Napoleon usually bid the eminent and remarkable men who had come to Erfurt, to see him. Every morning, he perused, with much interest, the list of new arrivals. One day, having noticed the name of Goethe among the number of newly-arrived visitors, he sent for him.

"Monsieur Goethe," he said to him on seeing him, "I am delighted to see you."

"Sire, I see that when your Majesty travels, you do not neglect to notice even the most insignificant persons."

"I know you are Germany's first dramatic poet."

"Sire, you wrong our country; we are under the impression we have our great men. Schiller, Lessing, and Wieland are surely known to your Majesty."

"I confess I hardly know them. However, I have read Schiller's *The Thirty Years War,* and that, I beg your pardon, seemed to me to furnish dramatic subjects only worthy of our boulevards."

"Sire, I do not know your boulevards, but I suppose that popular plays are given there. I am sorry to hear you judge so severely one of the greatest geniuses of modern times."

"You usually live in Weimar; is it the place where the most celebrated men of German literature meet?"

"Sire, they enjoy great protection there; but for the present, there is only one man in Weimar who is known throughout Europe; it is Wieland."

"I should be delighted to see Monsieur Wieland!"

"If your Majesty will allow me to ask him, I feel certain that he will come here immediately."

"Does he speak French?"

"He knows it, and has corrected several French translations of his works."

"While you are here, you must go every night to our plays. It will not do you any harm to see good French tragedies."

"I'll go willingly. I must confess to your Majesty that it was my intention, for I have translated, or rather imitated, some French pieces."

"Which ones?"

*"Mahomet* and *Tancred"* [by Voltaire]

"I shall ask Rémusat if he has any actors here to play them. I should be very glad for you to see them represented in our language. You are not as strict as we are in theatrical rules."

"Sire, unity with us is not so essential."

"How do you find our sojourn here?"

"Very brilliant, sire, and I hope it will be useful to our country."

"Are your people happy?"

"They hope to be so soon."

"Monsieur Goethe, you ought to remain with us during the whole of our stay and write your impressions of the grand sight we are offering."

"Ah! sire, it would require the pen of some great writer of antiquity to undertake such a task."

"Are you an admirer of Tacitus?"

"Yes, sire, I admire him much."

"Well, I don't; but we shall talk of that another time. Write and tell Monsieur Wieland to come here. I shall return his visit at Weimar, where the Duke has invited me. I'll be very glad to see the Duchess; she is a lady worthy of my esteem. The

Duke was troublesome enough, for some time. But he has been punished."

"Sire, troublesome though he may have been, the punishment was a little severe. But I am not a judge of such things; he protects literature and sciences, and we have nothing to say against him, but rather everything in his favour."

"Monsieur Goethe, come to-night to *Iphigenia*. [Racine's tragedy] It is a good piece. It is not, however, one of my favourites, but the French think a good deal of it. You will see in my pit a great number of sovereigns. Do you know the Prince Primate?"

"Yes, sire; almost intimately. He is very clever, very well informed, and very generous."

"Well, you will see him, to-night, fast asleep on the shoulder of the King of Württemberg. Have you already seen the Czar?" [Alexander I of Russia]

"No, sire, never; but I hope to be introduced to him."

"He speaks your language; should you write anything on the Erfurt interview, you must dedicate it to him."

"Sire, it is not my habit to do so. When I first commenced to write, I made it a principle never to dedicate anything to any one, in order that I should never repent it."

"The great writers of Louis the Fourteenth's time were not of your opinion."

"But your Majesty cannot be sure they never repented doing what they did."

"What has become of that scoundrel, Kotzebue?" [Political pamphleteer and author of comedies]

"Sire, they say he is in Siberia and that his Majesty will solicit his pardon from the Czar."

"But he is not the man for me."

"Sire, he has been very unfortunate, and is a man of great talent."

"Good-bye, Monsieur Goethe."

I followed Goethe to invite him to dine with me. On coming home, I wrote this first conversation, and, while at dinner, I ascertained, by different questions I put to him, that what I had written was correct. On rising from table, Goethe went to the theatre; I was anxious that he should be near the stage, but that was difficult enough, for the seats in front were occupied by the crowned heads, and the chairs placed behind them were taken up by the hereditary princes, while the seats still farther off were filled by ministers and princes. I, therefore recommended Goethe to Dazincourt who, without wounding propriety, found the means of placing him advantageously.

## THE EMPEROR AS LITERARY CRITIC

*For a long time Goethe kept the details of his conversation with Napoleon a secret. It was only in 1824 that he, urged by a friend, put on paper an outline of the interview. But even then Goethe did not specify the nature of Napoleon's criticism of "Werther." According to other sources Napoleon objected primarily to the mingling of the love-motive with that of offended ambition in Werther's suicide. Here is Goethe's sketch:*

I WAS ORDERED to the presence of the Emperor at 11 A.M. A stout chamberlain, a Pole, intimated to me to stay. The crowd dispersed. Presented to Savary and Talleyrand. I am called to the cabinet of the Emperor. At the same time Daru [intendant general of the imperial household] sends in his name, and is at once admitted. I therefore hesitate. Am again called. Step in.

The Emperor sits at a large round table, taking breakfast. At his right hand stands Talleyrand at some distance from the table, at his left, rather near, Daru, with whom he converses on war-reparation affairs. The Emperor nods to me to come forward. I stand at a suitable distance from him. Having looked at me attentively, he said. "Indeed, you are a *Man.*" I bow.

He asks, "How old are you?"

"Sixty years."

"You carry your age well.—You have written tragedies?"

I answered what was necessary. Here Daru took up the word. In some measure to flatter the Germans on whom he had to work so much woe, he spoke of German literature; being also well-conversant with Latin and himself editor of Horace. He spoke of me in much the same way as my patrons in Berlin might have spoken; at least, I recognised in his words their mode of thought and sentiment. He then added that I had translated Voltaire's "Mahomet" from the French.

The Emperor replied, "It is not a good piece," and stated forthwith in great detail how unsuitable it was for the conqueror of the world to give such an unfavourable description of himself. He then turned the conversation on "Werther," which he seemed to have studied thoroughly. After various very pertinent remarks he pointed out a certain passage and said, "Why have you written so? It is not according to nature"; opening up his meaning at large and setting forth the matter with perfect accuracy.

I listened to him with a serene face, and answered with a pleased smile, that I did not know, to be sure, whether any one else had made this same criticism; but I considered it entirely just, and confessed that there was something untrue to be found in this passage. But, I added, perhaps the author is to be pardoned if he employs a not easily detected artifice in order to produce certain effects, which he could not have achieved in a simple, natural way.

The Emperor seemed to be satisfied with this explanation, came back to the drama, and made some very significant remarks, such as one would make who had studied the tragic stage, as a judge studies a criminal, with the closest attention, and had felt very keenly the departure of the French theatre from nature and truth. Then he spoke also of fatalistic dramas with disapproval, saying that they belonged to the dark ages. "What will they do with fate now?" he said—"*Politics* is fate."

He next turned again to Daru, and spoke with him of the war-reparation affairs. I retired a little, and came to stand just at the corner where more than thirty years ago, along with many a glad hour, I had also experienced many a sad one, and had time to notice that to the right of me, towards the entrance, Berthier, Savary, and yet another person stood. Talleyrand had gone.

Marshal Soult was announced. This tall figure with a profusion of hair on his head entered. The Emperor inquired jocularly about some unpleasant events in Poland, and I had time to look round me in the room, and to think of the past. Here, still, was the same old tapestry. But the portraits on the walls had vanished. Here had hung the likeness of the Duchess Amalia in masquerade dress, a black half-mask in her hand, the other likenesses of governors and members of the family, likewise all gone.

The Emperor rose, went up to me, and by a kind of manoeuvre separated me from the other members of the row in which I stood. Turning his back on them, and speaking to me in a lower voice he asked whether I was married, had children, and other personal matters of usual interest. In the same manner, likewise, he inquired after my relations to the princely house, after the Duchess Amalia, the Prince, the Princess, etc. I answered him in a natural way. He seemed satisfied, and translated it into his own language, only in a somewhat more decisive style than I had been able to express myself.

I must remark, generally, that in the whole conversation I had to admire the multiplicity of his expressions of approval, for he seldom listened without some response, either nodding reflectively with the head or saying, "Yes," or "That's right," or such like. Nor must I forget to mention that when he had finished speaking, he usually added, "What do you think of it, Monsieur Goethe?"

And so I took the opportunity of asking the Chamberlain by a sign whether I might take leave, which he answered in the affirmative, and I then without further ado took my departure.

## BETTINA TO GOETHE

Vienna, May 28, 1810

It is Beethoven of whom I want to speak now, and in whom I have forgotten the world and you. I may not be qualified to judge, but I am not mistaken when I say (what perhaps no one realizes or believes) that he is far in advance of the culture of all mankind, and I wonder whether we can ever catch up with him! I doubt it. I only hope that he may live until the mighty and sublime enigma that lies in his soul may have reached its highest and ripest perfection. May he reach his highest ideal, for then he will surely leave in our hands the key to a divine knowledge which will bring us one step nearer true bliss!

To you I may confess that I believe in a divine magic which is the element of spiritual nature, and this magic Beethoven employs in his music. All he can teach you about it is pure magic; every combination of sounds is a phase of a higher existence, and for this reason Beethoven feels that he is the founder of a new sensuous basis in the spiritual life. You will probably be able to feel intuitively what I am trying to say, and that it is true. Who could replace this spirit? From whom could we expect anything equivalent to it? All human activity passes to and fro before him like clockwork; he alone creates freely from his inmost self the undreamed of, the uncreated. What would intercourse with the outside world profit this man, who is at his sacred work before sunrise and scarcely looks about him before sunset, who forgets bodily nourishment, and who is borne in his flight by the stream of inspiration past the shores of superficial, everyday life. He himself said to me, "Whenever I open my eyes I cannot but sigh, for all I see is counter to my religion and I must despise the world which does not comprehend that music is a higher revelation than all wisdom and philosophy. It is the wine which inspires new creations, and I am the Bacchus who presses out this glorious wine for men and intoxicates their spirit! . . . I have no friend and must ever be alone, but I know that God is nearer to me in my art than to others, and I commune with him without fear; I have always recognized Him and understood Him. Nor have I any fears for my music; it can meet no evil fate, for he to whom it makes itself intelligible will be freed from all misery with which others are burdened."

All this Beethoven said to me the first time I saw him, and I was filled with a feeling of reverence when he expressed himself to me with such friendly candor, since I must have seemed very unimportant to him. Besides, I was astonished, for I had been told that he was exceedingly reticent and avoided conversation with anyone; in fact, they were afraid to introduce me to him, so I had to look him up alone. He has three dwellings in which he alternately conceals himself—one in the country, one in the city, and the third on the bastion, in the third story of which I found him. I entered unannounced and mentioned my name. He was seated at the piano and was very amiable. He inquired whether I did not wish to hear a song that he had just composed. Then he sang, in a shrill and piercing voice, so that the plaintiveness reacted upon the listener, "Knowest thou the land?" [Mignon's song by Goethe] "It is beautiful, isn't it, very beautiful!" he cried, enraptured; "I'll sing it again;" and was delighted at my ready applause. "Most people are stirred by something good, but they are not artistic natures; artists are fiery—they do not weep." Then he sang one of your songs that he had composed lately, "Dry not, Tears of Eternal Love."

Yesterday I went for a walk with him through a beautiful garden at Schönbrunn that was in full blossom; all the hothouses were open and the fragrance was overpowering. Beethoven stopped in the burning sun and said, "Goethe's poems exercise a great power over me, not through their content alone, but also through their rhythm, and I am incited and moved to compose by his language, which is built up as if by the aid of spirits into a sublime structure that bears within it the mystery of harmonies. Then from the focus of my inspiration I must let the melody stream forth in every direction; I pursue it, passionately overtake it again, see it escaping me a second time and disappearing in a host of varying emotions; soon I seize it with renewed ardor; I can no longer separate myself from it, but with impetuous rapture I must reproduce it in all modulations, and, in the final moment, I triumph over the musical idea—and that, you see, is a symphony! Yes, music is truly the mediator between the spiritual and the sensuous world. I should like to discuss this with Goethe; I wonder whether he would understand me! Melody is the sensuous life of poetry. Does not the spiritual content of a poem become sensuous feeling through melody? Do we not in the song of Mignon feel her whole sensuous mood through melody, and does not this sensation incite one in turn to new creations? Then the spirit longs to expand to boundless universality where everything together forms a channel for the *feelings* that spring from the simple musical thought that otherwise would die away unnoted. This is harmony; this is expressed in my symphonies; the blending of manifold forms rolls on to the goal in a single channel. At such moments one feels that something eternal, infinite, something that can never be wholly comprehended, lies in all things spiritual; and although I always have the feeling of success in my compositions, yet with the last roll of the drum with which I have driven home my own enjoyment, my musical conviction, to my hearers, I feel an eternal hunger to begin anew, like a child, what a moment before seemed to me to have been exhausted.

"Speak to Goethe of me, and tell him to hear my symphonies. Then he will agree with me that music is the sole incorporeal entrance into a higher world of knowledge which, to be sure, embraces man, but which he, on the other hand, can never embrace. Rhythm of the spirit is necessary to comprehend music in its essence; music imparts presentiments, inspirations of divine science, and what the spirit experiences of the sensuous in it is the embodiment of spiritual knowledge. Although the spirits live upon music as a man lives upon air, it is a very different matter to *comprehend* it with the spirit. But the more the soul draws its sensuous nourishment from it, the riper the spirit becomes for a happy mutual understanding . . ."

He took me to a dress rehearsal with full orchestra, and I sat back in a box all alone in the large, unlighted hall, and saw this mighty spirit wield his authority. Oh, Goethe! No emperor, no king, is so conscious of his power, so conscious that all power radiates from him, as this same Beethoven is, who only now in the garden was searching for the source of his inspiration. If I understood him as I feel him, I should be omniscient. There he stood, so firmly resolved, his gestures and features expressing the perfection of his creation, anticipating every error, every misconception, every breath obeyed his will, and everything was set into the most rational activity by the superb presence of his spirit. One might well prophesy that such a spirit will reappear in a later reincarnation as ruler of the universe!

## GOETHE TO F. ZELTER

Weimar, February 28, 1811

I HAVE READ of the illustrious Oldenburg, first Secretary of the London Society, that he never opens a letter before he has placed pen, ink and paper in front of him, as he writes his answer immediately after the first reading. And thus, it seems, he gets through an immense amount of correspondence very easily. Could I have imitated this virtue, less people would have had to complain of my silence. But now the arrival of your dear letter, recalling the activity of our summer life, excites in me such a desire to answer it that I address these lines to you, though not at the first reading, at least on my awakening the morning after. . . .

It is very good of you not to have neglected my "Theory of Colors;" taken in small doses, it will have a very good effect. I know very well that my way of treating the subject, natural as it is, is very different from the usual method and I cannot expect everyone to recognize and to adopt its advantages immediately. Mathematicians are cranky people and they are so far from having the slightest notion of the real issue that one must be indulgent to their conceit. I am very curious to see who will be the first to understand the thing and behave honestly about it: for they cannot all be blind, nor maliciously inclined. Moreover, I have, in this instance, become more and more conscious of the fact—of which I have been aware for some time—that the training given to the mind by mathematics is extremely one-sided and limited. Voltaire even ventures to say somewhere, "I have always observed that geometry leaves the mind where it finds it." Franklin also has a peculiar aversion to mathematicians and expresses this plainly and clearly when speaking about social intercourse and referring to their spirit of pettiness and contradiction as being intolerable.

As far as the real Newtonians are concerned, they are like the old Prussians in October 1806. They thought they might yet win by tactics, although they had long been beaten by strategy. When once their eyes are opened, they will be surprised to see that I have already been to Naumburg and Leipzig, while they are still rummaging about in the vicinity of Weimar and Blankenhain. But that battle was lost beforehand, and it is the same here too. That doctrine is already extinguished, though these gentlemen still think they may despise their adversary. Pardon my big way of talking; I am as little ashamed of it as those gentlemen are of their petty minds.

*In his "Theory of Colors," the first part of which appeared in 1810, Goethe published the result of his studies with which he occupied himself for twenty years. He expounded his theory in passionate opposition to Newton, explaining the phenomena of color as modifications of the white light through more or less transparent media. Goethe's work, full of new observations and original ideas, was almost completely ignored by the scientists of his time.*

## BEETHOVEN TO GOETHE

Vienna, April 12, 1811

YOUR EXCELLENCY—

The pressing business of a friend of mine, one of your great admirers (as I also am), who is leaving here in a great hurry, gives me only a moment to offer my thanks for the long time I have known you (for I know you from the days of my childhood)—that is very little for so much. Bettina Brentano has assured me that you would receive me in a kindly—yes, indeed friendly, spirit. But how could I think of such a reception, seeing that I am only in a position to approach you with the deepest reverence, with an inexpressibly deep feeling for your noble creations? You will shortly receive from Leipzig, through Breitkopf and Haertel, the music to "Egmont," this glorious Egmont, with which I, with the same warmth with which I read it, was again through you impressed by it and set it to music. I should much like to know your opinion of it; even criticism will be profitable for me and for my art, and will be as willingly received as the greatest praise.

Your Excellency's great admirer,
LUDWIG VAN BEETHOVEN.

## GOETHE TO BEETHOVEN

Carlsbad, June 25, 1811

I HAVE RECEIVED your kind letter with great pleasure, my very respected sir, through Herr von Oliva. I am heartily grateful to you for the feelings expressed in it and I can assure you that I reciprocate them with sincerity: for whenever I have heard great artists or even amateurs play one of your compositions it was never without wanting to admire you personally at the piano and to delight in your extraordinary talent. Dear Bettina Brentano certainly deserves the interest you have shown in her. She speaks with enthusiasm and lively sympathy about you and considers the hours spent with you among the happiest of her life.

I think, when I come home, I shall find there the music you wrote for "Egmont." I am already grateful for it in advance, because I have heard several people praise it and I am planning to perform it together with my play in our theatre this winter. Thus I hope to prepare a rare treat for myself as well as for your many admirers. Most of all, however, I hope I have understood Herr von Oliva correctly who has given us hope that you will be able to visit Weimar on the occasion of a trip you are planning. If it would only take place at a time when both the Court and the entire music-loving public is still together. You may be certain of finding a reception worthy of your merits and your reputation. But no one of course can be more interested in it than I who, with the best wishes for your well-being, desires to be kindly remembered and to express his sincerest gratitude for the many good things he has already received from you.

Friedrich Wilhelm Riemer

August von Goethe

*Drawings by J. J. Schmeller*

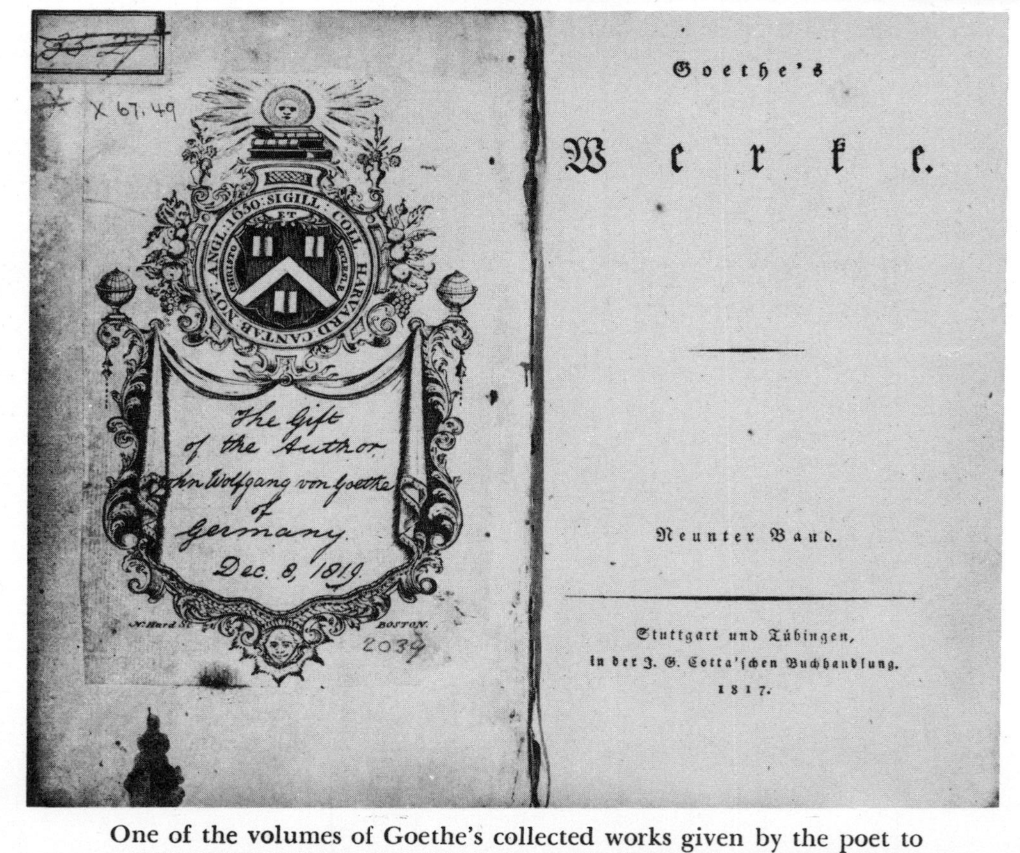

X 67.49

SIGILL: COLL: HARVARD: CANTAB: NOV: ANGL: 1650

CHRISTO ET ECCLESIAE

The Gift
of the Author
John Wolfgang von Goethe
of
Germany.
Dec. 8, 1819.

N. Hurd Sc. BOSTON.

2039

Goethe's

Werke.

Neunter Band.

Stuttgart und Tübingen,
in der J. G. Cotta'schen Buchhandlung.
1817.

One of the volumes of Goethe's collected works given by the poet to Harvard in 1819. Courtesy of the Library of Harvard University

Karl Friedrich Zelter. Drawing by G. Schadow

Felix Mendelssohn-Bartholdy at the age of eleven

## GOETHE TO F. ZELTER

*Goethe made Beethoven's personal acquaintance in the summer of 1812. His diary records on July 20 an excursion with Beethoven and, on the next morning, a visit at his house where he "played delightfully."*

Carlsbad, September 2, 1812

I MADE BEETHOVEN'S ACQUAINTANCE in Teplitz. His talent astounded me; but unfortunately his natural temperament is wholly uncontrolled and although he is, indeed, not at all wrong in thinking the world detestable, still, in doing so, he does not make it more pleasant, either for himself or for others. However, he is greatly to be forgiven and much to be pitied, for he is losing his hearing which perhaps affects the musician less than the social human being. As it is, he is laconic by nature and is now becoming doubly so through this defect.

*Zelter had informed his friend in a preceding letter of his stepson's suicide.*

Weimar, December 3, 1812

YOUR LETTER, my beloved friend, announcing the great misfortune that has befallen your house, has greatly afflicted, in fact, crushed me, for it reached me when I was in the midst of very serious meditations on life, and it was only through you yourself that I was able to rise again. On the black touchstone of death you have proved yourself genuine and refined gold. How wonderful a character appears when it is built on mind and soul, and how beautiful must that talent be which rests on such a fundament!

As to the deed or misdeed itself I can say nothing. When the *taedium vitae* seizes a man, he is only to be pitied, not blamed. That all the symptoms of this strange disease, as natural as it is unnatural, at one time raged furiously through my own innermost being, no one who knows my "Werther" will probably doubt. I am fully aware of the resolutions and effort it cost me in those days to escape the waves of death; and with the same difficulty I saved myself and recovered from many a later shipwreck. And so it fares with all sailors' and fishermen's stories.

When one sees how the world in general and the young world in particular not only yields to its lusts and passions, but how, at the same time, all that is nobler and better in it is abused and perverted by the serious follies of the time so that everything which should have led to its blessedness becomes its curse—not taking into account the inexpressible pressure from without—one is not astonished at the misdeeds by which man rages against himself and others. I could trust myself to write a new "Werther" which would make people's hair stand more on end than the first one. Let me add one other remark. Most young persons, conscious of some merit in themselves, make more demand upon themselves than is fair. To this, however, they are urged and driven by their crushing environment. I know half-a-dozen such persons who are certainly being ruined and whom it would be impossible to help, even if one could enlighten them as to their real advantages. No one easily comes to the conclusion that reason and a strong will are given us so that we may not only hold back from evil, but also from extreme good.

Now let us pass on to other things in your letters, which have done me good, and first of all, accept my thanks for your remarks on the pages of my biography. I had already, in a general way, heard many kind and friendly things said about them; you are the first and only one who has entered into the matter itself.

## THE DESTINY OF GENIUS

*Johannes Daniel Falk was one of the first of Goethe's admirers to record systematically his conversations with the poet. His religious disposition made Falk particularly receptive to Goethe's speculations about a future life.*

On the day of Wieland's funeral [January 25, 1813] I noticed such a solemn tone in Goethe's whole manner, as we were seldom accustomed to see in him. There was something so softened, I may almost say so melancholy, about him; his eyes frequently glistened; even his voice, his manner of speaking, were different from what was usual. This might possibly be because our conversation took a direction toward the supernatural, for which Goethe commonly showed repugnance, if not contempt: completely on principle, as it appears to me, for it was more consonant with his natural disposition rather to confine himself to the present and to the pleasant objects which nature and art in the sphere open to us have to offer to eye and observation.

Our departed friend was naturally the principal subject of our conversation. Without deviating greatly from it, I asked him on one occasion, when he spoke of the continuance of existence after death as a matter-of-course, "And what do you think is at this moment the occupation of Wieland's soul?"

"Nothing petty, nothing unworthy, nothing out of keeping

with that moral greatness which he all his life sustained," was the reply. "But not to be misunderstood; as we have entered on this subject, I must go somewhat deeper into it. It is something to have passed a life of eighty years in unblemished dignity and honor; it is something to have attained to that tender and elegant way of thinking, which predominated so delightfully in Wieland's soul; it is something to have possessed that industry, that iron persistency, in which he surpassed us all."

"Would you not willingly assign him a place near his Cicero with whom he busied himself so cheerfully up to the time of his death?"

"Do not disturb me, if you want me to develop my ideas along a continuous line. The destruction of such spiritual powers is a thing that in nature could never, and under no circumstances, even be considered. Nature is not such a prodigal spendthrift of her capital. Wieland's soul is one of Nature's treasures; a perfect jewel. What adds to this is, that his long life had increased, not diminished, these noble intellectual endowments. Again, I entreat you, consider this carefully. Raphael was scarcely thirty, Kepler scarcely forty, when they suddenly terminated their lives, while Wieland—"

"How," interrupted I with some surprise, "do you speak of dying as if it were a spontaneous act?"

"That I often allow myself to do," replied he; "and if you are pleased to consider it under a different aspect, I will (since at this moment I may be permitted to do so) tell you my thoughts upon the subject from the very beginning."

I begged him most earnestly not to withhold any of his opinions from me.

"You have long known," he resumed, "that ideas which are without a firm foundation in the world of the senses, whatever may be their value in other respects, bring no conviction for me; for in everything that concerns nature, I want knowledge and not merely conjectures or belief. With regard to the individual existence of the soul after death, my course has been as follows:

This hypothesis stands in no sort of contradiction with the observations of many years, which I have made on the constitution of our species, and all other species; on the contrary, these observations furnish fresh evidence in its support. But how much or how little, of this individual existence is worthy to last is another question, and a point we must leave to the Deity. At present I will only make this preliminary remark. I assume various classes and orders of the primary elements of all existence, of the germs of all phenomena in nature; these I would call souls, since from them proceeds the animation of the whole. Or rather monads– Let us always stick to that term of Leibnitz; a better can scarcely be found, to express the simplicity of the simplest existence. Now, as experience shows us, some of these monads are so small, so insignificant, that they are at best adapted only to subordinate use and being. Others, again, are strong and powerful. These latter, accordingly, draw into their sphere all that approaches them, and transmute it into something belonging to themselves; i.e. into a human body, into a plant, an animal, or, to go higher still, into a star. This process they continue till the small or larger world, whose completion lies predestined in them, at length comes bodily into light. Such alone are, I think, properly to be called souls. Hence it follows, that there are monads of worlds, souls of worlds; as well as monads of ants and souls of ants; and that both are, if not identical, of cognate origin. Every sun, every planet, bears within itself the germ of a higher fulfilment, in virtue of which its development is as regular, and must take place according to the same laws, as the development of a rosetree, by means of leaf, stalk and flower. You may call the germ an idea, or a monad, as you please; I have no objection. Enough that it is invisible, and antecedent to the visible external development. We must not be misled by the larvae or imperfect forms of the intermediate states which this idea or germ may assume in its transitions. One and the same metamorphosis, or capacity of transformation in nature, produces a flower, a rose out of a leaf, a caterpillar out of an egg, and again a butterfly out of the caterpillar.

The inferior monads, too, obey a superior one because they have to and not because it would give them particular pleassure. This takes place in general naturally enough. Let us observe this hand, for instance. It contains parts which are every moment at the service of that chief monad, which had the power, at their first inception, to attach them inseparably to itself. By means of them I can play this or that piece of music; I can make my fingers fly as I will over the keys of the pianoforte. They certainly thus procure me a delightful intellectual pleasure: but they are deaf; it is the chief monad alone that hears. I may therefore presume that my hand, or my fingers, are little, or not at all, interested in my playing. The exercise of monads, by means of which I procure enjoyment for myself, is very little for the good of my subjects; unless, perhaps, that it may tire them a little. How much better off they would be as to sensual enjoyment, could they, instead of idly roaming over the keys of my piano, fly about the meadows like busy bees, perch in a tree, or revel among its blossoms; and doubtless a disposition for all this exists in them. The moment of death, which is most appropriately called *dissolution,* is that in which the chief or ruling monad dismisses all those subordinate monads which have hitherto been faithful vassals in her service. I therefore regard leaving life, as well as being born into it, as a spontaneous act of this chief monad; which from its very constitution, is utterly unknown to us.

All monads are by nature so indestructible that even in the moment of dissolution they do not abate or lose anything of their activity, but continue it uninterruptedly. They part from their old connections only to enter into new ones at the same instant. In such changes, all depends upon the degree of strength of the germ of fulfilment contained in this or that monad. Whether the monad be that of a cultivated human soul, of a beaver, of a bird, of a fish, makes an immense difference. And here, we come again to the class or order of the souls which we are compelled to assume when we desire to explain to ourselves to any extent the phenomena of nature. . . . Annihilation is utterly out of the question; but the possibility of being caught on the way by some more powerful, and yet baser monad, and of becoming subordinated to it,—this is unquestionably a very serious consideration; and I for my part, have never been able entirely to divest myself of the fear of it on the basis of mere observation of nature. . . ."

I asked him whether he believed that the transition between these several stages were accompanied with consciousness in the monads themselves. To which Goethe replied: "That monads may be capable of a general historical review, I will not dispute, any more than that there may be among them higher natures than ourselves. The superior mind of a monad of the universe can and will elicit many things out of the dark bosom of its memory, which seem like divinations, though they be at bottom only dim recollections of some forgotten state, in other words memory; just as human genius discovered the laws concerning the origin of the universe not by dry study but by a lightning flash of recollection illuminating the darkness, because such genius itself was a party to their composition. It would be presumptuous to set bounds to such flashes in the memory of higher beings, or to attempt to determine at what point this illumination must stop. Thus, universally and historically viewed, the permanent and individual existence of the monad of a world appears to me by no means inconceivable. As to what more nearly concerns ourselves, it seems to me as if the former states or circumstances through which we and our planet have passed, were too insignificant and mediocre for much of it, in the eyes of nature, to have been worthy remembering again. Even the circumstances of our present condition would stand in need of great selection, and our chief monad, will, at some future time, grasp the whole of it at once, and summarily, i.e. in a few great historic stages. . . ."

"If we give ourselves up to our conjectures," said Goethe,

continuing his remarks, "I really do not see what should prevent the monad to which we are indebted for Wieland's appearance on our planet, from entering in its new state into the highest combinations this universe can present. By its industry, by its zeal, by its high intellect, which enabled it to master so large a portion of the history of the world, it has claim to everything. I should be so little surprised that I should find it entirely in accordance with my views on the subject, if thousands of years hence I were to meet this same Wieland as the monad of a world; as a star of the first magnitude; if I were to see him, and witness how he cheered everything that approached him by his beautiful light. To fashion the misty substance of some comet into light and clarity—that would be a truly welcome, pleasant task for the monad of our Wieland; as indeed, speaking generally, if we suppose the eternity of the actual state of the world, we can admit no other destiny for monads, than, as happily co-operating powers, to share eternally in the immortal joys of the gods. The work of creation is entrusted to them. Called or uncalled, they flock together of their own accord; in every way, from all mountains, out of all seas, from all stars—who may stop them? I am as certain, as you see me here, that I have been there a thousand times already, and hope to return a thousand times again."

"Pardon me," I interrupted, "I know not whether I should call a return without consciousness a return: for only he returns who knows that he has been in the same place before. During your observations of nature, bright recollections, and points of light from another state of the world, at which your monad was perhaps itself a co-operating agent, may have burst upon you; but all this rests upon a *perhaps;* I wish we were in a condition to attain greater certainty on matters of such moment, than we can obtain for ourselves through obscure divinations, and those flashes of genius which sometimes lighten the dark abyss of creation. Should we not come closer to our goal, if we only figured *one* loving chief monad as the central point of creation, which ruled all subordinate monads of this universe, in the same manner as our soul rules the inferior monads subordinate to her?"

"Against this conception, considered as faith, I have nothing to say," replied Goethe; "only I am accustomed to attach no exclusive value to ideas which have no foundation in the perceptions of the senses. Aye, indeed, if we did but know the structure of our own brain, and its connection with Uranus, and the thousandfold intersecting threads along which thought runs hither and thither. But as it is, we become conscious of the flashes of thought only when they strike. We know only ganglions, portions of the brain; of the nature of the brain itself we know nothing. What then can we pretend to know of God? Diderot has been greatly censured for saying: If there is not a God, then, perhaps there will be one. According to my views of nature and her laws, however, one may easily conceive of planets out of which the higher monads have already taken their departure, or in which they have not yet been called into activity. A constellation is required, such as is not to be had every day, to dissipate the waters and to dry up the land. As there are planets for men there may just as well be planets for fishes or for birds.

In one of our former conversations, I called man the first dialogue that nature held with God. I have not the least doubt that this dialogue may, in other planets, be kept up in a language far higher, deeper, and more significant. At present we are deficient in a thousand of the requisite kinds of knowledge. The very first that is wanting to us is self-knowledge; after this come all the others. Strictly considered, I can know nothing of God but what the very limited horizon of sensible perceptions on this planet affords ground for; and, that, on all points, is little enough. However, it is by no means asserted that, by this limitation of our observations on visible nature, limits are likewise set to our faith. On the contrary, the case may easily be, that with the immediacy of divine feelings in us, knowledge will appear piecemeal, and this especially on a planet which, wrenched out of its connection with the sun, leaves all observation imperfect, which for this very reason receives its full completion alone by faith. I have already taken occasion to remark in the *Theory of Colors* that there are primary phenomena, which, in their divine simplicity, we ought not to disturb and disarrange by useless enquiries, but leave to reason and faith. Let us endeavour to press forward courageously from both sides, only let us rigidly observe the boundaries at the same time. Let us not attempt to demonstrate what cannot be demonstrated! Otherwise sooner or later, we shall make our miserable deficiencies more glaring to posterity in our so called works of knowledge. Where knowledge is full and satisfactory, indeed, we stand not in need of faith; but where knowledge falls short, or appears inadequate, we must not contest with faith its rights. As soon as we set out from the principle that knowledge and faith are not given to destroy each other, but to supplement each other, we shall come near to an accurate estimate of the right."

It was late today when I left Goethe. He kissed my forehead at parting, contrary to his custom. I was going downstairs in the dark, but he would not permit me, and held me fast by the arm, till he rang for some one to light me out. At the door he warned me again to take care of myself, and to be on my guard against the rough night air. Never, before nor after, did I see Goethe in a softer mood than at the time of Wieland's death. . . .

On my return home, I wrote down the foregoing conversation; and I worked it out into certain results which have remained not without the greatest influence on the course of my life.

## FROM GOETHE'S DIARY

*Christiane, ill for many years, suffered from spasms, a condition which became so frighteningly bad that no one was able to stay with her for any length of time. She died shortly after her fifty-first birthday.*

June 2, 1816

MY WIFE'S CONDITION worsens. Minchen [a nurse] fell sick.

June 3

I SPENT a restless night worrying. The cook who was gripped by the same spasmodic fits had to go to bed. Frau von Heygendorf is with my wife who is still in great danger.

June 4

MY WIFE is still in the utmost danger. Kräuter [his secretary] stayed up with her during the night. I went with Hofrat Meyer for a ride. The air was very cool. We had luncheon together. Chancellor von Müller came after lunch. Suddenly I began to run a high fever and had to go to bed.

June 5

I HAVE SPENT the whole day in bed. My wife is still in the utmost danger. Our cook and Minchen are in fair condition. My son is now helper and counselor, in fact, the only solid point in this confusion. Kräuter was with me last night.

June 6

I HAVE SLEPT well and am feeling much better. My wife's end is approaching. The last terrible struggle of her life. She passed away about noon. Emptiness and deadly silence within me and outside of me.

# TWO AMERICANS IN WEIMAR

*In 1816 George Ticknor and Edward Everett completed their education at the then famous University of Göttingen. During a trip taken by the two Americans, George Ticknor kept a journal from which the following is an excerpt.*

Weimar, October 25, 1816

We sent our letters to Goethe this morning, and he returned for answer the message that he would be happy to see us at eleven o'clock. We went punctually, and he was ready to receive us. He is something above middle size, large but not gross, with gray hair, a dark, ruddy complexion, and full, rich, black eyes, which, though dimmed by age, are still very expressive. His whole countenance is old; and though his features are quiet and composed they bear decided traces of the tumult of early feeling and passion. Taken together, his person is not only respectable, but imposing. In his manners, he is simple.

He received us without ceremony, but with care and elegance, and made no German compliments. He spoke naturally of Wolf [distinguished scholar] as one of our letters was from him,—said he was a very great man, had delivered thirty-six different courses of lectures on different subjects connected with the study of antiquity, possessed the most remarkable memory he had ever known, and in genius and critical skill surpassed all the scholars of his time. In alluding to his last publication, he said he had written his "Life of Bentley" with uncommon talent, because in doing it he had exhibited and defended his own character, and in all he said showed that he had high admiration and regard for him.

Of Lord Byron, he spoke with interest and discrimination, —said that his poetry showed great knowledge of human nature and great talent in description; Lara, he thought, bordered on the kingdom of spectres; and of his late separation from his wife, that, in its circumstances and the mystery in which it is involved, it is so poetical, that if Lord Byron had invented it he could hardly have had a more fortunate subject for his genius. All this he said in a quiet, simple manner, which would have surprised me much, if I had known him only through his books; and it made me feel how bitter must have been Jean Paul's disappointment [famous German novelist] who came to him expecting to find in his conversation the characteristics of "Werther" and "Faust." Once his genius is kindled, and in spite of himself he grew almost fervent as he deplored the want of extemporary eloquence in Germany, and said, what I never heard before, but which is eminently true, that English is kept a much more living language by its influence. "Here", he said "we have no eloquence, our preaching is a monotonous middling declamation, public debate we have not at all, and if a little inspiration comes to us in our lecture-rooms, it is out of place, for eloquence does not teach." We remained with him nearly an hour, and when we came away he accompanied us as far as the parlor door with the same simplicity with which he received us, without any German congratulations.

October 28

Professor Riemer, who is second librarian of the public library, called on us and amused us above an hour, by describing Goethe's mode of living, peculiarities etc.—facts one cannot get in books, or from any source but the knowledge of an intimate acquaintance. Riemer lived nine years in Goethe's house, and knew him, of course, from the lowest note to the top of his compass. He said that Goethe is a much greater man than the world will ever know, because he always needs excitement and collision to rouse him to exertion, and that it is a great misfortune that he is now without such influence and example as when Herder, Wieland and Schiller were alive.

I asked what had been his relation with those extraordinary men. He replied that, from holding similar views in philosophy, Goethe and Schiller were nearest to each other, and Herder and Wieland; but that after the death of Schiller and Herder, Goethe became intimate with Wieland. Schiller, he said, had profited much by his connection with Goethe, and borrowed much from his genius,—among other pieces, in his "Wilhelm Tell", which Goethe had earlier thought to have made the subject of an epic poem; but now they are all dead, and since 1813 Goethe has been alone in the world.

He has much on paper which has never been published, and much in his memory which has not been put on paper, for he writes always by an amanuensis, to whom he dictates from memoranda on a card or scrap of paper, as he walks up and down his room. Of his views in physics and comparative anatomy, he has published little, but a programme by a medical professor at Jena [Oken] has lately made a great noise, in which the doctrine that the brain is formed from the medulla spinalis was, no doubt, from hints first given by Goethe.

Among the many unpublished things he has on hand, are parts of a continuation of "Faust," which Riemer had seen, in which the devil brings Faust to court and makes him a great man; and some poems in the Persian style and taste which he wrote during the last war, to give a relief to his imagination and feelings by employing himself on something that had no connection with Europe.

He lives now, in his old age, in unconsoled solitude; sees almost nobody, and rarely goes out. His enjoyment of life seems gone, his inclination for exertion gone, and nothing remains to him, that I can see, but a very few years of cold and unsatisfied retirement.

## J. G. COGSWELL TO MRS. DAVEIS

*Joseph Green Cogswell joined his friend George Ticknor at the University of Göttingen to take courses in Natural Sciences. Goethe took a special liking to the young American and kept up a correspondence with him about scientific matters.*

Berlin, April 17, 1817

I WENT to Weimar almost for the sole purpose of seeing Goethe, but he was absent on a visit to Jena, where I pursued him and obtained an audience. From all that I had heard of him, I was prepared to meet with the most repulsive reception, but, as I actually experienced the directly opposite, you will naturally infer that I felt not a little flattered, and therefore will not be surprised if I should give you a more favorable picture of him than you find in the "Edinburgh Review." I sent him my letters of introduction, with a note, asking when he would allow me to wait upon him. In one of the letters it was observed that I had some fondness for mineralogy, and was desirous of seeing the great cabinet, belonging to the society of which he is president, at Jena. In a few moments he returned me an answer, that he would meet me in the rooms of the society at noon, and there show me all that was to be seen. I liked this, as it evinced some degree of modesty in him, inasmuch as it implied that there was something, beside himself, worthy of my notice, and as it was very polite, too, in offering to take upon himself the trouble of going through the explanation of a collection, filling numerous and large apartments.

At noon, then, I went to meet this giant of German literature, the creator and sole governor of their taste. His exterior was in every respect different from the conceptions I had formed. A grand and graceful form, worthy of a knight of the days of chivalry, with a dignity of manners that marked the court rather than the closet, such as belong to Goethe, are not often the external characteristics of a man of letters. Soon after being introduced to him, with the politeness of a real gentleman, he turned the conversation to America, and he spoke of its hopes and promises, in a manner that showed it had been the subject of his inquiries, and made juster and more rational observations, upon its literary pretensions and character, than I ever heard from any man in Europe. We talked, also, of English and German literature. I told him of the interest we were now taking in the latter, and found a very convenient opportunity to introduce a few words of compliment to himself, which was the least return I could make for his civility.

That you may not think I have made too great progress in German, I just observe that this conversation which lasted an hour, was carried on in French. I suppose I might have managed the former; but I was afraid of going wrong, sometimes, with the titles of the Herr Minister von Goethe, and therefore proposed to him to adopt French, where I had only "Votre Excellence" to handle.

After we finished our literary discussions he carried me through the whole cabinet, and explained to me all its remarkables with a facility that could not have been exceeded by a Professor of Mineralogy. When we parted he invited me to call on him, whenever I should be in Weimar, and so managed the whole interview I had with him, that I left him inclined to enter the lists in his defense, if I should ever have occasion.

## GOETHE TO J. G. COGSWELL

*Goethe presented Harvard, about which he was well informed through his American visitors, with a set of his collected works and a number of other publications. In his letter of dedication to the University Goethe expressed his "deep interest in its high literary character."*

Weimar, August 11, 1819

YOU WILL RECEIVE with this, my dear friend, through Messrs. Bassange & Co., a parcel containing my poetical and scientific writings, mentioned in this list. They are well packed, and I desire they should not be taken out. Perhaps, on account of the long journey, you will have them enclosed in a box; but this I leave to you.

If you can, when forwarding to your dear fellow countrymen these results of my studies and labors, represent me kindly to them, I shall acknowledge the favor gratefully.

I also am preparing for a journey to Carlsbad, but still beg you will send me here the news of the safe arrival of the parcel. I should have wished very much to be able to study with you some remarkable points in that important mountain region. If you will let me know what numbers, in your collection of Carlsbad minerals, are wanting, I can perhaps send them to you.

In making a careful study of Mr. Warden's very interesting works [studies about the U. S. A.] I often find myself transported to your home, where I shall visit you diligently in thought and feeling, if you really leave us.

Be happy and content, and let us hear from you frequently, as well on this side as on that. I am eagerly expecting the promised periodicals. Faithfully—GOETHE.

## J. G. COGSWELL TO MRS. PRESCOTT

Leipzig, August 28, 1819

I HAVE JUST RETURNED here from the journey of leave-taking which I wrote you I was about to make. I went first to Weimar to see Goethe, and as he was absent at Jena I followed him there. They say in Germany that he is proud and has no heart, but it has ever been my good fortune to see him when he showed none of his pride, and to be received by him as if he had a heart, and a feeling one too. I know not when I was more touched at parting from a person to whom I was bound by no particular tie, than from him.

When I reached Jena he was from home. I waited several hours to see him, and, as he did not return till nearly night, I could remain but a few moments with him. "What brings you to Jena?" said he. "To take leave of you." "And how long will you stay with me?" "Half an hour." "I thank you from the heart for this mark of your regard. It delights me to find that you take such an interest in me in my old age, as to come so far to see me. Keep me, I beg you, in friendly remembrance." "Shall I write to you when I return to America?" "Yes, but you'll not wait till then I hope. Let me hear from you while you remain in Europe." A little further conversation and I parted from him. He embraced and kissed me affectionately according to the German custom, and the tear in his eye convinced me that he felt, not feigned, what he expressed.

Do not think I mean to make out of this a case to flatter my own vanity. Goethe's attention to me has been highly grateful, I confess, but it gives me no occasion to be vain, because I saw clearly it was my heart and not my mind which interested him.

Another great satisfaction I enjoyed in this part of my journey was the visit I made to the Grand Duke of Weimar, and that not because he is a Grand Duke, but because being a Grand Duke, he is also highly estimable as a man. He is a great patron and friend of science, and, what is better as a prince, a great friend to his subjects, and if he were a little more moral in some respects, he would be a pattern of a sovereign. He was very curious to know what I thought of Europe. His idea was, that everything here must appear to me to be in ruins, having lived in a land where freshness and youth are the characteristics of every object. He was candid enough, too, to say he supposed we were free from moral and political corruptions, and I should have confirmed him in the belief if I could have done it with truth.

## F. ZELTER TO GOETHE

Vienna, August 16, 1819

BEETHOVEN has gone to the country, but no one knows where; he has just written a letter from Baden to one of his lady friends, but *he* is not at Baden. He is said to be intolerably *maussade;* some say he is a fool,—that's easily said. Heaven forgive us all our sins! The poor man, they say, is completely deaf. I know how I feel when I look at the fingering here, and I—poor devil!—one finger of mine after the other gets useless.

Recently, Beethoven went to an inn, sat down at a table and, after an hour's meditation, called out to the waiter: "How much do I owe you?"

"Why, Your Honor has not yet eaten anything. What shall I bring you?"

"Bring what you like, but leave me alone!"

His patron is said to be the Archduke Rudolf, who allows him 1,500 Gulden (paper money) a year. With this he must try to manage like all other artists in Vienna. They are kept there like cats, and anyone who does not understand the art of mousing will hardly save anything, and yet, in spite of this, they are all as round and jolly as weasels.

September 14

THE DAY BEFORE YESTERDAY I went to Mödling to pay Beethoven a visit. He was just on his way to Vienna, and meeting each other on the road we got out of our carriages and embraced each other most heartily. The poor man is so deaf that I could hardly keep back my tears. I then continued to drive to Mödling and he to Vienna . . .

I must tell you a joke which I enjoyed uncommonly. My travelling companion on this occasion was Steiner, the music publisher, and as one does not get much talk with a deaf man on a public highway, it was arranged that Beethoven and I should meet properly in Steiner's music shop at four o'clock in the afternoon. Directly after lunch, we drove back to Vienna. Full as a badger and dog-tired I lay down and slept so soundly that I forgot everything. Then I strolled away to the theatre and, when I saw Beethoven in a distance, I felt quite dumbfounded. He was evidently undergoing the same process when discovering me, but this was not the place to come to an understanding with a deaf man. But the point of the story is yet to come.

In spite of all kinds of criticism to which Beethoven, rightly or wrongly, is here exposed, he enjoys that respectful consideration which is only given to distinguished men. Steiner had immediately made public that Beethoven would appear in person in his narrow shop, which holds some six or eight people, at four o'clock for the first time. He had also invited some guests so that fifty learned men crowded in the street for want of room were waiting there in vain. I myself only learned the real state of things next day when I got a letter from Beethoven in which he excused himself (in a way that pleased me admirably), because like myself he had happily slept away the time of the rendezvous!

# A CRITICAL APPRAISAL

*As a youth of nineteen the historian George Bancroft was studying at the University of Göttingen. On a holiday trip he visited Jena and made the following entry in his diary:*

October 12, 1819

I VISITED GOETHE towards noon. He was talkative and affable, began at first with speaking of common affairs. Then the discourse came on German philosophy, Kant was mentioned with reverence. The state of America then became the subject of conversation. He seemed to think he was quite well acquainted with it. He spoke of several books on the country, of Warden's Statistical Account etc. Then too, Cogswell had given him an essay on American literature, which had appeared in Edinburgh. This essay Goethe praised much for the beauty of its style and for the liveliness and fancy with which it was written, and smiled as he mentioned the freedom with which he spoke of the different professions. Then the talk was of Cogswell—"a man of great excellence." He spoke with pleasure of the visits Cogswell had paid him.

At length I, gathering courage from talking with him, took occasion to bring upon the British poets. Byron he praised in the highest terms, declared himself one of a large party in Germany who admired him unboundedly and seized on and swallowed everything that came from him. Of Scott we had time to talk; of Wordsworth, Southey he knew nothing; of Coleridge the name—had forgotten however his works. The author of "Bertram," C. R. Maturin, was praised. The tragedy, said Goethe, has many beautiful passages. Byron, however, seemed to remain the most admired of all. After this, Goethe asked after my pursuits, praised me, on my mentioning them, for coming to Germany, and spoke a word or two on Oriental matters. After this he asked what way I was to take the next day, and finding I was going to Weimar, offered me at once a letter which should make me welcome to the library. After a few more remarks I departed. . . .

As for his person, Goethe is somewhat large, though not very, with a marked countenance, a fine clear eye, large and very expressive features, well built, and giving at once a favorable impression. In his manners he is very dignified, or rather he has a sort of dignified stiffness, which he means should pass for genuine dignity. He walks amazingly upright. I found him quite in dishabille. He had on a surtout, but no waistcoat, a ruffled shirt, not altogether clean, a cravat like the shirt, fast inclining to dark complexion. His boots were of quite an ordinary cut. No dandy would have worn them. He received me in the garden.

## MARIANNE VON WILLEMER TO GOETHE

*In the fall of 1819 the "West-Eastern Divan" was published, a cycle of poems that reflect Goethe's tender relationship to Marianne von Willemer, young wife of a Frankfort banker. Marianne was the inspiration for the figure of Suleika who inflamed the aging Persian poet Hafis to new love and passion. The following letter makes allusion to the fact, discovered only many years later, that Goethe had included in his volume a number of poems composed by Marianne herself, who had so sensitively absorbed the poet's world of thoughts that her verses needed only slight changes.*

October, 1819

I HAVE READ and re-read the "Divan;" I can neither describe nor even explain to myself the feeling which gripped me with each familiar tone. If my being and my inmost soul have become as clear to you as I hope and wish, in fact, as I am sure of—since my heart lay bare before your eyes—then it does not need a description which could be only highly imperfect. You felt and knew exactly what was going on in me; I was a puzzle to myself. Humble and proud at the same time, ashamed and delighted, everything seemed to me an enraptured dream in which one recognizes one's own image beautified and ennobled and in which one likes to accept everything lovable and praiseworthy that is spoken and done in this exalted condition. In fact, even the unmistakable co-operation of a mighty, higher being—inasmuch as it attributes merits to us, which we perhaps do not possess, and discovers others, which we did not think we possessed—is so enchanting in its cause that one cannot do anything else but accept it as a gift of the gods if life has such silver views. Be indulgent with me and my confused ideas, the greatest happiness is always least comprehensible.

## A MUSICAL TEST

*In November, 1821, Zelter brought his star pupil Felix Mendelssohn to Weimar. The then 12-year-old Felix, was not only a brilliant pianist, but also an artist whose improvisations indicated already the future composer. The writer, Ludwig Rellstab, tells in his autobiography how Goethe put the youthful prodigy to the test.*

IN THE EVENING, we assembled in Goethe's rooms for tea; for he had invited a large party of his Weimar musical acquaintances to make them acquainted with the boy's extraordinary talents. Presently Goethe made his appearance: he came from his study, and had a habit—at least I generally noticed it—of waiting till all the guests were assembled, ere he showed himself. Till that period, his son and daughter-in-law did the duties of host in the most amiable way. A certain solemnity was visible among the guests, prior to the entrance of the great poet; and even those who stood on terms of intimacy with him underwent a feeling of veneration. His slow, serious walk; his impressive features, which expressed the strength rather than weakness of old age; the lofty forehead; the white, abundant hair; lastly, the deep voice, and slow way of speaking—all united to produce the effect. His "good evening" was addressed to all; but he walked up to Zelter first, and shook his hand cordially. Felix Mendelssohn looked up, with sparkling eyes, at the snow-white head of the poet. The latter, however, placed his hands kindly on the boy's head, and said, "Now you shall play us something." Zelter nodded his assent.

The piano was opened, and lights arranged on the desk. Mendelssohn asked Zelter, to whom he displayed a thoroughly childlike devotion and confidence, "What shall I play?"

"Well, what you can," the latter replied, in his peculiarly sharp voice; "whatever is not too difficult for you."

To me, who knew what the boy could do, and that no task was too difficult for him, this seemed an unjust depreciation of his faculties. It was at length arranged that he should play a fantasia; which he did to the wonder of all. But the young artist knew when to leave off; and thus the effect he produced was all the greater. A silence of surprise ensued when he raised his hands from the keys after a loud finale.

Zelter was the first to interrupt the silence in his humorous way, by saying aloud, "Ha! you must have been dreaming of kobolds and dragons: why, that went over fine!" At the same time there was a perfect indifference in his tone, as if there were nothing remarkable in the matter. Without doubt, the teacher intended to prevent, in this way, the danger of too brilliant a triumph. The playing, however, as it could not well do otherwise, aroused the highest admiration in all present; and Goethe, especially, was full of the warmest delight. He encouraged the lad, in whose childish features joy, pride, and confusion were at once depicted, by taking his head between his hands, patting him kindly, and saying jestingly, "But you will not get off with that. You must play more pieces before we recognize your merits."

"But what shall I play?" Felix asked: "Herr Professor,"—he was wont to address Zelter by this title,—"what shall I play now?"

I cannot say that I have properly retained the pieces the young virtuoso now performed; for they were numerous. I will, however, mention the most interesting.

Goethe was a great admirer of Bach's fugues, which a musician of Berka, a little town about ten miles from Weimar, came to play to him repeatedly. Felix was therefore requested to play a fugue by the great old master. Zelter selected it from the music-book; and the boy played it without any preparation, but with perfect certainty.

Goethe's delight grew with the boy's extraordinary powers. Among other things, he requested him to play a minuet.

"Shall I play you the loveliest in the whole world?" he asked with sparkling eyes.

"Well, and which is that?"

He played the minuet from "Don Giovanni."

Goethe stood by the instrument, listening; joy glistening in his features. He wished for the overture of the opera after the minuet; but this the player roundly declined, with the assertion, that it could not be played as it was written, and nobody dared make any alteration in it. He, however, offered to play the overture to "Figaro." He commenced it with a lightness of touch,—such certainty and clearness as I never heard again. At the same time he gave the orchestral effects so magnificently that the effect was extraordinary; and I can honestly state, that it afforded me more gratification than ever an orchestral performance did. Goethe grew more and more cheerful and kind, and even played tricks with the talented lad.

"Well, come," he said, "you have only played me pieces you know; but now we will see whether you can play something you do not know. I will put you on trial."

Goethe went out, re-entered the room in a few moments, and had a roll of music in his hand. "I have fetched something from my manuscript collection. Now we will try you. Do you think you can play this?"

He laid a page, with clear but small notes, on the desk. It was Mozart's handwriting. Whether Goethe told us so, or it was written on the paper, I forgot, and only remember that Felix glowed with delight at the name; and an indescribable feeling came over us all, partly enthusiasm and joy, partly admiration and expectation. Goethe, the aged man, laying a manuscript of Mozart, who had been buried thirty years, before a lad so full of promise for the future, to play at sight,—in truth such a constellation may be termed a rarity.

The young artist played with the most perfect certainty, not making the slightest mistake, though the manuscript was far from easy reading. The task was certainly not difficult, especially for Mendelssohn, as it was only an adagio: still there was a difficulty in doing it as the lad did; for he played it as if he had been practising it for years.

Goethe adhered to his good-humored tone, while all the rest applauded. "That is nothing," he said: "others could read that too. But I will now give you something over which you will stick; so take care."

With these words, he produced another paper, which he laid on the desk. This certainly looked very strange. It was difficult to say if they were notes or only a paper, ruled, and splashed with ink and blots. Felix Mendelssohn, in his surprise, laughed loudly. "How is that written? who can read it?" he said.

But suddenly he became serious; for while Goethe was saying, "Now guess who wrote it?" Zelter, who had walked up to the piano, and looked over the boy's shoulder, exclaimed, "Why, Beethoven wrote that! any one could see it a mile off. He always writes with a broomstick, and passes his sleeve over the notes before they are dry. I have plenty of his manuscripts. They are easy to recognize."

At the mention of the name, as I remarked, Mendelssohn had suddenly grown serious,—even more than serious. A shade of awe was visible on his features. Goethe regarded him with searching eyes, from which delight beamed. The boy kept his eyes immovably fixed on the manuscript; and a look of glad surprise flew over his features as he traced a brilliant thought amid the chaos of confused, blurred notes.

But all this lasted only a few seconds; for Goethe wished to make a severe trial, and give the performer no time for preparation. "You see," he exclaimed, "I told you that you would stick. Now try it: show us what you can do."

Felix began playing immediately. It was a simple melody; if clearly written, a trifle, I may say no task, for even a moderate performer. But to follow it through the scrambling labyrinth required a quickness and certainty of eye such as few are able to attain. I glanced with surprise at the leaf, and tried to hum the tune; but many of the notes were perfectly illegible, or had to be sought at the most unexpected corners, as the boy often pointed out with a laugh.

He played it through once in this way, generally correctly, but stopping at times, and correcting several mistakes with a quick "No, so!" then he exclaimed, "Now I will play it to you." And, this second time, not a note was missing. "This is Beethoven, this passage," he said once turning to me, as if he had come across something which sharply displayed the master's peculiar style. "That is true Beethoven. I recognize him in it at once."

With this trial-piece Goethe broke off. I need scarcely add, that the young player again reaped the fullest praise, which Goethe veiled in mocking jests.

## FELIX MENDELSSOHN TO HIS FAMILY

Weimar, November, 1821

Now, stop and listen, all of you. Today is Tuesday. On Sunday, the sun of Weimar—Goethe—arrived. In the morning we went to church, and they gave us half of Händel's 100th Psalm. The organ is large, but weak; the Marien-organ [at Berlin] small as it is, is much more powerful.

Afterwards I went to the Elephant-Hotel, where I sketched the house of Lucas Cranach. Two hours afterwards Professor Zelter came and said: "Goethe has come—the old gentleman's come!" In a minute we were down the steps and in Goethe's house. He was in the garden, and was just coming round a corner. Isn't it strange, dear father, that was exactly how you met him? He is very kind, but I don't think any of the pictures are like him.

He was looking over his collection of fossils which his son had arranged for him, and kept saying, "I am very much pleased." After that I stayed in the garden with him and Professor Zelter for half an hour. Then came dinner. One would never take him for seventy-three, but for fifty. After dinner Fräulein Ulrike, the sister of Frau von Goethe, asked for a kiss, and I did the same. Every morning I get a kiss from the author of "Faust" and "Werther" and every afternoon two kisses from my friend and father Goethe. Think of that!

After dinner I played for Goethe for two hours and more, partly Bach fugues, and partly extempore. In the evening they played whist, and Professor Zelter, who played with them at first, said, "Whist means that you are to hold your tongue!" What a good saying! We had supper all together, even Goethe too, though generally he never eats anything in the evening. Now, my dear grumbling Fanny, [Felix's sister] yesterday morning I took your songs to Frau von Goethe, who has a pretty voice. She is going to sing them to the old gentleman. I told him that you had written some, and asked if he would hear them. He said, "Yes, yes, very willingly." Frau von Goethe liked them very much, which is a good omen. He is to hear them today or tomorrow. . . .

Every afternoon Goethe opens the Streicher-Piano with these words, "I have not heard you at all today, so you must make a little noise for me." Then he sits down by me, and when I have finished (generally improvising) I beg for a kiss, or else I take one. You can have no conception of his goodness and kindness, nor of the quantity of minerals, busts, engravings, statuettes, and large drawings which this polar-star of poets has in his possession. That he has an imposing figure, I cannot see; he is really not much bigger than father. But his look, his language, his name, they are imposing. His voice has an enormous sound in it, and he can shout like ten thousand fighting men. His hair is not yet white, his walk is steady, and his manner of speaking gentle.

Zelter wanted to go to Jena on Tuesday, and from there on to Leipzig. On Saturday, Adele Schopenhaur [the sister of the philosopher] came to us, and, contrary to his custom, Goethe stayed the whole evening. The conversation turned upon our departure, and Adele proposed that we should all go and throw ourselves at Professor Zelter's feet and implore for a few days' grace. He was dragged into the room, and then Goethe burst out with his thundering voice, scolded Professor Zelter for wanting to take us away to the old nest, commanded him to be silent, to obey without a word, to leave me here, to go to Jena alone and then come back—in fact he so completely drove him into a corner that he will do everything that Goethe wishes. After this Goethe was assailed by everybody with kisses on his mouth and hands, and whoever could not reach these, stroked and kissed his shoulders; if he had not been at home, I think we should have taken him to his house, as the Roman people did Cicero after the first Catiline oration. Fräulein Ulrike also had thrown herself upon his neck, and as he is making love to her, and she is very pretty, the effect of the whole was capital.

# FROM F. VON MÜLLER'S DIARY

*After an unusual career in the judicial service of Saxe-Weimar, Friedrich von Müller in 1815 became the chief justiciar of the Grand-Duke, a position from which he derived the title "Chancellor." Though the relationship of this rather independent personality with Goethe was in the beginning not without friction, Müller in later years became one of the close friends of the poet.*

February 3, 1823

I MET GOETHE at about 6 o'clock in the evening quite alone; only his little grandson was scanning a picture book and his frequent lively questions were patiently answered by the old man from time to time. But finally, with a great deal of persuasion, he went to sleep on the bed in the small adjacent room.

The important news of the day, the war with Spain, gave the foundation to our conversation. . . . The opposition of the people of Württemberg to the supreme power of Austria seemed to him absurd, as would any opposition which, at the same time, did not strive toward something positive.

"If I had the misfortune of belonging to the opposition, I'd rather instigate uproar and revolution than move in the sinister circle of constant censure of everything that exists. Never in my life have I desired to place myself in inimical, senseless opposition to the powerful stream of the crowd or to the ruling principle; I'd rather retreat into my own shell and there dwell to my liking. We can see in Knebel where constant opposition and ill-tempered criticism and negation leads; it has made him the most dissatisfied and the unhappiest man;

his innermost soul eaten up as if from cancer; one cannot live with him in peace for two days, because he attacks everything that is dear to us."

In the course of our conversation we spoke of the election for the diet and of various members of the council whom I had to depict according to their individualities, and we also spoke of Riemer and his present ill-humor. Goethe stated that he has more talent and knowledge than he is able to bear according to the strength of his character. I carefully tried to make Goethe contribute to Riemer's encouragement through friendly attention, which finally showed good results.

Then he began to speak of an actual theory of dissatisfaction. Whatever we nourish in ourselves grows; that is an eternal law of nature. There is an organ of displeasure, of dissatisfaction in us, as there is one of opposition and doubt. The more food we provide for it and the more we practice it, the mightier it becomes, until it turns from an organ into a malignant ulcer and banefully eats up its environment, drains and strangles all the good humors of the body. Then repentence, self-reproach and other absurdities are added to it, we become unjust toward others and ourselves. The joy at one's own success and action as well as that of others is lost, in our desperation we finally look for the reason of all evil outside ourselves instead of finding it in our mental perversion. One should see every person and every event in its real light, one should step beyond oneself to be able to return to oneself all the more free.

February 18

AT NOON, with General von Egloffstein, I was startled by the news which my brother had just been told by Dr. Rehbein that Goethe had suffered a serious heart attack. I ran there immediately after lunch and was told that they had bled him. I met Dr. Huschke, saw the polluted blood and heard from the physicians' lips that the probability of saving his life was 2 to 10.

Ulrike von Levetzow

Verlaßt mich hier, getreue Weggenossen!
Laßt mich allein am Fels, in Moor und Moos;
Nur immer zu! euch ist die Welt erschlossen,
Die Erde weit, der Himmel hehr und gros;
Betrachtet, forscht, die Einzelnheiten sammelt,
Naturgeheimniß werde nachgestammelt.

Mir ist das All, ich bin mir selbst verlohren,
Der ich noch erst den Göttern Liebling war;
Sie prüften mich verliehen mir Pandoren,
So reich an Gütern, reicher an Gefahr;
Sie drängten mich zum gabeseligen Munde,
Sie trennen mich, und richten mich zu Grunde

The last stanzas of the "Marienbader Elegy" in Goethe's own handwriting

Johann Peter Eckermann

Friedrich von Müller

*Drawings by J. J. Schmeller*

Ottilie von Goethe

February 22

From Thursday to Saturday his condition changed continuously, improved and relapsed. Every afternoon I spent an hour with his son or with Ottilie or Ulrike. He was often unconscious, sometimes he spoke as if in delirium, but in between he seemed to speak intelligibly and with interest. . . .

Once he said to his servant Stadelmann in a low tone: "You can't imagine how sick I am, how *very* sick." He often admonished the doctors to think seriously about his condition, whereby he did not conceal that he had some disbelief in their art. "Continue your tricks and devices, it's all right with me; but you won't be able to save me." Several times he asked for a hot bath which was considered too daring. Once when the physicians spoke with each other in a low voice, he said: "There go the Jesuits, they can consult with each other, but they can't help or save me." He lamented that everybody gave him such arbitrary, confounded stuff to swallow and that his good children Ottilie and Ulrike were misused to make him swallow it.

Whenever he felt better for a moment, he wanted his daughter-in-law to indulge in her usual social pleasures, to go to the theatre and to Court. Every service rendered was acknowledged with gratitude and nice words or an obliging gesture. "Well, you bunnies, why do you tiptoe like this," he said to Ottilie Saturday morning when she came close to his bed. Almost constantly he sat on his bed or in the grandfather chair which Frau von Egloffstein, a lady-in-waiting, had sent him and which he praised a great deal saying: "With this present she assured herself a step on the stairway to heaven."

Saturday he was permitted to drink a glass of champagne which had no visible effect. With great delight he ate a pear and strawberry jelly. Once he spoke half aloud to himself: "I only wonder whether this entity, so torn asunder and tortured, will be able to reappear as an entity and take new shape." He said to Ulrike: "Ah, you can't believe how many ideas are tormenting me, how they zigzag and confuse me."

February 23

HIS CONDITION was worse on Sunday. Early in the morning he said to his son: "Death is standing in all corners around me." Several times to Dr. Huschke: "I am lost." Once he is supposed to have said: "O Christian God, how much suffering you pile up for your poor creatures and yet we shall laud and praise you for it in your temples." In the morning I was in Stadelmann's chamber next to his room, in the evening before I went to Court I was in his house for an hour again. Dr. Rehbein told him: "Inspiration comes easier than expiration." —"Of course, it does," he answered, "I feel it most, you dogs!"

February 24

IN THE AFTERNOON, from 4 to 9, I was with Goethe, in the adjacent room. The night had been very bad. His pulse often stopped, they feared a stroke. He was told that the Grand-Duke often wanted to come to him, but he was dissuaded from going to see him. He replied: "If I were a *Prince,* no one could keep me from doing what I want. The prince must force his way through, he must not take notice of such conspiracies." In the afternoon, he became very violent in his attitude towards the physicians, demanded impetuously some Kreuzbrunnen saying: "If I have got to die, then I'll die in my own way." He really drank a small bottle of Kreuzbrunnen with obviously good result. Previously he had said to his son: "This is the struggle between life and death."

## GOETHE TO AUGUSTE ZU STOLBERG

*After forty years of silence Auguste wrote to Goethe and expressed her apprehension about his spiritual welfare in her letter. Here is Goethe's answer.*

Weimar, April 17, 1823

I WAS GREATLY MOVED and delighted to receive again the handwriting of a dear friend of pleasant memories, whom my eyes have never seen, but who is well known to my heart. Nevertheless, I hesitate, undecided, as to what I could say in reply. Let me speak more in general terms, since we know nothing about each other in particular.

To live long means to survive a great many things, beloved and hated people and those to whom we feel indifferent, to survive kingdoms, great cities, and also forests and trees which we sowed and planted in our youth. We even survive ourselves and certainly realize it with gratitude, even if only a few gifts of body and mind may remain. We accept all these transient events; if only the eternal is with us every moment, then we don't suffer from fleeting time.

I have dealt with myself and others in sincerity all my life and, whatever I have done here on earth, I have always aimed at the most sublime. So have you and your like done. Therefore, let us continue to work as long as there is day for us, for others the sun will shine too, they will excel themselves in its rays and, by doing so, give us a brighter light.

And so we can remain unconcerned about the future! There are many provinces in our Father's realm and, since He allows us to settle down in such a joyful manner here on earth, then certainly both of us will be provided for in the beyond. Maybe, we will then succeed in what we could not achieve up to now, to meet face to face and to love each other all the more deeply. Remember me with calm faithfulness.

The above was written immediately after the arrival of your kind letter, but I did not dare send it, since—against my will and knowledge some time ago—I hurt the feelings of your noble, brave brother with similar utterances. Now, however, since I have returned to life from a deadly disease, this page shall nevertheless reach you to report at once: that the Almighty has granted me the privilege to see the beautiful light of his sun again; may the day seem friendly to you too and may you think of me with good and kind thoughts as I do not cease remembering those days when all that afterwards was separated still worked in harmonious effort.

May we all find each other again in the arms of our all-loving Father.

# ECKERMANN COMES TO WEIMAR

*Johann Peter Eckermann came to Weimar to solicit Goethe's recommendation for the publication of his own literary work. The young man, who had struggled hard to get his education, made such a favorable impression on Goethe that the poet thought of means to retain him in Weimar. He used Eckermann first to help him in editing his early writings and made him later his main assistant. Eckermann's collection of conversations with Goethe, a project in which the poet himself took an active interest, has long since become a classic. The selections here presented are from a modernized translation of "Goethe's Conversations with Eckermann" to be published by New Directions.*

Weimar, June 10th, 1823

I ARRIVED HERE a few days ago, but did not see Goethe till today. He received me with great cordiality; and the impression made on me was such that I consider this day as one of the happiest in my life. Yesterday, when I called to inquire, he fixed today at twelve o'clock as the time when he would be glad to see me. I went at the appointed time, and found a servant waiting to lead me to him.

The interior of the house made a very pleasant impression on me; without being showy, everything was extremely simple and noble. The casts from antique statues, placed on the stairs, indicated Goethe's especial partiality for plastic art and Grecian antiquity. I saw several ladies moving busily about in the lower part of the house, and one of Ottilie's beautiful boys [Goethe's grandson] came familiarly up to me and looked fixedly in my face.

After I had glanced around, I went up the stairs with the very talkative servant to the first floor. He opened a room, on the threshold of which was the motto *Salve* as a good omen of a friendly welcome. He led me through this apartment and opened another, somewhat more spacious, where he asked me to wait while he announced me to his master. The air here was most cool and refreshing. On the floor was spread a carpet; the room was furnished with a crimson sofa and chairs, which gave a cheerful appearance. On one side stood a piano; and the walls were decorated with many pictures and drawings of various sorts and sizes. Through an open door opposite, a farther room, also hung with pictures, could be seen through which the servant had gone to announce me.

It was not long before Goethe came in, dressed in a blue frockcoat and with shoes. What a sublime form! The impression upon me was surprising. But he soon put me at my ease with the kindest words. We sat down on the sofa. I felt a happy perplexity because of his look and his presence, and could say little or nothing.

He began by speaking of my manuscript. "I have just come from *you,*" he said; "I have been reading your writing all the morning; it needs no recommendation—it recommends itself." He praised the clearness of the style, the flow of the thought, and the unusual fact that all rested on a solid basis and had been thoroughly considered. "I will forward it soon," he said; "Today I shall write to Cotta [Goethe's publisher] by post, and send him the parcel tomorrow." I thanked him by words and looks. We then talked of my proposed excursion. I told him that my plan was to go into the Rhineland, where I intended to stay at a suitable place, and write something new. First, however, I would go to Jena, and there wait for Herr von Cotta's answer. Goethe asked whether I knew anyone at Jena. I replied that I hoped to meet Herr von Knebel and he promised me a letter which would insure me a more favorable reception. "And while you are in Jena", he said "we shall be neighbors, and can see or write one another as often as we please."

We sat a long while together, in a quiet, affectionate mood. I was close to him; I forgot to talk for looking at him—I could not look enough. His face is so powerful and brown, full of wrinkles, and each wrinkle full of expression! And everywhere such nobleness and firmness, such repose and greatness! He spoke in a slow, confidant manner, such as you would expect from an aged monarch. You realize by his bearing that he relies on himself, and is elevated far above both praise and blame. I was extremely happy near him; I felt calm like one who, after many efforts and tedious hopes, finally sees his dearest wishes gratified.

## GOETHE'S LAST PASSION

*During one of his summer trips to Bohemia Goethe made the acquaintance of the family Levetzow and was, on this occasion, gripped by a passionate feeling for the 19-year-old Ulrike. When the 74-year-old poet realized the impossibility of an alliance with the young girl, he once more went through all the sufferings of renunciation. He gave a most moving expression to his feelings in his "Marienbader Elegy." Ulrike von Levetzow, who never married, described her relationship to Goethe many years later as follows:*

GOETHE never spoke of marriage, neither to my mother nor to me, although he called me his "darling," but most of the time his "dear daughter."

In 1823, we were in Marienbad with him for only a short time, since my mother had to stay in Carlsbad. But Goethe came there for a few days, stayed in the same house with us and was always with us, for breakfast and all other meals. In the evenings he would make us read aloud, alternately, but my sister Amalie could never make up her mind to do so, and then Goethe and she would tease each other a great deal, as she was a very vivacious girl.

It so happened that he also spent his birthday in Carlsbad and, since mother noticed that he did not want us to know that it was his birthday, she also forbade us to mention it. The day before, Goethe said that he wished we would drive to Elbogen with him early in the morning and that we ought to be his guests for that day, as he had been our guest all the time. Mother accepted and gave the cook a day-off. When Goethe came down for breakfast at seven o'clock in the morning, he found a beautiful plate with an ivy wreath design at his place.

After looking at it for a while, he turned to my mother: "Why this beautiful plate?"

"To remind you of our friendship. Ivy is a symbol for friendship, isn't it?"

Goethe seized my mother's hand: "How very nice, I shall keep it as a prized souvenir."

Soon after we drove out, and Goethe was very gay all the time telling us of a great many cheerful events, particularly those that occurred in Carlsbad where he often stayed. In Elbogen he showed us all the remarkable sights. When it came time to eat, we found that he had sent his servant ahead to Elbogen in order to make all necessary preparations. But mother had brought with her a wonderful cake, a genuine birthday cake, and two bottles of old Rhine wine of which Goethe was very fond. These stood on the table, and Goethe remarked immediately: "What a wonderful cake!"

Mother again replied: "I too wanted to contribute something to the dinner, and so I chose the cake and wine which you like so much."

"My attentive little friend! But again what a beautiful glass do I see here engraved with yours and your children's names!"

My mother replied: "We wish, above all, not to be forgotten, and that you may keep us in mind and also this wonderful day we spent together, and that you will always remember it."

Goethe smiled, thanked her and continued in his gay mood. At the end of the meal his servant brought him a pile of letters and notes which he partly read, often saying: "Those good people, they are very friendly and nice," probably expecting us to ask him about it, which however we did not do. Thus, in a gay mood, we drove back to Carlsbad; from afar we could see many people gathered on the meadow before the house, waiting for us with music. When we stepped out of the carriage, Goethe was immediately surrounded by them. Mother beckoned us, bade Goethe a "goodnight" and we went upstairs with her.

Since it was already late, we did not see Goethe before the next morning, when his first question was: "You knew that yesterday was my birthday, didn't you?"

Mother said, "How could I help but know it? You shouldn't have had it published!"

Laughing, he beat his forehead and said: "Then let us call it the day of the public secret," and as such he referred to it later in his letters.

I can only repeat what I have said often enough: It was a wonderful time we spent with this amiable man. Goethe contributed a great deal to mine and my sister's knowledge and education, since he spoke about so many subjects with us and also gave my mother some hints and advice.

I could tell a great deal more about this time, but I think this will suffice to refute all the fantastic things which were printed about us—because: it was no love affair.

## GOETHE TO F. ZELTER

Eger, August 24, 1823

YOUR NICE LETTER, dearest friend, reached me at a very fortunate moment. In accordance with my promise, I shall—before quitting the enchanted spheres of Bohemia—again address a letter to you which you will welcome the more kindly and affectionately, as I have only good news to communicate.

First of all, let me say that during the time I lately spent in Mariendbad I was spared sufferings of any kind, in fact, I was cheerful and as if returning to life again, and now I am feeling better than I have been feeling for a long time.

Furthermore, I must tell you that, after receiving that kiss, the bestower of which you probably guessed [a pupil of Zelter], I was favored by another splendid gift from Berlin; for I have heard Madame Milder sing four little Lieder which she contrived to make so great that the remembrance of them still makes my eyes well with tears. Now, the praise I have heard bestowed upon her for so many years past, is no longer a cold theoretical word, but awakens true and deeply felt emotion. Give her my kindest remembrances. She asked me for something from my own hand and will receive through you the first offering that is not absolutely unworthy of her.

Madame Szymanowska, an incredibly fine pianist, affected me just as powerfully, though in quite a different way. I dare compare her to our Hummel, only that she is a lovely and amiable Polish lady. When Hummel stops playing, a gnome rises up before our eyes who, by the help of powerful demons, has performed such wonders that one scarcely dares to thank him for them; but when she stops playing and looks at us, we do not feel sure whether we may not consider ourselves fortunate that she has stopped. Give her a friendly welcome when she gets to Berlin, which will probably be before very long; remember me to her and help her when you can. . . .

It is comfortless to listen to political discussions from any quarter. To get rid of all such things—as well as of aesthetic conversations and lectures, I devoted myself to a very pretty child [Ulrike von Levetzow] for six weeks and was thus perfectly secured against all outward discomfort.

But now for the strangest thing of all! The immense power that music had over me in those days! Milder's voice, the rich sounds of Szymanowska and even the public performances of the local Jägercorps relaxed me just as one lets a clenched fist gently spread itself out. Trying to explain it to myself, I say: 'For more than two years you have not heard any music at all, except Hummel twice, and therefore this faculty—so far as it exists in you—has been lying shut up and apart; now the Heavenly One suddenly falls upon you and through the intervention of great talents exercises her full power over you, claims all her rights, and awakens all your dormant recollections.' I feel perfectly convinced that I should have to leave the hall at the very first bar I might hear from your *Singakademie.* And when I now consider what it is to hear an Opera—as we give them but once a week,—a *Don Juan* or a *Matrimonio Segreto,* renewing it within oneself and assimilating this feeling with the others that form part of an active life, then, for the first time, do I understand what it means to have to dispense with such an enjoyment which, like all the higher enjoyments of life, carries a person away taking him out of himself and above himself, at the same time lifting him out of the world and above it.

How good, how imperative it would be for me if I could now spend some time with you! By gently guiding and directing me, you would cure my morbid irritability which, after all, must be regarded as the cause of the above phenomenon and you would, little by little, enable me to absorb the whole wealth of God's fairest revelation. Now I must see how I can get through a dull and monotonous winter which, to some extent, I look forward to with horror. However, we must endeavor, with good humor and courage, to make the black days useful to ourselves and to our friends.

## FROM F. VON MÜLLER'S DIARY

October 24, 1823

GOETHE entertained in honor of that interesting Polish piano virtuoso, Madame Marie Szymanowska, about whom he had already told us a great deal and who had arrived yesterday with her sister Casimira Wolowska to visit him. He had written for her those wonderful touching stanzas in Marienbad which he had read to us the other day and which express his gratitude for her deep sympathy that calmed his feelings for the first time since the separation from the Levetzow's which had wounded him so deeply [the poem "Reconciliation"].

Goethe was very gay and gallant the whole evening, he greatly enjoyed the acclamation Madame Szymanowska received both because of her personality and of her sensitive playing of the piano.

November 4

FINALLY TODAY, after much trouble and many conflicting difficulties, Madame Szymanowska's public concert took place. Even a few hours earlier, this enterprise would have failed because there was no good instrument to be had, but the Grand-Duchess magnanimously put her own at Madame Szymanowska's disposal. After the concert we dined with the Egloffsteins at Goethe's who played the host with the most lovable *Gemütlichkeit.* When on the occasion of the many toasts one was also offered to the memory of old times, he uttered the following words with intensity:

"I cannot reminisce as you do, since that is only an awkward form of self-expression. Any great, beautiful, important experience need not be recalled from the outside, need not be secured as it were. In fact, from the very beginning it must blend with our inmost soul, must become an entity with it, build a new and better ego in us and thus, constantly molding, live on in us creatively. There should be nothing in the past which we want to recall, there is only the eternally new taking shape out of the ramified elements of the past. Genuine longing must always be productive and create something new and better."

He added with great emotion: "Have not all of us experienced this during the last few days? Don't we all feel deeply refreshed, within improved through this warm noble figure who is about to leave us again, has not our horizon been widened through her? No, she cannot vanish, she has become part of our inner selves, she lives in us and with us, and however she may try to escape us, I will always hold her embraced within me."

November 5

WHEN, in the afternoon, I went to see Goethe, I met him still sitting at the table with Madame Szymanowska. She had just presented the whole family down to her favorite, the little Wolf [Goethe's grandson] with the sweetest little souvenirs, partly the work of her own hands. The old man was in the most wonderful mood. He intended to be gay and full of fun, but the sadness of the farewell was noticeable in whatever he said.

At five o'clock she was expected at the farewell audience with the Grand-Duchess. According to court mourning she had dressed in black which enhanced Goethe's painful feelings. The carriage drove up and she disappeared in it without his knowledge. It seemed very doubtful whether she would ever come again.

Then the man in Goethe became so obviously clear; he most sincerely asked me to make her come back, not to let her go without saying goodbye. A few hours later his son and I came back to him with Madame Szymanowska and her sister.

"I go from you enriched and comforted," she said to him. "You have confirmed my belief in myself, I feel better and worthier knowing that you respect me. Let there be no good-bye, no thank you; let us dream of seeing each other again. Oh, if only I were much older and expected a grandson soon, I should baptize him *Wolf*, and the very first thing I would teach him to say would be your dear name."

"Well," Goethe replied, "your fellow countrymen have gone to so much trouble to chase away the *wolf* from their door, and now you want to bring one back to them?" But all attempt at humor did not help keep back his tears, without saying anything more he embraced her and her sister and his eyes followed them for some time as they disappeared through the long row of open rooms.

"I have to be grateful to this wonderful woman for a great deal," he told me later, "my acquaintance with her and her great talent have made me find my old self again."

## GOETHE TO F. ZELTER

*In December, 1823, Zelter visited Goethe who was suffering from a severe ailment after the emotional strain of the preceding months. Zelter's presence contributed much to the recovery of the patient.*

Weimar, January 9, 1824

To GET a clear picture of conditions in 1802, I looked through the correspondence of those days, and there I found your really wonderful and good, friendly and profound words which prove right to this very day. And thus the test of those critical weeks which we spent together add a great many and good spans to the many-year-old fabric of our friendship! Joy and misery we have both experienced, together and separately, during these twenty years, and your dear presence in my painful condition again was most refreshing; I felt it and I know it, and I am glad that the others too realize it who can never actually perceive what one person is and can be to another.

That you so faithfully repeated the content of the poem [Marienbader Elegy] with your sincere sympathy was nothing else but a repetition of what you have given me through your compositions for so long. But it was nevertheless peculiar that you could read and read again, that you could let me hear several times through your soft, sensitive voice what is dear to me to a degree which I do not dare admit and which has become even more part of myself, now that I feel that it has become part of you. I must not give it away, but should we live together, you would have to read it to me aloud and to sing it until you knew it by heart. . . .

However, I must say to myself: I should have taken better care of myself immediately after my return this year, and I should take care of myself now. For the great excitability brought forth by music—as you know already from what happened in Bohemia—is actually dangerous for me, although I cannot very well reject it, since it is this mood to which I must be grateful for the poem which, from time to time, gives new life to my mind and imagination.

## THOMAS CARLYLE TO GOETHE

*Thomas Carlyle was twenty-nine when he first established contact with Goethe. Madame de Staël's book about Germany had aroused Carlyle's interest in the literature of that country, which was then little-known to English readers. He studied German assiduously and became in the next few years the foremost promoter in England of German poets. Carlyle's translation of "Wilhelm Meister's Apprenticeship," which occasioned the first letter to Goethe, had just been published in Edinburgh.*

London, June 24, 1824

Permit me, Sir, in soliciting your acceptance of this translation to return you my sincere thanks for the profit which, in common with many millions, I have derived from the Original.

That you will honor this imperfect copy of your work with a perusal I do not hope: but the thought that some portion of my existence has been connected with that of the man whose intellect and mind I most admire, is pleasing to my imagination; nor will I neglect the present opportunity of communing with you even in this slight and transitory manner. Four years ago, when I read your "Faust" among the mountains of my native Scotland, I could not but fancy I might one day see you, and pour out before you, as before a father, the woes and wanderings of a heart whose mysteries you seemed so thoroughly to comprehend, and could so beautifully represent. The hope of meeting you is still among my dreams. Many saints have been expunged from my literary calendar since I first knew you; but your name still stands there, in characters more bright than ever. That your life may be long, long spared, for the solace and instruction of this and future generations, is the earnest prayer of, Sir, your most devoted servant,

THOMAS CARLYLE

# COUNSEL FROM A REALIST

*William Emerson, oldest brother of Ralph Waldo Emerson, studied theology at Göttingen. The influence of German philosophy aggravated the young man's doubts about his vocation for the ministry. William Emerson talked to Goethe about his personal problems and the poet recommended, as it seems, a realistic attitude. The following excerpt from William Emerson's travelling journal is here reprinted by courtesy of Columbia University Press from Dr. Haven Emerson's publication of the manuscript.*

Weimar, September 19, 1824

WE ARRIVED IN the pleasant town of Weimar at noon, and I immediately repaired to Goethe's house, and sent up my card, on which I had previously added "Boston, N. America," to my name. He sent me word that he was then surrounded with company, but if I would call at four, he would see me. It may be supposed, that I did not forget the appointment. I was shown into a room, that was filled with works of art. A huge bust of Minerva was placed over one of the doors. A large case with books, which from their great size, must have been drawings, stood in one corner.

Goethe, the gentle and venerable poet, entered almost immediately. I was so struck with the difference between him who came into the room, and the formidable portrait that is commonly to be seen of this great man, that I almost expected to see another person behind him. His address and manner were perfectly simple and unconstrained. After finding out my profession, he led the conversation immediately upon the state of religion in the United States and afterwards upon the states and hopes of our country in general. His tone became gradually that of an instructor, and yet it ceased not to be unassuming, but all was uttered quietly, as a mere private opinion. He said he thought we had nothing to do with the different systems of philosophy, but that the highest aim of life should be for each one to accommodate himself as perfectly as possible to the station he was placed.

He asked many questions, and talked willingly, yet seemed not too loath to be interrupted. The only thing that was American, a number of the "Palladium", I ventured to offer him, as newspapers are a great curiosity in Germany. He accepted the trifle very graciously, and said it was two years since he had seen one. He shook me kindly by the hand when I took leave. I left Weimar immediately but I shall not hastily forget this exceedingly interesting visit.

He was of common size, with pleasing but not striking features; his dress was a blue surtout, over a white vest. I should not have judged him to be more than sixty-five, yet he is said to be about ten years older.

# HEINRICH HEINE
# TO R. CHRISTIANI

*Heinrich Heine visited Goethe on October 2, 1824, at a time when he was still unknown as a poet.*

I WAS FRIGHTENED to the depth of my heart at the sight of Goethe; his face sallow and mummy-like, his toothless mouth anxiously moving, his whole figure a picture of human frailty. Maybe, all this is the consequence of his last disease. Only his eyes were clear and bright. These eyes are the sole remarkable thing that Weimar now possesses.

Goethe's deeply and humanly warm anxiety about my health was touching. The late Wolf had spoken to him about it. In many traits I recognized the Goethe to whom life, its preservation and beautification, as well as all specific practicality, is the highest good. Only then I felt quite clearly the contrast between his nature and mine to which everything practical is unpleasant, which attaches little value to life and would defiantly give it away for an idea. Just this is the conflict within me that my reason is in constant struggle with my innate tendency toward sentimental ecstasy. Now I also became aware of why—in the depth of my soul—I have always found Goethe's writings repugnant, however much I respected them in regard to their poetical quality and however much my own basic outlook on life harmonizes with Goethe's thinking. Thus I am actually at war with Goethe and his works in the same way as my *Weltanschauung* is fighting against my inherent propensities and hidden emotional disposition.

But do not worry about it, my good Christiani, these wars will never show on the surface. I shall always belong to the Goethean Volunteer Corps, and whatever I shall write will arise from artistic thoughtfulness and never from foolish enthusiasm.

## GOETHE TO THOMAS CARLYLE

Weimar, October 30, 1824

IF I DID NOT, my dear Sir, promptly inform you of the safe arrival of your welcome present, the reason was, that I had not the intention of writing a mere acknowledgement, but of adding thereto some deliberate words concerning your work which does me such honor. My advanced years, continually burdened with many indispensable duties, have, however, prevented me from leisurely comparing your translation with the original; which might perhaps prove a harder task for me than for some third person thoroughly at home in German and English literature. But now, since I have an opportunity of sending the present letters safely to London, by favor of the Lord Bentinck, and at the same time of bringing about an acquaintance agreeable to both parties, I do not delay to express my sincere thanks for your hearty sympathy in my literary work, as well as in the incidents of my life, and to beg earnestly for a continuance of it in the future. Perhaps I shall hereafter come to know much of you. Meanwhile I send together with this a set of poems, which you can hardly have seen, but which I venture to hope may prove of some interest to you.

# THE GENTLEMAN FROM WASHINGTON

*George H. Calvert, who visited Goethe in March, 1825, published this account twenty years later in "Putnams Magazine." A writer on various subjects, Calvert became one of the first Goethe-exponents in America.*

LEARNING THAT GOETHE dined at two, I waited till a quarter past three, and then walked to his house in the *Frauenplan.* I had no letter, and knowing that Goethe refused unlabelled visitors, I rang the bell with misgivings. The servant said, the Herr Geheimrat had not yet risen from table. There, cried I vexedly to myself as I turned away, by my impatience I have forfeited the at best doubtful chance of seeing the great man. The summons of his waiter from the dining-room to the door, he will feel as an intrusion on his privacy and comfort, and be thereby jarred into an inhospitable mood. I walked into the park, enlivened on a sunny Sunday afternoon with Weimar's quiet denizens. Towards four I was again ringing Goethe's bell. The servant asked my name, I gave him my card on which I had written, "from Washington, America." My home being near the capital, of this I availed myself to couple my name with that of the sublime man—honored by all the hundred millions in Christendom—the presenting of which to the imagination of a great poet might, I hoped, kindle an emotion that would plead irresistibly in my behalf. The servant quickly returned and ushered me in. I ascended the celebrated wide, easy, Italian staircase. On the threshold I was about to pass, my eye fell pleasantly on the hospitable SALVE, inlaid in large mosaic letters. The door was opened before me by the servant, and there, in the center of the room, tall, large, erect, majestic, Goethe stood, slightly borne forward by the intentness of his look, out of those large luminous eyes, fixed on the entrance.

In 1825, Americans were seldom seen so far inland. In his whole life Goethe had not probably met with six. The announcement of one for the unbusied moments of an after-dinner, was, I dare say, to the ever-fresh student and universal observer, a piquant novelty. His attitude and expression, as I entered, were those of an expectant naturalist, eagerly awaiting the transatlantic phenomenon. Goethe was then in his seventy-sixth year; but neither on his face nor figure was there any detracting mark of age. Kindly and gracefully he received me; advancing as I entered, he bade me be seated on the sofa, and sat down beside me. In a few moments I was perfectly at ease. At such an interview the opening conversation is inevitably predetermined. How long I had been in Europe; the route by which I had come; the sea-voyage. When he learned, that for fifteen months I had been a student at Göttingen, he inquired with interest for several of the professors. . . .

The news of the election of John Quincy Adams to be president of the United States had just reached Germany. Three days before, I had read it, while at Gotha in a Frankfort Newspaper. Goethe wished to understand the mode and form of election. This I explained to him in full: the first process through electors and then, as in this instance, the second by the House of Representatives. In stating that the people did not directly choose, but voted for a small number of electors, and that these then voted for one of the candidates, I used the word *gereinigt* (cleansed) to describe how the popular will, to reach its aim, was sifted through the electoral colleges. The term *gereinigt* pleased Goethe much. I used it because, being of one of the most federal of federal families, and not having yet begun to think for myself on political subjects, the breadth and grandeurs of democracy were still unrevealed to me; and it pleased Goethe, broad and deep as was his sympathy with humanity, he was after all not omnisentient any more than omniscient.

## THE THEATRE ON FIRE

*For 26 years Goethe was director of the Weimar theatre, or rather dictator, as his critics said. Though Goethe retired from the management in 1817, forced by an intrigue, he always kept a vivid interest in theatrical affairs. Here is Eckermann's report about the fire which destroyed the old theatre building.*

Weimar, March 22, 1825

LAST NIGHT, SHORTLY after twelve o'clock, we were awakened by a fire alarm; we heard cries, "The theatre is on fire!" I at once threw on my clothes, and rushed to the spot. The excitement was very great. Only a few hours before we had been enjoying the excellent acting of La Roche in Cumberland's "Jew", and Seidel had been arousing laughter with his comedy and jokes. And now, in the place so recently the scene of intellectual pleasures, the most terrible element of destruction was raging.

The fire, which started from the heating system, appears to have broken out in the pit; it soon spread to the stage and the dry lathwork of the wings, and, feeding on so much combustible material, it was not long before the flames burst through the roof, and the rafters gave away.

There was no lack of fire-fighting apparatus. The building was surrounded by engines, which poured an immense quantity of water upon the blaze. But it was all useless. The flames raged upwards filling the dark sky with glowing sparks and burning particles which drifted over the town on the breeze. The noise of the cries and calls of the men working the fire-ladders and engines was very great. All seemed determined to subdue the flames. On one side, as near to the spot as the fire allowed, stood a man in a cloak and military cap, smoking a cigar with the greatest composure. At first glance, he appeared to be an idle spectator, but such was not the case. There were several persons to whom in few words, he gave commands, which were immediately executed. It was the Grand Duke Carl August. He had soon seen that the building itself could not been saved; he therefore ordered that it should be left to fall, and that all the superfluous engines should be turned upon the neighboring houses, which were exposed to the fire. He must have been thinking with princely resignation—

> "Let *that* burn down,
> With greater beauty will it rise again."

He was not wrong. The theatre was old, by no means beautiful, and for a long time, it had ceased to be roomy enough to accommodate the ever-growing public. Nevertheless, it was sad to see the building irreparably destroyed, with which so many reminiscences of the past, illustrious and endeared to Weimar, were connected.

I saw in beautiful eyes many tears, which flowed for its downfall. I was no less touched by the grief of a member of the orchestra. He wept for his burnt violin. As the day dawned, I saw many pale faces. I noticed several young girls and women of high rank, who had been watching the fire all the night and were now shivering in the cold morning air. I returned home to take a little rest, and in the course of the forenoon I called upon Goethe.

The servant told me that he was unwell and in bed. Still Goethe had me called to his side. He stretched out his hand to me. "We have all sustained a loss," said he; "what is to be done? My little Wolf came early this morning to my bedside. He seized my hand, and looking full at me, said, 'So it is with human things.' What more can be said, than these words of my beloved Wolf, with which he tried to comfort me? The theatre, the scene of my love-labors for nearly thirty years, lies in ashes. But as Wolf says, 'so it is with human things.' I hardly slept all night; from my front windows, I watched the flames incessantly rising toward the sky. You can imagine that many thoughts of old times, of my years' work with Schiller, and of the progress of favorite pupils passed through my mind, and not without causing some emotion. So I intend wisely to remain in bed today."

I praised him for his forethought. Still he did not appear to me in the least weak or exhausted, but in a very pleasant and serene mood. This lying in bed seemed to me to be an old stratagem of war, which he likes to use after an extraordinary event, when he fears a crowd of visitors.

Goethe begged me to be seated on a chair near his bed, and to stay a little while. "I have thought much about you and pitied you," he said. "What will you do with your evenings now?"

"You know," I answered, "how passionately I love the theatre. When I came here two years ago I knew nothing at all about it except three or four plays which I had seen in Hanover. It was all new to me, actors as well as plays. Following your advice I gave myself up entirely to absorbing impressions in the theatre, without much thinking or reflecting, and I can honestly say that during these two winters, I have spent at the theatre the most harmless and yet agreeable hours I have ever known. I became so infatuated with the theatre that I not only never missed a performance, but also obtained admission to the rehearsals. And not even content with that, if, as I passed the theatre in the daytime, I happened to find the doors open, I would go in and sit for half an hour on the empty benches in the pit, imagining scenes which might at some time be played there."

"You are a madman," said Goethe, laughing; "but that is what I like. If only the whole public consisted of such children! And in fact you are right. Anyone who is young enough and not too spoiled, could hardly find any place that would suit him better than a theatre. No one asks you any questions: you don't need to open your mouth unless you want to; you sit at your ease like a king, and let everything pass before you, enjoying your thoughts and sensations to your heart's content. There is poetry, there is painting, there are singing and music, there is acting, and more besides. When all these arts, and the charm of youth and beauty raised to a level of significance, work together on the same evening, it is a bouquet to which no other can compare. But even when part is bad and part is good, it is still better than looking out of the window, or playing cards at a stuffy party in an atmosphere of cigar smoke. The theatre at Weimar need not to be despised; it has still the old trunk from our best time, which new talents have branched. We can still produce something which charms and pleases, and at least gives the appearance of an organized whole."

"If only I could have seen it twenty or thirty years ago!"

"That was certainly a time," replied Goethe, "when we were assisted by great advantages. Consider that the tedious period of French taste was just past; that the public was not spoiled by over-excitement; that the influence of Shakespeare was in all its first freshness; that the operas of Mozart were new; and lastly, that the plays of Schiller were first produced here year after year, and were given at the theatre of Weimar in all their first glory, under his own direction. Consider all that, and you can imagine how, with such dishes, a fine banquet was given to old and young, and we always had a grateful public."

I remarked, "Older people, who remember those times, cannot praise highly enough the reputation which the Weimar theatre had."

"I will not deny that it was something," returned Goethe. "That main point, however, was this, that the Grand Duke left my hands quite free, and I could do just as I liked. I did not try for magnificent scenery nor a brilliant wardrobe but I looked for good plays. From tragedy to farce, every species was welcome; but a play had to have something in it to find favor. It had to be great and clever, cheerful and graceful, above all healthy and containing some pith. Everything morbid, weak, lachrymose, and sentimental, as well as anything frightful, horrible, or offensive to decorum, was utterly excluded; I would have been afraid with such stuff of spoiling both actors and audience. By choosing good plays, I improved the actors; for the study of excellence, and the continued practice of excellence make something of any man whom nature has not left ungifted. I myself was constantly in personal contact with the actors. I attended the first reading of the play and explained his part to each one. I was present at the rehearsals, and discussed with the actors any improvements that might be made. I went to the performances, and pointed out the next day anything which did not seem to be right.

"In these ways I also tried to raise the whole class of actors in the esteem of society, by introducing the best and most promising into my own circle, thus showing the world that I considered them worthy of social intercourse with myself. The result was that the rest of higher society in Weimar followed my lead, and actors and actresses mixed in the best circles. By so doing, they acquired personal as well as external culture. My pupils, Wolff in Berlin, and our Durand here, are people of the finest tact in society. Oels and Graff are cultivated enough to do honor to the best circles.

"Schiller agreed with me about these principles. He had a great deal of contact with actors and actresses. He, like me, was present at every rehearsal; and after every successful performance of one of his plays, it was his custom to invite the actors, and to spend a merry day with them. They celebrated the success together and discussed anything which might be done better the next time. But when Schiller joined us he already found both actors and the public highly cultivated. Naturally this was the basis for the rapid success of his plays."

It gave me great pleasure to hear Goethe speak in such detail on a subject of such interest, and which, because of the fire, was uppermost in my mind.

"This burning of the house," I said, "in which you and Schiller accomplished so much, closes a great epoch, which will not soon return for Weimar. You must have derived great pleasure from your direction of the theatre and its extraordinary success."

"And plenty of trouble and difficulty," replied Goethe, with a sigh.

"It must be difficult to keep such a many-headed creature under control."

"A great deal," said Goethe, "may be done by severity, and more by love, but most by clear thinking and impartial justice which pays no respect to persons. I had to beware of two enemies which might have been dangerous to me. One was my passionate love of talent, which might easily have made me partial. The other I will not mention, but you can guess it. In our theatre there was no lack of women who were beautiful and young, and who also had great mental charms. I felt a passionate inclination toward many of them, and sometimes it happened that I was met half way. But I restrained myself, and said: No further! I knew my position, and what I owed to it. I was there, not as a private man, but as head of an establishment whose prosperity meant more to me than a momentary gratification. If I had involved myself in a love affair I would have been like a compass which cannot point right when under the influence of a magnet at its side. By thus keeping myself quite clear and always remaining master of myself I also remained master of the theatre and received the respect without which all authority is very soon at an end."

This confession of Goethe's deeply impressed me. I had already heard something of this kind about him from others, and I was glad to hear its confirmation from his own mouth. I loved him more than ever, and took leave of him with a hearty pressure of the hand.

I returned to the scene of the fire, where flames and columns of smoke were rising from the great heap of ruins. People were still occupied in extinguishing and pulling to pieces. I found near the spot a burnt fragment of a written part. It contained passages from Goethe's "Tasso".

## GOETHE TO F. ZELTER

Weimar, August 12, 1826

I MUST TELL you about a strange thing that happened. A young porcelain painter from Brunswick instilled in me such confidence in his work which he showed me and so very much struck my fancy that I yielded to his pressing entreaty and sat for him for several hours. The picture proved to be a good one, to the satisfaction of everyone. If it gets safely through the firing process, it will, both on its own account and for the sake of the beautiful ornament, be a good recommendation for him at home. His name is Ludwig Sebbers; he passed through here on his travels.

Sibylline-like, of all its youth bereft,
My face with vanity is yet acquainted!
For still the less of it to paint is left,
More often do the painters want to paint it!

In all fairness, this is how I have made fun of these endeavors; but one must submit to them.

*The portrait of Goethe painted by Ludwig Sebbers on a china cup is considered the best likeness of the poet in his old age.*

## A TIMID ADMIRER

*The Austrian poet Franz Grillparzer who successsfully continued the tradition of Goethe and Schiller in his plays, visited Weimar in September, 1826. In his autobiography he describes his journey.*

AT LAST I arrived in Weimar and took quarters in "The Elephant," a hostelry at that time famous throughout Germany and the ante-room, as it were, to the living Valhalla of Weimar. From there I dispatched the waiter with my card to Goethe, inquiring whether he would receive me. The waiter returned with the answer that His Excellency, the Privy-councilor, was entertaining some guests and could not, therefore, receive me at the moment. He would expect me in the evening for tea.

I dined at the hotel. My name had become known through my card and the report of my presence spread through the town, so that I made many acquaintances.

Toward evening I called on Goethe. In the reception-room I found quite a large assemblage waiting for His Excellency the Privy-councilor, who had not yet made his appearance. Among these there was a court councilor, Jacob or Jacobs, with his daughter, whom Goethe had entertained at dinner. The daughter, who later won a literary reputation under the pseudonym of Talvj, was as young as she was beautiful, and as beautiful as she was cultured, and so I soon lost my timidity and in my conversation with the charming young lady almost forgot that I was in Goethe's house. At last a side door opened, and he himself entered. Dressed in black, the star on his breast, with erect, almost stiff bearing, he stepped among us with the air of a monarch granting an audience. He exchanged a few words with one and another of his guests, and finally crossed the room and addressed me. He inquired whether Italian literature was cultivated to any great extent in our country. I told him, which was a fact, that the Italian language was, indeed, widely known, since all officials were required to learn it; Italian literature, on the other hand, was completely neglected; the fashion was rather to turn to English literature, which, despite its excellence, had an admixture of coarseness that seemed to me to be anything but advantageous to the present state of German culture, especially of poetry. Whether my opinion pleased him or not, I have no means of knowing; I am almost inclined to believe it did not, inasmuch as he was at that very time in correspondence with Lord Byron. He left me, talked with others, returned, conversed I no longer remember on what subjects, finally withdrew, and we were dismissed.

I confess that I returned to the hostelry in a most unpleasant frame of mind. It was not that my vanity had been offended—on the contrary, Goethe had treated me more kindly and more attentively than I had anticipated—but to see the ideal of my youth, the author of "Faust," "Clavigo," and "Egmont," in the role of a formal minister presiding at tea brought me down from my celestial heights. Had his manner been rude or had he shown me the door, it would have pleased me better. I almost repented having gone to Weimar.

Consequently I determined to devote the following day to sightseeing, and ordered horses at the inn for the day following. On the morning of the next day visitors of all sorts put in an appearance, among them the amiable and respected Chancellor Müller, and, above all, my fellow-countryman Hummel, who for many years had been occupying the position of musical director in Weimar. He had left Vienna before my poetry had attracted attention, so that we had not become acquainted with each other. It was almost touching to witness the joy with which this ordinarily unsociable man greeted me and took possession of me. In the first place I probably revived in him memories of his native city, which he had left with reluctance; then, too, it probably gave him satisfaction to find his literary countryman honored and respected in Weimar, where he heard nothing but disparaging opinions regarding the intellectual standing of Austria. And, finally, he had an opportunity of conversing with a Viennese in his home dialect, which he had preserved pure and unadulterated while living among people who spoke quite differently. I do not know whether it was the contrast, or whether this really was the worst German I had ever heard in my life. While we were planning to visit some points of interest in Weimar, and while Chancellor Müller, who had probably noticed my depression, was assuring me that Goethe's formality was nothing but the embarrassment always displayed by him on meeting a stranger for the first time, the waiter entered and handed me a card containing an invitation from Goethe to dine with him the next day. I therefore had to prolong my stay and to countermand the order for the horses. The morning was passed in visiting the places that had become famous through their literary associations. Schiller's house interested me most of all, and I was especially delighted to find in the poet's study, really an attic-room in the second story, an old man who is said to have acted as prompter at the theatre in Schiller's time, teaching his grandson to read. The little boy's open and intelligently animated expression prompted the illusion that out of Schiller's study a new Schiller might some day emerge—an illusion which, to be sure, has not been realized.

The exact order of events is now confused in my mind. I believe it was on this first day that I dined with Hummel en famille. There I found his wife, formerly the pretty singer, Miss Rockel, whom I could well remember in page's attire and close-fitting silk tights. Now she was efficient, a respected housewife, who vied with her husband in amiability. I felt myself strongly drawn to the whole family and, in spite of his rather mechanical disposition, I honored and venerated Hummel as the last genuine pupil of Mozart.

In the evening I attended the theatre with Chancellor Müller, where an unimportant play was being given, in which, however, Graff, Schiller's first Wallenstein, had a role. I saw

Goethe. Portrait on a porcelain cup. By L. Sebbers, 1826

Goethe. Drawing by L. Sebbers, 1826

nothing particularly remarkable in him, and when I was told that, after the first performance, Schiller had rushed upon the stage, embraced Graff, and exclaimed that now for the first time did he understand his Wallenstein, I thought to myself—how much greater might the great poet have become had he ever known a public and real actors! It is remarkable, by the way, that Schiller, who is not at bottom very objective, lends himself so perfectly to an objective representation. He became figurative, while believing himself to be only eloquent—one more proof of his incomparable genius. In Goethe we find the exact opposite. While he is ordinarily called objective and is so to a great extent, his characters lose in the actual representation. His figurativeness is only for the imagination; in the representation the delicate, poetic tinge is necessarily lost. However, these are reflections for another time; they do not belong here.

At last the momentous day with its dinner-hour arrived, and I went to Goethe. The other guests, all of them men, were already assembled, the charming Talvj having departed with her father the morning after the tea-party and Goethe's daughter-in-law being absent from Weimar at the time. To the latter and to her daughter, who died when quite young, I later became very much attached. As I advanced into the room Goethe came toward me, and was now as amiable and cordial as he had recently been formal and cold. I was deeply moved. When we went in to dinner, and Goethe, who had become for me the embodiment of German Poetry and, because of the immeasurable distance between us, almost a mythological being, took my hand to lead me into the dining-room, the boy in me manifested itself once again and I burst into tears. Goethe took great pains to conceal my foolish emotion. I sat next to him at dinner and he was more cheerful and talkative than he had been for a long time, as the guests asserted later. The conversation, enlivened by him, became general, but Goethe frequently turned to me individually. However, I cannot recall what he said, except a good joke regarding Müllner's "Midnight Journal." Unfortunately I made no notes concerning this journey, or, rather, I did begin a diary, but as the accident I had in Berlin made it at first impossible for me to write and later difficult, a great gap ensued. This deterred me from continuing it, and, besides, the difficulty of writing remained, even in Weimar. I therefore determined to fill in what was lacking immediately after my return to Vienna, while the events were still fresh in my mind; and therefore I retained in my memory nothing but general impressions of what I had almost called the most important moment of my life. Only one occurrence at dinner stands out in my memory—namely, in the ardor of the conversation, I yielded to an old habit of breaking up the piece of bread beside me into unsightly crumbs. Goethe lightly touched each individual crumb with his finger and arranged them in a little symmetrical heap. Only after the lapse of some time did I notice this, and then I discontinued my handiwork.

As I was taking my leave, Goethe requested me to come the next morning and have myself sketched, for he was in the habit of having drawings made of those of his visitors who interested him. They were done in black crayon by an artist especially engaged for the work [Johann Joseph Schmeller], and the pictures were then put into a frame which hung in the reception-room for this purpose, being changed in regular rotation every week. This honor was also bestowed upon me.

When I arrived the next morning the artist had not yet appeared; I was therefore directed to Goethe, who was walking up and down in his little garden. The cause of his stiff bearing before strangers now became clear to me. The years had not passed without leaving some traces. As he walked about in the garden, one could see that the upper part of his body, his head and shoulders, were bent slightly forward. This he wished to hide from strangers, and hence that forced straightening-up which produced an unpleasant impression. The sight of him in this unaffected carriage, wearing a long dressing-gown, a small skull-cap on his white hair, had something infinitely touching about it. He looked like a king, and again like a father. We walked up and down, engaged in conversation. He mentioned my "Sappho" and seemed to think well of it, thus in a way praising himself, for I had followed fairly closely in his footsteps. When I complained of my isolated position in Vienna he remarked what we have since read in his printed works, that man can do efficient work only in the company of like-minded or congenial spirits. If he and Schiller had attained universal recognition, they owed it largely to this stimulating and supplementing reciprocal influence.

In the meantime the artist had arrived. We entered the house and I was sketched. Goethe had gone into his room, whence he emerged from time to time to satisfy himself as to the progress of the picture, which pleased him when completed. When the artist had departed Goethe had his son bring in some of his choicest treasures. There was his correspondence with Lord Byron; everything relating to his acquaintance with the Empress and the Emperor of Austria at Carlsbad; and finally the imperial Austrian copyright of his collected works. This latter he seemed to value very highly, either because he liked the conservative attitude of Austria, or because he regarded it as an oddity in contradistinction to the usual policy pursued in literary matters by this country. These treasures were wrapped separately in half-oriental fashion in pieces of silk, Goethe handling them with reverence. At last I was most graciously dismissed.

In the course of the day Chancellor Müller suggested my visiting Goethe toward evening; he would be alone, and my visit would by no means be unwelcome to him. Not until later did it occur to me that Müller could not have made the suggestion without Goethe's knowledge.

Now I committed my second blunder in Weimar. I was afraid to be alone with Goethe for an entire evening, and after considerable vacillation decided not to go. Several elements combined to produce this fear. In the first place, it seemed to me that there was nothing within the whole range of my intellect worthy of being displayed before Goethe.

Secondly, it was not until later that I learned to place the proper value upon my own works by comparing them with those of my contemporaries, the former appearing exceedingly crude and insignificant in contrast with German poetry. Finally I had left Vienna with the feeling that my poetic talent had completely exhausted itself, a feeling which was intensified in Weimar to the point of actual depression. It seemed to me an utterly unworthy proceeding to fill Goethe's ears with lamentations and to listen to words of encouragement for which there seemed to be no guarantee of fulfilment.

Yet there was some method in this madness after all. Goethe's aversion at that time for anything violent and forced was well known to me. Now I was of the opinion that calmness and deliberation are appropriate only to one who is capable of introducing such a wealth of thought into his works as Goethe has done in his "Iphigenia" and "Tasso." At the same time I held the opinion that everyone must emphasize those qualities with which he is most strongly endowed, and these in my case were at this time warmth of feeling and vividness of imagination. Occupying, as I then did, the viewpoint of impartial observation, I felt that I was far too weak to defend against Goethe the causes of such divergence from his own views, and I had far too much reverence for him to accept his exposition with pretended approval or in hypocritical silence.

At all events I did not go, and that displeased Goethe. He had good cause to feel astonished that I should display such indifference to the proffered opportunity of enlightening him concerning my works and myself; or else he came nearer to the truth, and imagined that "The Ancestress" and my predilection for similar effusions, which were repugnant to him, were not entirely quenched within me; or perhaps he divined my entire mood, and concluded that an unmanly character was bound to ruin a great talent. From that time on he was much colder toward me.

But as far as this unmanliness is concerned, I confess, as I have previously done, to falling a prey to this weakness whenever I find myself confronted with a confused mass of sensations of lesser importance, especially with good-will, reverence, and gratitude. Whenever I was able to define the opposing factors sharply to myself in the rejection of the bad as well as in the perseverence in a conviction, I displayed both before and after this period a firmness, which, indeed, might even be called obstinacy. But in general it may safely be asserted: Only the union of character and talent produces what is called genius.

On one of these days I was also commanded to appear before the Grand Duke, whom I met in all his simplicity and unaffectedness in the so-called Roman House. He conversed with me for over an hour, and my description of Austrian conditions seemed to interest him. Not he, but most of the others, hinted at the desire of acquiring my services for the Weimar theatre—a desire that did not coincide with my own inclination.

When on the fourth day of my stay I paid my farewell visit to Goethe, he was friendly, but somewhat reserved. He expressed astonishment on my leaving Weimar so soon, and added that they would all be glad to hear from me occasionally. "They," then, would be glad, not he. Even in later years he did not do me justice, for I do consider myself the best poet that has appeared after him and Schiller, in spite of the gulf that separates me from them. That all this did not lessen my love and reverence for him, I need scarcely say.

# A FORECAST FOR THE U. S. A.

*Alexander von Humboldt, the famous scientist and explorer, whose book occasioned the following conversation with Eckermann, had visited Goethe a few months before.*

Weimar, February 21, 1827

DINED WITH GOETHE. He spoke much and with admiration, of Alexander von Humboldt, whose work on Cuba and Columbia he had begun to read, and whose views as to the project for making a passage through the Isthmus of Panama appeared to have a particular interest for him. "Humboldt," said Goethe, "has with a great knowledge of his subject, suggested other points where, by making use of some streams which flow in the Gulf of Mexico, the canal may perhaps be cut more easily through than at Panama. All this will take time and require bold planning. But this much is certain: if they succeed in cutting so large a canal that ships of any tonnage and size can be navigated through it from the Gulf of Mexico to the Pacific Ocean, innumerable benefits would result for the whole human race, civilized and uncivilized. But I would be surprised if the United States were to let slip an opportunity of getting such a project into their own hands. It may be foreseen that this young state with its movement towards the West, will, in thirty or forty years, have occupied and peopled the large area of land beyond the Rocky Mountains. Furthermore, along the whole coast of the Pacific Ocean, where Nature has already formed very large and secure harbors, important commercial towns will gradually arise, leading to extensive trade between China and the East Indies and the United States. In such a case, it would not only be desirable, but almost necessary, that a more rapid communication should be maintained between the eastern and western shores of North America, both by merchant and warships, than has hitherto been possible with the tedious, disagreeable, and expensive voyage round Cape Horn. I therefore repeat that it is absolutely indispensable for the United States to effect a passage from the Gulf of Mexico to the Pacific Ocean; and I am certain that they will do it.

I wish that I might live to see it!—but I shall not. I should like to see another thing too—a junction of the Danube and the Rhine. But this undertaking is so gigantic that I have doubts of its completion, particularly when I consider our German resources. And thirdly, I should wish to see England in possession of a canal through the Isthmus of Suez. If only I could live to see these three great works! It would be well worth the trouble to last some fifty years more for that."

## GOETHE TO F. ZELTER

Weimar, March 19, 1827

HOW SHOULD A FRIEND answer his friend in such a case? [Zelter's only remaining son had died] A similar calamity drew us so close to each other that the bond between us could not be more intimate. The present sorrow does not change our feelings and that in itself is a great deal.

The Fates are never weary of relating to one another the old myth of the Night, breaking in a thousand thousand times, and yet once more. To live long means to outlive many; this is the pitiful refrain of our vaudeville-like, listless life; it comes round time and again, fretting us and yet goading us to fresh and earnest endeavor.

The circle of persons with whom I come most in contact seems to me like a roll of Sibylline leaves which, being consumed by the flames of life, vanish one after the other into the air, thus making those that are left more precious from moment to moment. Let us work until we, in our turn, either before or after one another, are summoned by the Spirit of the Universe to return to the ether. And may the Eternally-Living not deny us new activities, like those in which we have already been put to the test! Should He, father-like, add to these the remembrance and after-feeling of the rectitude and virtue we desired and achieved even in this world, we should certainly plunge all the more eagerly in amongst the wheels of the world's machinery.

The Entelechean Monad must preserve himself only in restless activity; if this becomes his other nature, it can never, throughout Eternity, be in need of occupation. Forgive these abstruse expressions! But, at all times, people have lost themselves in such regions and tried to impart their thoughts by this kind of speech, wherever Reason did not prove sufficient and yet where one would not, by choice, allow Unreason to prevail.

## THOMAS CARLYLE TO GOETHE

Edinburgh, April 15, 1827

It is now more than two years since Lord Bentinck's servant delivered to me at London the packet from Weimar, containing your kind letter and present; of both which, to say they were heartily gratifying to me, would be saying little; for I received them and keep them with a regard which can belong to nothing else. To me they are memorials of one whom I never saw, yet whose voice came to me from afar, with counsel and help, in my utmost need. For if I have been delivered from darkness into any measure of light, if I know aught of myself and my duties and destination, it is to the study of your writing more than to any other circumstance that I owe this; it is you more than any other man that I should always thank and reverence with the feeling of a Disciple to his Master, nay of a Son to his spiritual Father. This is no idle compliment, but a heartfelt truth; and humble as it is I feel that the knowledge of such truths must be more pleasing to you than all other glory.

The books [Carlyle's *Life of Schiller* and his translation of *Wilhelm Meister's Travels*] which I here take the liberty to offer you, are the poor product of endeavors, obstructed by sickness and many other causes; and in themselves little worthy of your acceptance: but perhaps they may find some favor for my sake, and interest you likewise as evidences of the progress of German literature in England. Hitherto it has not been injustice but ignorance that has blinded us in this matter: at all events a different state of things seems approaching; with respect to yourself, it is at hand, or rather has already come. This "Wilhelm Meister's Travels" which I reckon somewhat better translated than its forerunner, I in many quarters hear deeply, if not loudly, praised; and even the character with which I have prefaced it, appears to excite not objection but partial compliance, or at worst, hesitation and inquiry.

Of "Wilhelm Meister's Apprenticeship" I am also happy to give a much more flattering account than I could have anticipated at first. Above a thousand copies of the book are already in the hands of the public; loved also, with more or less insight, by all persons of any culture; and, what it has many times interested me to observe, with a degree of estimation determined not less by the intellectual force than by the moral earnestness of the reader. One of its warmest admirers known to me is a lady of rank, and intensely religious.

I may mention further that, some weeks ago, a stranger—a London bookseller—applied to me to translate your "Truth and Poetry," a proposal which I have perhaps only postponed, not rejected.

All this warrants me to believe that your name and

doctrines will ere long be English as well as German; and certainly there are few things which I have more satisfaction in contemplating than the fact that to this result my own efforts have contributed; that I have assisted in conquering for you a new province of mental empire; and for my countrymen a new treasure of wisdom which I myself have found so precious. One day, it may be, if there is any gift in me, I shall send you some work of my own. . . .

About six months ago I was married: my young wife, who sympathizes with me in most things, agrees also in my admiration of you; and would have me, in her name, beg of you to accept this purse, the work, as I can testify, of dainty fingers with true love; that so something, which she had handled and which had been hers, might be in your hands and be yours. In this little point I have engaged that you would gratify her. She knows you in your own language; and her first criticism was the following, expressed with some surprise: "This Goethe is a greater genius than Schiller, though he does not make me cry!" A better judgment than many which have been pronounced with more formality.

## GOETHE TO THOMAS CARLYLE

Weimar, July 20, 1827

IN A LETTER of May 15, which I despatched by post, and which I hope will have reached you in due time, I informed you how much pleasure your present had brought me. It found me in the country where I could examine and enjoy it in greater quiet. I am now, in my turn, about to send you a packet, of which I request your friendly acceptance.

Let me, first of all, my dear Sir, commend most highly

your biography of Schiller. It is remarkable for the close study it shows of the incidents of his life, while it also manifests a sympathetic study of his works. The accurate insight into the character and distinguished merit of this man, which you have thus acquired is really admirable, and so clear and just as was hardly to have been expected from a foreigner.

In this an old saying is verified: "Love helps to perfect knowledge." For precisely because the Scotsman regards the German with kindliness, and honors and loves him, does he recognize most surely his admirable qualities, and thus he rises to a clearness of view, to which even the great man's compatriots could not in earlier days attain. For their contemporaries very easily fall into error concerning eminent men;—personal peculiarities disturb them, the changeful current of life displaces their points of view, and hinders their knowledge and recognition of such men.

Schiller, however, was of so exceptional a nature, that his biographer had but to keep before his eyes the ideal of a pre-eminent man, and by maintaining it to the end, through individual fortunes and actions, see his task fulfilled . . .

Let me add some general considerations, which I have long cherished in silence, and which have been stirred up afresh in me by the present works.

It is obvious that the effects of the best poet and aesthetic writers of all nations have now for some time been directed towards what is universal in humanity. In each special field, whether in history, mythology, or fiction, more or less arbitrarily conceived, one sees the traits which are universal always more clearly revealed and illumining what is merely national and personal.

Though something of the same sort also prevails now in practical life, pervading all that is earthy, crude, wild, cruel, false, selfish, and treacherous, and striving to diffuse everywhere some gentleness, we cannot indeed hope that universal peace is being ushered in thereby, but only that inevitable strife will be gradually more restrained, war will become less cruel, and victory less insolent.

Whatever in the poetry of any nation tends to this and contributes to it, the others should endeavour to appropriate. The peculiarities of each nation must be learned, and allowance made for them, in order by these very means to hold intercourse with it; for the special characteristics of a nation are like its language and its currency: they facilitate intercourse, nay they first make it completely possible.

Pardon me, my dear Sir, for these remarks, which are perhaps not altogether coherent, nor to be comprehended at once; they are drawn from that ocean of meditations which, as years advance, swells and evermore deepens around every thinking person. Allow me to add yet something more, which I wrote on another occasion, but which may be immediately applied to your present pursuits:

A genuine, universal tolerance is most surely attained, if we do not quarrel with the peculiar characteristics of individual men and races but only hold fast the conviction, that what is truly excellent is distinguished by its belonging to all mankind. To such intercourse and mutual recognition, the German people have long contributed.

Whoever understands and studies German finds himself in the market, where all nations offer their wares; he plays the interpreter, while he enriches himself.

And thus every translator is to be regarded as a middle-man in this universal spiritual commerce, and as making it his business to promote this exchange: for say what we may of the insufficiency of translation, yet the work is and will always be one of the weightiest and worthiest undertakings in the general concerns of the world.

The Koran says: "God has given to each people a prophet in its own tongue!" Thus each translator is a prophet to his people. Luther's translation of the Bible has produced the greatest results, though criticism gives it qualified praise, and picks faults in it, even to the present day. What indeed is the whole enormous business of the Bible Society, but to make known the Gospel to all people in their own tongue?

Here, though one might run on endlessly on this topic, let me close. Gratify me soon with some reply, that I may know the present packet has reached you. In conclusion, permit me also to greet your dear wife, for whom I give myself the pleasure of adding some trifles in return for her charming gift. May a happy life together be your portion for many years.

After all this I still find myself prompted to add a word. May Mr. Carlyle take in friendly part what I have written above, and by continued musing convert it into a dialogue, so that it may seem to him as if we stood face to face in person.

I have indeed still to thank him for the pains he has expended on my works; for the good and kindly feeling with which he has been pleased to speak of me personally and of the incidents of my life. Assured of this feeling, I venture to congratulate myself on the anticipation that hereafter, if other works of mine should become known to him, especially if my correspondence with Schiller should appear, he will not change his opinion either of my friend or of me, but rather by many particulars will find it still further confirmed.

## THOMAS CARLYLE TO GOETHE

Edinburgh, August 20, 1827

YOU ARE KIND ENOUGH to inquire about my bygone life. With what readiness could I speak to you of it, how often have I longed to pour out the whole history before you! As it is, your works have been a mirror to me; unasked and unhoped-for, your wisdom has counselled me; and so peace and health of soul have visited me from afar. For I was once an Unbeliever, not in Religion only, but in all the Mercy and Beauty of which it is the Symbol; storm-tossed in my own imaginations; a man divided from men; exasperated, wretched, driven almost to despair; so that Faust's wild curse seemed the only fit greeting for human life; and his passionate "Accursed be, above all, patience!" was spoken from my very inmost heart. But now, thank Heaven, all this is altered: without change of external circumstances, solely by the new light which rose upon me, I attained to new thoughts, and a composure which I should once have considered as impossible. And now, under happier omens, though the bodily health which I lost in these struggles has never been and may never be restored to me, I look forward with cheerfulness to a life spent in literature, with such fortune and such strength as may be granted me; hoping little and fearing little from the world; having learned that what I once called happiness is not only not to be attained on earth, but not even to be desired. No wonder I should love the wise and worthy men by whose instructions so blessed a result has been brought about. For these men, too, there can be no reward like that consciousness that in distant countries and times the hearts of their fellow-men will yearn towards them with gratitude and veneration, and those that are wandering in darkness turn towards them as to loadstars guiding into a secure home.

I shall still hope to hear from you, and again to write to you, and always acknowledge you as my teacher and benefactor. May all good be long continued to you, for your own sake and that of mankind!

Edinburgh, January 17, 1828

IN ADDITION to the valued marks of your regard already conferred on me, I have now to solicit a favor of a more practical and as I may justly fear, of a more questionable nature. If the liberty I take is too great, let me hope that I shall find in your goodness an excuse.

I am at present a candidate for the Professorship of Moral Philosophy in our ancient Scottish University of St. Andrews; a situation of considerable emolument and respectability, in which certain of my friends flatter me that I might be useful to myself and others. The Electors to the Office are the Principal and actual Professors of the College; who promise in this instance, contrary indeed to their too frequent practice, to be guided solely by grounds of a public sort; preferring that applicant who shall, by reference perhaps to his previous literary performances, or by testimonials from men of established note, approve himself the ablest. The qualifications required, or at least expected, are not so much any profound scientific acquaintance with Philosophy properly so called, as a general character for intelligence, integrity, and literary attainment; all proofs of talent and spiritual worth of any kind being more or less available. To the Electors personally I am altogether a stranger.

Of my fitness for this, or any other office, it is indeed little that I can expect you to know. Nevertheless, if you have traced in me any sense for what is true and good, and any symptom, however faint, that I may realize in my own literary life some fraction of what I love and reverence in that of my instructors, you will not hesitate to say so; and a word from you may go further than many words from another. There is also a second reason why I ask this favor of you: the wish to feel myself connected by still more and still kinder ties with a man to whom I must reckon it among the pleasures of my existence that I stand in any relation whatever. For the rest, let me assure you that good or ill success in this canvass is little likely to affect my equanimity unduly; I have studied and lived to little purpose, if I have not, at the age of thirty-two learned in some degree "to seek for that consistency and sequence within myself, which external events will for ever refuse me." I need only add, on this subject, that the form of such a document as I solicit is altogether unimportant; that of a general certificate or testimonial, not specially addressed at all, being as common as any other.

# GOETHE'S TESTIMONIAL TO CARLYLE

*Goethe's document arrived after considerable delay. "Mustard after dinner"—as Carlyle put it in a letter to his brother. His candidature for a professorship at St. Andrews had already been rejected.*

True conviction proceeds from the heart; the soul; the real seat of the conscience, judges concerning what may be permitted and what may not be permitted far more surely than the understanding, which will see into and determine many things without hitting the right mark.

A well-disposed and self-observant man, wishing to respect himself and to live at peace with himself, and yet conscious of many an imperfection perplexing his inner life, and grieved by many a fault compromising him in the eyes of others, whereby he finds himself disturbed and opposed from within and from without, will seek by all methods to free himself from such impediments.

When once, however, he has fought his way faithfully and perseveringly through these discordant elements, and has recognized that only by striving and by doing can he vanquish his sorrow and suffering, for each defect a merit, for each fault amends must be sought and found, then does he feel himself at peace, as a new man.

But then, too, an innate good impulse at once impels him to lighten the burden of others and to save them from like sufferings, to enlighten his fellow-creatures as to their inner nature, and the outer world, to show them whence contradictions come in and how they are to be avoided and reconciled. At the same time, however, notwithstanding all this, he must confess that in the course of life, the outer and the inner remain in incessant conflict, and that he must therefore daily arm himself to maintain the ever-renewed struggle.

It may now be asserted without arrogance that German literature has done much for humanity in this respect, that a moral-psychological tendency pervades it, introducing not ascetic timidity, but a free culture in accordance with nature, and in cheerful obedience to law, and therefore I have observed with pleasure Mr. Carlyle's admirably profound study of this literature, and I have noticed with sympathy how he has not only been able to discover the beautiful and human, the good and great in us, but has also contributed what was his own, and has endowed us with the treasures of his genius. It must be granted that he has a clear judgment as to our aesthetic and ethic writers, and, at the same time, his own way of looking at them, which proves that he rests on an original foundation and has the power to develop in himself the essentials of what is good and beautiful.

In this sense, I may well regard him as a man who would fill a Chair of Moral Philosophy, with single-heartedness, with purity, effect and influence; enlightening the youth entrusted to him as to their real duties, in accordance with his disciplined thought, his natural gifts and his acquired knowledge, aiming at leading and urging their minds to moral activity, and thereby steadily guiding them towards religious completeness.

# THE ESSENCE OF GENIUS

*For some time Eckermann suffered from an indisposition, but disregarding Goethe's advice he hesitated to see a physician. It was this little dispute which prompted one of the most remarkable conversations.*

Weimar, March 11, 1828

As I DID not appear to Goethe very gay and cheerful today after dinner, he lost his patience and could not refrain from smiling at me ironically and teasing me a little.

"You are a second Shandy," said he, "the father of that renowned Tristram, who was annoyed half his life by a creaking door but could not work up the resolution to remove the daily annoyance with a few drops of oil. But so it is with us all! The darkness and enlightenment of man make his destiny. The demon ought to lead us every day with strings, and show us what to do on every occasion. But the good spirit leaves us in the lurch, and we grope about in the dark.

Napoleon was the man! Always enlightened, always clear and decided, always with sufficient energy to carry through whatever he considered advantageous and necessary. His life was the stride of a demigod, from battle to battle, and from victory to victory. It might be said of him that he lived in a state of continual enlightenment. His destiny was more brilliant than any the world had seen before him, or perhaps will ever see after him. Yes, my good friend, that was a man whom we cannot imitate."

Goethe paced up and down the room. I had placed myself at the table, which had been already cleared, but upon which there was left some wine with biscuits and fruit. Goethe poured a glass for me and insisted that I eat. "You have," he said, "not condescended to be our guest at dinner today, but still a glass of this wine, a present from good friends, ought to do you good." I did not refuse these good things, and Goethe continued to walk up and down the room, murmuring to himself in an excited state of mind, and from time to time uttering unintelligible words.

What he had just said about Napoleon was in my mind, and I endeavored to lead the conversation back to that subject. "It appears to me," I began, "that Napoleon was especially in that state of enlightenment when he was young and his powers were still growing, when he seemed to be enjoying divine protection and all his luck was good. In later years this enlightenment seems to have forsaken him, as well as his good fortune and guiding star."

"What do you expect?" returned Goethe. "I was not able to repeat my 'love songs' or 'Werther'. That divine enlightenment, which inspires everything, is always found with the productive period of youth, as in the case of Napoleon, who was one of the most productive men that ever lived. Yes, my friend, you don't need to write poems and plays to be productive; there is also a productiveness of action, which in many cases is more important. A physician may be productive if he really intends to heal; if he is not he will only succeed now and then, as if by chance; on the whole he will be only a bungler."

"By productiveness you seem to mean what is usually called genius."

"One lies very near the other," replied Goethe. "For what is genius but that productive power by which actions are accomplished that can display themselves before God and Nature, and are therefore permanent, producing results. All Mozart's works are of this kind; there is in them a productive power which affects generation after generation, and yet is never diminished or used up. It is the same with other great composers and artists. What an influence Phidias and Raphael have had upon succeeding centuries, and Dürer and Holbein, too. The man who first invented the forms and proportions of the old German architecture, so that in the course of time a

Strasbourg cathedral and the one at Cologne were possible, was also a genius: for his thoughts had a power that is continually productive and still operates. Luther was a genius of a very important kind; he has been an influence for a long time and we cannot imagine when he will cease to be one in the future. Lessing would not accept for himself the lofty title of genius; but his permanent influence testifies against his modesty. On the other hand, we have considered in literature men who were important in their lifetime as great geniuses, but whose influence ended with their life, and who were therefore less great than they and others thought. For, as I said before, the test of genius is a productive power of permanent influence. Furthermore, genius does not depend upon the business, the art, or the trade which a man follows, but may be found in anyone. Whether a person shows himself a man of genius in science like Oken and Humboldt, or in war and statesmanship like Friedrich, Peter the Great and Napoleon, or whether he composes a song like Béranger, it all comes to the same thing; the only point is whether the thought, the discovery, the deed, is living, and can live on.

"Then I must add that it is not the quantity of creations or acts which indicate the productive man. We have in literature poets who are considered very productive because volume after volume of their poems has appeared. But, in my opinion, these people ought to be called thoroughly unproductive because what they have written is without life and durability. Goldsmith, on the contrary, has written so few poems that their number is not worth mentioning; but I would call him a thoroughly productive poet, because the little that he has written has an inherent life which can sustain itself."

There was a pause during which Goethe continued to pace up and down the room. But I was anxious to hear more on this significant point, and so attempted to arouse Goethe again.

"Does this productiveness of genius lie in the mind of a great man, or is it also in his body?"

"The body," said Goethe, "has the greatest influence upon

it. There was a time in Germany when a genius was always thought of as short, weak, or hunch-backed, but my genius is one who has a well-proportioned body. When it was said of Napoleon that he was a man of granite this applied particularly to his body. What did he not venture? From the burning sands of the Syrian deserts to the snowy plains of Moscow what an incalculable number of marches, battles, and nights in the open he went through! And what fatigues and bodily privations he was forced to endure! Little sleep, little nourishment, and yet always ready for the highest mental activity. After the awful exertion and excitement of the eighteenth Brumaire, at midnight, although he had not tasted anything the whole day, without thinking of strengthening his body with food, he felt power enough in the depth of the night to draw up the well-known proclamation to the French people. When you consider what he accomplished and endured, you might imagine that when he was in his fortieth year not a sound particle would be left in him; but even at that age he still was fit to be a perfect hero. But you are quite right: the real peak of his brilliance came in his youth. And it is something to say that a man of obscure origin, coming of age at a time in history which aroused great capacities, so distinguished himself as to become at twenty-seven the idol of a nation of thirty millions! Yes, my good friend, one must be young to do great things. And Napoleon is not the only one!"

"His brother Lucien," I suggested, "also did a great deal at an early age. We see him as president of the five hundred and afterwards as minister of the interior, when he had just passed twenty-five."

"Why name Lucien?" put in Goethe. "History gives us hundreds of clever people, who while still young, have carried through most important matters with great success both in the council room and in the field."

"If I were a prince," he went on with animation, "I would never place in the highest offices people who have gradually risen by birth and seniority, and who in their old age move on leisurely in their accustomed groove, for in this way little talent is brought to light. I would have young men; but they must have capacities, and be endowed with clearness and energy, and also with the best intentions and character. Then there would be pleasure in governing and improving one's people. But where is there a prince who would like this system and put it into service? I have great hopes of the present Crown Prince of Prussia. From all that I hear and know of him he is a very distinguished man; and that is essential for recognizing and choosing qualified and clever people. For, say what we will, like can only be recognized by like; and only a prince who himself possesses great abilities can properly acknowledge and value great abilities in his subjects and servants. 'Let the path be open to talent' was the well-known maxim of Napoleon, who really had a particular flair in the choice of his subordinates, who knew how to organize the spheres of his executives, and who therefore was served in all his great undertakings as scarcely anyone had been served before him."

Goethe delighted me particularly this evening. The noblest part of his nature appeared alive in him, while the sound of his voice and the fire of his eyes were full of power, as if he were inspired by a fresh gleam from the best days of youth. It seemed strange to me that he, who at so great an age was filling an important post, should speak so decidedly in favor of youth, and should wish the big jobs in the state to be filled, if not by youths, at least by men still young. I could not help mentioning some Germans of high standing, who at an advanced age did not appear to lack the necessary energy and youthful activity for the direction of the most important and most various affairs.

"Such men are natural geniuses," said Goethe. "They are special cases; they experience a renewed puberty, while other people are young only once. Every soul is a piece of eternity, and the few years which it is bound to the earthly body does not make it old. If this soul is of a trivial kind, it will exercize little control during its bodily confinement; the body will predominate, and when the body grows old the soul will not hold and restrain it. But if the soul is powerful, as is the case in men of natural genius, then with its animating penetration of the body it will not only strengthen and ennoble the organism, but it will also be able to confer perpetual youth. So it is that in men of superior endowments, even in old age, we constantly perceive fresh epochs of singular productiveness; they seem constantly to grow young again for a time, and that is what I call a repeated puberty. Still youth is youth, and however powerful a soul may prove, it will never become entirely master of the corporeal, and it makes a wonderful difference whether it finds in the body an ally or an adversary.

"There was a time in my life when I had to write a whole printed sheet every day, and I accomplished it with ease. I wrote my 'Brother and Sister' in three days and my 'Clavigo' in a week. Now I can do nothing of the kind, and yet I can hardly complain of want of productiveness considering my age. But whereas in my youth I wrote well every day and under all circumstances, now I am at my best only periodically and under certain favorable conditions. Ten or twelve years ago, in the happy time after the war of independence when the poems of the 'Divan' were inspiring me, I was often productive enough to compose two or three in a day, and it was all the same to me whether I was in the open air, in the carriage, or in an inn. Now I can only work at the second part of my 'Faust' during the early part of the day, when I feel refreshed and revived by sleep, and have not been perplexed by the trifles of daily life. And how much do I get done? Under the most favorable circumstances, a page of writing, but generally only a few inches on the page, and often, when in an unproductive mood, still less." . . .

Goethe sat down opposite me, and we talked about all sorts of things. We spoke of Lord Byron and the many misfortunes which had embittered his later life until in the end a noble will but an unhappy destiny drove him to Greece and entirely destroyed him.

"You will generally find," continued Goethe, "that in middle age a man frequently experiences a change; if in his youth everything favors him and goes well for him, suddenly everything is completely reversed, and misfortunes and disasters are heaped upon each other. Do you know my opinion on this matter? —*Man must be ruined again!* Every extraordinary man has a certain mission which he is called upon to accomplish. If he has fulfilled it, he is no longer needed upon earth in the same form, and Providence uses him for something else. But as everything here below happens in a natural way, the demons keep tripping him up till he finally falls. It was like that with Napoleon and many others. Mozart died at thirty-six. Raphael at almost the same age. Byron only a little older. But all of them had perfectly fulfilled their missions and it was time for them to go so that other people might still have something left to do in a world made to last a long while."

## RACE AGAINST TIME

*As a young girl, Jenny von Pappenheim often visited Goethe's daughter-in-law Ottilie who, with August and their three children, lived on the top floor of Goethe's house. In her memoirs Jenny von Pappenheim tells of a small incident which occurred on the occasion of a visit of the writer Ludwig Tieck in October 1828.*

FESTIVE PARTIES had been arranged in honor of Tieck, once by Ottilie on the top floor, once in Goethe's living quarters. First, Goethe invited only the family for dinner; though my presence was not desired, I dared, with the prerogative of youth, to invade the inner sanctum in order to accompany the Tiecks to Ottilie's, while the old man received other guests. In the course of the conversation they spoke of Walter Scott whom Goethe very much respected, at which my heart —taken in by the English—rejoiced; I only ventured to interject that "The Fair Maid of Perth" was not always too amusing, whereupon I met with a punishing side glance and the remark that "children always want nothing but colorful picture books."

A few days later we had tea with Ottilie. We stood about, speaking in low voices, and at the least noise we would turn awed toward the door as if we were expecting a spectre. But it did not appear. Ottilie was supposed to conjure it up, but the worldly as well as the celestial spirits are stubborn. The company became restive, Tieck turned pale and bit his lips. I approached Eckermann who was placidly standing in a corner and who had just put his "inevitable" note book into his pocket. "He does not want to appear," he said.

At that I took courage and went downstairs. The first few steps I took in great haste, then I slunk along slowly, for I was somewhat afraid nevertheless and might have turned back, had I not felt ashamed of myself, since Friedrich had already seen me. He did not want to announce me; "go in," he said.

Goethe was standing at his desk with his long house coat open, a pile of old manuscripts in front of him. He did not notice me come in; I said coyly: "Good evening!"

He turned his head, looked at me with wide-open eyes, cleared his throat—the most conspicuous sign of his suppressed anger. I raised my hands beseechingly. "What does the girl want from me?" he growled.

"We are all waiting for Your Excellency, and Tieck—"

"Ah, for heaven's sake," the old man blustered, "do you, little girl, think that I will run to everyone who is waiting for me? What would happen to me then?" And at that he pointed at the loose sheets of paper. "When I am dead, no one will do it for me. Tell that to the whole lot of them up there. Good evening."

I trembled at the sound of his voice which was constantly

growing louder and said in a low voice: "Good evening." But I might have sounded rather sad, because Goethe called me back, looked at me in a friendly manner and continued in a quite different tone: "An old man who still wants to work must not change his mind to please anyone. If he does, posterity won't like it at all. Now go, my child, your cheerful youth will make them feel much more at ease up there than my meditative age, tonight."

## GOETHE DICTATING

*Johann Christian Schuchardt, who worked as Goethe's secretary for several years, gave the following description of the poet's method of working.*

DURING THE TIME in which I held the position of secretary to Goethe, the final edition of his works were brought out. He dictated new and reworked old material for it, among other things also "Wilhelm Meister's Travels," whereby I had the occasion of admiring the strength, security and clarity of his mind at such an advanced age. He dictated, sure of himself, as fluently as anyone else would only be able to read out of a printed book.

Had all this happened in quiet and without any outside disturbance and interruption, it would have hardly struck me. But in between came the barber, the hairdresser (every second day Goethe had his hair curled and had his hair done daily), an attendant from the library, several times my predecessor, the librarian Kräuter, and the clerk, who all had permission to enter without being announced. Then the butler would announce a stranger with whom—if allowed to enter—Goethe conversed for some time; in between a member of the family would also come in. The barber and hairdresser spoke of what had happened in the city, the library attendant brought his reports from the library, and so forth.

When his sonorous "Come in!" sounded, I finished the sentence and waited until those present left again. Then I repeated as much as it seemed necessary for the context, and then his dictation continued until the next disturbance, as though nothing had happened. This seemed so incredible to me that I looked around the room to see whether there might have been a book somewhere, a rough draft or sketch in which Goethe could have glanced in passing (while he dictated he walked up and down without interruption, mostly around the table and around where I was sitting), but I was unable ever to discover anything.

When I expressed my surprise about it to Hofrat Meyer, Goethe's friend of long standing, whom I saw daily, he accepted it as something well known to him and told me of another incident: On the occasion of a long slow trip from Jena to Weimar Goethe told him the plot of the entire novel "Elective Affinities," reciting it as fluently as if he had a printed copy before him; and yet, at that time, not a single word had been written down.

While he dictated, it often happened that Goethe suddenly stopped as one might do when faced unexpectedly by a group of people or an object, momentarily attracting one's attention. Immediately he seemed to group them and to bring them into artistic form. With his hands stretched out and his body bent to one or the other side, he brought the object into balance and artistic position. When he seemed to have succeeded, he would say: "That's right! Quite right!"

# A DISCOURSE ON ENGLISH POETRY

*Henry Crabb Robinson, who met Goethe first in 1801, returned to Weimar in 1829. In his reminiscences Robinson tells the story of this second visit.*

August 2, 1829

A GOLDEN DAY! Voigt and I left Jena before seven, and in three hours were at Weimar. Having left our cards at Goethe's dwelling-house, we proceeded to the garden-house in the park, and were at once admitted to the great man. I was aware, by the present of medals from him, that I was not forgotten, and I had heard from Hall and others that I was expected. Yet I was oppressed by the kindness of his reception. We found the old man in his cottage in the park, to which he retires for solitude from his town-house where are his son, his daughter-in-law, and three grandchildren. He generally eats and drinks alone; and when he invites a stranger, it is to a tête-à-tête. This is a wise sparing of his strength. Twenty-seven years ago I thus described him: "In Goethe I beheld an elderly man of terrific dignity; a penetrating and insupportable eye. . . ." Now I beheld the same eye, indeed, but the eyebrows were become thin, the cheeks were furrowed, the lips no longer curled with fearful compression, and the lofty, erect posture had sunk to a gentle stoop. *Then* he never honored me with a look after the first haughty bow, *now* he was all courtesy. "Well, you are come at last," he said; "we have waited years for you. How is my old friend Knebel? You have given him youth again, I have no doubt." In his room in which there was a French bed without curtains, hung two large engravings: one, the well-known panoramic view of Rome; the other, the old square engraving, an imaginary restoration of the ancient public buildings. Both of these I then possessed, but I have now given them to the University Hall, London. He spoke of the old engraving that it delighted him by showing what the scholars thought in the fifteenth century. The opinion of scholars is now changed. In like manner he thought favorably of the panoramic view, though it is incorrect, including objects which cannot be seen from the same spot.

I had a second chat with him late in the evening. We talked much of Lord Byron, and the subject was renewed afterwards. To refer to detached subjects of conversation, I ascertained that he was unacquainted with Burn's "Vision." This is most remarkable, on account of its close resemblance to the "Dedication" to his own works, because the whole logic of the two poems is the same. Each poet confesses his infirmities; each is consoled by the Muse,—the holly-leaf of the Scotch poet being the "veil of dew and sunbeams" of the German. I pointed out this resemblance to Frau von Goethe; and she acknowledged it.

This evening I gave Goethe an account of De Lamennais [French philosophical writer] and quoted from him a passage that all truth comes from God, and is made known to us by the Church. He held at the moment a flower in his hand, and a beautiful butterfly was in the room. He exclaimed: "No doubt all truth comes from God; but the Church! There is the point. God speaks to us through this flower and that butterfly; and that's a language these rascals don't understand." Something led him to speak of Ossian with contempt. I remarked: "The taste for Ossian is to be ascribed to you in great measure. It was Werther that set the fashion." He smiled and said: "That's partly true; but it was never perceived by the critics that Werther praised Homer while he retained his senses, and Ossian when he was going mad. But reviewers do not notice such things." I reminded Goethe that Napoleon loved Ossian. "It was the contrast with his own nature," Goethe replied. "He loved soft and melancholy music. 'Werther' was among the books at St. Helena."

We spoke of the emancipation of the Catholics. Goethe

said: "My daughter will be glad to talk about it; I take no interest in such matters." On leaving him the first evening he kissed me three times. (I was always before disgusted with man's kisses) Voigt never saw him do so much to any other. He pressed me to spend some days at Weimar on my return; and, indeed, afterwards induced me to protract my stay. I was there from the 13th of August till the 19th.

I cannot pretend to set down our conversations in the order in which they occurred. On my return from Jena, I was more aware than before that Goethe was grown old; perhaps, because he did not exert himself so much. His expression of feeling was, however, constantly tender and kind. He was alive to his reputation in England, and apparently mortified at the poor account I gave of Lord Leveson Gower's translation of 'Faust'; though I did not choose to tell him that his noble translator, as an apology, said he did it as an exercise while learning the language. On my mentioning that Lord Leveson Gower had not ventured to translate the "Prologue in Heaven," he seemed surprised. "How so? that is quite unobjectionable. The idea is in Job." He did not perceive that that was the aggravation, not the excuse.

I spoke with especial admiration of his "Carnival at Rome" [In Goethe's account of the second journey in Rome] "I shall be there next winter, and shall be glad if the thing gives me half the pleasure I had in reading the description."—"Ay, my dear, but it won't do that! To let you into a secret, nothing can be more wearisome than that Carnival. I wrote that account really to relieve myself. My lodgings were in the Corso. I stood on the balcony, and jotted down everything I saw. There is not a single item invented." And then, smiling, he said: "We poets are much more matter-of-fact people than they who are not poets have any idea of; and it was the truth and reality which made that writing so popular." This is in harmony with Goethe's doctrine: he was a decided realist, and an enemy of the ideal, as he relates in the history of his first acquaintance with Schiller. Speaking this evening of his travels in Switzerland, he said that he still possessed all that he has in print called his "documents," that is, tavern-bills, accounts, advertisements, etc. And he repeated his remark that it is by the laborious collection of facts that even a poetical view of nature is to be corrected and authenticated. I mentioned Marlowe's "Faust." He burst out into an exclamation of praise. "How greatly it is all planned!" He had thought of translating it. He was fully aware that Shakespeare did not stand alone.

This, and indeed every evening, I believe, Lord Byron was the subject of his praise. He said: "There is no padding in his poetry." And he compared the brilliancy and clearness of his style to a metal wire drawn through a steel plate. In the complete edition of Byron's works, including the "Life" by Moore, there is a statement of the connection between Goethe and Byron. At the time of my interviews with Goethe, Byron's "Life" was actually in preparation. Goethe was by no means indifferent to the account which was to be given to the world of his own relations to the English poet, and was desirous of contributing all in his power to its completeness. For that purpose he put into my hands the lithographic dedication of "Sardanapalus" to himself, and all the original papers which had passed between them. He permitted me to take these to my hotel, and to do with them what I pleased; in other words, I was to copy them, and add such recollections as I was able to supply of Goethe's remarks on Byron. These filled a very closely written folio letter, which I despatched to England; but Moore afterwards assured me that he had never received it.

One or two of the following remarks will be found as significant as anything Goethe has written of Byron. It was a satisfaction to me to find that Goethe preferred to all the other serious poems of Byron the "Heaven and Earth", though it seemed almost satire when he exclaimed, "A bishop might have written it!" He added, "Byron should have lived to execute his vocation."—"And that was?" I asked. "To dramatize the Old Testament. What a subject under his hands would the Tower of Babel have been!" He continued: "You must not take it ill; but Byron was indebted for the profound views he took of the Bible to the *ennui* he suffered from it at school." Goethe, it will be remembered, in one of his ironical epigrams, derives his poetry from *ennui*; he greets her as the Mother of the Muses. It was with reference to the poems of the Old Testament that Goethe praised the views which Byron took of Nature. "He had not," Goethe said, "like me, devoted a long life to the study of Nature, and yet in all his works I found but two or three passages I could have wished to alter."

I had the courage to confess my inability to relish the serious poems of Byron, and to intimate my dissatisfaction with the comparison generally made between "Manfred" and "Faust." I remarked: "Faust has nothing left but to sell his soul to the Devil when he had exhausted all the resources of science in vain; but Manfred's was a poor reason,—his passion for Astarte." He smiled, and said, "That's true." But then he fell back on the indomitable spirit of Manfred. Even at the last he was not conquered. Power in all its forms Goethe had respect for. This he had in common with Carlyle. And the impudence of Byron's satire he felt and enjoyed. I pointed out "The Deformed Transformed," as being really an imitation of "Faust," and was pleased to find that Goethe especially praised this piece. I read to him the "Vision of Judgment," explaining the obscurer allusions. He enjoyed it as a child might, but his criticisms scarcely went beyond the exclamations "Too bad!" "Heavenly!" "Unsurpassable!" . . .

I took an opportunity to mention Milton, and found Goethe unacquainted with "Samson Agonistes." I read to him the first part, to the end of the scene with Delilah. He fully conceived the spirit of it, though he did not praise Milton with the warmth with which he eulogized Byron, of whom he said "the like would never come again; he was inimitable." Ariosto was not so daring as Byron in the "Vision of Judgment." Goethe said Samson's confession of his guilt was in a better spirit than anything in Byron. "There is fine logic in all the speeches." On my reading Delilah's vindication of herself, he exclaimed: "That is capital; he has put her in the right." To one of Samson's speeches he cried out, "O the parson!" He thanked me for making him acquainted with this poem, and said: "It gives me a higher opinion of Milton than I had before. It lets me more into the nature of his mind than any other of his works."

I read to him Coleridge's "Fire, Famine, and Slaughter"; his praise was faint. I inquired whether he knew the name of Lamb. "O yes! Did he not write a pretty sonnet on his own name?" Charles Lamb, though he always affected contempt for Goethe, yet was manifestly pleased that his name was known to him.

I informed Goethe of my possession of Wieland's bust by Schadow. He said: "It is like a lost child found. The Duchess Amalia sent for Schadow to do it, and when done gave it to Wieland. He died when the French were here, and we were all away. Wieland's goods were sold by auction, and we heard that the bust was bought by an Englishman." I related to him how I had bought it at the recommendation of Flaxman, who deemed it "a perfect work." Goethe then said: "You must be sensible that it ought to be here. A time will come when you can no longer enjoy it. Take care that it comes here hereafter." This I promised. And I have in my will given it to the Grand Duke, in trust, for the public library in Weimar. Goethe expressed to me his pleasure that I had retained so lively a recollection of Weimar at its best time, when Schiller, Herder, and Wieland all lived. I remember no other mention of Herder, nor did I expect it. Goethe spoke of Wieland as a man of genius, and of Schiller with great regard. He said that Schiller's rendering of the witch-scenes in "Macbeth" was "detestable." "But it was his way; you must let every man have his own character." This was a tolerance characteristic to Goethe.

I have already mentioned Goethe's fondness for keeping portrait memorials, and can only consider it as an extreme instance of this that I was desired to go to one Schmeller to have my portrait taken,—a head in crayons, frightfully ugly, and very like. The artist told me that he had within a few years done for Goethe more than three hundred. It is the kind of *Andenken* he preferred. They are all done in the same style,—full face. I sat to Schmeller also for a portrait for Knebel,—a profile, and much less offensive.

In this way I spent five evenings with Goethe. When he took leave of me, it was very kindly, and he requested me to write every three or four months, when I came to an interesting place. But this I did not venture to do. I went upstairs and looked over his rooms. They had little furniture, but there were interesting engravings on the walls. His bed was without curtains,—a mere couch. I saw much of his daughter-in-law; he is said to have called her, "a crazy angel," and the epithet is felicitous.

## A. E. ODYNIEC TO KORSAK

*Anton Eduard Odyniec, writer and translator, visited Goethe together with his friend, Adam Mickiewicz, the eminent Polish poet.*

Weimar, August 20, 1829

YESTERDAY, AT NOON, the elegant carriage of Frau Ottilie called for us at our hotel, and a quarter of an hour later we stepped out of it in front of the garden door leading to Goethe's cottage where an old servant of his was waiting for us. He guided us through the garden, opened the door to the salon, bade us enter and left. We waited there for almost fifteen minutes, speaking to each other in whispers. Adam Mickiewicz asked me whether my heart was beating rapidly. In fact, this was like a vigil, as if for a supernatural appearance. He himself remembered how he had envied Madame Szymanowska for having seen Goethe and having spoken to him. At that we heard someone walking above us. Adam quoted, with emphasis, the verse from Zgierski's 'Ciszka': "You hear a walking and a lofty stride"—and he had hardly cited this fitting quotation when the door opened and through it entered—Jupiter! I flushed. And it may be said without exaggeration that there is something Jupiter-like about him. His appearance was colossal, his figure tall, his face dignified, impressive, and his forehead—that is what is Jupiter-like about him. Without any diadem, it radiates majesty. His hair, not yet white, is only somewhat gray above his brow. His clear and lively eyes are distinguished by one peculiarity, namely a light gray, enameled line which encompasses the iris of both eyes. Adam likened them to the rings of Saturn. Never before had we seen anything like this on anyone. He wore a dark brown coat buttoned from top to bottom. Around his neck he wore no collar but a white scarf, held crosswise together by a pin.

Like a ray of sun breaking through clouds a wonderfully lovely, benevolent smile transfigured the austerity of his physiognomy, as he entered and greeted us with a bow and handshakes. He said in French: "I apologize, gentlemen, for having kept you waiting. I am very much pleased to meet friends of Madame Szymanowska who honors me with her friendship." I must tell you that Goethe was a great admirer of Mme. Szymanowska and, speaking of her, said: "She is as charming as she is beautiful; and gracious as she is charming."

Then, when we had sat down, he turned to Adam and assured him that he knew he was at the head of a new movement which had been taken up by the literati in his country as well as in the whole of Europe. "I know out of my own experience," he added, "what a difficult thing it is to swim against the tide."

"We know too," Adam replied, "according to Your Excellency's experience how a great genius while swimming can make the tide turn." Goethe nodded slightly, as a sign that he understood the compliment and continued talking saying he regretted that he knew only a little of Polish literature and that he did not understand any Slavic language. "But everyone has so much to do in this life." Yet he added that he knew Adam from the magazines as well as from fragments of his new work, 'Wallenrod,' which Madame Szymanowska had been kind enough to have sent him in a German translation. Meanwhile Adam interjected a few words about my translation of Bürger. I thought I found an expression of benevolent kindness in Goethe's eyes which met mine looking up at him. Then, at Goethe's request, Adam outlined the entire development of Polish literature very concisely and clearly, from the earliest to the latest period, solidifying it by comparing it to the historical epochs. When Goethe's eyes rested on him there was not only an expression of profound respect, but also of a lively interest in what was said. The finger movements of his hand seemed to indicate the same. By the way, I forgot to mention that, at the beginning of the conversation, Goethe spoke in German; but as soon as Adam gave him to understand that he was able to speak German, but did not dare use it in his presence, he immediately spoke French again. In the course of the conversation Goethe maintained that, with the striving for general truth—which constantly became more noticeable—poetry and literature as a whole would have to accept a more universal character; but he granted Adam that it would never lose its peculiar national traits. From that the conversation turned to folk-songs, and Goethe asked about and then listened with great interest to what Adam, and partly I too, could tell him about the characteristic differences and the melodies of our provincial songs. He repeated all this later at luncheon for the benefit of the others. Thus our literary conversation ended.

# W. M. THACKERAY'S RECOLLECTIONS

*As a young man William Makepeace Thackeray lived for some time in Weimar. In 1855 Thackeray contributed this account of his reminiscences to G. H. Lewes' "Life of Goethe."*

FIVE-AND-TWENTY YEARS AGO, at least a score of young English lads used to live at Weimar for study, or sport, or society; all of which were to be had in the friendly little Saxon capital. The Grand-duke and Duchess received us with the kindliest hospitality. The court was splendid, but yet most pleasant and homely. We were invited in our turns to dinners, balls, and assemblies there. Such young men as had a right, appeared in uniforms, diplomatic and military. Some, I remember, invented gorgeous clothing: the kind old court marshal of those days, M. de Spiegel (who had two of the most lovely daughters eyes ever looked on) being in nowise difficult as to the admission of these young Englishmen. Of the winter nights we used to charter sedan chairs, in which we were carried through the snow to those pleasant court entertainments. I for my part had the good luck to purchase Schiller's sword, which formed a part of my court costume, and still hangs in my study, and puts me in mind of days of youth the most kindly and delightful.

We knew the whole society of the little city, and but that the young ladies, one and all, spoke admirable English, we surely might have learned the very best German. The society met constantly. The ladies of the court had their evenings. The theatre was open twice or thrice in the week, where we assembled, a large family party. Goethe had retired from the direction, but the great traditions remained still. The theatre was admirably conducted; and besides the excellent Weimar company, famous actors and singers from various parts of Germany performed starring engagements through the winter. In that winter I remember we had Ludwig Devrient in Shylock, Hamlet, Falstaff and "The Robbers"; and the beautiful Schröder in "Fidelio." . . .

In 1831, though he had retired from the world, Goethe would nevertheless very kindly receive strangers. His daughter-in-law's tea-table was always spread for us. We passed hours after hours there, and night after night with the pleasantest talk and music. We read over endless novels and poems in French, English, and German. My delight in those days was to make caricatures for children. I was touched to find that they were remembered, and some even kept until the present time; and very proud to be told, as a lad, that the great Goethe had looked at some of them.

He remained in his private apartments, where only a very few privileged persons were admitted; but he liked to know all that was happening, and interested himself about all strangers. Whenever a countenance struck his fancy, there was an artist settled in Weimar who made a portrait of it. Goethe had quite a gallery of heads, in black and white, taken by his painter. His house was all over pictures, drawings, casts, statues and medals.

Of course I remember very well the perturbation of spirit with which, as a lad of nineteen, I received the expected intimation that the Herr Geheimrat would see me on such a morning. This notable audience took place in a little antechamber of his private apartments, covered all round with antique casts and bas-reliefs. He was habited in a long grey or drab redingote, with a white neck-cloth and a red ribbon in his buttonhole. He kept his hands behind his back, just as in Rauch's statuette. His complexion was very bright, clear and rosy. His eyes extraordinarily dark, piercing and brilliant. I felt quite afraid before them, and recollect comparing them to the eyes of the hero of a certain romance called "Melmoth the Wanderer," which used to alarm us boys thirty years ago; eyes of an individual who had made a bargain with a Certain Person, and at an extreme old age retained these eyes in all their awful splendour. I fancied Goethe must have been still more handsome as an old man than even in the days of his youth. His voice was very rich and sweet. He asked me questions about myself, which I answered as best I could. I recollect I was at first astonished, and then somewhat relieved, when I found he spoke French with not a good accent.

I saw him but three times. Once walking in the garden of his house in the *Frauenplan;* once going to step in his chariot on a sunshiny day, wearing a cap and a cloak with a red collar. He was caressing at the time a beautiful little golden-haired granddaughter, over whose sweet fair face the earth has long since closed too.

Any of us who had books or magazines from England sent them to him, and he examined them eagerly. "Frazer's Magazine" had lately come out, and I remember he was interested in those admirable outline portraits which appeared for a while in its pages. But there was one, a very ghastly caricature of Mr. Rogers, which, as Madame de Goethe told me, he shut up and put away from him angrily. "They would make me look like that," he said; though in truth I can fancy nothing more serene, majestic, and healthy looking than the grand old Goethe.

Though his sun was setting, the sky round about was calm and bright, and that little Weimar illumined by it. In every one of those kind salons the talk was still of Art and letters. The theatre, though possessing no very extraordinary actors, was still conducted with noble intelligence and order. The actors read books, and were men of letters and gentlemen; holding a not unkindly relationship with the aristocracy. At court the conversation was exceedingly friendly, simple and polished.

The Grand-duchess, a lady of very remarkable endowments, would kindly borrow our books from us, lend us her own, and graciously talk to us young men about our literary tastes and pursuits. In the respect paid by this court to the patriarch of letters, there was something ennobling I think, alike to the subject and sovereign. With a five-and-twenty years' experience since those happy days of which I write, and an acquaintance with an immense variety of human kind, I think I have never seen a society more simple, charitable, courteous, gentlemen-like than that of the dear little Saxon city, where the good Schiller and the great Goethe lived and lie buried.

## THE DEATH OF AUGUST

*In April 1830 Eckermann accompanied Goethe's son August on a trip to Italy. The travelling companions separated at Genoa and August continued alone his journey to Rome. It was there that he died of a brain stroke on October 27, in his 41 year. August von Goethe was buried in the Protestant cemetery near the Pyramid of Cestius, a place which had once impressed his father so strongly by its romantic beauty that he expressed the wish to be buried there himself. Eckermann reports in the following passage his reflections on the way home to Weimar.*

On the afternoon of November 20th, I left Nordheim, and set off for Göttingen, which I reached at dusk. In the evening, at the dinner table, when the landlord heard that I had come from Weimar, and was on my way back, he calmly told me that the great poet Goethe had had a severe misfortune in his old age, since according to the last papers, his only son had died of paralysis in Italy.

I spent a sleepless night. This event which affected me so

closely was constantly before my eyes. The following days and nights, which I spent on the road, and in Mülhausen and Gotha, were no better. Being alone in the carriage, under the influence of the gloomy November days, and in desert fields, where there was no external object to distract my attention or to cheer me, I vainly tried to think of other things. While among the people at the inns, I constantly heard of the mournful event as the news of the day. My greatest fear was that Goethe, at his advanced years, would not be able to surmount the violent storm of paternal feelings. And what impression, I thought, will my own arrival make—when I went away with his son, and now come back alone. It will seem as though he has not really lost him till he sees me.

With these thoughts and feelings, I reached the last station before Weimar, on Tuesday, the 23rd of November, at six o'clock in the evening. I felt, for the second time in my life, that human existence has heavy moments through which one must pass. I was communing in thought with higher beings above me, when I was struck by the light of the moon, which came from amid thick clouds, and after shining brightly for some moments was wrapped in darkness as before. Whether this was chance, or something more, I took it as a favorable omen from above, and thus received unexpected encouragement.

I just greeted the people at my residence, and then set off at once for Goethe's house. I first went to Frau von Goethe. I found her already in mourning, but calm and collected, and we had a great deal to say to each other.

I then went downstairs to see Goethe. He was standing erect and firm in his room and embraced me heartily. I found him perfectly serene and calm. We sat down and talked immediately of practical matters, and I was very happy to be near him again. He showed me two letters which he had started to write me but had not sent off. We then talked about the Grand Duchess, about the prince and many other things. Not a single word, however, was said about his son.

## GOETHE TO F. ZELTER

*Two days after he had seen Eckermann again, the travelling companion of his unfortunate son, Goethe suffered a hemorrhage.*

Weimar, December 10, 1830

HAD I NOT KEPT the clockwork of my life's activities in good order, I could scarcely continue to exist in so pitiful a condition. This time, however, the hand has only been put back a few hours, and now everything is going again in the old steady way.

However, I have another confession to make about the events of November. The loss of my son weighed heavily upon me in more than one way, so I decided upon a piece of work that should completely absorb me. The fourth volume of my *Autobiography* had lain quietly aside for more than ten years, in the form of sketches, only partially worked out. I had not ventured to take it up again. But now I plunged myself into it with force and have so far succeeded that the volume might go into print as it is now, were it not for my hope to make the subject matter more substantial and important, and the treatment of it still more perfect.

Well, I got so far in a fortnight, and there can be no doubt, that the suppressed grief and such a strenuous mental effort brought forth that shock for which my body was predisposed. Suddenly, without any premonitory symptom or any distinct warning, I broke a blood-vessel in my lungs and the loss of blood was so great that, had not prompt and skilful help been at hand, the last boundary of things would, I suppose, have been drawn here. Next time I'll write about other things which I worked at industriously during the past sunless summer in the hope that they would prove satisfactory later as they have done at present . . .

May we both have strength and consolation given us to persevere actively unto the end. Therefore, while sometimes looking back, let us go bravely forward in this silly game of life!

## TRUTH AND POETRY

*Zelter's inquiry into the interpretation of one spot in Goethe's autobiography wherein he said that in his youth the teachers used to treat their pupils with cuffs and thumps, made the poet write this letter. Zelter bet 12 bottles of champagne that this remark did not imply that the poet himself was beaten when a schoolboy. Ambiguous as Goethe's reply was, the champagne was consumed anyhow.*

"As to the title of my life's confidences—*Truth and Poetry*—which is certainly somewhat paradoxical, I adopted it because of my experience that the public always entertains some doubt as to the truthfulness of such biographical efforts. To meet this, I acknowledged having written a kind of fiction, driven to it to some extent unnecessarily, by a certain spirit of contradiction. For it was my most earnest endeavor, as far as possible, to represent and express the genuine, fundamental truth which—inasmuch as I could be aware of it—had prevailed throughout my life. But if such a thing is not possible in later years without the co-operation of memory and one's imagination so that in one way or other we never fail to exercise the poetic gift, then it is clear that we shall present and bring into relief the results, and the past as it seems to us *now* rather than the individual events as they happened *then*. For does not the most ordinary chronicle necessarily embody something of the spirit of the time in which it was written? Will not the fourteenth century hand down the report on a comet more ominously than the nineteenth? In fact, in the same town you may hear one version of a striking event in the morning, and another in the evening.

"Under the word *Poetry* I included all that belongs to the narrator and the narrative so that I could make use of the truth of which I was conscious, for my own ends. Whether I have attained them I leave to the generous reader to determine, for then the question arises, 'Is what has been related consistent? Does it give an idea of the gradual development of a personality, already well known through his works?'

"In every History, even if it be written diplomatically, we always see the nation, the party, to which the writer belonged, peering through. The French speak of English History in a very different tone from that of the English themselves!

"I was lately very much struck by this in the memoirs of the Duke de St. Simon; you cannot fully enjoy the detailed reports of this highly educated and truth-loving man, unless you remember that they are written by a Duke and a Peer. It is the reflection of a period in which grand people find less to win than they must fear to lose."

I felt it my duty to write the above, my dear friend, in reply to a question very much like yours, which was put to me by one whom I highly honor; I give you the answer I gave him, as it is to the point in both instances. Remember that with every breath we draw, an ethereal stream of Lethe runs through our whole being so that we have but a partial recollection of our joys and scarcely any of our sorrows. I have always known how to value, profit by, and enhance the use of this precious gift of God.

Therefore, as far as the question of the cuffs and thumps are concerned with which Fate, our lady-loves, our friends and foes have put us to the test, the recollection of such things has—in the mind of a good and resolute man—long ago vanished into air.

It would be difficult, in fact, impossible for me to specify any particular instance as you request. Still, to please you, I bethink myself that our schoolmaster used to wield, as an emblem of majesty, a flexible ruler which was otherwise not unserviceable and with which he dealt occasional whacks by way of punishment or encouragement. Yet even in those days of rigorous pedagogues, a humanizing means of information had been discovered, foreshadowing that, which since Beccaria's time, has had so gracious an influence on our Criminal Code,—for those who were to be punished were made to hold out a hand and submit again and again to canings more or less severe. This gave one an opportunity of boldly stretching out one's hand, like Mucius Scaevola, and gaining an heroic martyr's wreath, without moving a muscle of one's face. Now, whatever may be the prospect of your winning or losing the dozen bottles of champagne, I wish to bring forward my testimony to the best of my recollection with the greatest show of Truth and leaving Poetry out of the account entirely.

# FIFTEEN ENGLISH FRIENDS OF GOETHE

*Fifteen English admirers of Goethe, among them Thomas Carlyle, Walter Scott and William Wordsworth, presented the poet with a highly wrought seal as a gift for his 82 birthday. The impression on the seal was a star encircled with the serpent-of-eternity, and this motto from one of Goethe's Xenien: Like a star, without haste, yet without rest. The gift was accompanied by the following letter:*

SIR— Among the friends whom this so interesting Anniversary calls round you, may we "English friends," in thought and symbolically, since personally it is impossible, present ourselves to offer you our affectionate congratulations. We hope you will do us the honour to accept this little birthday gift; which as a true testimony of our feelings, may not be without value.

We said to ourselves: As it is always the highest duty and pleasure to show reverence to whom reverence is due, and our chief, perhaps our only benefactor is he who by act and word, instructs us in wisdom,—so we undersigned, feeling towards the poet Goethe as the spiritually-taught towards their spiritual teacher, are desirous to express that sentiment openly and in common. For which end we have determined to solicit his acceptance of a small English gift, proceeding from us all equally, on his approaching birthday; that so, while the venerable man still dwells among us, some memorial of the gratitude we owe him, and think the whole world owes him, may not be wanting.

And thus our little tribute, perhaps among the purest that men could offer to man, now stands in visible shape, and begs to be received. May it be welcome, and speak permanently of a most close relation, though wide seas flow between the parties!

We pray that many years may be added to a life so glorious —that all happiness may be yours, and strength given to complete your high task, even as it hitherto proceeded, "like a star, without haste, yet without rest."

We remain, Sir, your friends and servants—Fifteen English Friends.

## ". . . YOU TOO WILL SOON FIND REST"

*Goethe spent his 82nd birthday, the last he was to see, in the Thuringian village Ilmenau. The mine supervisor, Johann Christian Mahr, reported on this visit:*

ON THE EVENING of the 26th of August, 1831, Goethe arrived here in Ilmenau and stayed at the inn "Ye Lions" with his two grandsons and servants. A clear sky, without any clouds, afforded the most wonderful weather. His arrival was immediately reported to me and he had asked me to visit him, but it so happened that I did not come home from the Kammerberg mines until late in the evening. Therefore, I visited him on the morning of the 27th. He had already been busy at his desk since four o'clock in the morning. His joy, he said, was very great to see this countryside again which he had not visited for thirty years, though he had been here so often before and for such a long time. Both his grandsons had already set out for the mountains accompanied by the butler and would stay there until luncheon. After several inquiries as to whether anything noteworthy had happened there to report in a geognostic respect, he then asked whether it was possible to get up to the Kickelhahn [peak in the Thuringian forest] easily by carriage. He desired to see the little hunting house again on the Kickelhahn which was still a remarkable sight in his memory since those early days, and he wanted me to accompany him there.

We drove in nice weather on the forest road via Gabelbach. On the road he enjoyed seeing the metaphyr rock dug out during the building of the road not only because of its remarkable rarity in the porphyry, but also because of its wonderful sight from the road. Furthermore, he was pleasantly surprised by the layout of the avenues and the paved roads arranged by König, superintendent of forests, and he compared them to the utterly bad roads through the woods of earlier times, still alive in his memory.

We reached the highest point on the Kickelhahn quite easily. He stepped out, delighted about the splendid view from the roundel, and enjoyed the sight of the grand forests. He then exclaimed: "Ah, if only my good Grand-Duke Carl August could have seen this beauty once more!" Then he asked: "Isn't the little house in the woods somewhere here? I can walk there and the carriage can wait for us here."

Indeed, with vigorous strides he walked along the crest of the mountain through rather high bilberry bushes to the two-storied hunting-box, well known to him, built of timber and planks. A steep staircase ran to the upper floor; I offered my help to support him, but he rejected it with youthful gaiety, though he celebrated his 82nd birthday the very next day, and with the words: "Don't think I can't climb up those stairs any more; I still can manage fine."

When entering the upper room, he said: "Quite some time ago I spent eight days here with my servant during one of those summers and I then wrote a little verse here on the wall. I'd like to see that verse once more, and should the day be written underneath have the kindness to note it." I led him

Goethe's study in the house at Weimar

Goethe. Lithograph by D. Maclise based on a sketch by W. M. Thackeray, 1830

Goethe. Drawing by K. A. Schwerdgeburth, 1831

Goethe on his deathbed. Drawing by F. Preller, 1832

immediately to the southern window of the room, where to its left was written with pencil:

There is hardly a breeze,
Peace dwells in the top of the trees
And upon the mountain crest.
The birds in the woods are still.
Wait, and you too will
Soon find rest.

September 7, 1780

Goethe reread this short verse and tears were running down his cheeks. Quite slowly he took his snow white kerchief out of his dark-brown coat, dried his tears and said in a soft woeful voice: "Yes, wait, and you too will soon find rest!" Then he fell silent for half a minute, looked once more out the window into the sinister dark fir woods and turned towards me with the words: "Well, let's go again!"

## GOETHE TO MARIANNE VON WILLEMER

Weimar, February 10, 1832

WHILE I SERIOUSLY EMPLOY the time granted to me to going through this boundless amount of papers which have accumulated with time, to shifting them and to determining what to do with them, certain leaves particularly seem to reflect the most beautiful days of my life; some of them, however, kept separate for a long time, are now packed and sealed.

Such a package [Marianne's letters] lies in front of me with your address on it, and I would like to forward it at once to anticipate all possibilities. But the only promise I request of you is to keep it unopened until a not yet determined hour. Such pages give us the pleasant feeling of having lived; these are the most wonderful documents on which we may rest.

Since, moreover, you hold as I do: to secure each day and to make it as beautiful as possible and to counteract suffering immediately with some kind of activity, so you remain like myself unchangeable in your most friendly feelings.

## GOETHE TO W. VON HUMBOLDT

*For many years Goethe conducted a stimulating correspondence with the brothers von Humboldt, Alexander, the explorer, and Wilhelm who besides being a diplomat was a distinguished philologist. Wilhelm von Humboldt had inquired about the Faust-manuscript which Goethe had completed in August, 1831, and then put under seal, to be published only after his death. This is the last letter that Goethe dictated.*

Weimar, March 17, 1832.

AFTER A LONG, involuntary pause I begin as follows, and yet simply on the spur of the moment. Animals, the ancients say, are taught by their organs. I add to this, men also, although they have the advantage of teaching their organs in return.

For every act, and, consequently, for every talent, an innate tendency is requisite, working automatically, and unconsciously carrying with itself the necessary predisposition; yet, for this very reason, it works on and on inconsequently, so that, although it contains its laws within itself, it may, nevertheless, ultimately run out, devoid of end or aim. The earlier a man perceives that there is a handicraft or an art which will aid him to attain a normal increase of his natural talents, the more fortunate he is. Moreover, what he receives from without does not impair his innate individuality. The best genius is that which absorbs everything within itself, which knows how to adapt everything, without prejudicing in the least the real fundamental essence—the quality which is called character—so that it becomes the element which truly elevates that quality and endows it throughout so far as may be possible.

Here, now, appear the manifold relations between the conscious and the unconscious. Imagine a musical talent that is going to compose an important score; consciousness and unconsciousness will be related like the warp and the woof, a simile that I am so fond of using. Through practice, teaching, reflection, failure, furtherance, opposition, and renewed reflection the organs of man unconsciously unite, in a free activity, the acquired and the innate, so that this process creates a unity which amazes the world. This generalization may serve as a speedy reply to your query and as an explanation of the note that is herewith returned.

Over sixty years have passed since, in my youth, the conception of Faust lay before me clear from the first, although the entire sequence was present in less detailed form. Now, I have always kept my purpose in the back of my mind and I have elaborated only the passages that were of special interest to me, so that gaps remain in the second part which are to be connected through the agency of a uniform interest. Here, I must admit, appeared the great difficulty of attaining through resolution and character what should properly belong only to a voluntarily active nature. It would, however, not have been well had this not been feasible after so long a life of active reflection, and I let no fear assail me that it may be possible to distinguish the older from the newer, and the later from the earlier; which point, then, we shall intrust to future readers for their friendly examination.

Beyond all question it would give me infinite pleasure to dedicate and communicate these very serious jests to my valued, ever thankfully recognized, and widely scattered friends while still living, and to receive their reply. But, as a matter of fact, the age is so absurd and so insane that I am convinced that the candid efforts which I have long expended upon this unusual work would be ill rewarded, and that, driven ashore, they will lie like a wreck in ruins and speedily be covered over by the sand-dunes of time. In theory and practice confusion rules the world, and I have no more urgent task than to augment, wherever possible, what is and has remained within me, and to safeguard my peculiarities, as you, worthy friend, surely also do in your castle.

## THE LAST DAY

*Goethe contracted a feverish cold which led to violent pains in his chest and limbs. Though the treatment of his physician, Dr. Karl Vogel, mitigated the pain, the end of the octogenarian could no longer be put off. K. W. Mueller reported about the last day's events on March 22, 1832.*

IN THE MORNING about six o'clock he asked to sit up in his easychair and took a few steps from his bedroom into his work room. There he found his daughter-in-law who had kept hidden in this room during the night and to whom he said in a friendly and jocose tone: "There, now, woman! have you really come down again?"

However, he felt very weak and immediately went back again to the easychair in his bedroom . . . Though the physician had explicitly declared that there was no hope of saving him from the catarrhal fever which had abated, nevertheless all those friends present in the front room refused to believe this painful news, all the more that the barometer had risen decidedly since the day before and they knew from experience what a strong influence the atmospheric condition exerted on Goethe's health. Even the patient expressed the hope of regaining his health and strength when speaking to his daughter-in-law in the morning, saying that April would bring storms, but also beautiful days in which he would get strong again by moving around in the open air; he even asked his doctor not to give him medicine any more, since he felt quite well.

Toward sunrise his condition worsened noticeably, as the physician had predicted, and more and more his strength failed him. The room was kept quite dark in order to keep the patient calmer, but he said: "Let me have light; the darkness is unpleasant." However, his eyes soon seemed to bother him, because repeatedly he held his hand before them like a screen, as if he wished to protect them or to discern something at a distance. They gave him the green eyeshade which he usually wore in the evening when he read. He then asked his daughter-in-law to sit by him, seized her hand and held it for a long time.

At about nine o'clock Goethe asked for water mixed with wine, and when it was brought to him, he straightened up in his easychair, took hold of the glass with a firm grip and emptied it, but not before he had asked the question: "There isn't too much wine in it?" Then he called John to him and, supported by him and his butler, he got up from the chair. Standing before it, he asked what day of the month it was and to the answer that it was the 22nd replied: "Then spring has begun, all the easier will it be to recover."

Then he sat down again in his arm chair and a gentle sleep with pleasant dreams embraced him, for he spoke in his dream among other things: "Behold that beautiful female head—with its black curls—in magnificent shades—against the dark background." The arts seemed to occupy him entirely, because shortly afterwards he said: "Friedrich, give me the folder with the drawings standing over there." Since there was no folder but a book at the designated place, the servant held it out to him, but the patient said: "Not the book, the portfolio!" The servant assured him that there was no portfolio, only a book. Then Goethe, awakening from his drowsy state, said jocosely: "Well, then it must have been a spectre."

Shortly thereafter he demanded cold poultry for breakfast. It was brought to him; he took a bite and asked for a drink. Friedrich gave him a glass of water and wine of which he drank only a little, putting the question to his servant: "I hope you didn't put any sugar into the wine, as it is harmful to me?" He then ordered what he wanted to eat for lunch and, moreover, for Sunday he ordered the favorite dish of Hofrat Vogel who was supposed to eat with him that day . . .

Again Goethe straightened up with the help of his copyist John and Friedrich to go into his work room, however, he only reached the entrance, tottered, and soon again sat in his easychair. Sitting thus for a while, he wished to see a manuscript by Kotzebue. There was no manuscript to be found, and he was told so. Whereupon he replied: "Then someone must have taken it." Later it turned out that this demand for a Kotzebue manuscript was not caused by his feverish imagination; a few days previous he had busied himself with his adaptation of Kotzebue's "Guardian Spirit"—a play he loved very much—and had given it to his grandson Wolf as a present. Some time later it was found on Wolf's desk.

Thereupon his mind became occupied with his friend Schiller who had preceded him into death. Namely, when he saw a piece of paper lying on the floor, he asked why Schiller's letters were lying around, one should put them safely away. Immediately afterwards he called to Friedrich: "Why don't you also open the other window in the room, so that more light can come in!" These were his last words.

Now when speaking became more and more difficult for

him, yet he still felt the urge to make himself understood, he first drew in the air with his hand raised, as he used to do in his healthy days; then with the forefinger of his right hand he wrote a few lines in the air. Since he was weakening, his arm sank lower, and he wrote lower and lower and finally—as it seemed he was writing the same over and over again—on the blanket which covered his legs. One could notice that he put in exact punctuations, and one could recognize the capital letter W; it was impossible to decipher the other signs . . .

As his fingers began to become blue, someone took the green eyeshade from his eyes and found that they had already grown dim. From minute to minute his breath became heavier, however without turning into a rattle. The dying man pressed himself comfortably into the left side of the easychair, without the least sign of pain, and the breast which had created, carried and nurtured a world in itself, no longer breathed.

## ECKERMANN'S FAREWELL

THE MORNING AFTER Goethe's death a strong desire seized me to look once again upon his earthly garment. His faithful servant, Friedrich, let me into the room where he was laid out. Stretched upon his back, he reposed as if asleep; there were profound peace and security in the features of his sublimely noble face. The mighty brow seemed still to harbor thoughts. I would have liked a lock of his hair; but reverence prevented me from cutting it off. The body lay naked, only wrapped in a white sheet; large pieces of ice had been placed near it, to keep it fresh as long as possible. Friedrich drew aside the sheet, and I was astonished at the divine magnificence of the limbs. The breast was powerful, broad, and arched; the arms and thighs were full, and softly muscular; the feet were elegant, and of the most perfect shape; nowhere, on the whole body, was there a trace of fat or of leanness and decay. A perfect man lay in great beauty before me; and the rapture which the sight caused made me forget for a moment that the immortal spirit had left such an abode. I laid my hand on his heart—there was a deep silence—and I turned away to give free vent to my suppressed tears.

## BURIED LIKE A PRINCE

*Goethe's burial took place in the afternoon of March 26. The London magazine "The Athenaeum" published the following account of the interment.*

Weimar, March 31, 1832

The Grand Duke appointed Monday last for the celebration of Goethe's funeral obsequies. His corpse was laid out on a couch, overlaid with sable trappings, and resplendent with wax lights. Here it remained exposed to the sorrowing inspection of the public at large, during the entire forenoon of that day. The body itself lay on its couch in the centre of the apartment, resting upon pillows of white satin. A wreath of fresh laurel encircled the head; and a Roman toga, likewise of satin, was tastefully disposed round the corpse. On its right was a column, from which a crown of laurel, worked in pure gold, relieved with emeralds (a tribute from Frankfort, his native town, on the occasion of his academic jubilee,) hung suspended. Behind his head rose another column to which was attached a lyre and a basket—the latter inclosing rolls of parchment, symbolical of the writer's literary labors, and a third column was placed on the left of the body, against which his several diplomas were displayed. At the feet were three other columns, to which the insignia of the numerous orders which princely favour and esteem had conferred upon the illustrious departed, were suspended.

Large cypresses were disposed on either side behind the couch of state; and on each side stood twenty candelabra of silver; guards of honour of all ranks and classes, keeping watch beside them. Three splendid stars, in allusion to Goethe's transition to a heavenly state, hung over his remains. Multitudes came from far and near to bid them a last farewell. The coffin was removed at five o'clock in the afternoon, in order that it might be borne to the destination assigned it by the late Grand Duke, his enlightened and munificent patron—namely, by the side of Schiller, in the sepulchre of the Grand Ducal family. It was for this reason that the whole ceremony was ordered on a scale of commensurate splendour.

Upon its removal the corpse was placed in the Grand Ducal hearse of state, which was drawn by four horses, and surrounded by members of the cabinet and household, and those of our learned and scientific bodies, part of the clergy and their assistants, military men, and, in short, almost every respectable inhabitant of Weimar following on foot behind. Amongst this throng of mourners, the students of Jena, with roses attached to their sable scarfs, were not the least conspicuous. The train was closed by a line composed of the Grand-Ducal carriages, in one of which sat Baron de Spiegel, as the representative of the reigning prince.

The chief portion of the clergy in conjunction with a numerous choir, were stationed in the sepulchre. A beautiful hymn greeted the entrance of the funeral procession; to this succeeded a discourse, in which the preacher dwelt upon the heavy account which is required at the hands of those on whom nature has shed her richest gifts; and this was followed by one of Goethe's pieces, the music to which was composed by his oldest surviving friend, Zelter, director of the orchestra at Berlin, and performed under the superintendence of the celebrated Hummel.

The coffin was then delivered into the custody of the Lord Marshal; immediately after which the chapel was cleared, and the ceremonies terminated. The coffin is of oak lined with lead, and the external inscription is simply the following:

Goethe:
Born the 28th August, 1749
Died the 22nd March, 1832

It is a remarkable circumstance that the carpet, on which the coffin was laid within the chapel, was an heirloom in Goethe's family; that his parents stood upon it at the celebration of their marriage; and that in the instance of the poet himself, it covered the floor on which the several ceremonies of his birth, marriage and burial were performed. On the evening of his funeral the theatre, which had been closed several days out of respect for his memory, was opened with the representation of his "Tasso."

## SOURCES

Amelung, Heinz, editor. *Goethe als Persönlichkeit.* München, 1914

Arnim, Bettina von, *Goethe's Correspondence with a Child.* Translated by Wallace Smith Murray. In "The German Classics." New York, 1914

Austin, Sarah, editor, *Characteristics of Goethe.* London, 1833

Bamberg, Eduard von, editor. *Erinnerungen der Karoline Jagemann.* Dresden, 1926.

Bell, Edward, editor. *Early and Miscellaneous Letters of J. W. Goethe.* London, 1889

Bergemann, Fritz, editor. *Bettinas Leben und Briefwechsel mit Goethe.* Leipzig, 1927

Biedermann, Flodoard von, editor. *Goethes Gespräche.* Gesamtausgabe. Leipzig, 1909-1911

Bielschowsky, Albert, *The Life of Goethe.* Translated by William A. Cooper. New York, 1905

Burkhardt, C. A. H., editor. *Goethes Unterhaltungen mit dem Kanzler von Müller.* Stuttgart, 1898

Coleridge, A. D., editor. *Goethe's Letters to Zelter.* London, 1887

Emerson, Haven, editor. *William Emerson's Travels Abroad.* In "Charaka Club Proceedings," New York. Columbia University Press, 1935

Gibbs, Alfred S., editor. *Goethe's Mother.* New York, 1880

Goethe, Johann Wolfgang von, *Gesamtausgabe der Werke, Briefe und Tagebücher.* Weimar, 1887-1912

———. *Annals.* Translated by Charles Nisbert. London, 1884

———. *Miscellaneous Travels.* Translated by A. J. W. Morrison and R. Farie. London, 1882

———. *Poetry and Truth.* A revised translation by Minna Steele Smith. London, 1908

Goethe, *Travels in Italy*. Translated by A. J. W. Morrison and Charles Nisbert. London, 1885

*Goethe's Conversations with Eckermann*. A modernized translation. New Directions. (In preparation)

GRILLPARZER, FRANZ, *My Journey to Weimar*. Translated by Alfred Remy. In "The German Classics," New York, 1914

HECKER, MAX, editor. *Goethes Briefwechsel mit Marianne von Willemer*. Leipzig, 1922

LAMPADIUS, W. A., *Life of Felix Mendelssohn-Bartholdy*. Translated by William Leonhard Gage. New York, 1865

LEWIS, GEORGE HENRY, *The Life and Works of Goethe*. London, 1875

MENDELSSOHN-BARTHOLDY, KARL, *Goethe and Mendelssohn*. Translated by M. E. von Glehn. London, 1872

NORTON, CHARLES ELIOT, editor. *Correspondence between Goethe and Carlyle*. London, 1887

RIEMER, FRIEDRICH WILHELM, *Mitteilungen über Goethe*. Leipzig, 1921

ROBINSON, HENRY CRABB, *Diary, Reminiscences and Correspondence*. London, 1872

SCHMITZ, L. DORA, editor. *Correspondence between Schiller and Goethe*. London, 1877

SIMPSON, LEONARD, editor. *Correspondence between Schiller and Körner*. London, 1849

STAËL-HOLSTEIN, ANNE LOUISE GERMAINE DE, *Germany*. Translated by O. W. Wight. New York, 1861

TALLEYRAND, PRINCE DE, *Memoirs*. Translated by R. L. de Beaufort. New York, 1891

TICKNOR, A. E., *The Life of J. G. Cogswell*. Cambridge, 1874.

TICKNOR, GEORGE, *Life, Letters and Journals*. Boston, 1876

# INDEX